Loomshuttles, Warpaths

Ines Doujak, John Barker

Loomshuttles, Warpaths

An Eccentric Archive 2010 – 2018

Spector Books

published in conjunction with

Württembergischer Kunstverein Stuttgart, curators Hans D. Christ, Iris Dressler
Lentos Kunstmuseum Linz, curator Hemma Schmutz

on the occasion of the exhibitions

Not Dressed For Conquering, October 2016 – January 2017
SALE, February 2018 – May 2018

it contains

a *collection* of forty-eight Andean textiles; an *inventory*; *communications* with the items in the collection; *posters* as visual manifestations of each textile; *numerical dates* related to workers' struggles; the colonial histories of *cloths and colours*; *archived images* with captions; and the figure of *The Investigator.*

with communications from

* textcollages by Doujak / Barker
° based on interviews by Doujak / Seefranz, abridged by Barker / Doujak

Sonia Abian
Fahim Amir
Zdenka Silvia Ballon°
John Barker
Cristina Bubba°
Anja Büchele / Matthew Hyland
Guiseppe Campuzano°
T.J. Clark
Liz Conor
Alice Creischer / Andreas Siekmann
Max Jorge Hinderer Cruz
Cordula Daus
Ines Doujak
Edgar Endress
Antke Engel
Judith Fischer
Nipples Hasno Gender / Julia Fuchs / Mara Gheddon
Simryn Gill
Elena and Nora Izcue°
Luis Jacobs
Waldo Jordan°
Thomas Kilpper / Jens Risch
Anja Kirschner / David Panos
Cornelia Klinger
Peter Linebaugh
Catherine Lord
Luciano
Ruth Noack
Boris Ondreička
Prabhakar Pachpute
Beatriz Canedo Patiño°
Lukas Pusch
Juan Quispe°
David Riff
François Rabelais*
Edgar *Huracán* Ramírez°
Pedro G. Romero
Hedwig Saxenhuber
Ferdinand Schmatz
Simon Sheikh
Irene Silverblatt
Evelyn Steinthaler
Imogen Stidworthy
Shooshie Suleiman
Graham Townsley*
B. Traven*
Grant Watson
Markus Wörgötter

A rudimentary pedal loom exposed to the cold wind and rain in the Huancavelica Department of Peru.

Preface

In 2006 an elaborately tattooed 1500-year-old mummy of a young woman from the pre-Inca Moche culture was discovered in northern Peru. The tomb yielded a rich array of funeral objects, from gold sewing needles and weaving tools to numerous weapons, including two massive war clubs.

The *Eccentric Archive* presented here is one product of an eight-year investigation *Loomshuttles, Warpaths*. Its starting point is a collection of forty-eight Andean textiles assembled over 35 years, which includes the ancient and contemporary, natural and synthetic fibres and a variety of production techniques. It contains descriptions of its items, the *inventory*, which is contextual, anecdotal, autobiographical, and technical. *Communications* with each item have been produced by a variety of people either in a text or visually. *Posters* consisting of visual interpretations of each textile include *numerical dates* which refer to specific instances of the continuing class conflict in the making of cloth and clothes over the last 600 years; and of rebellion by style of dress, a form of contestation well articulated by the idlers of 18th-century Lima, who when asked why they were not working said they were 'not dressed for conquering'. On the posters are also imprinted the names of *colours and cloths*, with texts showing how entangled with imperialist history they have been, and also describing the impacts of shifts in technologies and the perception of colours themselves. *Archived images* with *captions* that are the off-cuts of the archive are included as an accompaniment. The figure of *The Investigator* was created both to play with and challenge ethnographic notions; it is at once naked and full of eyes.
Its adventures in the present-day Andes and then in Europe are described in a coda. The archive is eccentric in the literal sense of being off-centre, both in its movement in time and space and in its composition. It is also an archive that travels, having been shown in exhibitions worldwide at different stages of its creation.

Communications

Andean textiles are perceived as animate entities with whom – since their energies do not disappear after the cloth is created or worn – it is possible actively to communicate. Items of the collection were sent out in the hope that they might speak to people outside of their communities. Some items evoked personal memories and sensations, for cloth is "such a stuff to be seen and touched", as was most vividly the case for some poor women of Paris, sexually aroused by the sound and feel of 'fresh' silk that was discarded once used. The sensuality of fabric is given free rein in the imagination of Rabelais, communicating from the past, and, more prosaically in the modern day, by a weaving that "is not hard or rough, but firm". In this instance, cloth that would have been used to wrap food when visiting the dead on All Saints' Day evoked feelings about a dead mother and the proximity of her things. In other *communications* the relation of cloth to the body shaped by clothes, either imposed as alien and body-warping, or self-shaped over time, is brought to life. Cloth can be useful and beautiful – in the Andean aesthetic this is the 'well made' – or it can give sheer pleasure as fabric on skin. In other communications cloth provides comfort, as a poncho does in one case, though this is comfort in a world of unasked for violence. For violence too is communicated: sometimes the pieces of the collection move out into the harshness of the world of free trade, drug wars and killer drones; while another correspondent feels with stark immediacy the blood and bruises of Andean ritualised violence; and in another a comic dimension bursts through. These *communications* are all grounded in the materiality of the inventory's items, their descriptions and their place in a world of dispersed manufacture, financial derivatives and digitalisation, from which they nevertheless express their own particular and autonomous cosmology. Within that, a geography of landscapes, memories, expectations and desires encompasses perception of and responses to a shared sense of belonging to the natural world in which knowledge is not of a reality constituted by objects but is full of movement. The self-confidence of these cosmologies in the 'global' world as expressed in the inventory's range is remarkable, and in only one case did the communication with a textile appear violent, causing havoc in an ordered Europe to which that item had not wished to travel.

The Exact and the Ecstatic

Developed over millennia, Andean cloth-making, in which "every known weaving technique was used", came from a passion for the exact and the ecstatic, mathematics and dance.

Its survival in the face of the colonial onslaught – both demographic, cultural and environmental – that followed the first appearance of Columbus in the Americas, is a testament to both the importance of textiles and to the extent to which they were grounded in the principles of balance and reciprocity that are fundamental to the region's cosmology. In the modern world the textile tradition exists not as a nostalgic relic but continues to shape all levels of life. It also anchors the beauty that textiles can possess, even in the ugly and colonial-inflected relations of production worldwide, just as it did for the 19th-century silk weavers of Lyon despite their lack of power in relation to merchant capital, the 'manufacturers without factories'.

It is these parts of the *Eccentric Archive* – the textiles and the descriptions of and communications with them – that give substance to beauty, adventure and social significance in the world of cloth, so that the subtlety of light and shade in silk velvet, the beauty of 17th-century Indian damask – only the more exclusive cloths are likely to have survived – or the refinement of colour and stripe spacing of an Andean potato sack can be appreciated regardless of for whom they was made. Early weavers chose different coloured grasses to make patterns even when life was precarious and survival a priority. This desire surfaces in production that could have been solely functional. At the same time the beauty or ugliness of what is consumed is often a consequence of how it is produced. The forced labour in the Spanish textile 'workshops' of the 17th and 18th century of what is now Bolivia and Peru, where only poor quality cloth for local markets was made and from which "many preferred to escape to the most distant and unknown regions and would seek to die by whatever means", is one example. In our times the deadly fires in South Asian factories, have occurred in those factories that produce the cheapest 'throwaway' clothes such as when 286 Karachi workers were killed in 2012 in one where jeans were made for the German textile discounter KiK[1], while conditions in the mills making the cheapest synthetic cloth in modern Indian Gujerat are the worst in the region.

A Warped Globalisation

Textiles, not just luxury items, were among the first goods to be traded at distance, and this long preceded the outbreak of European colonialism. Indian cloths for ordinary people were in evidence in 11th-century Cairo. By the 15th century, they were sold across the Indian Ocean in East Africa. Forms of exploitation of labour in the textile business were already prevalent in 13th- and 14th-century Flanders; and land grabs for sheep and their wool had already begun in England by the time that Columbus set off in 1492. Nevertheless, the rapid spread of European colonialism that followed his accidental coming upon the Americas, along with Vasco da Gama's more planned arrival in India via the Cape of Good Hope, changed everything. Both voyages were aggressive naval ventures launched by a militarised culture keen on acquiring high-quality Asia commodities like Indian cloths. They were prompted by the blocking of the old trade routes that took place after the Ottomans took over what had been Constantinople. The colonialisms that followed created a wholly distorted and unequal international division of capital, labour and consumption. Cloth-making and its main raw materials, wool and cotton, was an avant-garde in the process. Its dirty footprints remain visible in today's Western-retail dominated chains of textile production.

In the case of the Andes, initially the silver from the fabled Bolivian mine of Potosí not only provided the liquidity needed to kick-start European capitalism, but gave its early-phase merchants a commodity that Asian producers of sought-after commodities actually wanted. Some – silks from China, Indian cloth and carpets from Persia – came directly to the 16th- and 17th-century nouveaux-riche of Potosí, who enjoyed an orgy of globalised textiles including linen from Germany, wool from England, lace points from France, and taffeta from Spain. In the process the Andean population was nearly destroyed by the Spanish invasion, a population of approximately 10 million reduced to 1.5 million in the 50 years leading up to 1571, decimated by a genocidal mixture of disease, violence and overwork. The mass deaths of the Indigenous peoples of the whole American continent also prompted the invaders' need for slave labour, not only for extraction of the continent's precious metals but also for the plantations that had been established for the growing of coffee, sugar, indigo and cotton. Cotton was like wool[2] in involving the seizure of land but was different in being 'effort-intensive', requiring also a mass of labour. It became integral to the slave trade. At first cottons from India, re-exported from Europe, were used to buy African slaves and the cheapest were used to clothe, albeit minimally, the

1 KiK being short for *Der Kunde ist König* – literally *The Consumer is King.*

2 The seizure of land for wool production never stopped: from 19th-century Scotland and Australia to 21st-century Argentina.

slaves themselves. Later, a conjunction of the massification of North American slave-plantation cotton-growing and the mechanisation of spinning and weaving, especially in Britain and partly financed by profits from the slave trade, tightened the relation. In the globalised world of cotton, a price increase determined in Liverpool could, as a consequence, dislodge more Native Americans from their lands and increase the use of the whip on the plantation.

Categorical Imperatives

In the dynamic worldview of Andean communities, the production process is just as important as the finished product, and everything, including the means of production, possesses the same degree of vitality. The external aspect of cloth is always a reflection of the interior, and its creative animation results not only from the process and the various individuals involved but is perceived as an entity in itself. Numerous studies deal with the semiology and politics of fashion and clothing; or with present-day globalised 'chains' of production. The *Eccentric Archive* attempts to avoid such a division of concern, which reflects what is distinctive about modern capitalism, the rigid separation of 'the consumer' from the 'producer'. Even though in the universe of the rich, of celebrities and fashion bloggers, the consumer can influence shifts in what is produced, there is a gross and bogus flattery involved in the notion that the generic 'consumer is king' when the majority of consumers are also most likely to be exploited producers. Another commonplace is the unwarranted assumption that the wearers of clothes will be intrinsically passive and are the deserving targets of moralising for being 'consumerist'. The theme is an old one. It is poor servant girls and seamstresses who are attacked as 'unpatriotic' by Daniel Defoe for wearing calicos at the start of the 18th century, when the 'calico craze' was posing a threat to the English wool business. In the same century in Quito it is two slave women working for a court judge who tear down an edict demanding a stop to the 'scandalous excess' in clothes worn by the non-white population of the city; while North American slaves often found ways to dress 'beyond their station'. The ideological separation of 'consumer' and 'producer' has, as a main function, the hiding of what has been involved in the making of what is bought. It can also be all too real, as when Jane Collins describes how in a present-day Mexican clothing *maquiladora* a worker will never be able to afford the $100 jeans she is making.

Just as with these modern production sites, means of control were always central to the structure of the pioneer mechanised textile mills and factories. There were precedents in the ways that merchant capitalists organised and profited from labour in a previous era, but most of all the mill owners learned from the discipline imposed on African slaves on plantations, from which labour cost-accounting first emerged. "While English society increasingly condemned the institution of slavery, it approved experiments in labour discipline which appeared to gravitate towards the plantation model. Slaveholders and industrialists shared a growing interest not only in surveillance and control but in modifying the character and habits of their workers".[3]

The slave plantation used a 'managed gang system' in which 'the most able hands' set the pace, exactly the same as is laid down in Taylorism, the management religion of the early 20th century. The ability to increase the quotas that are demanded for the same wages is still basic to the extraction of maximum surplus value. For post-slavery small-scale cotton growers, the loss of their own sources of food along with taxation, debt and a falling price meant that even more labour had to be performed in order simply to survive. In the factories the same production quota is imposed on a smaller number of workers, as in the '1851' text, or else each worker must look after more machines, which is what crippled the radical 'barefoot aristocracy' of spinners in the late 19th-century USA and was later imposed on the knitting factories of North Carolina in the 1970s. English colonialist landowners in mid-18th-century Ireland imported the plantation model for the spinning and weaving of linen, making use of what was essentially the slave labour of the workhouse and of orphanages. One, Sir Richard Cox, planned to 'modify' the worker by abolishing traditional communal festivals and, as a replacement encouraging rituals of individual competition. In effect a redefining of the calendar, subsequently taken up by the factory systems of shift work and piece rates.

Patriarchy Reassures Foreign Investors

The modern-day textile clothing industry is one of 'Bloody Taylorism'[4]. It added to the 'team' speed-ups of the plantation a new element in the form of the subdivision of tasks. Adam Smith's

3 Susan Buck-Morss, *Hegel, Haiti, and Universal History*, University of Pittsburgh Press, 2009.

4 Bloody Taylorism is a phrase of coined by Alain Lipietz to describe low-wage, export-oriented and relatively unskilled production, broken down into simple and repetitive actions as per the management model of F.W. Taylor. It is in large part situated in poorer parts of the world, and stands in contrast to heavily capitalised 'Fordism', in which wages were set at such a level as to promote domestic markets, so that the car worker could himself buy a car.

idea of such divisions of labour as neutral is entirely misleading when the division is subject to capital and both gendered and internationally hierarchised. The technological limits to dealing with a 'limp' material like cloth means that the sewing machine, mostly operated by women, is still essential to making garments. A common consequence is a woman worker in the formerly colonised world doing 12-hour shifts sewing just the same one end of the same belt-loops for trousers[5], with men as foremen and managers. Patriarchal social relations have been embraced and encouraged by merchant capitalists and factory owners alike, despite modern capitalism's discourse of cultural liberalism. The capitalist's drive to constantly increase production is now aided by new and newer production surveillance technology in which "Quality, while not dropping speed, is achieved not by developing workers' skills but by intensifying control".
Other forms of labour discipline were and are used against female factory workers. These were first imposed on spinners in factory dormitories, the archetypes of which were 18th-century Catholic model-factory villages in Spain and Mexico. They then spread to Japanese-colonised Korea; then Japan itself; and today they proliferate in China and Thailand. The female spinner and sewing machinist is favoured by capital because of an assumed 'docility', one which, if it doesn't exist in the first place, can often be created by means of "verbal abuse and sexual harassment". For women earning their own wage away from the likely-as-not patriarchal social relations of the village from which they are recruited, wage labour is very often also a form of 'liberation' that allows for an autonomy in personal and collective life. But the factory may not be a free choice, as in countries where violent land-grabbing of peasant farms is still rife[6]. In Cambodia and Honduras, those who have shown the greatest leadership and courage in defending their land have been women. Collectively, and as is shown in many of the numerical date entries in this book women workers have been at the forefront of fights against the owners of capital in textiles: as spinners in the mills of early-20th-century Barcelona, the north-east USA and Mexico, in mid-century Japan, modern-day Egypt and in the clothes factories of Cambodia. They have fought speed-ups, for better wages, for independent unions and in solidarity with sacked fellow workers.

Dirty Footprints

Such resistance takes place within an international division of labour that is by and large a 'legacy' of colonialism. In textiles this is articulated in 'dispersed chains of production' where what is 'value-added' is determined in the 'First World'. This means that although "the ability to work at high-speed is a skill in itself", a skill characteristic of both cloth and clothes production as it was with cotton-picking, it does not figure in the scale of 'value-added'. Instead the retail giants and clothing labels – modern-day 'manufacturers without factories' – keep a tight control on design and marketing. They may also maintain or sub-contract R&D (research and development) within the richer part of the world, focusing on new textile materials, dyes and automated cutting. The design-execution split and the massively differential incomes that go with it stand in sharp contrast to the skill of the Andean weaver of whom "no evidence existed to suggest that weavings were executed by a weaver according to cartoons made by someone else"[7]. Today this split is set in stone; and it is concretised by capital's constant threat to move production elsewhere when higher wages are demanded by those at the bottom end of the division of labour. This threat is likely to be backed up by the repressive force of states. Such force has been exerted on behalf of textile export capitals from 14th-century Flanders to present day Bangladesh and is implicit in the dynamic, bilateral 'Free Trade' deals that are formed between more and less powerful states. In the case of modern-day Peru, such deals with the USA and then China have endangered the livelihoods of cotton farmers and textile producers alike in the interests of mining capital. This is one reason why so many of the country's people are leaving the land, as is described in one *communication* with an item in the collection, a woven potato sack.

No Claim Bonus

While the *Eccentric Archive* gives full scope to the special nature and importance of cloth in Andean culture and takes this as its starting point, the context of a worldwide past and present helps it sidestep the claims of research territoriality and the whole minefield of professionalised and selective ethical accusation that goes with it. It avoids too the binaries associated with authenticity, tradition and modernity[8]. The very question of what really is traditional in the

5 This is the one-sided nature of the producers' product as against the many-sided nature of their needs taken to the nth degree.

6 In recent years there has developed something of a 'victim-agency axis', along which academic positions are fixed and political and professional battles are fought out. This is most graphic in the instance of second-wave feminism talking of 'the prostitute' as victim as against the third wave's 'sex worker'.

7 Anni Albers, *From Bauhaus to Black Mountain*. Virginia Gardner Troy: Ashgate, 2002.

8 Having previously been misused in the interests of monopoly claims, authenticity is now being pre-emptively trashed by other claimants. It still, however, carries weight in the world of clothes. In China and Brazil, designated as the biggest consumers of fake products, those in the know can tell a real pair of Levi's from a fake: an art of discernment that implies a 'tribal' exclusiveness and in turn reinforces the value of the label, the authentic product.

sphere of historical narrations is examined in Giuseppe Campuzanos' *communication*, where he takes apart the myth of sexualised and de-sexualised gender roles in Peru. In a section on Tartan, the way in which both the pattern and the kilt were taken up as traditional dress by the leaders of Scottish clans is revealed to have its origins in cheap cloth for slaves in the West Indies and a style rendered safe by the destruction of Highland society. In Bolivia itself, the collector Waldo Jordan talks about his embarrassment at discovering during a celebratory festival that his beautiful coca bag was in a style appropriate for funerals, while the designer Beatriz Patiño is pleased with her 'inauthentic' combination dress for the inauguration of Evo Morales, the country's first Aymará president. Morales meanwhile refused to play any dress-code game on his first trip to Europe in 2006, choosing to wear neither Western suit nor 'Indigenous' clothing but instead the kind of pullover favoured by many Bolivians.

The same considerations prevent us from making a big deal out of 'hybridity'. It is too easy for its realities to be treated so uncritically that they become prescriptive as when one critic warned diasporas, which are intrinsically mediums of process, to be careful to avoid 'idealising the past'. Hybridity may be better than performing such ersatz authenticity, but the all-purpose 'Other' should not be expected to 'perform' this new virtue either. Especially not when hybridity is more a case of pragmatic but no-choice improvisation, as in two of the items described in the *inventory*: a suit whose lining is made from the material of a flour sack and sandals from rubber tyres. In her communication with the suit, Antke Engel goes further and asks why, in the form of the *mestiza*[9], hybridity is confined to the anthropological and given no weight in the political world. Hybridity is something Andean weavers just do, as exemplified in several items of the collection and as discussed in a number of archive texts. Take, for example, their use of Chinese acrylic thread admired for its colour, but re-spun on drop spindles by Andean women on the grounds that the manufactured synthetic yarn is perceived to be of poor textural quality. Their ancestors were equally sophisticated: 120 hues have been identified in 2000-year-old Nazca weavings, while the wide range of dyeing plants used till now can be found listed in the acrylic rope item in the *inventory*.

The Wonder Colour

The attraction of colour and the history of dyes is a thread that runs right through the *Eccentric Archive*. In pre-colonial Europe colours were only for the rich, while for the poor the world was colourless. Colours themselves – black, reds, blue, green, purple, grey, and ultramarine – have their own say, moving in and out of fashion, the symbolism, function and hue of each in constant historical flux. For textiles it is the dye and its fastness that matters; its 'raw materials' from the colonised world were highly sought after, and for Spain the financial benefits from Mexican cochineal was second only to gold. Always there was also something magical in the process. Early use of indigo first needed to be treated with a 'reducing agent' which made it colourless, only for it to turn back to blue on exposure to the air. "Think of the existential agony of the proto-chemist, to have gained the coloured dye with so much labour, then to be forced to watch its colour disappear, hoping, hoping that it will comeback." This experience of the 'magic' of colour must, as Roald Hoffman writes, have recurred on many occasions; and the experience was repeated yet again when 19th-century chemistry produced bright colours from coal tar. Some of this sense of the miraculous is given in the text dealing with Devil's Food, which was the name given to indigo in 16th- and 17th-century Europe when the dye was a threat to the domestic woad business. The text describes the drawn-out process of dyeing deep indigo on a particular Indonesian island, where it is a secretive business known and practised only by women. In consequence of colour's status as a luxury, dyeing was a restricted form of knowledge everywhere, with Sumptuary Laws related to cloth colour strictly enforced. Specific Guilds kept a tight control over knowledge of processes and ingredients; Imperial Rome had a firm grip on its exclusive Tyrian purple dye works; the Spanish invaders a monopoly on their own stolen knowledge of the production of cochineal; the French in India spied on the use of dyes by printers and painters on cloth; the British Empire held a near monopoly on natural indigo; and later the German synthetic dye business took out a huge array of patents. Indigo was doubly paradigmatic of the devastation and distortion wrought by colonialism. Slave workers in its dye baths would not survive seven years of such work before they succumbed to respiratory illness, as did the slaves of the first South Carolina boom of the 18th century[10]. These had been chosen for their expert

9 Literally women of mixed European and Amerindian descent; metaphorically used to talk of people living in a figurative borderlands or imbued with cross-border consciousness.

10 In the modern world the production of genuinely faded denim involving the blasting of the cloth with gravel guns has, like indigo baths, caused respiratory illness and in a 'race to the bottom' been moved on from Turkey to Bangladesh.

knowledge of the plant. Although threatened by severe punishment, they used some of the indigo for themselves to colour the drab cloth they were forced to wear, as described in the text 'Negro Cloth'. Later the farmers of colonial Bengal were pressured by the instruments of tax and debt into growing indigo as an underpaid cash crop, losing their self-sufficiency in food, just as would happen to those forced into cotton monoculture. This loss of self-sufficiency is spoken of openly in the B. Traven communication included in the *Eccentric Archive*, where its rejection is conjoined with a pragmatic understanding of how beauty in the production of useful objects is destroyed by the same process of repetitive single-crop or -item production. In the 19th century, the destruction of India's position as the world's leading cloth producer was a precondition for the colonial imposition of its new role as a producer of raw cotton and indigo. "The larger population now employed in spinning and weaving would be made available for agricultural labour and cultivation [of cotton] extended", a colonial administrator confidently boasted in 1869.

The Active Mask

With this grim part of the modern world in mind, the poster that goes with 'Denim Triumphant' shows a ship facing us, brow on, displaying an impressive bulk that would have once have come proudly out of a shipyard, but which is here run aground with its metal rusted and rotten. The date 2009 speaks of modern dashed hopes, the suicides of Indian farmers producing raw cotton with GM seed and falling into debt. Against this there is proud defiance in the poster for 'Alpaca', in which a woman is shown holding the red flag of the São Paulo homeless movement, whose very existence recalls the against-the-odds survival of the alpaca in the early years of the Spanish invasion. The date, 1903, relates to a panic by the Council of La Paz at the costume of the poor, who were considered to be either underdressed or dressed beyond their station. The image for the 'Velvet' poster was taken from a German newspaper and features a right-wing demonstrator in Moscow with an Andean facemask in which lips, eyes and nose are emphasised, creating a look that is both sinister and melancholic. The shoe-shiners of La Paz who figure on the 'Devil's Food' poster (and in one event in The Investigator's travels) also wear masks, though for a different reason, in their case because of the perceived humiliation of their work. The resonances here move back and forth across the world in time and space, for the 'Velvet' poster is a response to a modern full-head, balaclava-like mask in the collection that mimics the colonial and Creole master during the time of the invasion. Such mask mimicry has a long history in both Peru and Bolivia during carnival, where mask-making remains a highly specialised craft. At the same time reference to the European 'Other' represents only a small part of both craft and use. More common are masks for dances, ceremonies and entertainments relating to varieties of Andean cosmology. High up at 5000 metres in the Andean highlands specifically, woollen balaclavas offer protection against the cold, but have also been used ceremonially, like by shamans conducting rituals for missing dead persons in the recent civil war between the Peruvian state and Sendero Luminoso (Shining Path). In an instance of the politicisation of dress, the balaclavas were banned during the war, at a time when many peasants supported the guerrilla movement. The communication with the same mask moves beyond its Peruvian significance to make an immediate connection to the activist intervention by Pussy Riot in a Russian Orthodox church; its relation to representational politics, with a reference to the present-day Zapatistas; and to the renewed oppression of post-USSR Russian women. The beauty of velvet that is identified by the poster is given full due in the corresponding text, which shows how its indulgence led to violent death in Renaissance Italy. The date, 1954, tells of a most unexpected strike victory – unexpected certainly by owners, society and the state – by 'docile' women in Japan, which was at that time the dominant nation in world cotton cloth production.

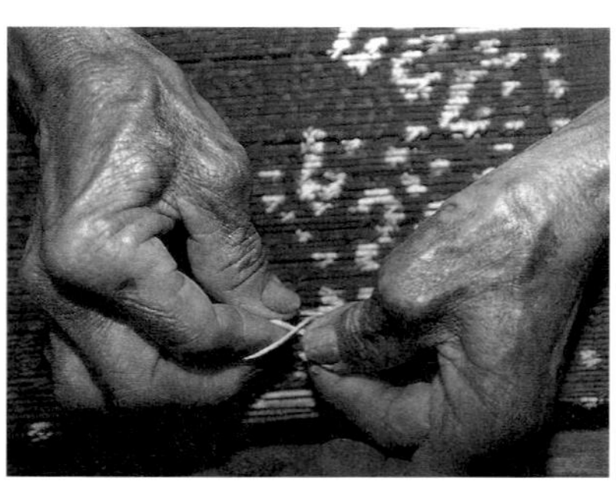

Among Indigenous groups in Borneo female weavers held the same social status as headhunters – the highest. The loom was equated with their warpath.

Velvet

in der Nähe des Kreml die Gewalt. Faschisten und Fußballfans fallen gemeinsam über Ausländer her und liefern

DENIM TRIUMPHANT
2009

Calico
0208

Human Hair
1685

INDIGO
1944

Remix

Dye Spy
1794

CASHMERE
0803

TWILL

2013

Scarlet
1907

PURPLE
1978

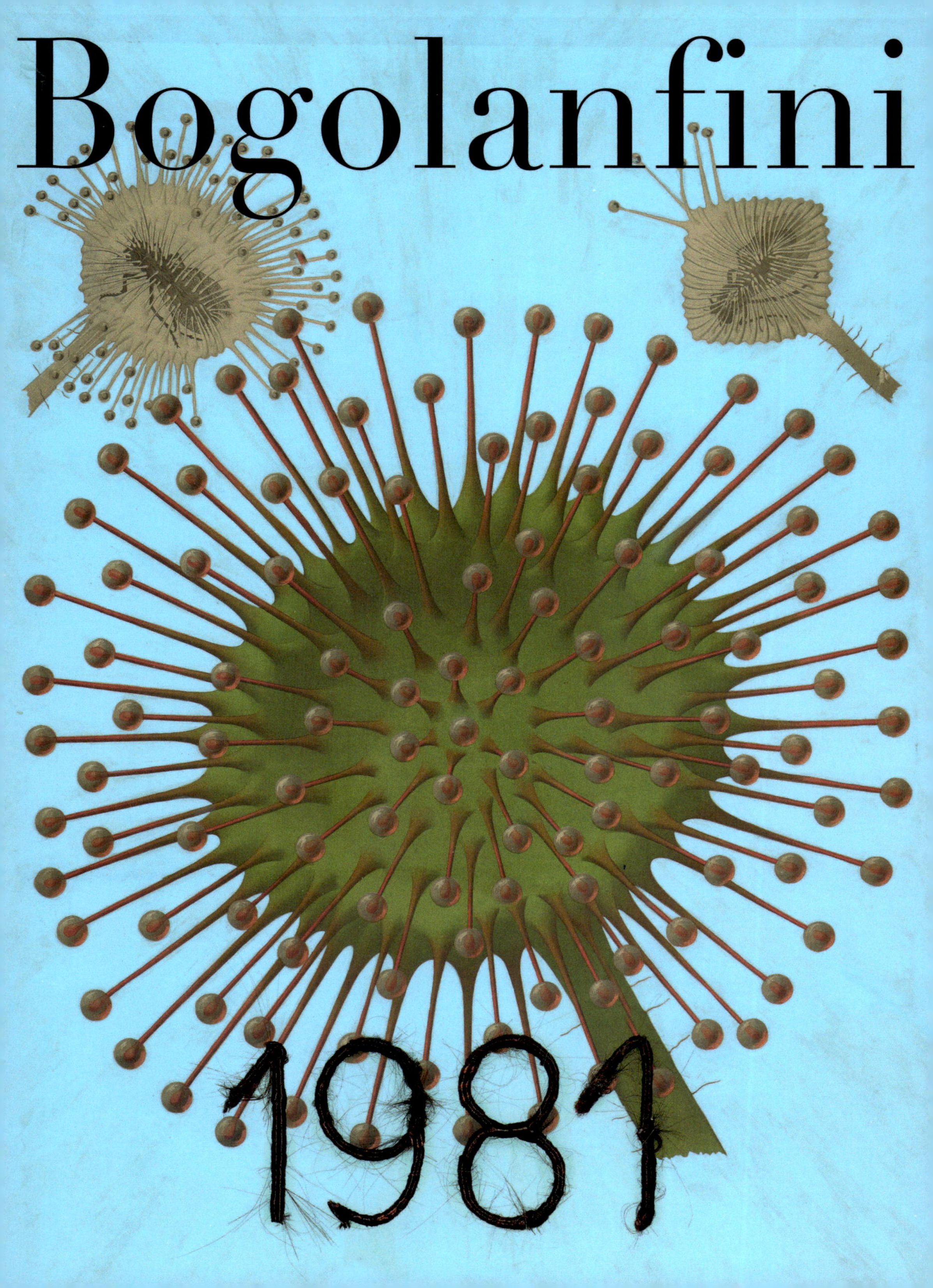
Bogolanfini
1981

SKINS
680

Cochineal

MONUMENTO NACIONAL
PROHIBIDO PINTAR
y
FIJAR CARTELES
LA IDENTIDAD CULTUR
REFLEJADA EN NUESTRA
ADOLESCENCIA Y JUVENTU
En Concierto...!
ALDIA DEL NUEVO MILENI
2000
tus ojos ante el
BORN TO KILL
1738

Waq'ollo / 3 Facial Masks

1

Sheep wool and acrylic, late 20th century; acquired from street vendors in El Alto, La Paz, Cuzco, Lima between 2005 and 2010. The modern full-head, balaclava-like masks in the collection – machine-woven acrylic but hand sewn – mimic the colonial and Creole master. They are used for instance in the *Qhapaq Qolla* dance, which represents the rich merchants from the region around Lake Titicaca who used to bring products from the jungle to trade or exchange. During the annual pilgrimage known as *El Señor de Qoyllur Rit'i* (resplendent snow), that usually draws about 40,000 worshippers and which started out hundreds of years ago as a rite to the *apus*, the climax of the festival was until recently when the *ukukus* (spectacled bears), their faces covered with the *waq'ollo*, and who are the only ones allowed to make the last bit of the pilgrimage up to the altitude of 5600 metres, carried down heavy blocks of ice tied to their backs. The glacial ice is deemed to be holy water, revered as the *apu*'s semen, a healing elixir good for fertilising *Pacha Mama*. The *ukukus* are also considered to be the only ones capable of dealing with *condenados*, the cursed souls said to inhabit the snowfields. Since 1993 the mystical bear-men have been worried that the removal of the ice might be causing the glacier to shrink, and these days cutting ice is all but taboo. The National Commission on Climate Change in Lima predicts that Peru could lose all its glaciers below 5500 metres in elevation in the next 10 years and that within 40 years they all will be gone. According to local myth, when the snow disappears from the tops of the mountains, it will herald the end of the world. In the highlands woollen balaclavas not only have a pragmatic use but are also worn by shamans, as in the ceremony for a missing peasant victim in the recent war between the Peruvian state and the *Sendero Luminoso* (Shining Path guerrillas). In an instance of the politicisation of dress, the masks were banned during this war, in which many peasants supported the guerilla movement whose leader, Guzmán, has now been joined in prison by the country's wartime president, Alberto Fujimori, such was the level of state violence. In the Andes every mask must be in motion and animated within a context of human relationships, social, historical and mythic. The masks are passed down, constantly absorbing new elements and adapted according to the interests, feelings and condition of the people.

Velvet

On the 26th December 1476, Duke Galeazzo Sforza, ruler of Milan, was murdered by his own courtiers angered at losing their places to favourites and at unprecedented taxes placed on them by the Duke's extravagance. Clothes were his obsession, designing the costumes for court personnel and his mistress himself; a bureaucracy for clothes was created and the whole court's wardrobe was renewed three times a year. Velvet woven with silk was a speciality of Italian city-states and the most expensive material of the time. It became a chief cause of the Duke's downfall. Spending on this material alone increased by 500% in the six years between 1469 and 1475, absorbing not just a large part of the city's budget, but requiring a large loan from the Medicis. His was a dramatic case but even in England a duke might spend half his annual rents on a velvet doublet with gold thread inlaid.

Italy, starting with Lucca in the late 13th century, became famous for its velvet production from then on, and city-states like Venice became rich from its production. Originally the material was imported from Cairo, which from early in the same century was the largest producer of silk cloth, using yarn that came from China and India via Baghdad. From the 10th century the city was possibly the biggest textile producer in the 'Old World'. Another aristocratic enthusiast of this time was Musa I, ruler of the Mali Empire, who found the fabric as he passed through the Egyptian city on his pilgrimage to Mecca in 1324 and brought velvet-weavers back to Timbuktu. A locally produced crimson velvet caftan was made for subsequent rulers. At the same time that Duke Galeazzo's velvet fetish was costing him his life, Mehmet II, ruler of the Ottoman Empire, had no such problems. Using silk from Bursa, Turkey, he was able to have even assistant cooks dressed in blue-coloured dresses, conical hats and baggy trousers all made from the material.

During these periods this 'three-dimensional' cloth, which allowed for shifts in its lighting and changes of colour as it moved, was woven only with silk, and its highly specialised craftsmen in Italy enjoyed far higher wages than those of other weavers. Fortunes were built on its manufacture, banking dynasties like the Medici evolving from the money it made. Conversely wearing velvet was a means of showing off wealth and power and the object of various 'sumptuary laws', which banned most classes of people from wearing it. Originally it was reserved just for the aristocracy but the advance of the merchant-banking dynasties made a de facto shift in the matter of its wearing. The Duke's case was extreme but a showy vulgarity was not unique. More cloth was being used for each garment, "an excessive, pompous and improper use, an open and lavish wastage of resources: growing size of outfits, trains dragging on the ground, linings more valuable than the outfits themselves." The cut and line of clothes was spoiled simply to show the amount of cloth used, but it also functioned to show off one's status in a more brazen manner: "The outfits increasingly featured forms that hindered movement, accentuating all those features that had nothing to do with manual labour such as the excessive length and volume of the gowns and exaggeratedly long and ample sleeves." This changed and has continued to change as first linen, cotton and wool were used in the complex weaving of the fabric, and nowadays a variety of synthetic mixes with natural fibres and synthetic themselves. Its democratisation first begins in its use on interior furnishings and how it became a must-have for opera houses and then theatres, and the curtains, trim and even seats of cinemas. The deep red plushness of it all is an integral part of the pleasure of being taken into another, often exotic world on the screen.

opposite page

A Peruvian shaman conducts funeral rites for one of the 'disappeared' on the Peruvian civil war of the 1980s.

Zapatista women, defending Indigenous peoples liberated area, Chiapas, Mexico.

Mothers of the thousands "disappeared" by the Argentine military dictatorship protested every week in Buenos Aires.

A pioneer cosmetic surgeon during World War I.

Black Lives Matter protests following police shootings of two unarmed black men, New York, 2016.

Female *Kurdistan Workers Party* fighters with a displaced Yazidi woman.

DESAPA
MADRES de PL
MAYO
DRES de PL
MAYO

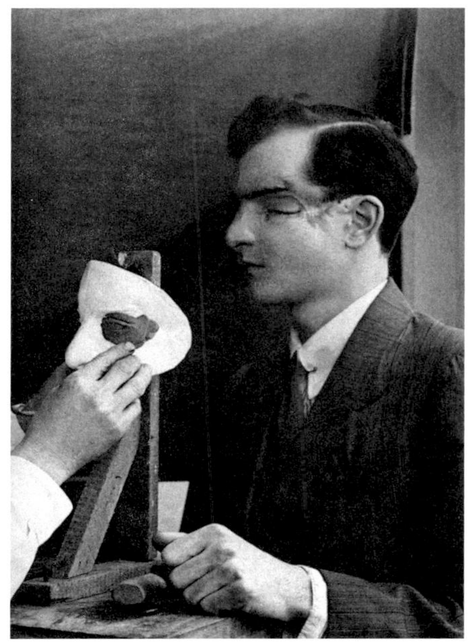

FERGUSON IS EVERYWHERE
STOP
POLICE
BRUTALITY
& MURDE
Speaks:
REVOLUTION—
NOTHING
LESS!
revcom.us

1954

On 2nd June 1954 a strike seen as a 'human rights strike' at the Omi Kenshi Spinning Company in Japan – a silk and thread factory – began. By this time, Japan had resumed its pre-war position of being the world's largest exporter of cotton cloth, having first supplanted the British in the mid-1930s, thanks to the demand created by the Korean War of 1950–53. Cotton cloth was crucial to the country's 'economic miracle', and the significance of its global role can be seen in tussles with the USA over the volume of textile imports. Many of the workers were young women from rural areas, considered to be 'docile' by the especially authoritarian company. This 'style' of production had been developed and refined in Japanese colonial Korea where textile factories recruited young women from the most impoverished countryside and housed them in factory dormitories, most of them strictly prohibiting the women from 'leaving the premises, visiting home and writing or receiving letters'. Even in these circumstances women organised strikes as at the Silk Reeling factories in 1931–32. The post-war women of Japan itself were however assumed to be thoroughly 'docile'. The Omi company held monthly conferences to select and fire workers who were sick or otherwise could not work hard enough; had a comprehensive spy work which included the opening of personal letters and searching of personal possessions; imposed unpaid overtime; imposed Japanese state Shintoism as the company religion; controlled the non-working hours of employees; and would not recognise the Trade Union. There is a suspicion that this fast-growing company had annoyed the 'Top Ten' textile companies and that they encouraged the Unions to make an issue of these conditions. If so, they misjudged the situation because the workers surprised everyone: women marched with placards in front of the company's buildings; and they held out for 106 days to win the freedoms they had demanded, and also gained approval of the new Union, overtime pay, and paid vacations. The government was seriously alarmed and tried to crack down on Unions following the Omi Kenshi strike but it inspired another by 140,000 workers the following year of 1955 both for higher wages from the major 'Top Ten' companies themselves and for recognition of the Zensen Union. Government and employers were shocked by popular support for the strike and after 20 days during which the media's useful idiots tried to characterise it as the 'caramel' strike – because the amount of money involved was small and the workers were women – a compromise was reached.

Fashion chain Primark is selling in 2017 "My First Bra" targeted to young girls roughly aged 7–13 years old. Twitter user @MissTylerB posted to the social network showing the bra and claiming it sexualises children. Primark reponded that "these bras are moulded, not padded and are designed and constructed purely for support, comfort, and modesty ... ."

It favoured the Union, whose membership, which had been just 67,000 in 1946, rose to 600,000 by 1973. More directly for the women themselves it lead to the de-emphasising of piece rates with the result that they stayed longer in the same jobs while the significance of the strike can hardly be over-emphasised, given the position of the industry both in Japan and internationally.

David Riff

"A representation which is divorced from the consciousness of those whom it represents is no representation. What I do not know, I do not worry about." Nothing is immune to cooptation, and some cooptations are very odd. La Paz is an unlikely destination for even the most adventurous Russian football hooligan. But still. The mask is obviously from there. Maybe it was bought or traded via eBay. Who knows. The loving detail of the patterns, the finely knit alpaca nose and nostrils gives you a soft clue: these masks might have had an artistic-ritual use in carnivals or other religious processions, where they could serve to hide the wearer's identity and to turn him or her into an avatar of some more abstract force, perhaps even that of some fundamental anonymous violence: the knit mask's face could be that of an exploitative white clown, especially if it were historicised by the mustache of a Spanish *conquistador* like some masks are. The one in *Die Zeit*'s picture from the Manege riots of December 2011 in Moscow doesn't have a mustache. The mouth is embroidered, a hockey mask reminiscent of Hannibal Lecter: a Friday-the-13th guarantee of anonymity for nationalist football maniacs out on an axe-murder rampage. What scares the German *Bildungsbürger* here is an intentional misunderstanding:

it presents something like a post-colonial black bloc self-image of generic protest anywhere at all where tear gas is deployed. The result is strangely flattering for the Russian nationalist football fan. He can lose his identity and join in an unconscious solidarity much bigger than himself. Something is wrong in this picture.

Things changed again with Pussy Riot. I thought their bank robber balaclavas looked extremely familiar, though I couldn't figure out why. It was only when they performed their punk-prayer that I got it. This is much closer to some inner solidarity with Aymará women who donned these masks to become their conquistador-oppressors, inhabiting that heartbeat of a heartless world that pulses through prayers. Here, I have to think of the half a million pilgrims who stood in line to touch a relic of the Virgin Mary's pregnancy belt at Christ the Savior Cathedral in late November 2011, right before the opposition's constituents underwent their political epiphanies. Unconsciously, this grotesque procession looked like an update of 19th-century Russian realism in the age of immaterial labour: pensioners, off-duty security guards, clerks, office workers, waitresses all devoutly crawling through the cordon as the mirror image of our own pilgrimages to Opposition meetings. "Black robes and golden epaulettes", "an Easter procession of black limousines", while "gay-pride is sent off to Siberia in shackles", as Pussy Riot sang in their recent punk-prayer at the same church, in which they ascended onto the dais of the altar to perform a song with the brutally clear chorus "Mother of God, chase Putin away".

What makes this quick-and-dirty hyperbole, lip-synched to go viral as a bad (or bad-ass) reproduction on YouTube so spicy as an image is that it consciously misrepresents the protests, reducing them to calls for insurrection and open violence through ultra-leftist radicals wearing Commandante Marcos balaclavas. This is exactly the kind of iconic image the protest movement has been trying to avoid, with its emphatically anti-revolutionary rhetoric, its consolidation around patriotic if not national-democratic values, and its respectful avoidance of any critique aimed at the Russian Orthodox Church as one of the state-ideological apparatuses that has filled the void left behind by the Communist Party. By resorting to such conscious hyperbole, Pussy Riot's incantation channels an apolitical indignation that otherwise cannot rise above the horizon of civic concern and fear at the most forcible possible repression.

Pussy Riot really seems to have hit the mark, and the repressive apparatus is immense. A intra-agency task-force was created to find and apprehend two of Pussy Riot's key activists on shaky legal grounds, stripping Maria Alyokhina and Nadezhda Tolokonnikova of their masks, and turning them into two beautiful young mothers who now may face up to seven years in jail. This overly harsh response has drawn the broadest criticism, and not only from the usual suspects: even leading clerics in the Russian Orthodox Church have come out in defence of the activists by asking for the mildest possible punishment, some even amplifying Pussy Riot's critique, and attacking the hypocrisy of their own institution. But even more importantly, Pussy Riot has raised an unexpected and under-represented feminist voice in the current opposition, putting the "miss back in representation" in the most decisively gendered way. This is not just about the president-elect and his machismo. Nor is just about what contemporary Russian capitalism has done to women over the last 20 to 30 years, how it has subjected them to a forcible regendering, replacing that contradictory thing called Soviet emancipation (though implicitly heterosexist and homophobic) with a consumerism rife with 1950s-style chauvinism, underpinned by the reinstated simulacra of traditionalist patriarchy. This re-gendering mirrors other similar processes of expropriation and re-subjectification that have taken place over the last 20 to 30 years. Former Soviet citizens from the Central Asian Republics – once subjects of all the contradictory and doubtful (inter)nationalism the Soviet Union offered – have become subaltern migrant workers from distant friendly dictatorships, (re)productive slave labour.

Eric Lafforgue/Constantine James

Clay, knitted cap, bought at the Alacitas market in La Paz, 2005. Eke'ko is a jolly little man offering an expansive gesture with his arms and sometimes accessorised with a burning cigarette thrust between his parted lips. *Eke'ko* means 'buy me' in the Aymará language. He is the pitch man for *Alacitas'* miniatures, some of which he carries on his arms and back. The *Eke'ko* is also linked to *pachamama*, the Andean earth mother, and is appropriately venerated as the sustainer of life. Despite the Catholic missionaries efforts to eliminate the cult of the *Eke'ko*, it has endured. At the time of the invasion, it was described as an 'image' of gold, silver stone or clay found in all homes in a 'preferential' place. Nowadays it is mostly made of plaster or plastic and it has acquired a *mestizo* look.

Bolivia Claims Repatriation of Alleged Illa Del Ekeko Statue from Historical Museum of Berne. April 13, 2014 by Nina M. Neuhaus. *Since 1929, a small-scale (16 cm in height) statue made of green stone and dating from the period between the 2nd century BC and 2nd century AD has been part of the permanent collection of the Historical Museum of Berne. The statue originates from the Andean highlands of Bolivia, where it was worshiped as a deity against thieves. In 1858, the Swiss natural scientist Johann Jakob von Tschudi acquired the statue from the indigenous people while on an excursion in Bolivia – allegedly in return for a bottle of cognac. After Tschudi's death, the Historical Museum of Berne purchased the statue from his estate. It was during a visit to the Historical Museum of Berne in 2012 that the Bolivian Ambassador to Switzerland first spotted the statue. Ever since, Bolivia has been undertaking efforts to effect the repatriation of the statue. At a first meeting between the Bolivian Ambassador and the Historical Museum of Berne in February 2013, the former claimed that the statue represented*

an Illa del Ekeko, a deity of wealth in the Aymará culture. As such, the statue was of outstanding cultural importance to the people of Bolivia. In January 2014, a second meeting took place between the parties. During this meeting, the Historical Museum of Berne acknowledged that it was in principle willing to follow justified claims for repatriation, referring to the ICOM Code of Ethics. ("Requests for removal from public display of human remains or material of sacred significance from the originating communities must be addressed expeditiously with respect and sensitivity. Requests for the return of such material should be addressed similarly. Museum policies should clearly define the process for responding to such requests.") However, the Historical Museum of Berne pointed out that it has not been established whether the statue was actually an Illa del Ekeko. Only one Bolivian scientist has so far claimed this, whereas all others were of the opinion that the statue represented either a deity of water, a deity of fertility or simply the depiction of a female figure. In order to clarify this question and as a basis for further negotiations, both parties agreed to commission a joint expert opinion. This dispute forms part of a bigger theme of how museums are dealing with the repatriation claims for cultural objects which were brought to Europe during colonial times. Although the Historical Museum of Berne stated in its press release of April 2014 that it was confident that the negotiations would lead to a solution favourable to both parties, it also pointed out that repatriation claims were usually very complex and time-consuming.

Denim Triumphant

"How did this utilitarian and unpretentious fabric become the stuff of legends that it is today?" asks Levi Strauss historian Lynn Downey. A starting point is 1930s America when Levi's jeans or 'waist overalls', which were still confined to the West of the USA, broke out of this regionalism in what has become rich territory for sociologists. Sandra Curtis Comstock points to a conjunction of "border-crossing Mexican and American intellectuals" on the one hand, and on the other of how returning Mexican migrant labour began to "conceive of blue jeans as a positive symbol of American style wage-work and market-oriented consumption", with the extra element of bohemian exclusivity contributed by those intellectuals. This was then augmented by the image of the cowboy as the authentic American, the mythic rugged individual of the American Dream. A dream of frontiers and pioneers who enclosed the land as cowboys did with wire fences. In the modern world denim is used by those trying to get into Europe through the Spanish enclave of Mellila to tie the struts and rungs of improvised ladders to be placed against the high and barbed wire fences that keep them out. In America, the pioneer image was promoted through the popularity of 'Westerns', cowboy films in epic landscapes, and followed up by Easterners taking holidays on the 'dude' ranches of California, Nevada and Arizona and going back home with their first Levi's. A further boost came from the many thousands of US troops who fought the Pacific War, returning home through West Coast ports and likely as not picking up a pair of Levi's on the way. The rebellious image that came to the fore in the 1950s is also attributed by Sandra Comstock to "Eastern college women offending the public by wearing jeans for war-work and leisure".

A double second revolution took place in the 1970s with what might be called 'designer jeans' and then 'designer denim', the impetus for which came from East Asia, from Hong Kong and Japan. In Japan this did not come from nowhere: based on the work of heavily exploited young women, the country had been a powerhouse in the export of cotton cloth, a country that grew no cotton yet was the world's largest exporter. After the war there developed a 'vintage boom' with people paying high prices for authentic vintage American Levi's and Wranglers. This in turn evolved into a style where vintage was re-created by the Osaka 5 denim companies with Evisu as the leading brand, and now Real Japan Blues. The process included the Japanese revival of original shuttle looms to make selvedge denim, and then the making of 'fake' selvedge with modern looms. It also prompted the production of high-class denim cloth including equally high-class Japanese indigo dyeing, and a reputation for attention to detail as well as expensive washes and finishes, specialised cottons, and the use of avant-garde textile designers. What took place was the *customisation* of denim, allowing for many small labels and appealing to the worldwide demand for what is *not* mass-produced. *Strike Gold, Pure Gold, Iron Heart* ranges have clearly understood how personal identity can be manifested in exclusive denim.

Der Mensch als Industriepalast
CRÉDITOS
sistema microfinanciero

2009

From 1991 to 2009, approximately 200,000 Indian farmers committed suicide. These were almost exclusively farmers of cash crops including cotton, and in most cases faced un-payable debt, despite 8 million having quit farming altogether. The incidence increased after 2002, which was when the agro business Monsanto's genetically modified Bt (*Bacillus thuringienesis*) cottonseed was introduced on a truly massive scale. One estimate is that 120,000 Bt cotton farmers have killed themselves. The statistics are not clear enough to state this as fact, but there is a clear correlation between this kind of cotton and the incidence of suicide, which goes against the claims of Bt apologists that the real causes were drought and alcoholism.
The reasons are clear enough: the promise is of greater yields and less pesticide use, but the seeds are relatively expensive and must be bought anew every time. They can neither be saved nor replanted, tangible evidence that despite capitalism's claims to produce abundance, it must reproduce scarcity. The other great claim for Bt was its resistance to bollworm infection, but in the case of rain-fed cotton this is irrelevant given the life-cycle of the bollworm and evidence from Chinese researchers, and even some in the USA itself at the University of Georgia, is that bollworm resistance is developing. Even before this, Bt crops also proved to be susceptible to sucking pests like jassids and to a resurgence of secondary pests including white-fly. In fact pesticide use has increased, furthering the costs incurred, while at the same time Bt cotton has required more water. Cash crop farmers are always at risk from the fluctuations of world prices as well as drought, but the risk has been greatly magnified by the fact that the additional costs of Bt cotton have not brought about across-the-board greater yields. It is a case of history repeating itself as tragedy. In the 19th century, the East India Company, following its role in the destruction of India's position as the world's predominant producer of cotton cloth, saw the country as a supplier of raw cotton. But the many varieties of rain-fed cotton that required no irrigation were not ideal for spinning machinery. The company's representatives were also aware that Indian cotton produced less per acre than the American cotton – a fact which they put down to ignorance, so that in 1840 the company employed ten American planters to demonstrate American-style cotton growing and gave them all the land they needed in Coimbatore. The experiment went on for thirteen years. In 1861 their supervisor Dr Wight reported that "In three years the American planters had completely exhausted the fertility of the soil by cropping it with cotton year after year". In the fourth and fifth years the crop was not worth gathering. George Watt, botanical advisor to the government noted that "It might almost be said that progression is deliberately stultified, the labours of centuries ruthlessly thrown away, and a large and important industry practically cornered or restricted in its possible development by interested parties ... since the existing traffic is aimed at the destruction of all the good features of the Indigenous fibre". Nevertheless the American seeds continued to be distributed by British colonial agents. These new seeds were one of the ways through which the mono-cultural cotton farmers of today came into being, a result of British colonial strategy. As early as 1840 worries were expressed about the dependence of the cotton textile industry on American slave cotton, and the whole country was surveyed region by region for its cotton potential. At this time Indian farmers wouldn't give up 'waste' land and precedence was given to food crops. The American planters complained of being obliged "to give way to the prejudices of workers" and of their "laziness". In 1841 the Bombay Chamber of Commerce said serious cotton growing would require wholesale change in the "customs and habits of a whole people". Given urgency by the American Civil War, this is what the British colonial state attempted to bring about, so that by the mid-1870s an official could boast that "Cotton is grown almost entirely for export. The manufacture of home cloth has been undermined by the importation of English piece goods and many of the weaver class have become ordinary labourers."

Cleaning cotton by hand in preparation for spinning at an Indian mill.

Markus Wörgötter

Montera Tarabuqueña / Felt Helmet

3

Cowhide, sheep wool, cotton, beads; late 20th century; acquired at the market in Tarabuco, Bolivia, 2008. The Tarabuco are a group of approximately 12,000 people inhabiting the south-east of Sucre in the provinces of Oropeza, Yamparaez and Zudaez (Department of Chuquisaca). They live in autonomous communities without a common political structure. These communities have constructed a collective identity through the Colonial and Republican periods but they do not share a generally accepted name. The term 'Tarabuco' is a popular term used to refer to the residents of the region by those who live outside it. Tarabuco was one of the few places where the Spanish were defeated – in the battle of Jumbate in the 19th century, by the Yamaraez warriors – and this *montera* mimics, or 'quotes', the helmet they would have worn. The victory was achieved by the people disguising themselves as trees to form a moving forest, like the tactic used by MacDuff in Shakespeare's *Macbeth*, written 200 years earlier. These helmet-like hats are made of a hard shell of dried moss, then covered with a thin piece of leather and decorated with sequins and beads. They are traditionally worn by the men from Tarabuco. If a man dies, his wife sometimes wears his hat as a sign of mourning.

Calico

Calico is a fabric finished from unbleached processed plain-woven cotton, that was cheap though made with bright colours and understated floral or abstract patterns by the traditional weavers of the city of Calicut, Kerala. They were so popular, the first cotton fabric to be so, that the English prohibited their importation in a series of Calico Acts (1690–1721) to protect the home wool market. The calico question was one of the major issues of National politics between the 1690s and the 1720s. Originally the law outlawed printed cottons, a measure that led to the importing of plain white cotton cloth and which gave a boost to the domestic business of calico printing. Dissatisfied with the smuggling of outside textiles after the original Act, Parliament passed a stricter addition, prohibiting the sale of most cottons, imported and domestic, and promoting the sale of wool.

The "calico crisis" depicted Indian textiles as a national threat not just to English trade but to gender roles. It contributed to a national debate about luxury, with women consumers of calico reproached in pamphlets which went on to attack working women who defied the "decorum of consumption". Opposition across Europe took on both a mercantilist and moral tone linked to class. Eastern luxuries were seen as corrupting and creating 'disorder and confusion' across the social hierarchy. In pamphlets and tracts in support of the wool trade, authors such as Daniel Defoe accused female domestic servants, who were subject to fewer sartorial constraints than their liveried male colleagues, of ruining England's wool industry and of causing widespread unemployment among male weavers. There were however few cases of prosecutions of those wearing calico except for an incident when angry mobs attacked women wearing it. However the bans did not effect re-exported cloth. That a considerable quantity of what the East India Company had, from early in the 17th century imported, was for re-export had been crucial in defending itself against the accusation that it was unpatriotic, an accusation that resulted from how much of what it paid in India was in bullion. That this was so was in large part because they had found no market there for even the finest English woollens. In their defence they pointed to re-export sales to the Levant. The exemption at the time of the bans resulted in merchants pretending to buy for foreign sales but on the ships supposedly for the continent secretly unloading at remote spots on the Kent and East Anglian coast. It was on such a scale, sold door-to-door by pedlars that by 1719 the Government admitted that despite its efforts "there were more Calicoes that pay no duty than what are painted and worn here that do pay duty".

18th-century wool weaving manufactury. The owner of the wool weaver's house in Dudeldorf was Master Carl Brand, who belonged to a family of weavers, controlled the whole wool making process, including even maintaining his own herd of sheep. The weaving business was often threatened by the lack of wool as raw material, which led to unstable market prices.

In France punishments were both more severe and pervasive, but in both countries attitudes changed and a 'crisis' became a 'calico craze'. Decadence was transformed into 'fashion' as a business that the country did not want to lose out on. Thus the mid-18th-century economist Jacob Nicolas Moreau talked of how "it is fashion ... a certain vanity that makes women of the lower classes so curious about calicoes. Dressed in light or printed cottons, they think of themselves no longer at the same level of women of their social station ... because ladies of quality too wear calicoes".

In Britain two forces were at work to change attitudes. First was the power of the East India Company, importers of the cloth. Between 1720 and 1770, Indian cotton textiles accounted for at least half their imports. They also soon discovered that British consumers wanted light coloured backgrounds different from the dark reds and blues of Gujarat and Coromandel. This in turn opened the door to European production, as the white backgrounds were not favoured by Indian printers. Thus when British manufacturers had worked out how to colour print cotton themselves, there was a change of tune. British officials were confident that Indian cottons could be replaced. There was one final complaint from the manufacturers. In 1782 they petitioned parliament that the East India Company had taken advantage of the "improvements introduced by them some years ago in printing on engraved metal and copper plates. By sending out plates and workmen to their Indian settlements where the price of labour is cheaper the petitioners are in danger of being ruined ... provisions were made against the seducing of workmen or the exportation of tools employed in their manufactures".

0208

One of the greatest scandals of the early 19th century in Lima was the arrest of Francisco Pro, a 20-year-old mulatto tailor. Pro was walking along the Alameda de los Descalzos one winter afternoon on 2 August 1803, dressed as a woman, with his head covered. Back in those days it was not unusual to see women "tapadas", nor for them to cover their faces as well. That day, Pro uncovered himself and revealed his identity. He was arrested and brought to trial, charged with sodomy. He was sentenced to a "public shame walk" in order to teach him a lesson and to make an example of him. The court argued that he was a pervert and a sodomite, and besides he had the "strange" profession in a man of tailoring. He was also sentenced to two months of forced labour, of which he ended up serving six, because of the sluggishness of the courts.

The veiled women of Lima, Peru, 19th century.

After the six months nothing else was known of him. His name does not appear in any other document. Maybe the authorities made him disappear, but it can be presumed that during his whole life he suffered public shame and condemnation, and that he was always considered a delinquent. The gay movement "Azúcar Rosales" decided to reclaim the significance of this historical figure on the day celebrating "Gay Pride".
There is no place on earth where women are so free and exercise so much power as in Lima. Their costume is unique. Lima is the only city in the world where it has ever appeared. The manto is always black. It completely covers the bust and most of the head, leaving only one eye uncovered. Oh! How enchanting they are, as first they draw their manto right over their face, than slyly draw it aside! I can say without fear of contradiction that if a lovely form and a magnetic glance were sufficient to ensure women the supremacy they are destined to possess, the women of Lima in their sayas would be proclaimed queens of earth. So these ladies go out alone to the theatre, to bullfights, to public gatherings, to balls, to churches and to pay visits; and they are accepted everywhere they go. If they wish to speak to anybody they do so, then take their leave, so that they remain free and independent. When the women of Lima want to make their disguise even more complete, they put on an old bodice, an old manto, and an old saya, which is falling into rags and losing its pleats; this is known as disfrazar. A disfrazada is looked upon as eminently respectable, so nobody ever accosts her; and it would be improper

and even dishonourable to follow her. It is supposed, and rightly, that if she has disguised herself it is because she has important reasons to do so. Freedom of action characterises everything she does.

The AIDS Memorial Quilt is the largest on-going community arts project in the world. It has grown exponentially since San Francisco gay rights activist Cleve Jones made the first coffin-sized panel in memory of his friend Marvin Feldman. In June of 1987, Jones teamed up with others to formally organise the NAMES Project Foundation.

Cristina Bubba Zamora

"Yes, I was angry about illegal trafficking in weavings, I'm a Bolivian, and that's how I got involved in Coroma and recovering them. What a battle that was. Because the weavings have sacred value. It's difficult to explain but they are a bridge between the people, the actual people, the members of the *ayllus** and the old ones, the first ancestors. It's how to stay in touch with them in the rituals, with the people that were living like 500 years ago and it's then that these old ones tell the people what they are supposed to be, keep alive in them the sacred geography of Coroma. People ask, how is it then, how can memories, even the name of an ancestor, be stored in a weaving, but that's how it is, an oral tradition. It's not like honouring the ancestors, no, it's how in certain ceremonies, in rituals they talk to the weavings. And in to this came the dealers, and the dealers they don't understand this, they just think, Oh this piece is beautiful or that piece is beautiful, what they think is beautiful. What they did was to wait till there was a festival, like for the All Saints' festival when the weavings are taken out of their *q'epis*, their bundles, and displayed in the festival, and then they took pictures and then sent Bolivian middlemen to Coroma with the pictures and money. Of course with money. The people there are very poor, and the middlemen kept coming back but the money they got, those that did sell, they didn't use it well. Like they kept fifty dollars and got drunk, and you know, bought themselves a radio, and all the time thinking fifty dollars was going to change their lives. And what happened was that people that sold the weavings, some of them are blind, committed suicide, they lost their animals. It's not a coincidence, it really happened. But something else happened, which is how we have got many of the weavings back where they belong, those pictures they took, the dealers, they used Polaroid photos, you remember them, and some they threw away, and the people they picked them up, and that's how we knew, how we could prove that these weavings, that were in the USA and Canada, that the dealers had sold there, belonged to the community. And we had to prove this, that they were stolen, because they were common property of the *ayllu* and no one has the right to sell them without permission because it belongs to all of them. That's how it is in Coroma, in Charazani it's different. The rituals are strong there too but the weavings aren't common property. But for Coroma, we got a clue from John Murra in San Francisco who'd seen a post-card with a Coroma weaving on it, and then we got support too from some people in those countries who knew it was wrong and they gave us support, and most of all it was other Indigenous people. Like one day, somebody was knocking at the door, and I opened and there were two Indigenous men from Canada to support Coroma because they are having to fight for their culture. And of course there are changes with the government making a stronger law and the UNESCO Cultural Property Convention, which is good, but what we had to do was to give it legal force, to enforce the Convention that these weavings are sacred. It's the first time in law history that the government recognises different values of the weavings. That's how all these things, that's how we got 48 pieces back from the USA and more from Canada in 2002. But it was a big fight. When I was in the USA with an elder from Coroma, out of the 1000 pieces the US Customs had confiscated from a dealer, we had recovered only 23 from Coroma and were ready to return to Bolivia. Only that night I had a dream with a black cloth in my arm, a dog, and the ancestors dressed in old clothes and agitated and I just knew we must look again. So I phoned the Customs and the lady she rang me back and said it was true that there was one box we hadn't seen. We went and she opened the box and there were another 25 weavings from Coroma. And then we had another big fight when they said that the weavings shouldn't go back to the *ayllus*, that the people would just sell them again. First the big museums they think they should have them. Then the authority, the main

The *jilaqata* (the highest authority of a *ayllu* or a community) Trifón Diaz dressed in a male ceremonial tunic, an *unku* or *qhawa*.

Monument to the victory of Indigenous warriors over the Spaniards in Tarabuco, Bolivia.

traditional authority they think they must control them, not the Coroma people. They think only of museums. So they built a museum in the village, but the people didn't want to put their ancestors there because it was like a jail. So the museum is built, and it is empty. Either the people must be able to live in the museum, to make rituals there, to look after them. And if they can't have that, then the museum should only be for pictures of the weavings. The people planning the museum they have no conception, all they talked of was a cafeteria and parking for cars. And we kept saying no, because it's not going to work like this. But what's good is that other communities have been inspired by what we did at Coroma."

* An *ayllu* is an Indigenous community whose members share a common focus.

Chuspa / Coca Bag

4

Cotton; Pachacámac, central coast, probably Early Intermediate Period, approx. 400–700 CE; acquired in Lima, 1978, loan to the archive. Embroidered onto the natural *Gossypium barbadense* cotton of the Pacific coast in its five natural colours, the bag is a highly unusual example of a textile illustrating the various types of plants, seeds, trees and roots, which played a vital role in ancient Peruvian agriculture. It is of particular graphic interest because of its visual inversion. The root motifs, when turned upside down, are transformed into prancing figures with waving arms. The flora of Peru, with a few exceptions, did not inspire textile artists. In an account of a procession in Potosí in 1555, Bartolomé de Arzáns de Orsúa y Vela tells us, "The whole part of the floor where the procession was going to pass was covered with rich woollen and cotton mantles that the Indians gave affectionately, and from more than 30 and 40 leagues they brought, in their devotion, in a few days, an infinite variety of fragrant flowers and herbs to cover these carpets so that the natural beauty of the fields substitute for the defects of their hand-made works".

Human Hair

There was a basket of brown wool made from human hair in the passage of my grandmother's house where I lived. She told me that they were woven from the braids of her own hair that were so long she could sit on them. In the period between the Wars she cut it off to get rid of lice but also because her family were so poor that they thought of making socks from it. As I passed the hairy wool everyday for fourteen years, looking at it first from below and than from above, touching it as often as I could though it made me shiver, for it felt both dead and alive, knowing that hair was something that grew and yet there it was, inanimate.

Nuns in colonial Latin America undertook a life of self-denigration. Atoning for their sins by suffering in imitation of Christ, they practiced mortification of the flesh, wearing a hair shirt during the day, flagellating themselves at night. When they were brought to the convents by their fathers at the age of thirteen the virgin-brides of Jesus had their hair shaved off and one of their first tasks was to make little wigs out of the hair for the statues of their blood-covered saviour. Before then the adoration surrounding the Inca Atahualpa could go to extraordinary lengths. The women surrounding him removed any hairs that fell on to his clothing and ate them, because he was very frightened of sorcery. In colonial Peru there was a hierarchy of scalps. Spanish heads of hair, though not disdained, were not as esteemed as those of Indians for the Chulupi of what is now the Bolivian Chaco. When the owners of the scalps died, their relatives would burn them on the tombs for the smoke to mark a path of easy access to paradise for the soul of the deceased. To them there is no smoke more noble than that of a Toba warrior scalp, their eternal enemies. In the myth of the *Inkarriy* (the Inca king), the Inca's head is buried like a seed in the earth where his hair will sprout again like roots and stimulate the eventual union of the head with the body, and so reconstitute the Inca's authority at some moment in the future. The fertility of the hair, whether the hair of the dead, the hair of new plants, pastures, or fleece, is essential to the reconstitution of a new being. In the ancient Andean worldview, hair was associated with the potentially wilful, wild and dangerous and therefore had to be contained, bound in braids. Fibre from the hair of camelids (sacrificial animals) or the seedpod (boll) of the cotton plant was considered sinuous and wild and as such had to be contained and ordered, that is, civilized by spinning into threads and yarn, in and of itself a quite miraculous transformational process, and which is then ordered further when woven into cloth. The colonial priests, having learned from the bible that Samson's strength came from his hair and that once cut he would lose it, had the Indigenous people shaved. In the Inca society prostitutes, *pamparuina*, had their hair shaved off in public.
The Africans brought to the Americas and the Caribbean as slaves were forced to give up their culture and adapt to the culture of their European masters. The entire life of the slave was changed: religion, speech, clothing, and even their hair. In 1905, Madame C.J. Walker invented the straightening comb. This invention not only made her the first African American woman millionaire, but now African American women no longer had to worry about the embarrassment of having nappy hair. Men also began to straighten their hair and Malcolm X describes the procedure: "When Shorty let me stand up and see in the mirror, my hair hang down in limp, damp strings. My scalp still flamed ... My first view in the mirror blotted out the hurting. I'd seen some pretty conks (the 'conk' was hair straightened at home by a method using lye, which burned the scalp), but when it's the first time, on your own head, the transformation, after the lifetime of kinks, is staggering ... on top of my head was this thick, smooth sheen of shining red hair, real red, as straight as any white man's ... This was my first really big Step towards self- degradation."
In the 1930s in Jamaica a religious movement emerged that sought to create a black identity with connections to the home of the slave, Africa. Rastafarianism offered Jamaicans a black identity through religion that was separate from the European religion imposed by colonialism. Letting the hair mat and grow uncontained is the visual expression of the dread experience of oppression.

1685

King Louis XIV of France revokes the Edict of Nantes that had allowed for religious tolerance, and instead declares Protestantism to be illegal in the Edict of Fontainebleau. From 1681 onwards he had started shredding the provision of Nantes, banning Protestants from working in various trades and pulling down churches, while also giving a green light to atrocities committed during the 'dragonnades' campaign of recantation enforced by military terror tactics. In response, an Edict of Potsdam, which encouraged Protestants, called Huguenots, to come to Brandenburg, was issued. But those who really gained from this exodus of skilled workers were the Netherlands and most of all England, which had earlier benefited from the expertise of refugees from Flanders. An estimated 50,000 Huguenots fled to England. Many went to Norwich, at that time the second-largest city in the country and one where there was already a colony of Flemish and Walloon weavers. These too had fled persecution and arrived in the

특수가발
대머리

pro-Protestant town in the great 'Stranger' immigration of 1567 and whose merchant house, The Strangers Hall survives to this day. Within 50 years the city's Huguenot master weavers had risen to become the wealthiest, most influential and cultivated class of entrepreneurs in the country. They were also present in Canterbury and then in Spitalfields, London, where they developed a silk-weaving industry with exports to the Americas and a London domestic market. The spun silk was imported from Italy and, via the East India Company, from India, Bengal and, depending on the scale of import duties, from China. Five of the seven main silk designers were Huguenots, known especially for their floral patterns. There was also an output of plainer silks. It was they who set up the Royal Lustring Company. Over the next 300 years their workshops and merchant houses in Spitalfields were used by new groups of immigrants, first Jews and then Bengalis who continued the work of general textile production. Nowadays these places are likely to be bars or art galleries. Meanwhile in the North of Ireland, where they were active supporters of the Protestant king William of Orange, one of them, Louis Crommelin is said to have planned the development of a linen industry and set up a factory at Lisburn, near Belfast. Other historians claim it was an earlier Huguenot who created linen manufacture, and that there were already 1000 looms in the North. Whichever version is true, by the end of the 19th century Belfast was the linen capital of the world, with more spindles than anywhere else and more power looms than in Britain and Europe combined.

François Rabelais

The ladies at the foundation of this order were apparelled after their own pleasure and liking; but, since that of their own accord and free will they have reformed themselves, their accoutrement is in manner as followeth. They wore stockings of scarlet crimson, or ingrained purple dye, which reached just three inches above the knee, having a list beautified with exquisite embroideries and rare incisions of the cutter's art. Their garters were of the colour of their bracelets, and circled the knee a little both over and under. Their shoes, pumps, and slippers were either of red, violet, or crimson-velvet, pinked and jagged like lobster waddles. Next to their smock they put on the pretty kirtle or vasquin of pure silk camlet: above that went the taffety or tabby farthingale, of white, red, tawny, grey, or of any other colour. Above this taffety petticoat they had another of cloth of tissue or brocade, embroidered with fine gold and interlaced with needlework, or as they thought good, and according to the temperature and disposition of the weather had their upper coats of satin, damask, or velvet, and those either orange, tawny, green, ash-coloured, blue, yellow, bright red, crimson, or white, and so forth; or had them of cloth of gold, cloth of silver, or some other choice stuff, enriched with purl, or embroidered according to the dignity of the festival days and times wherein they wore them. Their gowns, being still correspondent to the season, were either of cloth of gold frizzled with a silver-raised work; of red satin, covered with gold purl; of tabby, or taffety, white, blue, black, tawny, &c., of silk serge, silk camlet, velvet, cloth of silver, silver tissue, cloth of gold, gold wire, figured velvet, or figured satin tinselled and overcast with golden threads, in divers variously purfled draughts.

In the summer some days instead of gowns they wore light handsome mantles, made either of the stuff of the aforesaid attire, or like Moresco rugs, of violet velvet frizzled, with a raised work of gold upon silver purl, or with a knotted cord-work of gold embroidery, everywhere garnished with little Indian pearls. They always carried a fair panache, or plume of feathers, of the colour of their muff, bravely adorned and tricked out with glistering spangles of gold. In the winter time they had their taffety gowns of all colours, as above-named, and those lined with the rich furrings of hind-wolves, or speckled lynxes, black-spotted weasels, martlet skins of Calabria, sables, and other costly furs of an inestimable value. Their beads, rings, bracelets, collars, carcanets, and neck-chains were all of precious stones, such as carbuncles, rubies, baleus, diamonds, sapphires, emeralds, turquoises, garnets, agates, beryls, and excellent margarites. Their head-dressing also varied with the season of the year, according to which they decked themselves. In winter it was of the French fashion; in the spring, of the Spanish; in summer, of the fashion of Tuscany, except only upon the holy days and Sundays, at which times they were accoutred in the French mode, because they accounted it more honourable and better befitting the garb of a matronal pudicity.

opposite page

In 1840 Brittany Thomas Trollope watched hair dealers shearing peasant girls "like sheep". In 19th-century England inmates of prisons, workhouses and hospitals routinely had their head shaved, the sale of the hair providing an income to the institutions. The harvesting of hair is dependent on the poverty of the sellers. It is no coincidence that most hair now on the market is black, and these days 'virgin' hair from India and Brazil is big business.

In 1599, the Duke of Württemberg put on a spectacle whereby he and his courtiers dressed up in skins to simulate the nakedness of the 'Indians' of the Americas.

The men were apparelled after their fashion. Their stockings were of tamine or of cloth serge, of white, black, scarlet, or some other ingrained colour. Their breeches were of velvet, of the same colour with their stockings, or very near, embroidered and cut according to their fancy. Their doublet was of cloth of gold, of cloth of silver, of velvet, satin, damask, taffeties, &c., of the same colours, cut, embroidered, and suitably trimmed up in perfection. The points were of silk of the same colours; the tags were of gold well enamelled. Their coats and jerkins were of cloth of gold, cloth of silver, gold, tissue or velvet embroidered, as they thought fit. Their gowns were every whit as costly as those of the ladies. Their girdles were of silks, of the colour of their doublets. Every one had a gallant sword by his side, the hilt and handle whereof were gilt, and the scabbard of velvet, of the colour of his breeches, with a chape of gold, and pure goldsmith's work. The dagger was of the same. Their caps or bonnets were of black velvet, adorned with jewels and buttons of gold. Upon that they wore a white plume, most prettily and minion-like parted by so many rows of gold spangles, at the end whereof hung dangling in a more sparkling resplendency fair rubies, emeralds, diamonds, &c., but there was such a sympathy betwixt the gallants and the ladies, that every day they were apparelled in the same livery. And that they might not miss, there were certain gentlemen appointed to tell the youths every morning what vestments the ladies would on that day wear: for all was done according to the pleasure of the ladies. In these so handsome clothes, and habiliments so rich, think not that either one or other of either sex did waste any time at all; for the masters of the wardrobes had all their raiments and apparel so ready for every morning, and the chamber-ladies so well skilled, that in a trice they would be dressed and completely in their clothes from head to foot. And to have those accoutrements with the more conveniency, there was about the wood of Theleme a row of houses of the extent of half a league, very neat and cleanly, wherein dwelt the goldsmiths, lapidaries, jewellers, embroiderers, tailors, gold-drawers, velvet-weavers, tapestry-makers and upholsterers, who wrought there every one in his own trade, and all for the aforesaid jolly friars and nuns of the new stamp. They were furnished with matter and stuff from the hands of the Lord Nausiclete, who every year brought them seven ships from the Perlas and Cannibal Islands, laden with ingots of gold, with raw silk, with pearls and precious stones. And if any margarites, called unions, began to grow old and lose somewhat of their natural whiteness and lustre, those with their art they did renew by tendering them to eat to some pretty cocks, as they use to give casting unto hawks.

Awki, Chola and K'usillu; acquired at the Alacitas market of La Paz in 2010. On January 24th there begins a month-long observance of *Alacitas*, the annual festival of hope for a bountiful future in La Paz, Bolivia. A mix of Indigenous and European traditions, *Alacitas* encourage the purchase of miniatures in the belief that with enough faith and effort from the devotee, they will grow into the real thing before the next year. The miniatures have morphed over the years with advances in technology and expectations. Trucks, cars and houses, along with dollars and Bolivian currency, used to dominate, but these are now being replaced by global currencies. To add to their prospects, shoppers can also purchase a blessing. The blessers burn offerings of coca, honey and flower petals over tiny braziers and pass the miniatures through the smoke. Another technique employs intinction, using a flower dipped in solutions. The *awki* is a Carnival dance costume and in Aymará it also has another name, *achachi khumu*, which means hump-backed old man. The word derives from *achachila*, which is rich in meanings: grandfather, authority, ancestor, tutelary god. The dance reflects respect and homage to those who have attained wisdom and the outfit consists of breeches, frock coat, silk scarf, coca bag, parchment mask, tin hat, necklace of shells and seeds, and a crooked stick. It is danced bent over; the dancers pause to complain and to rub their aching hips and then fall, roll onto the floor, stand again, then complain once more. The *chola* accompanies her partner, the *ch'uta*, wearing luxurious finery along with the *pollera*, a heavily pleated skirt traditionally used by Spanish peasants of the 15th century, in which the multicoloured silks and velvets exceed 12 in number at the very least. The *k'usillu* is much more than a mere satire of libidinous white and mestizo authority figures, although he does portray their defects. He can take on the characteristics of the partridge, the fox, the *vicuña*, or the hunter. Also, following the changes brought about during the colonial period, he can represent the devil: not the fearsome but the mischievous one, bringing confusion as a reminder that not everything in life is serious, static and ordered. He inspires good humour and joy. Southern Peruvian peasants play the "pebble game".

Miniature iconic texts built out of pebbles make requests to powerful beings, and are used as a mode of communication. They operate on different assumptions about the relationship of form, substance, and human action than abstract alphabetic writing. A sense of this is given by Michael Sallnow's description of fooleries during the annual *Qoyllur Rit'i* pilgrimage around the time of Corpus Christi: "... some indulged in general horseplay, leaping and jumping around amid much shouting and laughter. Others played a game of make-believe. One ... bought a cow from a companion, in reality a lump of quartz, for which he gave a handful of scraps of paper representing money and which he tethered with a strand of wool from his cap. He then took his cow over to a group and proceeded to sell it to them in turn. The original vendor's scraps of paper, meanwhile, have become seeds, which he went off to plant. Others, meanwhile, occupied themselves in the construction of elaborate miniature houses and corrals out of rock, with stones representing llamas, alpacas, and sheep, to indicate the devotee's desires."

Indigo

"One hundred thousand slaves, Black or mulatto, work in sugar mills, indigo and cocoa plantations to gratify our newly acquired appetites ... things unknown to our ancestors", wrote Voltaire in 1756. In the period from around 1600 the production of indigo dye from India, from where it had gone to Europe through the Middle East for hundreds of years, could not meet the demand for the bright blue and variations of colour it could produce. This meant that until British colonialism finally established a ruthlessly organised indigo industry there, its profitability excited the colonialists of Spain, France, Holland and Britain in the 'New World' of the Americas. As early as 1609, the Spanish invaders required the Pipil Indians of the coastal plains of El Salvador to pick the wild variety of the plant as part of 'tax obligations', and were able to export 700,000 pounds of indigo from Veracruz, the atlantic port of Panama to Spain. It declined in the mid-17th century because of a fall in the population due to illness that was in part caused by the toxicity of dye-processing in vats.

Mask with dyer in the Afro-Brazilian Museum in Salvador, Bahia.

At this point, and in the developing industry in Guatemala, this problem was recognised and dealt with. African slaves as skilled labour with knowledge and experience of West African dye-making were bought to work the dye vats. The fermenting liquid smelled so foul that vats were always located well away from populated areas. The Africans were believed to be less prone to illnesses caused by the vapors as well as disease-carrying insects while Indigenous Indians were shifted to fieldwork. The French, despite banning the use of indigo in France itself, created plantations in Saint-Domingue (modern day Haiti) and also used imported slaves. By 1775 when the dye had been legalised in the 'home' country, the island was exporting 2 million pounds a year. As early as 1717 there were a hundred dye works, and fortunes were made. By 1789, at the time of the French Revolution, there were 1800 indigo plantations. This business collapsed as an unintended consequence of mulatto planters rebelling against all-white rulers. Both sides armed their slaves, hastening the revolution by the slaves themselves, a shock to rulers everywhere, a revolution still not forgiven by the West. The British, not to be left out, had invaded Jamaica in 1655 and 20 years later there were 60 slave-operated dye works there. Slowly, indigo gave way to sugar, an even more profitable slave economy, and the indigo business shifted to British controlled South Carolina, another business built on slavery. Hand-picked slaves who worked in the indigo dye-houses of South Carolina in the mid- to late 18th century when it was still British were easy to identify: their hands were stained blue, and the dyeing process was as toxic as ever. Over time the Africans proved as vulnerable to the effects of fermentation and precipitation from the vats as the

Indigenous had been. "From fifty to sixty hands work in the indigo factory; and such is the effect of the indigo upon the lungs of the labourers, that they never live over seven years. Every one that runs away, and is caught, is put in the indigo fields, which are hedged all around, so that they cannot escape again." This did not stop planters resenting the cost of replacing the slaves who died so young. Contemporary accounts also show that when prices were high, indigo dyestuffs could be exchanged for slaves. A planter could ride to Charleston and exchange "indigo pound for pound of negro weighed naked". Eventually the "blue gold" became a prized cash crop for the textile industry with a 1748 shipment of 130,000 pounds to English producers. The South Carolina bonanza in which fortunes were made and capital accumulated to be used in other business came to end late in the 18th century, by which time part of North America was independent and the British had started organised capitalist production in India. It is in the spirit of that time and this view of humanity that the directors of IG Farben, the self-styled 'Council of the Gods', should have called their chemical plant at Auschwitz, designed to make dyestuffs as well as synthetic rubber, Buna-Werke. In 19th century Bengal *buna* was the name given to the men who worked in the indigo vats.

1944

The bold working class urbanites of Cuzco, Peru, were the targets of the modernising project of the 1920s and its moralising tenets. The marketplace became the obsession of the social-cleansers: the marketsellers, the *mestizas* and their so-called filthy appearance were a constant source of worry to the city rulers. They proposed banning the *'vestido de castilla'*, a colourful woollen skirt with which *mestizas* marked their identity as self-respecting and successful Indigenous urbanites. To the elite male authorities, however, the skirt was a "favourite nesting material for bugs and filth of all sorts, a permanent carrier of bacteria". Instead of their usual dress, *mestizas* were to wear white, body-length aprons and short hair. In 1944, the market women created the *Sindicato de Mercados Unidos* (United Markets Union), one of the most active and regionally important among the many Unions of the city. Through their actions they became a symbol of popular classes' struggles. During a General Strike in the 1970s, which was called in response to a rise in the price of gasoline and therefore of transport costs, six female market vendors kidnapped the opposing General Daniel Vargas Dávila. "They grabbed him by the neck, pulled off his military jacket and his hat, and urinated in it" and forced him to negotiate an end to the strike. In the same period, at the end of the Second World War, the market women of Lagos, Nigeria supported a General Strike in the country which gave impetus to the decolonisation movement for self-determination. They were a well-organised group who from 1908 had combined on an ad hoc basis for specific struggles against the British colonial power such as that against the imposition of water rates. By the 1920s the Lagos Market Women's Association had been formed. Its initial test was to oppose a colonial government plan to impose a tax on them, and they then successfully resisted its plan to move the Ereko market to another location. When the War did start, regulations were imposed to raise revenue. The women organised mass protests against income tax, arguing that it was against customary practice to tax women; that it was they who were having to feed and clothe unemployed men; and, significant for the national liberation struggle, they argued 'No Taxation Without Representation', the slogan of the North American Revolution of 1776.

Bundles of cloth left during the day by rural day workers at the edges of a park in La Paz where they spend the night.

Waldo Jordan

"I can hardly believe it, it's more than thirty years since I began to work with textiles. In fact, my God, it's coming near to forty. It started this way when I was around 14 and I went with my mother who is from the Andean zone, to the central part of the country for some reason I don't remember, and in this little town I found a very large scarf, and I said, 'this scarf must be for a gringo' because it was so big, three, maybe four metres. But then I think no, it's impossible to use as a scarf even for a big guy. Anyway, I bought it and began to ask people how they wore it, and then I started collecting you know, with *ch'uspas*, the coca bags, then belts, the cheapest ones. The first things I showed, it was an exhibition in La Paz at the time of 150 years since the independence of the country and I showed two pieces, a wedding dress from Charazani and a dress for men from the Richu tribe, and can you believe it, they were the only two things from Indians in the whole show. And I was very happy that I'd done this but three or so years later I saw I had made a very big mistake because the *manta* (carrier cloth) covering the back was from my community, but the skirt was from another and the belt from another. It wasn't the last mistake either. I was making trips into the country and these nice old people invited me to a fiesta, a thanksgiving and this old guy, Pedro Vargas was his name, says to me, 'Waldo, you shouldn't wear that *ch'uspa*'. And I said, 'Why?' because it was very nice and he says, 'Yes, your *ch'uspa* is very nice, but this is a mourning piece, it's not for a festival.' I was so embarrassed but I learned my lesson. For something to be nice, to be beautiful, is not enough and I said to myself, never again use a piece if you don't know what it's for. This is part of what I've learned about weavings, which are not like making a shirt or pants where you cut the material. With those, anyone can have the same idea but with a weaving it's from inside you. First you have to ask permission from *pachamama*, from all the Cosmos to make a weaving because you are bringing your own life into it, who you are, what you will do. All your feelings are in the weaving and for the weaver it's alive like the woven bags are alive. Or it's a record, a memory of the life, which can be read. Not like you read a book in Europe because it is also something useful, like a woven table-cloth but at the same time it can be read. But of course we are losing many things because our young people, they don't know any more, they don't read them. And this is even now when the situation has changed, when it should be easier to be an Indian. Years ago, if you have an Indian name, if you looked like an Indian, it was very hard. The situation is better now, but not completely. For one thing the people are not appreciating their own culture enough. OK there are more Indians in the government. From the 1944 Constitution they said this is a multicultural country, but they make it in a folkloric way, because there is too much colour, too much story. That way the system is still using the Indians. Like the costume of Evo Morales, when he came to be President he didn't go straight to the palace, no, he went to Tiahauanco and the people prepared a pre-Hispanic piece for him, a cap and an *unku*. But in those times before the Spanish you were using the *unku* naked. Not the other thing inside. They were trying, but they got it wrong. I don't have anything against things being mixed in principle, it's not that, it was always that people living in the *altiplano* had to come down to the jungle or the sea, they needed coca leaves or a boat or they were escaping Spanish taxes. And then the Inca were moving a lot, moving themselves and whole communities, we have Bolivian communities from Lake Titicaca region living now in Salasaca, Ecuador. And in the past, from colonial times there was mix. Indians were prohibited to use their own dresses. Then they began to use all the Spanish dresses. But when they made the Indian ceremonies, revelations, they began to use some Indian dresses, because at those moments it's very important. Still now, when they go to some celebration, some parade, I don't know, what, que cosa, ah, yes it was when the people were asking to change the constitution, the new constitution, and the people were walking from, very near and far, I don't remember the city, and I was coming by bus from Cochabamba. Very far away from La Paz, we couldn't come any further, and then we began to walk, yeah, and the people were walking, I don't know, 1 week, 10 days, I don't know. But more Indians, with their own dresses, their music playing, it was very nice, and some people some people from La Paz were coming to meet them and all the people had the same *polleras* (skirts), but the *polleras de balleta*, the Indian *polleras*, the Indian materials, the Indian *mantas*, the white hats, not the black hats from the cities, the men with *ponchos*, and when they arrived at the city I went to take photos, it's very important to them, well they use the western dresses, but over the *poncho*, over the hat, when they come from the community. They come with jeans, but when they are close to the place, they opened their *mochilas* (backpacks) and they changed."

7 Aprons, 13 Photographs 6

Cotton and synthetic fibre, as worn by the market women, late 20th century; acquired in La Paz at a street market, 2008. Cretan fertility goddesses and Assyrian priests wore sacred aprons, and Egyptian rulers showed their status by wearing jewel-encrusted ones. In Europe

during the Middle Ages tradesmen and artisans began wearing aprons to protect their clothing and were in fact generally called 'apron men'. They were so common that several trades boasted distinguishing styles. As far as women's power to act is concerned, Andean society still works with constructs created by hegemonic European and androcentric historiography. Marisol de la Cadena's study on the market women of Cuzco in the period from 1930 to 1960 describes the situation differently, in that the categorisations of Indigenous people and *mestizas* are not analogised with a development process from the primitive to the civilised. Rather, in this study Indigenous perspectives reflect various social relations by means of endless relational classifications. She describes how ethnic categories are negotiated in specific interactions even though they are based on racist classifications. *Mestizas*, for example, claim authority on the grounds that unlike Indigenous women they are not servants, they live in the city, and they earn a respectable living as merchants. Based on the quality of a fabric, the shape of a blouse, the way a shawl is worn, the material of a hat, and so on, the *mestizas* and their customers fit themselves into a classification system that places the *india* (the Indian) and the *buen mestiza* (the good *mestiza*) in the lowest and highest position, respectively. Women, then, are perceived as *india*, *mestizas simples* (simple *mestizas*), *casi damas* (nearly ladies), *damas* (ladies), and *buenas mestizas* (good *mestizas*). Rank-specific clothing describes a power structure that generally refers to differing economic circumstances that are not necessarily ethnic. However, the ranking also permits a situation-dependent interpretation of interactions that can shift continuously. For instance, by changing clothing an *india* can become a *dama* or vice versa, thus expressing a social transformation preceded by the long process of learning how to wear clothes. In spite of prohibitions by the colonial master the Indigenous women's mantle, *aksu*, continued to be important. In the more remote communities it took more time for the Spanish to enforce their policies, but particularly in Bolivia the Indigenous women continued to wear the *aksu* over Spanish-style clothes. Worn as an apron over the full skirt, today's aprons of the market women might be seen as a variation.

Remix

In 15th-century Italy the showing off of wealth involved using too much velvet cloth for clothes, which led to vast portions being destined for the scrap heap. "In reality, of course, everything was saved and re-used in making shoes, purses, muffs and border, velvet with gold ground, which is especially strong structurally, were used right down to the smallest snippets and were always saved from discarded clothing and re-cycled in other items." The celebrated Navajo weavers would unwind red thread from a commercial wool flannel called *bayeta cloth*, like that from the blankets of Spanish soldiers in Mexico, and reweave it with other dyed and spun yarns. It was because although they had a range of wonderful dye colours they did not have satisfactory red. One step back from this and the very *bayeta* cloth was originally English bay (a coarse open woollen stuff), exported to Spain where it would be dyed red with that country's abundant supply of cochineal. It would have been easier for the Navajo when it became available from North America where it was being advertised in 1746. In West Africa Yoruba and Edo weavers used unravelled wool yarn from imported textiles to make their most vividly coloured brocaded patterns, and the *kente* cloth for the Asante elite of what is now Ghana relied on purchases of taffeta and other overseas textiles unravelled for their yarn.

Hand-woven Madras cottons from India with specific plaid and check patterns have been highly prized by the Kalabari people of the Niger Delta since the 1800s, when they came via England, as they still do today. Once in Nigeria, additional designs are added to the cottons by pulling white and bright threads: "design by subtraction". Using a needle and razor blade, one end of a thread is lifted up and cut, then pulled out to leave an empty space. By this means, a Madras is transformed into a *pelete bite*. Such cloths are treated as a precious commodity, to be used only for special events.

Jaime Saenz, a Bolivian poet, wearing a jacket of a loadcarrier, made out of textile scraps.

In Santiago de Chile under the Pinochet regime women from its slums embroider arpilleras with scraps of wool and old cloth. The arpilleras are sold in churches. That anyone buys them is incredible. The women are amazed: 'We embroider our problems and our problems are ugly'.

Contemporary Mayan women make 'bricolage' textiles "often constructed with more creativity than grace, they compose fragmented influences: wool and wild cotton, acrylic and synthetic metallic yarns; indigo and aniline dyes; rickrack, lace, gauze and polyester. This is more than 'making do', rather that the 'appropriations' and improvisations in women's textiles are deliberate and sometimes culturally subversive." Similarly the Chiriguano Guaraní agricultural festival has joined up with the *Criollo* carnival, "keeping its social cohesion and proprietary rites through a ceremony full of alien signs without losing its originality and its poetry. The masks used for the ceremony are of *Chané Arawak* origin, the top hats are a colonial legacy, the outfits show an Andean influence on *mestizo* clothes, the ornaments are Chiriguano, Criollo, Andean, Nivaklé, Lengua, maybe Mennonite. Some of the disguises, alongside jaguar skins, heron feathers and *caraguatá* textiles use motorcycle gloves, fake wigs and dark glasses.

Wooden *samuhú* masks are decorated with falcon wings that carry, like a collage, a face cut from a magazine, masks made from the fur of wild cats, *pecarí* or wild deer co-exist with others made of cardboard and plastic; representations of ancestors or mythological beasts share the festival with Batman and ET." In Kayapo culture in Central Brazil *õ nêkrêx*, refers to ornaments or specific rights that are individually inherited and are highly esteemed. Innovations in ornamentation become the ritual privilege of the inventor, though they may have originated with other groups. "After a fire destroyed one village the feather headdresses for the final dance of an important ceremony were lost. Without the headdresses it would be a shameful show. Someone had the idea of going to a town and buying up plastic drinking straws in different colours and with this made a headdress that, from a distance, looked just like the *áká* feather headdress. The monopoly right to make it was passed on as an inheritance, but the recipient generously 'lent' them to people who didn't have enough feathers or simply fancied wearing the new version."

The *aparapitas*, the load carriers of La Paz, were described in the 1970s thus: "He has patches in all colours and shapes, in all kinds of fabric ... Felipe saw patches as little as a thumb nail and as big as a hand; he saw patches from velvet and leather, from hessian from flannel, from silk, from floor-cloth, from wool cloth, from canvas, from rubber, from denim, from jute, from chamois leather, linen and oil cloth. He saw patches which were circular, square, triangular and many-sided, some fitted perfectly, others ugly, others neat, but all sewn very tight, and as a matter of course with the most diverse materials: thread, hemp, electric cable, shoe laces, wire and stripes of leather."

2002

In Saudi Arabia 14 Mecca schoolgirls at the Makkah Intermediate School No 31, Saudi Arabia, were killed by a fire. The school was run by the General Presidency for Girls' Education, a government agency controlled by conservative clerics. It had ignored warnings about the dangers of overcrowding in the school which was kept locked to ensure full segregation of the sexes, and where there was also a lack of fire extinguishers and alarms. The deaths however were made certain by the actions of members of the religious police, the Committee for the Propagation of Virtue and the Prevention of Vice, who stopped girls from leaving the building and hindered rescue workers because the girls were 'not properly covered', that is, in headscarves and black robes (*abayas*). In the eyes of the religious police there was a danger of physical contact between the girls and the civil defence forces, which might in turn create sexual enticement. One witness reported seeing three policemen beating girls to prevent them from leaving, and another reported being stopped in attempt to help them because "it is sinful to approach them". A Civil Defence officer said, "Whenever the girls got out through the main gate, these people forced them to return through another." This resembles the so-called "Shirokiya Incident" in Tokyo in 1932, which was a highly publicised tragedy that called attention to the kimono's shortcomings and prompted many women to adopt Western-style undergarments. In this incident, female employees dressed in kimono were trapped on the fifth floor of the Shirokiya department store when the building caught fire. Newspapers reported that many of these workers died in the fire because they did not want to leap from the building for fear that they would expose their lack of undergarments to those on the ground. Immediately a law passed requiring salesgirls to wear panties.

Aftermath of Bangladesh factory collapse in 2013. Nobody knows who they are or the relation between them, but perhaps they are trying to save each other in the last moments of life in the deathtrap of Rana Plaza.

That the Mecca schoolgirls died when prevented from escaping the fire also has a terrible similarity to a history of deaths by fire in Bangladeshi textile factories producing for First-World brands. Just one year earlier in August 2001 at the Mico factory 24 women workers died and a hundred were injured when trying to escape a 7th floor fire and finding they were trapped on the stairs to the exit where the doors were locked. It followed the deaths of 54 workers, mostly teenage girls, at the Chowdhury Knitwear factory in Shibpur. A fire broke out when they were doing enforced overtime and when trying to escape found the fire escape door and the main gates locked from the outside. Up to now this horror story of locked exits to police enforced overtime and fires caused by overloaded electricity circuits, has been repeated with regularity. The locked doors and window bars, the fear of theft of cloth greater than that of loss of life, featured again in the worst ever such fire, which took place at Ali Enterprises, Karachi in 2013, leading to the deaths of 283 people and to life-restricting injuries for many more. Though it is now alleged that the cause of the fire was the failure of the owners to pay protection money, it was the impossibility of escape that caused the deaths, and this was the case despite the factory having been given Western-approved safety certificates just one month earlier.

Ruth Noack

Pinafores. The parcel arrives from Somewhere via Vienna, where it had been opened, its contents taken out, aired and evaluated, then caressed for awhile – until it was time to put them back again, envelope them in their wrapping and bury them in their box.

I myself have never been to Somewhere. My imaginary relationship to the place is insufficient. Now, to some people, blankness is a potential, to be turned into colour and sound and diagrams and stories by conjecture or projection or research. Not to me. I cannot go to that blank space. What stands between me and Somewhere is not wisdom ("Better not go down *that* path, you might burn your fingers ..."). Between me and Somewhere stand those two, Vienna and the parcel. To Vienna I have been. Vienna I know. It is where she lives, she who sent the parcel to me. Vienna (and she) are attendant in my fantasies. They are ghosts that I find quite comfortable to live with. The parcel, on the other hand, is simply present. It appeared one day on my doorstep and now it is sitting in front of me, waiting to be opened. So I do. Open it, that is.

It contains aprons.

They must have been caressed by her, those aprons, I cannot imagine differently. She would find them endearing, in their plainness. It is not that they have no frills, just the contrary, they are certainly frilly. In fact, while I unpack them, they open like paper flowers. Starched ruffles start breathing, taking on a life of their own. Or so it seems in those first moments of our aquaintance.

But, boy, they are plain. Even their patterns are plain. Not kitschy, not conceptual either. I can divine no secret in those patterns, no meaning, not even heritage. They neither seem to say: "Chola", nor: "Made in China". All I can hear them murmuring is: "Pattern."
And look at the colours. Are those actually colours? Muddy browns, nowhere near those earthy tones easily associated with expensive natural fibres. Dispirited flowers huddling on darkish ground. As if they had been washed too many times. Even the pinks seem grey. I take flight to other associations: The Japanese, don't they have a knack for finding beauty in even the dullest fabric? If I adopt their perspective, I might ... – no, something is still off.
Let's look at the fabric. Not plastic. Definitely cotton. Thin though, but not thin enough to be cousin to those fancy transparents – christening robes, lace hankerchiefs, mantillas. Rather "thin as in cheap". No one would want to dry their hands on this kind of apron. Wet hands before drying. And disillusioned wet hands afterwards. I remember towels like these from communist times. No use value at all, even after the starch had been washed away. Wait, I also saw them in my neighbour's kitchens. On the wall. Towels as decor. Apples and birds flying all over the place.
Slowly, understanding dawns. From those strange animals – by now, I have unwrapped all and spread them out around me (a room full of aprons!) – from those strange animals, from those disheveled birds emanates a story. (More likely, I am projecting onto the poor things, yet, clearly, a bond has been formed between us.) It is wrong to call them aprons, they answer to another name, old fashioned, but much more astute: "Pinafore".
Imagine two resolute hands appearing from behind, taking up the pinafore, giving it a firm shake, thus making order of frills and folds and then placing it carefully before the body.
The halter goes over the neck; strings are tied round the midriff, a perfect knot and bow centred in the back/in front. Before coming to rest, both hands (still red from prior scrubbing) give the pinafore a last stroke, straightening all residue of willfulness from it, there, finished.
Her story is another one. As a girl, she wore two. One was part of every day. It was supposed to protect a dress from dirt. After all someone must clear men's dirty dishes from the table. Sauce sloshes over, seeping into cotton. Wet hands (or dirty ones) do indeed get dried (or cleaned) repeatedly. Maybe a nose is sneakily blown on a corner of the thing. And then comes Sunday. The dress is changed. Another one is taken out of the closet. A nicer one. Not that it is more comfortable; to tell the truth, it scratches at the neck, but so pretty, oh so pretty ...! And a new apron is pinned on as well.
Alas, even on the holiday, dishes need to be cleared away. And washed. Chores done, a girl might want to go out to play with the other kids. It is obvious, that this girl cannot be trusted to keep her pretty apron fine. The one only worn on Sundays, along with the scratchy dress. What do do, what to do? Her elders know to make things right, how to crush a spirit well. It is decreed that on Sundays, she wear two aprons, the dirty one on top of the virgin, protecting it (and the dress, and the body under it) from evil.
The girl has grown into a woman. She does not do protective gear. She cooks as she lives. Pleasure is at most an arm's length away. (Do not kid yourself though: These things are never just there. She has worked hard to get here.) She relishes her silken pants. Fully aware of the stains that might be.
I imagine the women to those pinafores. In my fantasy, they garb themselves with self-respecting womanhood. Their garments do more than embellish their bodies. Their bodies do more than embellish their garments. As the knots are tied and the folds stroked flat, their bodies become round and real to themselves. Is it truly the fabric that is caressed, not the thigh hidden under it? She, I know, neither caresses out of desire nor out of pity. She loves the thought that the women feel beautiful in their pinafores. And she likes that the pinafores are pretty, despite their lack in refinement. In fact, the multitude of their lacks (lack in practicality, lack in aesthetic finesse, and now, lack in intended usership) secretly delights her. They are autonomous things. For now.

Ch'ullus / 2 Woollen Caps

7

Probably due to an edict in 1572 by Viceroy Francisco Toledo, which prohibited the traditional skull deformations, Aymarán men started to wear European headgear. The patterns of the pointed knitted caps are derived from weavings. Often they are worn under felt hats. The image shows the two Mamani brothers from the north of Potosi in 1988.

opposite page

For the forests of Brazil it didn't stop with Brazil wood and for its Indigenous peoples the land grab continues.

Wool, acryl; handknitted; acquired in Puno, 2009. Ch'ullus are typically made and worn by men in the highlands (*altiplano*) region for daily use or during festivals, and a well-made *chullo* is a source of pride. Older *ch'ullus* were made from sheep's wool with natural dyes, but now they are mostly knitted with cotton or acrylic materials and are dyed with bright synthetic colours. They have a conical structure with a multitude of bold designs. Referring to the pointed tip, Elvira Especho tells us: *The Incas taught us, so they say, to make the head grow, tying it with cord, like a damned one. ... It's to have a good head, and that's why they have a large band hanging down to the backside, it's to make the head grow.* In the case of the two archival items, the producers, using colonial images such as lions, did the same as people like Sebastian Münster, whose *Cosmographia* (1544) is also a geographical-historical description of the whole world known at the time. Even though it appeared after 50 years of voyages pioneered by Columbus, it continued a long European tradition of imaginative travel writing and imagined creatures and lower forms of life. Columbus himself had read such writing avidly and formed his view of the world before he had even set sail. It was a world of dog-faced men, cannibals, men with their eyes and mouth in the upper chest, and headless folk.

In the making of the caps the strands are knitted bottom-up, starting with a rather complicated braided cast-on and typically a zig-zag pointed edging. Traditional patterns are the weaving patterns, but these are worked horizontally rather than vertically. The knitting of traditional *ch'ullus* came very close to disappearing in most regions. It's a significantly steeper learning curve than other forms of knitting, demanding the yarn-management and hand knowledge of a weaver in order to perform with any reasonable rate of speed. A skilled *ch'ullu* knitter can make one in about 2–3 nights, or one really long day. They're knitted with the smallest metal needles that can be found, and the needles are often made from bicycle spokes. The stranded colourwork patterns vary from village to village. One of the most visible differences is in the style of earflaps: some villages feature squared tabs about the size of postage stamps, while others are adorned with semicircles that stretch from brow to well behind the ear. It is said that there are

Women in Mahuaypampa dye yarn using cochineal.

200 different types of knitted hats in the Peruvian highlands. Knitters also create babies' and children's hats, purses and, as the market for Peruvian knitting has grown, have begun making contemporary pieces such as mufflers and cell-phone cases.

Not until 600–800 CE did precursors to knitting come into existence, and current-day knitting techniques arrived in the Andes with the Spanish in the mid-16th century. The European artisanal practice of male knitters is continued till today. *Ch'ullus*, whose colour and motifs signal specific cultural information about the wearer's home region, ethnic identification, status, and sometimes age, are among the oldest surviving examples of Andean knitting.

Dye Spy

Dye chemistry was the foundation of the development of the chemical industry as a whole; pharmaceuticals, fibres and plastics, it's that important. Not surprising then, that it should have been a prime site of espionage, just as it had been for pre-industrial cochineal. Its development from coal tar was mostly a German affair. Even William Perkin, celebrated as the creator of the first synthetic 'mauve', was working in England for the German chemist August Hoffman. He and others were enticed back to Germany, which, without empire, had no direct access to natural raw materials, but was by 1877 producing half the world's colour stuffs. It continued to be dominated by German companies like Bayer and Hoechst and BASF, producing a new generation of synthetic dyes. "The indanthrene colours ... were so stable, being light-fast, waterproof and boilable that they could out last the cotton they dyed. Hoechst labels for dyestuffs conjured up attractive high coloured scenes of exotic places, animals and so on." At this time the USA was playing catch-up mostly with the aid of German chemists, including Bayer with its own production facility on the Hudson

river, though it kept a tight grip on its patents. This did not prevent a 'dye famine' at the start of World War I, German dye factories switching to explosives, and a British naval blockade. It was seen as a disaster by Carl Duisberg, head of Bayer's works at Leverkusen – a catastrophe for which they were not prepared and which effected a nearly total disruption to trade. The price of sulfur black, so important to hard-wearing fabrics like denim, rose by over 15 times in the one year, 1914–1915. When the USA entered the war itself in 1917, its 'anti-German spy' campaign focused on the dye-chemical industry and took three forms: German chemists like Louis Hihn were arrested, charged with stealing samples and formulae; others were interned; and companies with German ownership were seized by the Alien Property Custodian. This distinctive tactic of opportunism and the pre-emptive strike included seizing all the US assets of Bayer itself including its patents.

"Those who journeyed along the Silk route gained useful information about competitors, as did the 7th c. AD Chinese traveller Husuan-Tsang who noted Persian silks were twice as wide as those of his own country. This mild form of industrial espionage was reinforced by artisans themselves; weavers were analysing competitors' weave structures in order to imitate them long before scholars were doing the same to understand them."

The patents however were 'too vague' to be useful, and Du Pont, which had entered the dye business, could not get around sulfur black production problems, and so after the war they entered the espionage business themselves. The German government had prohibited the issuance of passports to chemists, but in 1921 Du Pont offered huge sums of money to four Bayer chemists in Leverkusen to defect. The usual false bottom trunks were involved but discovered, and it took US diplomatic pressure and Du Pont masquerading to finally get the men out and lay the foundations for the company's leading position in the US dye industry. Soon after this however, the dynamics of international capital asserted themselves in the face of post-war depression, and the US company which had most benefited from the Bayer seizure in 1917 – Grasselli – negotiated a collaboration with Bayer in Germany in 1924. This was just before Bayer joined with BASF and Hoechst to form the near-monopoly IG Farben. The conglomerate, notorious from its pro-active collusion with the Nazi regime, in the meantime became through the Grasselli link-up a major player in the US chemical industry, operating as the General Aniline company, while keeping its patented knowledge under tight German control.

This didn't prevent further attempts to gain German technical secrets by the USA, then the British and the French. In 1927 Guido Meisel was convicted and imprisoned for a year when trying to recruit chemists for a small rival to General Aniline, the American Portsmouth Dye company, as were the two chemists he was recruiting. In the same year three Hoechst employees with an advance high-paid contract promised were caught carrying trade secrets to England in their socks. In 1928 a 'well-organised' spy ring for the French was discovered in Leverkusen.

A very different picture of the Weimar Republic from the popular image of decadence and disorganisation emerges, for in each case the 'spies' came up against the even better organised IG Farben intelligence department, which placed agents in all of its plants.

At the outbreak of World War II, the IG Farben-controlled General Aniline and Du Pont were the dominant producers of dyes in the USA. Despite the depression, production of dyes was at record levels in 1936. But as soon as the USA joined the war in December 1941, secret service agents moved into General Aniline's offices and plants and its German-born executives were removed. Two months later, just as in 1917, the government formally seized all its assets. This was at the same time IG Farben was producing Zyklon B poison gas for concentration camps and the methanol with which to burn the corpses. Following Americanisation, General Aniline became the main producer of vat dyes for military uniforms. After the war the dynamics both of national interest, and capital as international, were at work. While Chancellor Adenauer complained bitterly that the American grab of IG Farben patents gave it a ten year lead in the chemical industry, executives of the conglomerate including those indicted at the Nuremberg trials, even when they had served short prison terms, were soon again running the banking-industrial complex of Germany. The conglomerate itself was simply broken back up into its component parts of Bayer, BASF, Hoechst and Agfa, which carried on in the chemicals business.

1794

At the same time as the revolt of Haitian slaves against French plantation colonialism is underway, Eli Whitney invents the cotton gin in the USA. One consequence of the Haitian uprising was to amplify the huge increase in slave numbers in the American South – some from other Caribbean islands and "well acquainted with the culture of cotton" – that its production depended on, and which the gin invention, by speeding up cotton processing, made profitable and therefore widespread. Another consequence was the US slave revolts inspired by those of Haiti. The slaves in Haiti (then Saint-Domingue) were used in the business of both indigo and cotton as well as coffee. Taking their cue from the rhetoric of the French Revolution, the former slaves finally formed an independent state in 1804. In the process they fought off Napoleon's attempt to retake the island. This in turn prompted him to sell Louisiana to the USA and thereby dramatically increased the land space suitable for cotton there, the expansion financed by Barings with capital they had accumulated from government loans and East India engagements. All this took place at a time when slavery itself was a dying institution in the USA because of the decline of tobacco and indigo as cash crops. Whitney's gin transformed the situation. It increased the capacity of cleaning the cotton bolls by some 50 times so that slaves – as sowers, pickers and carriers – became a profitable proposition again. However, increased labour productivity did not, as normally, decrease the number of workers, here slaves, but the reverse. This was due firstly to the availability of land in the early 1800s the Creeks were forced to give up land in Georgia that was converted into cotton farms, and in 1823 were forced to sign the Treaty of Fort Jackson that ceded 23 million acres of Georgia/Alabama, and secondly to the astronomical increase in British industry's demand for raw cotton, which between 1783 and 1825 increased from 9 to 220 million pounds.

French male revolutionary vest, 1789–94. Made of linen canvas with silk needlepoint, embroidery and warpcut-pile trim. On the right pocket lapel is written *"L'habit ne fait pas le moine"* ("Do not judge the book by its cover").

In consequence, 80,00 new slaves were kidnapped from Africa in the years 1790 to 1808. In addition, between 1794 and 1860 some 1 million slaves born in the East of the USA, Virginia or Maryland, were sold to cotton plantations in Mississippi, Louisiana and Alabama. In the 1790s the slave population of Georgia nearly doubled. This internal displacement took place while slave importation was banned in 1808, because plantation owners feared that it might incite slave revolts.

A major centre of the slave trade existed close to the White House in Washington, which had itself been built by slave labour; price negotiations were conducted at slave 'pens'. The intensity of labour promoted by free use of the whip when quotas were not met meant that the ban on fresh slave importation did not in fact prevent uprisings. Records have shown anything between 250 and 313 slave revolts, where 'revolts' are defined as incidents involving ten or more slaves with "freedom as the apparent aim", and with "contemporary references labelling the event as an uprising, plot, insurrection or the equivalent of these". In 1816 the Seminole Wars were fought against an alliance of escaped slaves and Native Americans who'd made it to Spanish Florida. The later Vesey 'conspiracy' in 1822 and then Nat Turner's revolt in 1831, in which some of the hated 'Whites' were killed, resulted in mass executions of slaves. They, like the Gabriel 'conspiracy' of 1800, were all inspired by what had been achieved in Haiti. Gabriel, a literate blacksmith, had met with liberty-minded French soldiers and was directly inspired to rally at least a thousand slaves. He was defeated before the rebellion had hardly begun by a decision not to be secretive, then by the bad luck of unprecedented storms and finally due to betrayal by a slave who feared retribution in the event of failure. He and seven others were executed. Yet only 11 years later in Louisiana, with the Haiti example still alive, Charles Deslondes mounted "the largest and most sophisticated slave revolt in US history", defeated only when his army of over 100 men ran out of ammunition in a pitched battle 20 miles outside New Orleans. The reprisals were akin to those carried out in Tudor England and 20th-century European 'civil' wars: heads severed and placed on poles along the road to the city.

The zombie myth first appeared in Haiti in the 17th century. Half of the slaves brought in from Africa were worked to death within a few years. They believed that dying would release them back to *lan guinée*, literally Guinea, where they could be free. Those who took their own lives wouldn't be allowed to return, but were condemned to haunt the plantations for eternity, denied their own bodies and yet trapped inside them.

Shooshie Sulaiman

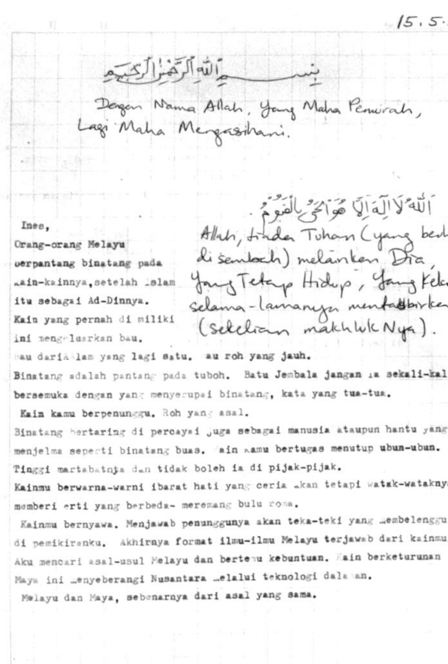

15.5.12

Dengan Nama Allah, Yang Maha Pemurah,
Lagi Maha Mengasihani.

Allah, tiada Tuhan (yang berhak di sembah) melainkan Dia, Yang Tetap Hidup, Yang Kekal selama-lamanya mentadbirkan (sekelian makhluk Nya).

Ines,
Orang-orang Melayu
berpantang binatang pada
kain-kainnya, setelah Islam
itu sebagai Ad-Dinnya.
Kain yang pernah di miliki
ini mengeluarkan bau.
Bau dari Alam yang lagi satu. Bau roh yang jauh.
Binatang adalah pantang pada tuboh. Batu Jembala jangan ia sekali-kali
bersemuka dengan yang menyerupai binatang, kata yang tua-tua.
Kain kamu berpenunggu. Roh yang asal.
Binatang bertaring di percayai juga sebagai manusia ataupun hantu yang
menjelma seperti binatang buas. Kain kamu bertugas menutup ubun-ubun.
Tinggi martabatnja dan tidak boleh ia di pijak-pijak.
Kainmu berwarna-warni ibarat hati yang ceria akan tetapi watak-wataknya
memberi erti yang berbeda- meremang bulu roma.
Kainmu bernyawa. Menjawab penunggunya akan teka-teki yang membelenggu
di pemikiranku. Akhirnya format ilmu-ilmu Melayu terjawab dari kainmu.
Aku mencari asal-usul Melayu dan bertemu kebuntuan. Kain berketurunan
Maya ini menyeberangi Nusantara melalui teknologi dalaman.
Melayu dan Maya, sebenarnya dari asal yang sama.

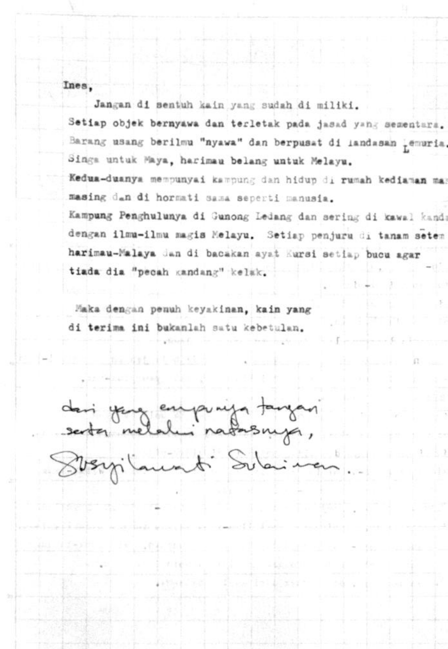

Ines,
Jangan di sentuh kain yang sudah di miliki.
Setiap objek bernyawa dan terletak pada jasad yang sementara.
Barang usang berilmu "nyawa" dan berpusat di landasan Lemuria.
Singa untuk Maya, harimau belang untuk Melayu.
Kedua-duanya mempunyai kampung dan hidup di rumah kediaman masing-
masing dan di hormati sama seperti manusia.
Kampung Penghulunya di Gunong Ledang dan sering di kawal kandangnya
dengan ilmu-ilmu magis Melayu. Setiap penjuru di tanam setem
harimau-Malaya dan di bacakan ayat Kursi setiap bucu agar
tiada dia "pecah kandang" kelak.

Maka dengan penuh keyakinan, kain yang
di terima ini bukanlah satu kebetulan.

dari yang empunya tangan
serta melalui nafasnya,
Shosyilawati Sulaiman.

page 1 Ines, the Malays have an unspoken taboo about animal depictions upon the fabric of their apparel, especially ever since Islam became their Ad-Din (Faith). The cloth that was once 'owned', emits a smell that was faint but intense. A smell of another realm. The smell of a distance soul. Animals are taboo for the body. Ancient people say that one's head must never come face to face with that which depicts animals. Animals with fangs are also believed to be humans and ghouls that transform into wild beast. Your cloth function to cover the fontanel; a place of high distinction, not to be stepped on. Your colourful cloth is like a heart that is light and cheerful; yet the characters give out the opposite, and it gave me an eerie feeling. My hairs stood on end. This cloth has Life. To find an answer to the spirit inside the cloth was a puzzle that challenged my thoughts and understanding. I have searched for the roots of Malays for a long time, and came to a dead end. However, in the end, the very format of Malay lore and teachings were revealed from your cloth - this cloth from the Mayas, that has crossed Nusantara (Malay Archipelago) via innate (internal) technology. Melayu (Malay) and Maya, are from the same origin.
page 2 Ines, do not touch this cloth that was once 'owned'. All objects have life and are placed in a temporary form. Old objects contain live knowledge, and are centred upon the landscape of Lemuria. The Lion for Mayas, the Tiger for the Malays. They each have their own villages (*kampong*) in which they live, and they are respected, just like humans. The Chief Kampong is in Gunong Ledang and is usually guarded by the lore of Malay 'magic'. A Panthera Tigris Malayensis stamp has been planted of each corner, and blessed with the verses of the Ayatul Kursi (The Verse of the The Throne, Holy Qur'an 2:255), to ensure that the tiger cannot break loose. Therefore, with absolute conviction, this cloth that I have received is not a coincidence.
From the owner of these hands, and one who breathes through Him. Shooshie Sulaiman

8

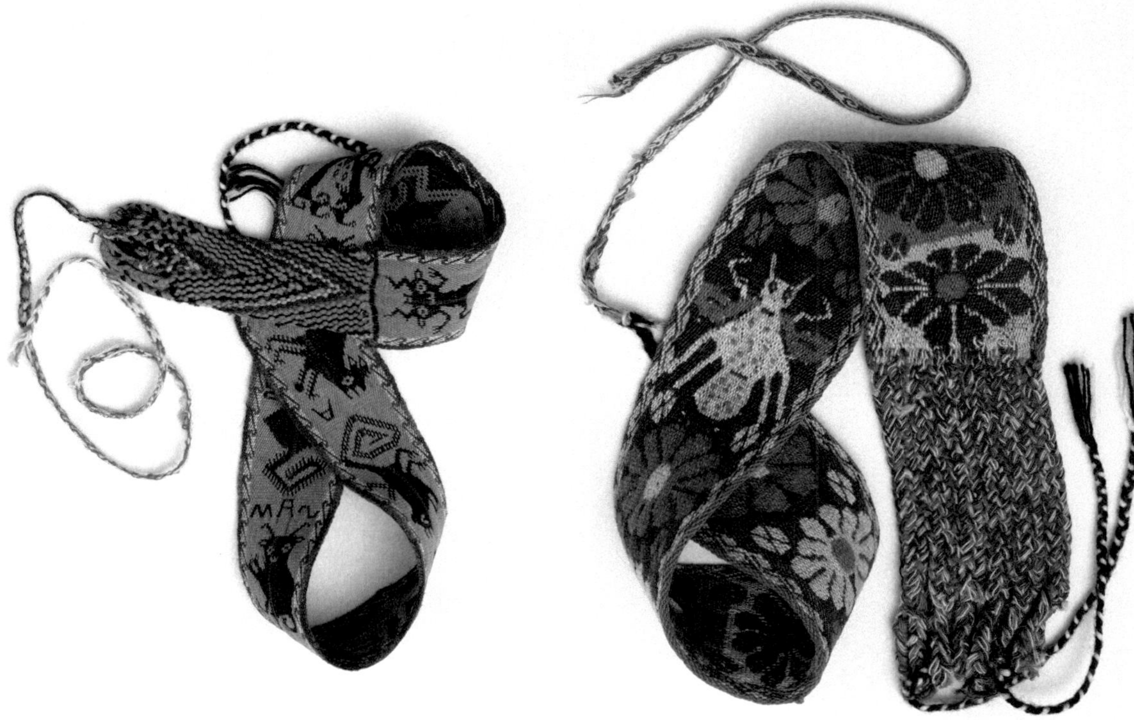

Beige and multicoloured synthetic dye palette, woven in warp-faced double cloth; ca. 1940; Jalq'a, Bolivia; acquired in a weaving shop, Sucre, Bolivia, 2010. Medium-size belts in all-over patterning with animal imaginary in oblique, interlaced units sewn and woven together ending in a looped interlaced tie. A belt is called *chumpi* or *wak'a* in Quechua. It can also be used as a headband, or *wincha*. For either use these weavings are part of the native costume indicating age, marital status, rank and group affiliation.

In one the centrepiece is a mosquito. However clear the importance of animals to Native American cultures, the spiritual basis of this shared human-animal trajectory is perhaps not widely understood. The animal-human continuum existing throughout the cultures of the Indigenous Americas flows from the high value placed on the experience of visions in shamanic thought and practice. A primary aspect of altered consciousness is the direct kinesthetic experience of becoming an animal, or several, and/or watching animals transform into other animals and beings. This is both a visceral and a visual experience.

Cashmere

The fleece of goats in Tibet and Ladakh has always produced an exceptionally fine yarn called *pashm*, but for centuries it was only spun and woven in the city of Srinigar in Kashmir from which comes the name of the cloth, as it is internationally known. This was the case despite the great distance and very difficult route involved. The 17th-century Treaty of Tingmosgang made official the near monopoly of Kashmir merchants which allowed them to pay "a most miserable price" to the nomadic goat herders. Those who carried the fleece had a worse time, underpaid for carrying 55 kilo loads over a period of 3 weeks over steep tracks slippery with ice.

"Many of the men who go from Kashmir to fetch loads of wool lose their lives or are crippled for ever", noted the Jesuit priest Ippolito Desideri in 1715. Meanwhile as an early lesson in 'value-added', the wool itself increased 13 times its original cost in the hands of merchants and factors. Kashmir changed rulers from different empires over the centuries, including, in the 16th century, that textile connoisseur the Mughal Emperor Akhbar, who encouraged the weaving tradition. During his rule he ordered experiments in dyeing so that soon 64 fast colours could be dyed. What all the different rulers had in common was to keep a grip on the business of spinning and then weaving the twill tapestry shawls that were known internationally for their brilliance of colour and design as well as their softness. Many different specialists were involved in making the shawls, including designers, design copiers and warp yarn threaders, but the weavers themselves also had a miserable time of it, "often little better than bonded labour, bound by debt and poverty to their masters and subject to oppressive laws and taxes". By age 50 they were either blind or dead from respiratory infections. When in 1865 during Srinigar's final 19th-century boom the business had become completely dominated by financiers, they demonstrated against these conditions. In response the Maharaja of Kashmir had them shot or imprisoned. The shawls became known in Europe through the ubiquitous East India Company and techniques studied by Western travellers like William Moorcroft, their curiosity transmuted into gentlemanly industrial espionage. Such shameless expropriation of the intellectual property rights of Indian textile producers was commonplace, and was documented in a range of texts, from the 18th-century *Processes Employed by the Natives on Dyeing Silk or Cotton in Bangalore* to Forbes Watson's 19th-century *Collection of Specimens and Illustrations of the Textile Manufacture of India*, which included hundreds of comprehensively described samples.

By the time the weavers were being shot in Kashmir, imitations of the shawl using both wool, silk and cotton were being industrially produced in France and Scotland; the yarn itself was also being imported by James Johnston of Elgin, Scotland, to make "Superior Cashmere tweed", a company which developed a mechanical means of de-hairing and cleaning the wool; and soon afterwards the Western fashion for the fabulously expensive authentic shawl that involved so much skill and labour-time was over. The firm of Dawson, also based in Scotland, became the biggest purchaser and processer of the fabric, supplying fashion houses, while another Scottish firm, Pringles of Hawick, pioneered the uses of cashmere for knitted hosiery and in 1933 introduced its famous sweater and twin-set. With cashmere, the usual historical ironies of cloth and colonialism apply. The authentic shawl from

real *pashm* has made a comeback for the new rich of an ultra-inegalitarian India, where it was always more than the passing fashion it had become in the West by the end of the 19th century. At the same time knitted yarn for scarves and sweaters was a huge business, and it is China with its own goats and those of occupied Tibet that is now the dominant force, rather than far-distant Scotland. From the time of the Revolution in 1949 up to 2004, due both to Western demand and Chinese migration policies, there has been a 10 times increase in the number of goats both in territory it controls and in Mongolia, where the numbers are "breaching the limits of sustainability". From 1980 China quickly learned the secret of processing the yarn, with Dawson overtaken, and also began to produce cashmere sweaters, with some 10 million exported to the USA in 2005, a 'downmarket' product in which pashma was mixed with other goat-based yarns. As with other sectors however it has begun to develop luxury-end cashmere as well as the mass product. As icing on the irony cake, Pringle is now owned by a Hong Kong company selling 'Made in Scotland'-labelled cashmere to the new rich of China itself.

0803

4 months after the 1905 Tsarist massacre of unarmed protesters in St Petersburg a strike was called on May 14th in the textile area of Russia, Ivanova, nicknamed 'cotton kingdom' and it was a kingdom in an empire expanding to grow more of its own cotton, and which had by 1900 become the world's fourth-biggest manufacturer of cotton cloth. Worker strikes in the industry were constant if discontinuous and more frequent at moments of economic upturn from 1870 onwards. Many workers were peasants with low literacy levels, which is supposed to lessen militancy but having the village as a safety net, being less susceptible to factory discipline, and their experience of the unanimity and anonymity of peasant protests, meant that the opposite was true. By this time, since the introduction of power looms, women had come to be numerically dominant in the industry. They had been involved in the Lazerev textile factory strike in Moscow in 1874 and at the Petrograd New Cotton Spinning Plant in 1878. This time, within days of the strike, support from all the area's workers led to the creation of the first ever 'soviet' (a model of self-organisation of workers), this was later disempowered by the Bolshevik party in wose name they ruled, on May 28th. It has been argued that again peasant experience was significant, this time of the village assemblies (*sel'skii skhod*) which all Russians with rural ties would be familiar with. Demands included shorter hours, better minimum pay, paid maternity leave, factory nurseries and freedom of association. On June 3rd soldiers disrupting a strike meeting opened fire, killing 28 workers in the process. The strike still held out, demands were won, and it was the greatest strike in Russian history in terms of hours lost, well over a million. Across Russia 8 million worker hours were 'lost' in this year as opposed to 1 million over the previous nine. In the Empire the weavers and spinner of the Polish textile city of Lodz stood up for their rights on June 23rd. Fighting with the army and especially the Cossacks lasted for 3 days and around 200 workers were killed. Some months later the state took revenge and set off a pogrom against workers leaders and Jews which culminated in its attack on the Moscow uprising in December which focused on the city's textile mills. Some months later however, the state took revenge and launched a pogrom against workers' leaders and Jews. In 1915 more workers were killed during a strike. But textile workers continued to be at the centre of struggles over working conditions, and for political change. So it was that in the vital period early in 1917 on international Women's Day March 8th (23rd February on the old Russian calendar), a Day Clara Zetkin had called for some years earlier at a meeting of international women socialists, women textile workers did a walk-out in Petrograd which prompted a city-wide strike that was directly instrumental in bringing about the fall of the Tsarist state. A few years earlier in 1893 the Austrian seamstress Amalie Ryba, who was only 17 and not yet an Union member, organised the first women's textile worker strike. The working conditions in the Viennese sweatshops around 1900 were horrendous: 13 hours of daily labour in rooms where the temperature were rising up to 52°C and where the bleach vapors made breathing a nightmare. The strike was successful, a 10-hours working day was won and a labour-free 1st of May.

The Russian Revolution begins in February 1917 in a mass demonstration of workers and citizens in Petrograd for food and was met with repression.

Simryn Gill

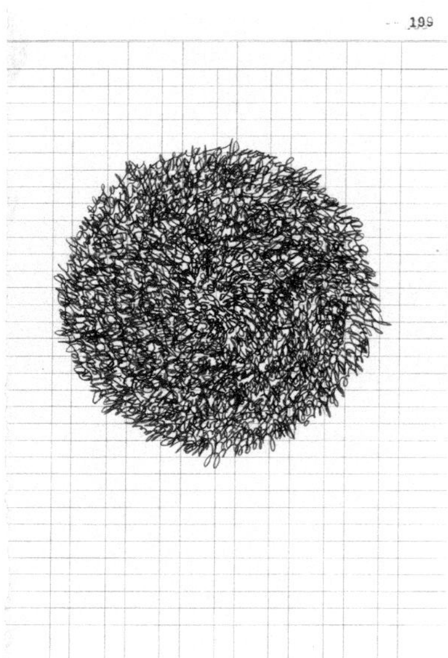

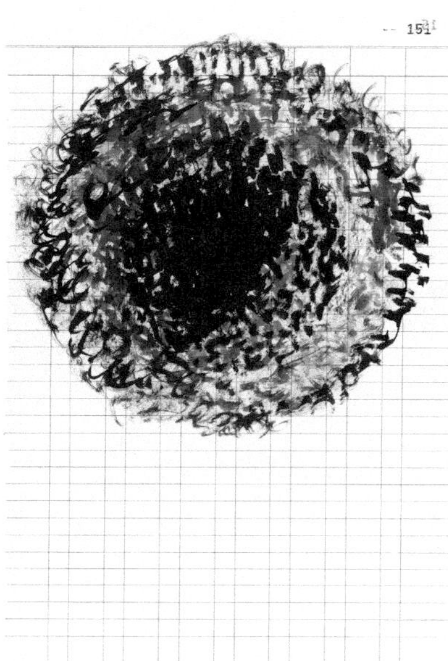

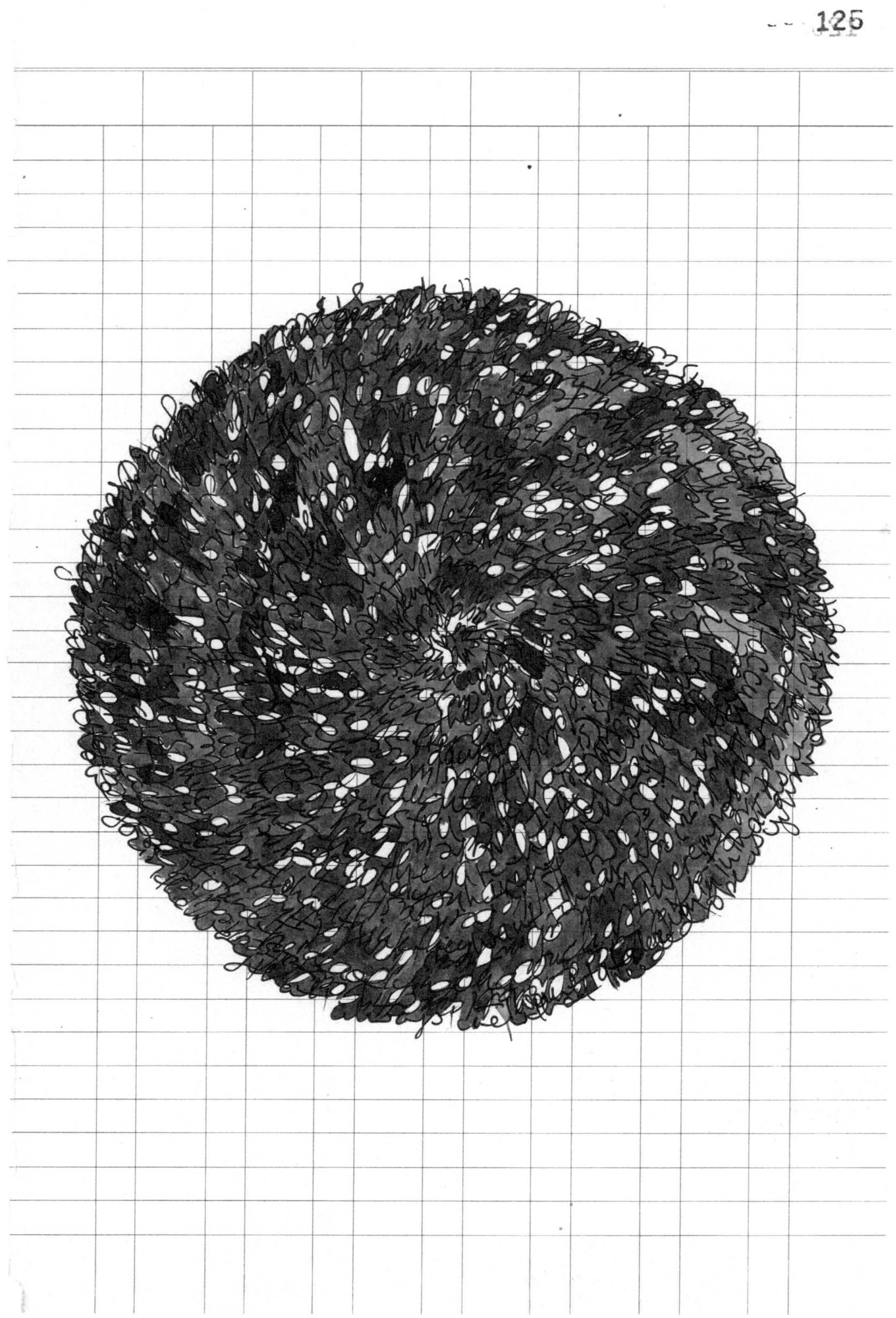

Fighting Glove

Macha; alpaca, acquired in La Paz from an antique shop, 2007. A ritual called *tinku* was once widespread throughout the Andean world, possibly as far back as 1100 CE. Early each February the people of Bolivia's highlands trek to the town of Sacaca. Mostly subsistence farmers, they dance, drink *chicha* (the fermented beverage made here from rye) and then fight one another until blood stains the earth. Men square off against each other on the streets, though sometimes women also enter the fray. Some of the men wear leather helmets and gloves, but the fighting can also be bare-knuckle. Bystanders sometimes step in to break up contests that become too uneven. In addition to bruised faces and limbs, deaths can occur. The periodic channelling of communal violence serves to reduce conflict during the rest of the year and can be a way to confirm or defend collective landholdings, or to bring good fortune at harvest time. Blood was required for participants to feel that they had consummated a harvest fertility rite. *Tinku* functions like a psychologist who helps to overcome collective and individual traumas.

The Academia Mayor de la Lengua Quechua in Cuzco, Peru, defines the verb *tinku* as to encounter, to meet. In Quechua the suffix 'y' at the end of most words adds the meaning of 'mine' or 'for me'. Literally *tinkuy* means the encounter with one's self. According to Andean Cosmology we live in three worlds, the Upper World or *Hanan Pacha*, the Middle World or *Kay Pacha*, and the Inner World or *Uku Pacha*. The Inner World is the world within us. *Tinkuy* is the act of reuniting with it. Catherine Allen describes encounters of these differing energies: "Through the *tinkuy*, social unity is created dialectically and expressed in terms of complementary opposition. Although *tinkuy* refers to ritual dance battles, the word has wider applications. It is not easily translated into English. ... When streams converge in foaming eddies to produce a single, larger stream they are said to be *tinkuy*, and their convergence is called *tinku*. *Tinkus* are powerful, dangerous places full of liberated and uncontrollable forces."

Twill

The period three to five thousand years ago could be described as a worldwide "Dye and Loom Age" in which the most sophisticated technologies were for the making of cloth. One of the first innovations was to go beyond plain weave known as Tabby, in which one weft passes over and under a single warp, and instead use the possibility of offsetting the 1-to-1 warp to weft relation

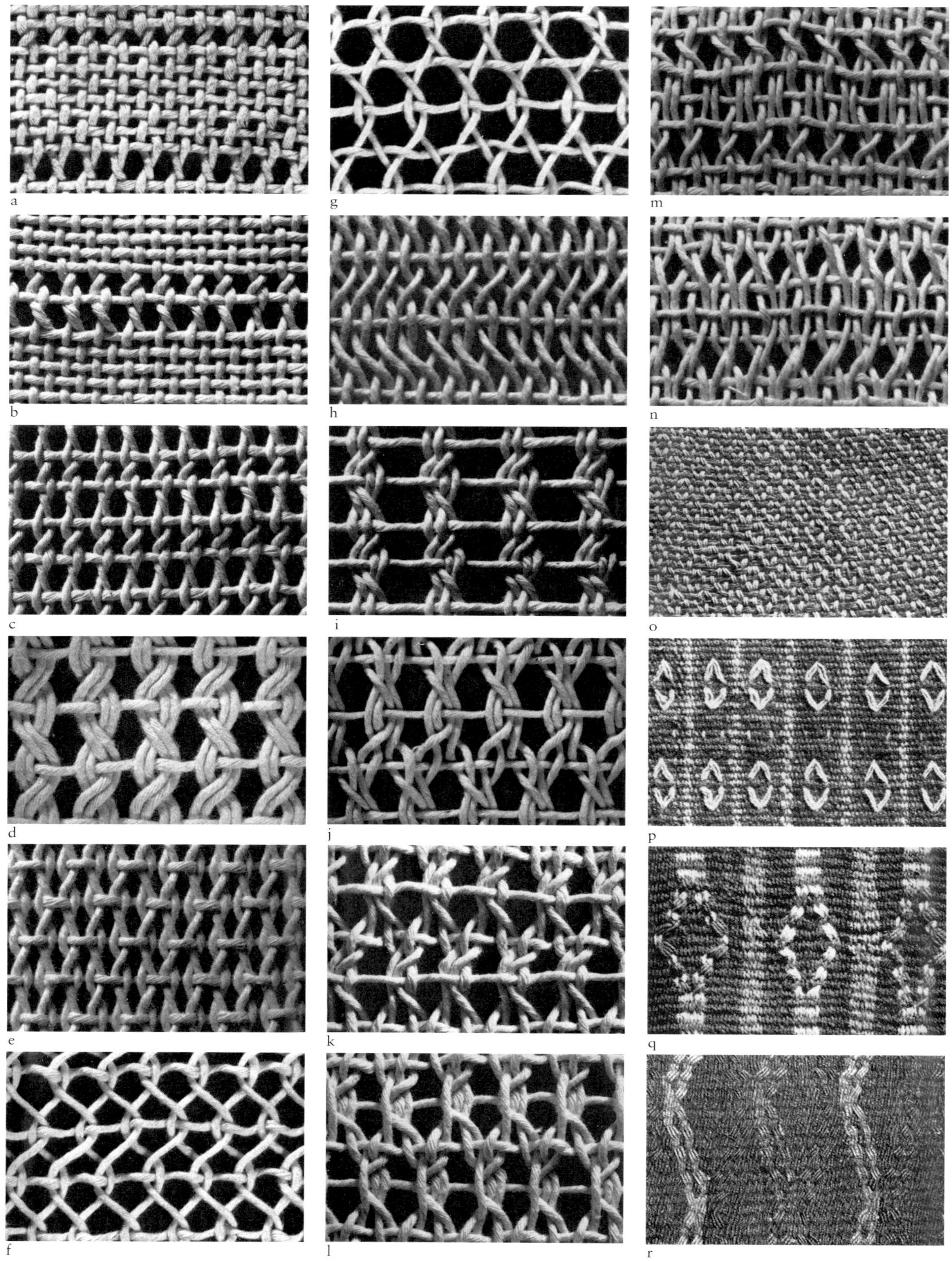

a/ Cross: Crossing alternate warps over intervening ones; b/ As above, plus re-crossing after a single weft shot; c/ Plain: Warps *and* wefts interwork; d/ Plain: with paired warps; e/ Plain: with directional variation by means of reversing the direction of warp shift in alternate pairs; f/ Simple alternating: warps interwork 2/1; wefts 1/1; g/ Alternating: intermediate non-holding wefts interlacing 1/1; h/ Simple alternating: higher warp than weft count; i/ Complex: vertically aligned groups of four interworking warps; j/ Complex alternating: two orders of weft interlacing and two different orders and sequences of warp; k/ Complex alternating: one out of every four warps floats free from 1/1 weft interlacing; l/ Reverse complex alternating; each fourth warp omitted; m/ Uneven crosses: when one warp crosses and re-crosses two warps which do not interwork with the other; n/ Opposite face of m/; o/ Peruvian: 'full-turn' countered with two non-holding wefts between holding wefts; p/ Peruvian: diamond patterns when pairs of extra-warp units alternately diverge and converge in diagonal floats; q/ Peruvian simple transposed-warp: 3 coloured warp stripes; r/ Chilean transposed-warp: series of right 2-coloured stripes in a warp-faced warp pattern of Tabby so as to produce a distinctive diagonal weave in diamond or chevron pattern, which in Bronze Age Europe, for example, needed the invention of a loom with more than one heddle. It would also have required the skill to plan out how the heddles would be used and in what sequence. There are cloth examples of this in the famous archeological site of Hallstatt in Austria in which horsehair, wool and linen were all woven.

Hallstatt's wealth was built on its salt mine and its people were Celts or proto-Celts. In the cloth that has survived, wool, both coarse and fine, is prominent, and it was by repeating the weaving sequences heddles made possible that distinctive diagonal patterns were made. In the Iron Age the stronger plied yarn was used as the warp, with the 2/2 diagonal twill occurring most frequently. As a cloth it had better heat retention than Tabby and was more pliable.

The exact moment at which a similar technique was used in what is modern day Peru is not known, but at least 3000 years ago weavers there developed it further. In their case they used both cotton and alpaca. The weft might go under two warp threads or over two and under one; either way the weft yarn is displaced from the weft yarn of the preceding row to the right and left selvages. The distinctive pattern of basic twill can be found in the modern cloths of denim, serge, jean and chino. With different coloured threads, tweed, and with a simple variation, herringbone is produced. By extending the principle to more than two wefts and by breaking up the regularity of the diagonal ridges, a more complex cloth like satin can also be manufactured. Its most widespread form in the modern world is denim, and here there have been complex varieties like 'broken twill' for Wrangler and an increasing dominance of 3:1 twill (whereas in the 1930s the lighter weight 2:1 was the norm).

"The Indians of that first age (pre-Inca) dressed like animals, because the only clothes they had was what nature gave them: their own skin" (Garcilaso de la Vega, 1609). In Quechua *q'ara* literally means peeled, like an animal hide that is worn bare. This is a pejorative term implying "non-human" and was applied to Europeans.

The Peruvian weavers understood these possibilities but they used the weave very little for monochrome cloth. What excited them was the possibility of different coloured warp and weft yarn to create complex woven patterns. What they learned was that either the warp or the weft could be used as the 'active' element, the one that covers the other. This reached new levels of sophistication in 'dual-lease' weaving in which what threads were hidden and what shown could be varied. This allowed for double-sided and more complex woven pattern. Junius Bird has described their textiles as "among the finest fabrics ever produced". This was in part because of how the weavers had an ability to conceive of pattern and the technical means to produce it as a continuity. On backstrap looms they made complex sequences of shed and heddle manoeuvres integral to the visual conception; a deep knowledge of mathematics and geometry allowed design and its realisation to be as one. "The true equipment of Andean weaving is the mental agility if the weavers themselves, who find in the simple looms no mechanical limits to their creative vision", as Ed Frequemont described this ability. It was at only the end of the 18th century in Europe with the Jacquard loom that such sophistication was 'mechanised', with a 'punch card' set of prearranged holes in a plate for different threads. It was this which inspired the 19th-century mathematicians Charles Babbage and Ada Lovelace to conceive of how this could be applied back to mathematics and of what has come to be the *computer.*

2013

In late November the Bangladeshi Minimum Wage Board announced a 76% increase in garment workers' pay. This victory, in a country which is the second-largest exporter of clothing in the world and pays the lowest wages to workers, did not come out of nowhere, and neither was it an end to the workers' fight both for better wages and for safe working conditions. Over the last 15 years there have been waves of mass protests by workers outside of official Trade Union institutions. They have frequently been met with violence from the police, Border Guard troops and the Rapid Action Battalion, a paramilitary force at the service of factory owners. They have not been passive: they have engaged in strikes and when attacked have themselves attacked factories and barricaded streets. Their demands have often been over unpaid overtime and back pay and, with a terrible regularity, for action when workers have been burned to death in factories.

Despite enquiries, agreements and promises these deaths have actually increased in frequency in the last three years. The deadly Tazreen fire killed over a hundred late in 2012, and early in 2013 over a thousand died when the Rana Plaza, a building that contained a factory producing for Western brands, collapsed. This prompted publicity worries for both labels and retailers, and prompted new promises and new structures for investigating the safety of factories. After so many deaths and so many conferences on the subject had changed nothing, the Bangladeshi Awami League government finally expressed concern about the country's image, as well as worries about its own electoral unpopularity.

With this background, a wave of strikes started in September and then again in November. Following a four-day shutdown of hundreds of factories by strikes and a series of violent confrontations, the government pushed through a deal whereby the minimum monthly wage would be increased by 77% from $38 to $68. It would still leave the wage level as the world's lowest but was initially opposed by the Bangladesh Garment Manufacturers' and Exporters' Association (BGMEA) who made the standard claim that by increasing their production cost "significantly it would destroy the industry in a fiercely competitive global market". Its leader claimed that they had only accepted the agreement because the prime minister had "assured us that she would look into our problems". On the other side the labour representative on the Minimum Wage Board, Sirajul Islam Rony, was not chosen by workers and said that "Seeing the owners will now be paying them more, I also hope that the workers will be considerate and enhance their productivity". He also hoped that "the workers will not engage in any further unrest". This was not to be. A large number of workers, saying that their demand had been for $100 a month and citing rental and food price increases running at 7–12%, whereas the agreement would lock them into a 5% yearly increase, walked out of factories in the garment production hub of Ashulia on the outskirts of Dhaka and into confrontations with police. For workers, however, the 77% increase has been a victory in real terms and has also had the effect of prompting the major European label retailer H&M to announce, soon after the minimum wage agreement, a pledge to pay a living wage to 850,000 textile workers in Bangladesh and Cambodia, with a trial of the scheme involving payments to three factories and the aim of expanding it to 750 in 2018. H&M said it would use the Fair Wage Method but did not put a figure on a living wage, which has prompted some scepticism, but the move did indicate a real concern about a new wave of worker militancy in these ultra-low cost countries. By 2017, however, government pressure on employers occasioned by the mass deaths at Tazreen and Rana Plaza proved to be cynically temporary. Promised compensation has not been fully realised. True, there have been no mass deaths fromfactory fires – though 11 were killed in 2017 by an exploding boiler that had defied safety regulations, but the mesh of interests between the BGMEA and the repressive apparatus of the state is stronger than ever. At the end of 2016 the Special Powers Act was invoked, allowing for arbitrary arrest after a strike wave that began in solidarity with 120 dismissed workers. The striking workers soon added a demand for an increase in the minimum wage, unchanged from the one that had been agreed in 2013. More dismissals followed, blacklists were enforced and workers imprisoned. Financial journals say the demand for higher wages is laughable – not enough 'value-added' is created – and yet state and privatised violence is used to repress it. In May 2017 workers at factories of the Azim Group in Chittagong, organising for union recognition, were beaten, and their families threatened by hired thugs: the 'race to the bottom' given a helping hand.

Goon squads and police on behalf of Bangladeshi factory owners.

"The feudal lord might flog or kill his serfs, but he was dealing directly with the human realities as the stockholder or the banker is not. The chivalrous Southerner whose interest is mounting up in the bank that lends money to the textile mill is not conscious that he has helped pull the trigger that murdered Ella May Wiggins." She, a mother and worker at the Loray Mill, Gastonia, was shot dead by its hired men during the 1929 strike.

Evelyn Steinthaler

1. Oruro, 2. Knitted combat mitten, 3. Catalina de Erauso

It surprises me that they want to know nothing of it. They do not know that the rules that truly apply are different.

They make fools of themselves, even as the blood drips to the ground. They make fools of themselves in their misery and in their joy. There they stand, proudly wearing their stitched-together helmets, as though by doing so they could save themselves.

As though they could possibly find a way out of a misery that they cannot hope to comprehend. They pray, make sacrifices to their Panchamama, they cling to one another, to the bloodshed, to their strange rituals.

Like naughty children, they take what they can get and try to deceive us but will not succeed, not by the rules we have brought them.

I have not come to preach them salvation. That is a task for others. The task of those who would also seek to bring me to salvation.

I have not refused salvation, my salvation is the sword.

They take what they can get, even salvation when they are so urgently enjoined to do so.

We are not equals.

I wear a suit of armor; they wear only a helmet that is no helmet at all. Cowhides sewn together with entrails and adorned with brightly coloured ribbons and tassels. As though – with their gay ribbons on their pointed helmet, as worn by Pizarro before them – they wanted to rob us of everything.

They do not understand that what they do here in Oruro makes no sense at all. If one were to talk of such a thing in Madrid, no one would be able to muster any appreciation for it. Least of all myself. They will never come to understand, regardless of what we offer them, no matter how much pressure we exert upon them and how many of them die.

Nothing will change: Here, in this place, they will continue to let drops of blood fall to the earth. Without wanting to know their motivation, I do believe I can guess what it is. I am beginning to understand what was never explained to me. I was only presented with incomplete facts. My family drew the cowl over me, but I am no nun. I wear a suit of armor, I am Catalina de Erauso.

Though they are more foreign to me than those I left behind in the convent, I understand them. Bloodshed, dying, killing comes easy to them, as it does me. Soil drenched in blood has nothing of a sacred place; it is eternal damnation.

I know why, but they see it differently. Meanwhile they are accustomed to constantly being surrounded by death. See the darkness, misery and irrevocable subjection. On this we agree.

It means they make sacrifices. Human sacrifices or just the one drop of blood necessary to continue living. I also understand them in this regard. The fact that the bloodshed, the sacrifice in battle has to happen seems clear. In this they wear their adorned helmets, approach each other openly and upright. And they strike each other: man against man, woman against woman. Until drops of blood fall to the earth. Without swords, without swords, without pistols, but armed nevertheless. Wool. Thick, earth-coloured wool.

Apart from a thin metal piece inserted between the fingers, the weapon is tightly knitted and wound around the combat hand.

A battle mitten.

I have tried this weapon.

Not on one of their holidays, not in the public square. I am as out of place there as I am in a convent or in the bed of a man.

I killed one of them with this weapon. It was simple. He had not anticipated that I would come so close. His bloody breath clung to me as he was laid low. I do not know how many came before him. It is also of no consequence. Not to me. And they are used to making sacrifices. On this we agree.

Textile Fragment

10

Nazca; probably 400 CE; acquired in Cuzco, 1978, private collection, loan to the archive.
This may be a fragment of a tunic; what is certain is that its production required an enormous amount of manual labour. It is estimated that 7 kilometres of different coloured threads were needed to complete one piece of this kind. Because of this it was worth more than its equivalent in gold or silver. Sometimes in other cultures the value of a robe of honour which marked status was explicit: the cost of the gold thread was sewn onto the robe on a label. The weaving was produced from the joining of two wool panels. Until the Spanish invasion the Andean world was an isolated one which invented its own autochthonous art. The interlocking warp and weft technique was brought to its fullest development in the Nazca 2 phase, where "the warp and weft are discontinuous in the sense that they do not travel from selvage to selvage but go back and forth only over a particular colour area". The principle involved is like tapestry, except that both warp and weft change colour at the edge of each section of the design, so that they are equally visible. The development of Nazca culture was in the valleys of Chincha, Pisco, Ica, Nazca, and Lomas. Each of these sections had highly stylised representations of people, animals, and plants in their textiles. Sex was also represented, as were musical instruments.

It was a culture of strong religious character and great astronomers who had an understanding of the movement of the stars and of the distinct stellar constellations. These were represented in the form of animals, as for example in the epic lines of the Nazca Pampa. Andean textiles are characterised by an interrupted warp and weft technique not found in any other culture around the world. The Andean textile tradition of South America forms the longest continuous textile record in world history. Fibre art survives in this region from approximately 10,000 BCE. Pre-loom textiles first appear in the Pre-Ceramic Period (3000–1800 BCE) in Northern Peru. By the Early Horizon Period (1800 BCE–0) loom woven textiles using nearly all techniques are found in the South highlands and Coastal Regions of Bolivia, Chile and Peru. In the Early Intermediate Period (0–500 CE) the Andean textile tradition was fully developed with the addition of discontinuous warp and weft techniques and a focus on embroidery. During the Middle Horizon Period (500–800 CE) textiles were worked in almost all known textile structures. Fine textiles were woven primarily in the interlocked tapestry technique in the South Central Andean region. Both camilid fibres (alpaca, llama and vicuña) and cotton were used, and because of the unique climactic conditions, a very large number of these ancient textiles survived.

opposite page

This advertisement for the Bayer Company's patented scarlet consciously plays at being both modern but somehow from a traditional world of dashing knights. It also shows a medal given to the company for participation in the Philadelphia International Exhibition of 1876, where it was commended for "the beauty of coal tar colours generally".

Scarlet

"Then the angel carried me away in the Sprit into a desert. There I saw a woman sitting on a scarlet beast that was covered with blasphemous names and had seven heads and ten horns." In the Book of Revelations (17:3), in a typically apocalyptic part of the Judaeo-Christian Bible, this is the scarlet Whore of Babylon. The colour itself denotes a slightly orange red colour often seen as the colour of fresh blood, and the word comes from the Persian 'sarqilat' which gives it the heathen connotation that the Whore carried with her. One account has her symbolising pagan, pre-Christian Rome, but ironically in the 13th century scarlet was declared to be the colour of the cassock and choir cassock of cardinals of the Roman Catholic Church. They were at this time still a purplish-red using a dye coming from the murex mollusc. After the fall of Constantinople in 1453 this was no longer available and instead kermes was used to produce more of a scarlet as was worn by Kings and Princes during the Middle Ages and the Renaissance which though varying in shade was famed for its brilliance and richness of colour. It was this which expressed wealth and power. The finest – *scarlatto* – came from Venice, produced by a protective guild, so protective that its members spread frightening tales of a white ghost who haunted the dye works. An even more vivid hue became available after the invasion of the Americas involved a Spanish grabbing of cochineal production and its first export to Europe from Mexico in 1523. Despite initial opposition from the Venetian guild it became scarlet's 'dye of choice'.

As for the cardinals with scarlet being the colour of blood they retrospectively decided that it symbolised their willingness to die for their faith. This also chimed with the colour being linked to death. "Since the days of Genghis Khan poets marvelled at how poppies as scarlet as blood tend to spring up in war-torn land." In the modern Anglo-Saxon world, where the state celebrates its own wars, the poppy has been used in this way since the popularisation of a jingoistic World War I poem by Lt Colonel John McCrae, "In Flanders Field". For the cardinals however a further irony was produced by their adherence to the colour in that a whole range of Protestant fundamentalists refer to the Roman Catholic Church itself as "the scarlet whore of Rome". It was such fundamentalists – the puritan New England of the modern USA - who re-established the colour's link to sexual transgression. In earlier periods sumptuary laws for prostitutes varied from place to place and it was only in Zurich and Hamburg that they had to wear scarlet headwear. For the Puritans however the biblical reference was absolute and their attitude made well-known by Nathaniel Hawthorne's *The Scarlet Letter*, in which Hester Prynne is forced to wear a scarlet A for adulteress on her clothes. She turns the tables on her accusers by refusing to remove the badge when permission to do so has been won by others on her behalf.

As a good novelist, Hawthorne gives substance to the symbol when he describes it as smelling of blood. After European use of cochineal had come to an end, the production of a scarlet dye involved a variety of additives including ox blood, also believed to have superhuman power. Others ingredients put in the mix were tin (tin boilers were also recommended), quercitron yellow and tartar. At the end of the 18th century experiments with different mixes and methods were made by men like Dr Edward Bancroft, who became notorious as a British-American double agent. Though it was agreed that this new scarlet was different to that which had been made using kermes, and that it was 'one of the most brilliant colours known to dyeing', it was accepted that it was not a fixed hue. Thus one variety might be very bright, while another, in which tin had been slowly dissolved in lemon juice, would be better described as 'inclining a little to yellow'.

1907

"I owe my soul to the company store": this folk song by Tennessee Ernie Ford talks about the conditions of US coalminers in the 1940s and it describes something that's been hated by workers all over the world. Back in 1907 Margarita Martinez, a textile worker, leads an attack on the company store of the French-owned factory Rio Blanco in Pueblo, Mexico. The country's cotton cloth industry was highly authoritarian even though the state's protectionist policy had been prompted by riots in Pueblo in the 1830s. For cotton pickers in the north of the country "the landlord's word was law backed by uniformed private police forces who used a specially made cage – the *cepo de campaña* – for troublesome workers". Those in the factories – landless

"The potential of textiles for popular propaganda has long been recognised ... but it is far too crude and naive a ploy to use textiles merely as bearers of printed pictures." The difficulties expressed here in 1928 USSR were manifested in consumer resistance to being made into "'walking billboards', especially when images of the modern tractor as idealised farm life contrasted with what was not working well in peasant life".

peasants and debt peons – were kept in isolation. This attack in 1907 also has its own history: It's the last years of the Porfirio Diaz dictatorship; they had struck before in 1903 over an abusive supervisor; and it ends with the death of anything from 50 to 200 of the workers and the imprisonment of 400. Not all one-sided, the weavers fought back. Some say that 25 federal soldiers were killed in the process. It began in 1906 with the formation of a workers' organisation the *Gran Circulo de Obreros Libres* (GCOL) and, on the other side, a *Centro Industrial Mexicano* formed by the predominantly French owners of 93 textile factories in central Mexico with the support of Diaz's Finance Minister, and marshalled by the most powerful French interests. Late in November it prohibited uncensored reading materials in company towns and required *identification passbooks, which were to include the discipline history of each worker.* The CGOL called a strike against the passbooks, the company store system, and for shorter hours and improved wages. The factory owners responded with an across-the board lock-out. "Now is the time", one of then declared, "to throttle these movements at their beginning." With 30,000 suddenly out of work and the Diaz regime touched by nationalist sentiment, it intervened much to the annoyance of the employers who, however, got much the best of the deal then made. The concessions to the workers were small: uniform wage rates across the industry; limiting child labour; and limiting wage deductions. A new leadership was imposed on the GCOL, with a timekeeper, Morales, as its leader. He accepted the deal, but a strong minority of workers rejected it. The attack on it began with the company store raid. The local political chief called in the peasant troops who refused to attack the workers and were arrested themselves when federal troops arrived. The troops then opened fire, killing 17 workers immediately and arresting many more. Soon afterwards the workers divide into two groups. One marches into town and releases the prisoners. They seize the railway station and cut down telegraph wire. The other group go to Santa Rosa and Nogales and set fire to company stores there. On their way back the army ambushes them and many were killed. On January 8th two of their leaders were executed as the army regained control, warmly praised for its action by the US consul. Blame for the violence was attached in normal fashion to 'anarchist agitators'. Meanwhile in the same year and running into 1908, the army was also required to arrest leaders of strikes and to occupy factories in the San Angel textile-manufacturing district near Mexico City.

Back in Rio Blanco an army garrison was established and impoverished peasant strike-breakers from neighbouring Oaxaca were brought into the factories. But despite this, and a desire by many to keep their heads down, the workers struck again in 1909 and closed the plant. In December 1911, taking advantage of the first phase of the Mexican Revolution, a general strike was called which closed down all the most important textile centres. It was so effective that on 20th January 1912 the owners, who had been so hard-line just a few years earlier, agreed to a 10% wage increase, reduction of the working day to 10 hours and a tripartite regulation system for the industry. Although textile workers did not fight in the ongoing Revolution, they continued to take advantage of it and shifted the balance of power over discipline in the factory, getting rid of unpopular supervisors and preventing the firing of workers. In this, remembering the events of 1907, they also used violence to contest managerial authority. Right through to the 1940s they won arguably the best working conditions in the world's textile industry though at the cost of an institutionalised labour hierarchy and the marginalisation of women.

Ines Doujak

Emma, an old Bolivian textile dealer, told me how to heal with threads, to carry that knowledge to Europe. Different coloured threads are required for different illnesses and should be broken over the body only on certain days; dark natural alpaca shades for serious illness on Fridays; lighter tones for starting a treatment and for the healing of less serious illnesses on Thursdays. The threads must be torn apart with great force over specific body parts, and the thread itself

opposite page

"A successful T-shirt has to make you think but then, crucially, you have to act. ... What's tragic is that most messages from the 1980s are still relevant today, nuclear weapons, world poverty and famine." Designer Katharine Hamnett

has to be left-spun, the one used for the weaving of ritual cloth. Right-spun thread is for the weaving of everyday wear.

Upon my return the items of the eccentric collection assembled in Peru and Bolivia were gathered in my flat in Vienna. After a while I began to feel exhausted, sick, burdened, not able to move for days on end. During this time, the entrance key to the block of flats which was in my bag bent 90 degree for no apparent reason. Suspecting that my own state must be linked to the presence of the textiles I resolved to iron them all, thinking that this might deal with whatever force they were creating. While I was ironing a specific poncho time somehow stopped and it seemed to go on for ever, I was covered with sweat. The rest was told to me by my assistant, a very decisive person who was, for once, mesmerised by what was happening. She saw me doubling in size and I started screaming without pause. After half an hour she seized the cloth away from me and threw it out of the window on to the grass outside. The grass had not been cut for some time. My assistant went downstairs to clean the poncho with palo santo, the smoke of the holy wood of the Andes which is used by shamans to cleanse evil spirits. When she had done this, she moved the weaving. In the space it had occupied, three precise turquoise circle outlines formed on the tops of the grass. At this point my assistant called me down for moral support and she moved the textile again while I watched. Other turquoise circles formed, and then others though the colour had got less intense.

The next days the circles were still there and they remained for four more days until this section of grass was due to be cut by the Municipality. But I was far more alarmed at what else happened the next morning: I picked two teeth out of my mouth. Worried but not connecting the facts I spoke on the phone with Frau Heidi who reads the cards for me and, incidentally, mentioned the teeth. She was seriously disturbed and decided I needed help immediately.

Designer Fong-Leng with model Mathilde.

She gave me the telephone number of an Austrian shaman. I found it unreal that I was doing such a thing as he murmured with a strong Lower Austrian accent down the phone until he finally assured me that everything was now all right. Frau Heidi also asked for help from her sister, a shaman in Germany. Things then got really out of hand, as her sister called for a shamanic conference there. Their verdict was serious, I must send all the textiles back to the Andes or burn them on the bank of a river. I must do this was the agreed opinion, because my life was under threat from spirits in the textiles. They did not want to be in Austria and were directing their aggression towards me.

I could not do this as my whole research was based on the collection of textiles. I also believe that once you have started something there is no easy way out such as burning and you have to find other solutions. So instead, I spent time trying to feel out which of the textiles so resented having been brought to Europe and remembering the circumstances in which I had acquired each piece. Finally I chose a weaving I had already hesitated to buy in La Paz, but finally did because of the dyeing technique used, and for having an Ikat pattern that is not so common in the region. Even though I had not bought it from Emma I was confident she would know how to deal with it and I prepared a parcel with gloves on in order not to touch the weaving anymore and addressed it to her and wrote on the back: DO NOT RETURN TO AUSTRIA.

Other textiles from the collection I had subsequently sent to many other artists to respond to in whatever way they might. A year later I took an 800 year old Nazca cloth from the collection to Korea with the idea of asking a Korean shaman to respond to it. The one I reached immediately said that she would not do it, and that if I came to visit her I must not bring the cloth with me. Having heard my story she told me that a black shadow was lingering behind me, that even if I sent off the textiles the spirits would remain with me. She advised me that I should prepare an altar with food and liqor. On the other hand she said that I was stronger than her, that what had happened to me would have killed her, but that on the basis that the spirits had not disappeared she would prepare a charm for me and that it would consist of 3 inscriptions in a bag, written with colured earth and oil. The only proviso was that

Syrian refugee children, as young as 11, are forced into work in Turkish textile factories. A Turkish worker on the minimum wage earns around $450 a month. A Syrian child, working 12 hours a day, earns as little as $160. The image of a monument showing Korean migrant workers.

I should not show the three papers to anyone else, and that I should not allow them to get wet. For whatever reason, the very next morning, needing to wash clothes, I forgot that I had left the charm in a pocket of a robe that was now in the washing machine. The bag emerged fine but the papers were pulp. I was not to panic she said, she would write three more and I could collect them the following evening, Sunday. In the afternoon of that day I returned to the Inwangsan forested hill that rises out of a cluster of high rise apartment blocks in Seoul, and is called the Shaman's hillside though there are also Buddhist temples. The first time I visited it had been surprisingly tranquil and uncrowded for such a beautiful place in such a populated city. This time I took the Nazca cloth with me to take some photographs in this place for the archival card. On arrival there I could hear the sound of drums and in different spots shamans were performing with no big deal being made of it. Other people carried dried fish with them to supply the cat that is the god of the hill. Offerings with food and flowers were made at springwaters and rocks, candles and incense lit, cloth was ritualistically torn over bodies, there was a magical feel to everything. One of those lovely golden autumn afternoons, full of colours and smells.
I photographed the textile under a sacred bush and at a retreat high up where two small areas had been levelled under a huge rock and thick polysterene slabs placed to lie on. On the level below a woman shaman sang and danced into a trance, unconscious of the few people who passed. Listening to her for a long time I caught a glimpse of her on the way back. She was throwing wooden sticks and dancing, winding a cloth around her. In the evening I went to the flat of the shaman I knew and got a new talisman with three dry inscriptions inside of them, this time to hang around my neck.

Chuku / Head Shawl, Ch'ullu Soltero / Single Man's Cap

11

Cap hand-knitted on four needles by Juan Quispe; wool; both acquired at Taquile 2005, and 2008. In 2005 Taquile and its textile art were recognised by UNESCO as a Masterpiece of the Oral and Intangible Heritage of Humanity. Taquile is a small island in Lake Titicaca, on the Peruvian side, in the Andean highlands at nearly 3,815 metres above sea level. This community's Quechua-speaking inhabitants are renowned worldwide for their dramatically coloured, finely handwoven textiles. The island's population was estimated at nineteen hundred in the year 2000. Taquilean female dress, with its many layers, gives girls and women the form of red-and-black triangles: the head forms the apex, as the navy blue or black head shawl (*chuku*) drapes over multiple skirts (*polleras*) with contrasting edge bindings. When worn, the elegant all-black *lliklla* (shawl or mantle) accentuates this impression, even as it covers the woman's shirt (*almilla*), which is white if she is unmarried or red if she is married. The long, woven plain-weave black head shawl (*chuku*) is made from handwoven yardage (*bayeta*) and decorated with a narrow, variegated crocheted edging and large multicoloured tassels (*t'ika*). When wearing the shawl, girls and women usually tuck one front corner into the wide belt; this helps keep the shawl neat and evenly balanced. Learning to wear the head shawl takes years because it threatens constantly to fall off and requires periodic adjustment.

Taquilean male clothing consists of a knit cap (*ch'ullu*), the colour and design of which ideally vary according to the wearer's age and social status. During the latter part of the 20th century and the early twenty-first, unmarried men wore a finely-knit cap (*ch'ullu soltero*) with a coloured base and white top, without earflaps. Married men, especially those who had completed community service, wore a red and navy blue striped knit cap (*pintay ch'ullu*), filled with design motifs along its length.

Starting in the 1970s, Taquileans increasingly purchased factory-spun wool or synthetic fibre yarn, a response to the decreased availability of fleece and the poor quality of dyes, along with the desire to reduce the time devoted to spinning and plying yarns, the most time-consuming phase in textile production.

Purple

Purple is a slippery colour word. Violet and mauve immediately come to mind, and even in Classical times in Europe when it had the highest status as a dye, it had considerable flexibility as a hue. This was when it was 'Tyrian' or 'Imperial' purple, made only from two Murex molluscs found in the Mediterranean Sea. "Who has not heard how Tyrian shells/Enclosed the blue, that dye of dyes/Whereof one drop worked miracle/And coloured Astarte's eyes." There was also a dye made from such creatures in Peru and Mexican fishermen extracted the liquid without killing them and dyed cotton from it. Such was the range of hue that many of the edicts made by Roman Emperors as to who could wear what referred to the Murex material being used rather than the colour itself. The dye was the most important colour technology of the Ancient European world. It was a hugely laborious and technically difficult process, with as many as 10,000 molluscs needed to make one and a half grams of dye. The Phoenecians kept its manufacture secret for many centuries but it is known that the variety of hue produced is not surprising given that, although in the production process it began as a colourless liquid and turned in seconds to purple, in the dyeing of the cloth itself it went from white to green to yellow before finally fixing again at purple.

The most precious colours always used to come from the South, and Europe was an eager market. Today dyers worldwide use synthetic colourants from Germany, the USA, France, and Japan.

All these circumstances meant such cloth was very expensive, and in Rome whose Julius Caesar was said to have been seduced by the colour at the court of the Egyptian queen Cleopatra, the purple dyers had their own fraternity within the dyers' guild. They also had to maintain their vats outside of the city walls, as had been the case in Athens, because of the horrible smell made by rotten shellfish soaked in stale urine mixed with wood ash and water. Even the clothes thus dyed had a distinctive smell of fish – but for many Romans, it was the smell of money. The cloth was something only the very rich could buy and various sumptuary laws existed to determine who could wear such coloured cloth. It was very beautiful, with writers of the time like Pliny and Philostratus commenting on its surface lustre. Its miracle, as described by Pliny, was that it was able to incorporate within itself both light and darkness. As light itself took on a transcendental quality in late Antiquity, this gave an extra importance to purple. It also had a reputation for its durability, keeping its sheen and brightness. Some witnesses said the brightness increased with age. These characteristics were so special that the Emperors Diocletian and Constantine used it for burial shrouds, and in the Roman Empire itself the cost of production and the wealth that required was not the only criterion for its use. Sumptuary laws as to who could wear what were often ignored but not those regarding the wearing of Tyrian purple. Only the Emperor could wear purple cape trimmed in golden thread and Senators a toga with a purple stripe. Pliny rationalised it, writing that "It distinguishes the senator from the knight; it is called on to appease the gods. It brightens every garment, and shares with gold the glory of the triumph. For these reasons we must pardon the mad desire for purple."

Purple retained its exclusive quality in the Byzantine Empire centred on Constantinople: Theodosius the Great declared that "The holy purple mollusc must be worshipped". The disappearance of Imperial purple as the ultimate in prestige coincided with the fall of that city and Empire in 1453 when knowledge of production techniques were lost. There are several explanations: that Mehmet II had the purple dye works destroyed; the supply of molluscs had run out; or because it was simply too expensive. A slightly cheaper though still exclusive red from kermes replaced it in the Church, where Cardinals were dressed in scarlet. Purple remained part of the dyeing trade in Florence into the 16th century, but it was a red-purple colour produced from the roots of the madder plant and then covered with a bath of woad-indigo. It reappeared as an important cloth colour in the form of mauve following William Perkin's discovery of the first synthetic dye as against the earlier cyanol blue in the mid-19th century. Its significance is given by the fictional ghost of Walter Rathenau, the assassinated Weimar Republic economic overlord, whose death occurred at a time when Germany still dominated synthetics: "A thousand different molecules waited in the preterite dung. This is the sign of revealing. Of unfolding. This is one meaning of mauve, the first new colour on earth, leaping to Earth's light from its grace miles and aeons below."

1978

The Korean 'economic miracle' was created by the hyper-exploitation of young women through the 1960s, '70s and '80s in textile and clothing 'factories' which attracted American and Japanese investment. These factories had the worst safety record in the world, with 1397 workers killed on the job in 1978 alone, while 70% of the country's exports were textiles or clothes and the World Bank hailed it as a "miracle". The post-war industry of independent South Korea copied the methods of the Japanese when they colonised the country from the beginning of the 20th century up to 1945, just as its succession of post-war dictators had been collaborators with the colonisers. In the Japanese-occupied 1920s the pattern was set, with factory recruiters searching the poorest areas of the countryside for obedient young women who were kept in factory dormitories surrounded by iron fences topped with barbed wire, and where "disciplinary devices such as cells, places and ranks were enacted in spaces that were architectural, functional and hierarchical". In the 1960s patriarchal norms were used to the full.

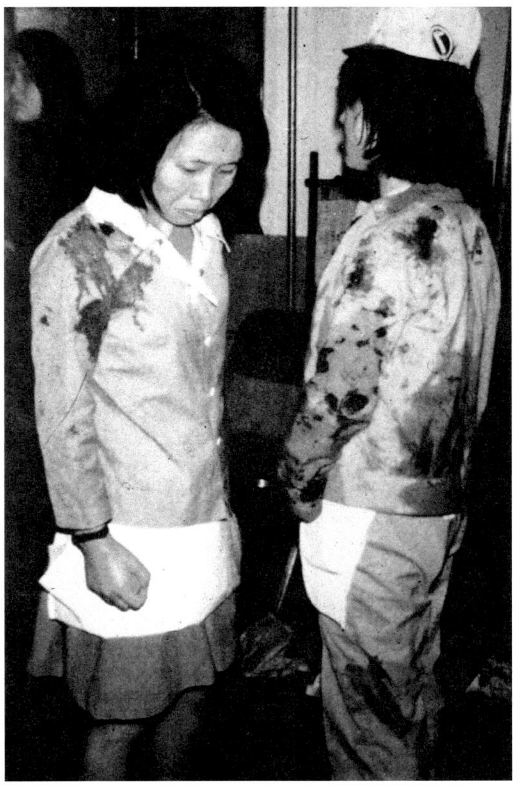

Dongil workers pose for photos after being splashed with human excrement by pro-company male workers.

Women outnumbered men by 9 to 1 in the factories but at the head of the apex was the *jaedansha*, the cutter, who was always male and who distributed the work. He had the power to hire and fire, to reject work as defective, to restrict the amount of work given to women he didn't like. The other form of discipline was the 'team-working' principle whereby the most experienced machinist was made leader and made responsible for dividing work and income between more junior machinists and the apprentices, the *shida*, who worked 16 hours a day. 'Team' was a form of divide and rule and it was one of the first oppressions dealt with by the courageous women who created the Chonggye Union despite the repression built into the 1972 Yushin constitution, the regime's own goon squad trade union and the constant 'Communist' accusation. One of the union's founders was stabbed to death; its education programme building was trashed. That in the face of all this it mobilised 8000 members and in 1974 participated in wage negotiations in which it got rid of the 'team' system – all wages would have to be paid directly by the employer – was the real 'miracle'.

At the Dongil company, meanwhile, 1100 women from a workforce of 1300, with the protection if the Christian outreach 'Urban Industrial Mission', developed a strategy to win the Presidency and Executive Committee control of the government-controlled union. They succeeded, and Choo Kil Ja was voted in as the first ever woman union President in 1973. She had a legally binding three-year term. It was a humiliation for both company and union, so that in 1976 threats of dismissal and bribes were used by both. And yet, another woman worker, Lee Yong Sook, was elected. She was promptly arrested on the grounds of causing a riot after women had thrown money at men in contempt as they tried to reverse the vote. In the demonstration for her release another 72 women were arrested and 14 hospitalised. The struggle continued for another 9 months until a binding vote for union president was held. Again a woman won. This was intolerable: despite the draconian Park dictatorship, foreign investors needed the reassurance of unmolested patriarchy. In February 1978 there were to be new elections for floor delegates, those with the power to vote for a President. When the women arrived at the union hall they found everything covered in excrement and men began to rub it in their faces. The Company then announced that 124 of women union members including all its officers had been sacked for causing damage to company property and the National Textile Union joined the attack by rescinding the charter of the local union. The sacked women were blackballed by the union, government and employers.

Nipples Hasno Gender, Mara Gheddon, Julia Fuchs

Balls of Wool

12

Sheep wool, dyed in natural and synthetic colours, right and left hand spun; acquired at the market of Pisac, 2010. The typical yarn in the Andes is Z-spun and S-plied, which is called *paña* or right. Yarns spun and plied in the opposite direction are called *lloq'e* or left. *Paña* and *lloq'e* are also philosophically contrasting concepts in Andean belief and ritual. The masculine paña is the path to the world of the spirits, while the feminine *lloq'e* is the path through which one accesses practical magic, such as healing or divination. Such yarns may be worn on the wrists or ankles as a protective device and are wrapped around injured or diseased parts during the curing ritual, after which the yarns are disposed of in the river. Pregnant women tie the yarns to their waists so that this thread will protect them. The yarns are also put around the necks of new-born animals to prevent bad energy from being received through the cloth whose wool they will provide.

Andean textiles and shamanic hallucination share a strong and central emphasis on colour. A spiritual value placed on strong, juxtaposed colours may have originated in the powerful visual experience of shamanic hallucination: brilliant colours are reported constantly by those who have taken a hallucinatory journey. If truth, power and inspiration are believed to have come from the other-worlds seen in visions, then their colourful nature can be regarded as driving this colourist fibre aesthetic. Colour was related both in the past and in the present to the domain of the sun and moon and the communal obligations of lands, flocks, and warfare.

The green threads represent pasture, red ones blood and war, and yellow ones the sun. To send black threads indicates "whoever would arrive at night", while such threads mixed with white indicates their arrival "with a moonlit night".

The ribbons to be seen on the archival poster are from the *Church of Senhor do Bonfim* in Salvador do Bahia in Brazil, which has long functioned as a place of healing. After pilgrims make their request they purchase a coloured ribbon stamped with the name of the church and tie it around their wrists. The issue should be resolved when it wears away. The photo was taken in front of the *Igreja de Nossa Senhora do Rosário dos Pretos* (The Church Our Lady of the Rosary of the Blacks), which was built over a period of a hundred years beginning in 1704 by the enslaved members of *O Irmandade de Nossa Senhora do Rosário dos Homens Pretos do*

Pelourinho (The Brotherhood of Our Lady of the Rosary of the Black Men of Pelourinho) for their own use, as they weren't allowed inside the other churches. Work on the church was always done at night so that the slaves' normal daytime work could carry on uninterrupted.

Berafula Cloth

Between the 11th and 14th centuries cotton cloth had such importance in parts of West Africa as to be treated as a currency. There was internal trade between the Guinea coast and cloth producers in the interior, and by the end of the 15th century imports of specific cloths from India and coloured woollen cloth from Europe, while weavers on the Bight of Benin coast were making cloth for regional export on treadle looms. The Atlantic slave trade made trading both more diverse and intense. One manifestation of this intensity was the development of a fully vertically-integrated cotton cloth industry on the Capo Verde islands as thorough-going, if on a smaller scale, as that of Inca-era production in the Andes, and it was one made with slave labour. What is extraordinary is that the islands were uninhabited when the Portuguese came upon them in the 15th century. Their only initial advantage was the lichen indigenous to the island called *Orchil* which yielded a purple blue dye that was profitable and was followed by experimental plant adaptation using the knowledge of inland Africans and their weaving skills. The cloth made there included a plain white cotton weave but the speciality was barafula cloth made of six strips alternating plain white with piece-dyed blue. It too was so important as to become a currency both on the islands and the Guinea coast. Weavers and spinners also made the necessary dye from orchil until the Portuguese in India brought back indigo which gradually replaced it. The Capo Verde islands, especially Fogo, also had a great geographical advantage however and become an important entrepot in the developing Atlantic slavery trade in which cloth itself was such an important trading commodity. Within a hundred years of the islands' discovery, a slave economy "grew, harvested, processed, spun and wove dyed cotton under merchant supervision". Cotton and indigo plantations were created and then the skill and knowledge of inland Bainuk and Karanga weavers and dyers was learned and copied so as to recreate the barafula cloth on a much larger scale. Pre-existing technologies were exploited in this production laboratory. During the 17th century with the aid of Afro-Portuguese and Jewish refugee traders the *panos* (wraps) of Capo Verde assumed a dominant position in the Guinea trade. The cloth produced, which as a currency was standardised, was then traded both to European slavers and regionally. It could buy gold, ivory or slaves; at one time in the 17th century the exchange rate was 60 barafulas for a slave. African chieftains insisted that such cloth be part of the mix of commodities they received in such trade. Its production in turn re-inforced the islands' importance in the grisly global trade in which slavery was so crucial, because slavers might need barafulas to trade with. For a time the General Company of Pará-Maranhão held a monopoly on the Amazon and Maranhão slave trade from the Guinea coast. It was formed using capital accumulated by Capo Verde and Bissau owners of cloth enterprises that controlled the slaves who made it and then getting a Portuguese crown licence to enter the 'slave business'. The trade remained through the 18th century until the abolition of slavery in the USA and Britain, though not in Brazil. What really bit into its market was an Indian cloth called *iniri* from Chennai. Its pattern was very similar but in black and white.

The Bolivian Pajchiri mountain, on the morning of the first of August. The *ch'amakani* Carmelo Quispe makes an offering consulting a radiating stone.

1932

An uprising begins on April 3rd in the cotton textile town of Vichuga in the Ivanavo Industrial region of the USSR, when food rations were cut on the first day of the month. Already workers there had shown their militancy by striking against 'socialist competition' (a form of increased intensity of labour) in 1927. The OGPU secret police had noted several episodes of unrest and absenteeism in the previous year with concerns also about high rents. The strike was initiated by workers – men and women, weavers and spinners – at the Nogen Mill. Attempts to prevent them meeting collectively, to break them into small groups, were resisted and they were joined by weavers at Shagov Mill No.1, who refused to start their machines the next day. The Krasnyi Mill was marched on and came out in support, with male supervisors showing support for their mostly female subordinates who were also demanding child care facilities. An all-factory workers conference was demanded which would involve some 18,000 workers. Communist Party Komsomol members defending Nogin's Mill were swept aside, machinery was smashed and scabs (strikebreaking workers) beaten. The following day, although one worker, Lurkin, had been arrested by the secret police, all factories were picketed, and the demand for his release lead to ransacking the police station, the beating of the police chief, and the occupation of the secret police building. The police fired live rounds and one worker was killed, but the pickets remained, scabs were ejected from factories, and an ad hoc committee of five was formed: three women and two men from across the three mills. A large number of police and secret police members were sent from Moscow with Kaganovich, Secretary of the Communist Party's Central Committee. On the 11th of April a meeting of 2000 workers sent a telegram to the USSR President Kalinin, but were told by local officials who had panicked three days earlier, that no concessions would be made till they went back to work. Knowing these officials could not be trusted the strike continued. The next day Stalin's representative Kaganovich addressed a crowd of 4000 workers at Nogin mill where he combined the usual accusations with a promise to address their concerns. By the end of April 13th several concessions were made with rations to be restored along with concessions on alternative supplies of food: suburban farming, 'Soviet bazaars', and allowing workers to attend to kitchen gardens. This was an assertion of an old tradition of workers maintaining a degree of independence. Back in the 1880s the new factory proletariat of the Moscow textile factories maintained allotments. Now, in 1937, despite selective repression, these gains were implemented soon after on a countrywide basis. Five years later, in the summer of 1942, the textile workers of Kiev formed the Dynamo Kiev football team. A game was organised by the German Nazi occupiers for its armed forces national team to play them. "The stadium is full. It goes silent when the occupying army scores the first goal but goes wild when Dynamo equalise and then take the lead. With the score 2-1 at half time, the army commander sends a warning to the Kiev dressing room. 'We have never lost in occupied territories', he says. And then the threat, 'If you win we will execute you.' The players return to the field. Within minutes, a third goal for Dynamo. Fourth goal and the crowd goes wild. Suddenly, before it is time, the referee stops the game. They shot the players still in their team kit by the edge of the ravine."

Between 1928 and 1933, designers, historians, artists, and critics continued to wage debates on what constituted appropriate textile design. Their opinions ranged from affirmations that Soviet textiles had ideological influence to calls for the elimination of all design because all style was bourgeois. This latter group claimed that the only slogans and text should represent the proletariat.

Judith Fischer

(1)

GHOST ARTIST: ENTANGLED, WRAPPED, SWALLOWED

Some months ago: Ines gives me this packet full of little, luminous, woolly, coloured balls. ("Please do not write about the packet!" she said to me.) I stow the box on the highest shelf in my work room, so that I can see it sitting up there. A casket.

I was given a collection of brightly coloured balls of wool, shamanic yarns, potentials, a repair kit as a loan object.

(I suddenly realise, a memory: That's how I grew up, left alone for hours in my mother's sewing room. Here, I had access to all the utensils for countless 'fort-da' games: threads in dozens (hundreds?) of shades and thread colours on spools made of wood or plastic spools with larger openings that would fit the Pfaff sewing machine, or also: paper spools.)

The cure is to become a curer. In being healed he is also becoming a healer.[1]

In Frankfurt, while researching at the Haus der Kulturen der Welt[2], I find a marvelous drawing in an ethnological research report and photograph this detail: (1)

With what will I correspond? In doing so, will I repeat myself or find a new pattern?

Which perspective? Will it be a submersion or an immersion or a seeing-through-the-eyelids, an allowing-myself-to-see-a-JUMBLE OF GRID LINES that covers everything and in which I can recognise order?

(Everything vague. Loose.)

From this point of view, every person wears a usually invisible pattern on his or her body (*yora quené*). In Frankfurt, I spend several long afternoons reading at a glass table in front of a floral

arrangement, sitting in a black leather chair and he writes that, in this sense, an entire cosmic region – the higher world – consists of patterns, a lattice work, a framework.[3]
And then – soon thereafter – a find, this place in the text, a poetic detail in the report, a shamanic vision:

A long line of tiny blue and violet hummingbirds descends upon the building. The birds are carrying little glass tubes in their beaks. They let them fall on the quietly seated, where they settle as a thin, brightly shimmering net.[4]

I have received a great deal of THE HELP OF STRANGERS during my stays in the field as a researcher, he writes.
So for the female shaman, I think, it has to do with a difficult vision, an activity that requires a great deal of preparation: They want to see the ghosts or cause of diseases or disease agent, the souls of the dead. The shaman want to become ghosts, can be the dead and have to find allies on their travels.[5]

The shamanic concept of the causes of a disease[6]: First there is a fright (called *susto*, *aniraté* or *raqueti*) and it is only through the resulting "opening" of the body that imaginary, pathogenic objects can invade the person, thus coercing, plaguing and threatening the soul, causing the illness.

How do they manage to become acquainted with these beings? Where do they reside and how much does this affect and alter the tectonics of our views and ideas? Do they stay there, are they contained in it or do they come for a visit?

(What do you know about it? Not enough.)

This one is entangled, wrapped, devoured. They are singing songs and surround her with a protective cocoon made of patterns. Tipsy. Travel. Animals. Feathers. Hallucinating in bright colours. Wrapping the dead in cloth and tying it with lianas. The hallucinogenic brew made of dead liana, a LIANA DRINK.

(This is how I leaf through a bundle of pictures in the language.)

SHAMANIC ACTION VERBS: disperse, loosen, distribute, cast off, wash off, grind, shoo away, destroy, detach, cast out, dismember, kill.

Ceremonies and rites of passage there (also, for example: attaining a position, new status & being most vulnerable at these times[7]) and then the textiles come into play. Even in funeral rituals. In Southeast Asia, the shroud used to wrap the bodies can only be woven by infertile and post-menopausal women.[8]
What higher effectiveness does this condition bestow?

(Buddha gave – so I read – the spiritual advice to only wear the clothing of the dead.)

I learn that in research, the unnamed creators of popular and/or classic textile patterns are referred to as GHOST ARTISTS.

(It occurs to me that I have read a lot of Wittgenstein recently. I toy with this thought.)

Shaman wool. Left weave. The ritual tearing of the woolen threads over the patient's body. A sacred tie. A cord. A string. Connecting lines. Try-outs. Threads of time. Threads of fate. Ariadne's thread. Suture. So much.

1 Taussig, Michael. *Shamanism, Colonialism, and the Wild Man: A Study in Terror and Healing*. Chicago: University of Chicago Press, 1987. p. 447.
2 Warmest thanks to Isabella Kresse for her hospitality in Frankfurt in February 2012.
3 Illius, Bruno. *Ani Shinan: Schamanismus bei den Shipibo-Conibo (Ost-Peru) (Ethnologische Studien)*. German. p. 12. Berlin-Münster: Lit Verlag, 1991. p. 162.
4 Illius, p. 58.
5 Eliade, Mircea. *Schamanismus und Archaische Exstasetechnik*. Berlin: Suhrkamp Verlag, 1975.
6 Illius, p. 179.
7 Fraser-Lu, Sylvia. *Handwoven Textiles of South-East Asia*. Oxford: Oxford University Press, 1990.
8 "Death blankets can only be woven by women who are barren or past their childbearing years." In: Sylvia Fraser-Lu, p. 78.

13

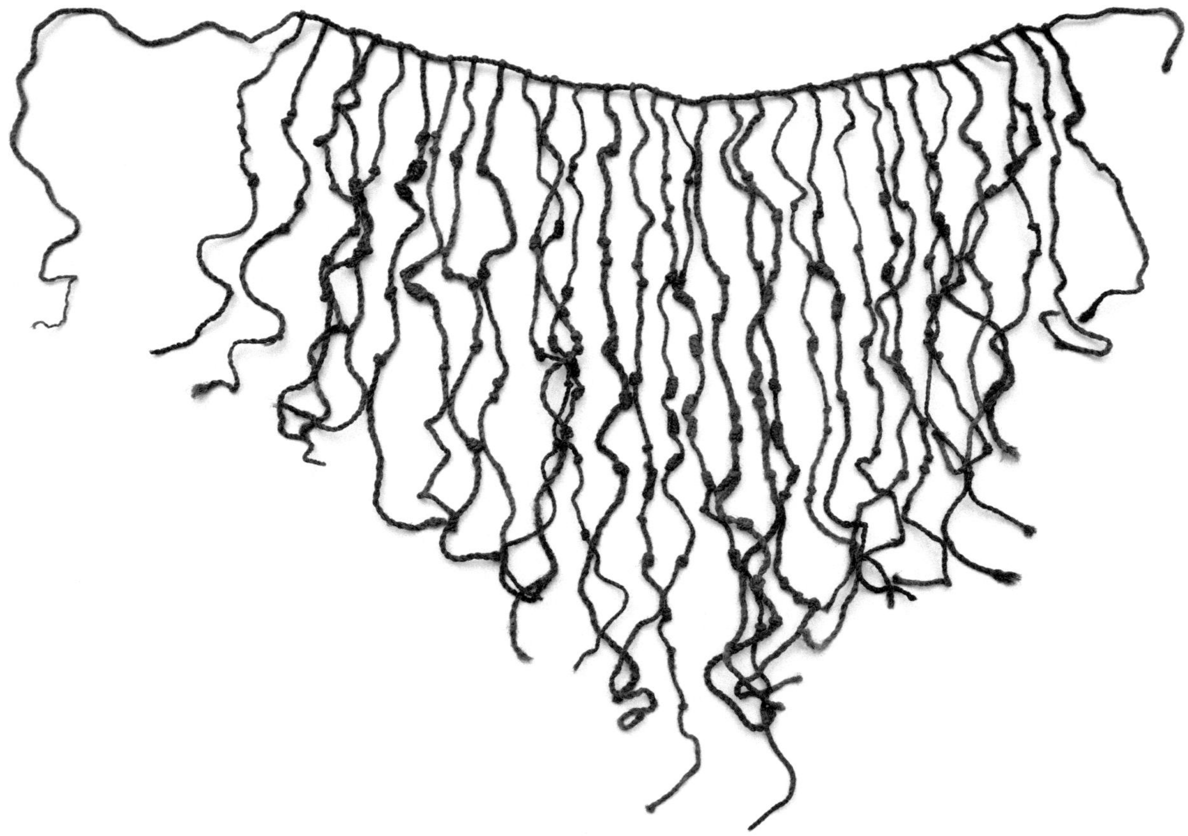

Cotton, wool; probably 1450 to 1533 CE; Inca; acquired in Lima, 1978, private collection, loan to the archive. "The *khipu* were knotted-string devices that were used for recording both statistical and narrative information, most notably by the Inca but also by other peoples of the central Andes from pre-Inca times, through the colonial and republican eras, and even – in a considerably transformed and attenuated form – down to the present day".

Consisting of a long horizontal rope with vertical strings dangling from it, the *khipu* encoded information in the patterns of knots tied into the vertical strings and could be read by running one's hands along the knots. In the 1580s the Spaniards ordered all *khipus* to be destroyed as 'idolatrous objects'. Only about 750 are known to have survived, and although the knots used to indicate numbers have been deciphered, scholars have not entirely broken the code as such. This symbolic knot language is always accompanied by the spoken word, by songs and other semantic media. In 1575, José de Acosta was appointed dean of the Jesuit College in Lima. The Jesuits introduced the printing press to South America in 1584. José de Acosta penned the catechism *Doctrina Cristiana y Catecismo para instrucción de los Indios*, the first book to be printed in South America. He also co-authored the *Confessionario para los Curas de Indios* (a "Confession manual for priests at Indio missions, with instructions to eradicate indigenous rites and admonishments to help natives make their peace with God before they die. Includes a list of privileges and marriage bans") for priests who were sent to Latin American missions. A whole executive apparatus was installed, supplementing the inquisition, to control the faith of the population. Communities were searched for shells, little animal figures, containers for offerings, mugs to brew *chicha*, mummies, and – *khipus*. Indigenous people were prepared to meet the persecution and destruction of local knowledge: "In order for your confession to be good and to God's liking, the first thing you have to do, my son, is think carefully about your sins, and mark them down in a *quipo*: the same way that, as the inn's foreman, you keep a *quipo* of what you

:h'uncho dancers at the *Qoyllur Rit'i* :estival.

give and what you are owed, you must keep a *quipo* of what you have done against God and against your fellow man, as well as of how many times: a lot or very few. And you must not only tell of your deeds, but also of your evil thoughts [...] because men are also condemned for the sins of the heart that are not seen. After reflecting on your sins and putting them down in a *quipo* according to the ten commandments, or whichever way you know best, you must ask God for forgiveness." Some male and female natives used "certain *quipos*, knots and stories which they bring to their confession, as their own writings and memorials. The fact is that these natives, particularly the females, teach the other females to confess with these knots and marks, which they have of many colours, in order to sort out the sins that they have committed or not, and the number of them. And they believe that having confessed with these knots and having declared their sins in such a way, they are then sanctified and can rightfully take communion".

Lace

In the comprehensive English sumptuary laws of 1482 saying who could wear what, there is no mention of lace, which only became fashionable in the mid-16th century when a law did then limit the use of expensive needle lace, then called 'cutworks'. At this time it was made with silk or linen and could also incorporate gold and silver thread. The fashion featured lace handkerchiefs and heavily starched ruffs, huge ones for necks and wrists. At the Diet of Blois when the French Estates General met to discuss the problem of inflation, blaming shipments of gold from the Americas, King Henry III blithely attended wearing 4000 yards of gold lace on what must have been a very heavy suit. In the middle of the 18th century these kind of excesses give way to a simpler style, but the demand slack was taken up in the Americas, "an outlet for lace designs no longer in fashion and otherwise unsellable on the Continent". The de Ullao brothers, travelling in 1735–44, commented on clothing in Lima, "In the choice of laces, the women carry their taste to prodigious excess, nor is this an emulation confined to persons of quality, but has spread through all ranks, except to the lowest class of Negroes ... These laces must be all of Flanders manufacture, no woman of rank condescending to look on any other." And a few years later, in 1751, Don Gerónimo de Uztáriz observed that "many families have been ruined by the great quantities of fine lace and gold stuffs they purchased of foreign manufacture, by which means Spanish America is drained of many millions of dollars." This led to controls on the import of lace trimmings, especially for Indigenous women, who instead succeeded in weaving lace patterns or 'motifs' into their mantles: women who were otherwise forbidden to attach more than a specified quantity in their garments.

A man races on a donkey to win the prize of a shift, lace and beribboned, at a village wake near Manchester, England.

In the early part of the 19th century inventions like that of John Heathcoat enabled the use of cotton for lace-making and more sophisticated machine-made lace so that its overuse returned from the Americas to Europe. In recent times such indulgence has been taken up by the rich of Nigeria. Up until 30 years ago, quality lace was being manufactured by Kano textile mills in the country, but has since declined, largely to the benefit of the Austrian textile industry of Vorarlberg where some 50 million Euros are spent every year on the material. Ironically, this really took off when a 1980s ban on such imports was in force. Much of the lace is used for ceremonies like weddings, but the Austrian manufacturers are aiming for a bigger market, and have sent their own designers to study Nigerian street fashion. Now they have started to use young Nigerian designers, saying, "We know that we have to adapt to the changes and modernisation taking place among the Nigerian buyers. Lace is seen as traditional and old fashioned, which is why we are now altering the perception by bringing these wonderful fabrics into the homes of the younger and more modern fashion crowd." Meanwhile in Austria, the Nigerian ambassador pleads for Nigerian cotton to be used in the making of lace, while each new design is copied, reaching Chinese manufacturers via India within a week of its appearance.

1971

When Salvador Allende became the President of Chile in 1970, the country's textile industry was in the hands of a largely Arab-owned oligopoly with limited competition and a management history that mixed paternalism with repression. The most important was the Yarur mill, which had been established in 1936 and was part of a group controlled by Amador Yarur, which included chemical and food manufacturing and the Banco Credito e Inversiones. The US Chase Manhattan Bank held much of its stock. The mill dominated cheaper cotton textile production for mass consumption. It developed a system of supervision and control through a strategy of favouritism and informing. Disloyalty meant harassment, suspension or dismissal. No talk of Trade Unions or national politics was allowed. Some times violence had been used as when the personnel manager ran over strikers in his car in 1963, and factory guards had shot at strikers. All this followed actions in 1962 against the enforcement of the crudest Taylorist factory discipline.

The Allende government's policy was one of limited nationalisation, the limits prescribed as the "Area of Social Property". The Yarur mill was not included, but in April 1971, and influenced by strikes at another mill where scabs had been hired and workers beaten by goon squads and

opposite page

Archangel Raphael, Cuzco School, a group of European and Indigenous painters active in Cuzco, Peru, from the 16th through the 18th century.

Source unknown.

Rafael Castro in a carnival costume, 1861.

Cowboy lovers.

As Lot and his family, forewarned by angels, fled the city of Sodom and Gomorrah, God rained down burning sulphur, destroying men, animals and vegetation.

by the repressive atmosphere at Yarur, the workers peacefully took over the plant. The government was embarrassed by the factory seizure, which was strictly a worker initiative and not part of its nationalisation plan, but after three days, they legitimised it. It has been suggested that this was easier to do because the textile sector was Arab-owned, but the takeover took place in a period of wider confrontation; of capital flight and economic sabotage by those who hated the Allende government. What stands out however is both the sustained policy of non-violence and the level of organisation of the textile workers. On the one hand worker participation in management had both an advisory and decision-making function while, almost uniquely in such a self-management enterprise, the independence of the Union was maintained. In the event the feeling of workers in this situation was that now they could work "tranquilly".

In 1972 they mobilised to defend the factory using only sharpened sticks rather than guns and bombs after another Yarur factory had been burned down by anti-government forces determined to sabotage this dangerous precedent of worker self-management. During August 1973 a truck belonging to the company – now named the ex-Yarur – was fire-bombed. The response was to take an undamaged truck into the city with fashions designed by the workers and a sign saying, "Here is the work of the workers", and to place the damaged truck next to it with a sign saying, "Here is the work of the fascists". Soon afterwards, on the day of the notorious, violent Pinochet military coup d'etat, the workers at Yarur decided that to defend their factory, full of inflammable cotton, was suicidal.

The decision, in the democratic spirit of the worker-controlled plant, was made by its last general assembly.

Thomas Kilpper / Jens Risch

die sprache der knoten – talking nodes; thomas kilpper knots the *quipu* with the work of jens risch
jutepiece, 1997, 100 m jute-thread tied, approx. 17x13x11 cm; photo: Ina Schoof

14

Early 20th century; acquired in Lima, 2008. The allegorical images that emerged and circulated in the 16th century depicted America as a voluptuous woman wearing little clothing but adorned with feathers and weapons and often accompanied by an exotic crocodile or armadillo. This popularised image and the diaries kept by the invaders attest to the fact that Spaniards felt that the Americas needed 'civilising', and that the main way to do so was through imposing Christianity. With this mindset, Francisco Pizarro and his entourage of nearly two hundred men conquered the Andean Inca Empire in 1532. Following or accompanying the invaders, Catholic missionaries were sent to the colonial Andes to set up centres of conversion, and to replace the Andeans' Inca faith with Christianity. The Incas rarely used naturalistic designs in their weavings: it was the Spanish who introduced concepts of visual narrative and naturalistic representations, though there were realistic depictions of animals, plants and humans in other pre-Hispanic textiles. One of the least known aspects of Andean life is their love of dancing. Pre-Columbians masked and danced, in festivals, pageants and pilgrimages. The history of their ancestry and pilgrimage routes is told through ritual dance steps. The costume is all about reflecting the light and fairly vibrates with a sway of gold fringe, embroidered gold dragons and scales of bright embellishment on a pale blue velvet outfit.

Bogolanfini Cloth

Bogolanfini is a type of mud cloth special to the Bamanan, the largest group of the Mande people in Mali. They were forcibly converted to Islam in around 1860, but the religion co-exists with an older Indigenous culture from which comes the cloth and its iconography. The story goes that once upon a time a hunter who was unsuccessful due to a "frivolous and undisciplined" nature was given a new outfit by his wife. Clearly a generous and forgiving woman. It was made of clean white cotton, 15-centimetre strips of cloth sewn together as was the style in West Africa. We are not told if he had woven the strips himself, though it was a job for men using treadle looms. Given his characterisation, probably not. Anyway, after a typically unrewarding day he fell asleep among leaves and then rolled into the muddy bank of a stream. Even a frivolous man might have felt anxious on his return home. We do not know what was said, but his wife went to a river to wash out the stains and found they would not come out. From then on superb textiles have been made that show striking white abstract designs with a complex iconography on rich brown backgrounds. No two pieces are alike, pattern and depths of colour vary. They can mark not just the status or occupation of the wearer, but his or her character. The designs are also used to mark different important stages in life: women will be wrapped in such a cloth after childbirth, boys in another for circumcision. What tallies with the original story is that although it may have been men who wove the cloth, this form of dyeing was the work of women. The story of origin may also be true, as such cloth was worn by hunters for camouflage, but the mud that is used, containing iron oxide, is fermented for anything up to a year before being used, stored in a clay jar. The whole process was described unkindly by J.B. Donne as "a strange and cumbersome technique". The cloth is first soaked in a dye bath of boiled or soaked leaves from the *n'gallama* tree, which gives the cotton a yellow tinge. The mud applied with bamboo sticks makes an outline of the design, and a spatula is used to fill in the background with more mud. Later the yellow is taken out with caustic soda mixed with peanuts and millet. What stands out in the finished cloth are deliberate 'mistakes' in what are otherwise regular geometric patterns. These are assumed to represent coded messages symbolising historical events, myth or contemporary 'issues' as well as moments of life transition. Cloth is still made in this 'cumbersome' manner in rural Mali, though in the urban world it is now being replaced by Bogolan, which uses the same imagery but can be created with a much simpler process. For one thing, the cloth itself will be machine-woven and woven in one piece rather than in strips, while stencils and chemicals are used to speed up the process. More significantly, as it has become an export market both within West Africa and outside, it has involved a major gender shift: Bogolan production is now dominated by men. The increase in demand for Bogolan is partly a matter of African urban male fashion and is also international. This followed the emergence of Malian cinema in the 1970s, which put the whole culture, music and dress, on the map. The major figure in giving Bogolan an international presence was the Malian fashion designer Chris Seydou who showed that the cloth patterns based on Bogolafini designs could be applied to Western clothing. This has been spearheaded by artists in the Groupe Bogolan Kasobané. Two women's cooperatives have also formed to make the cloth: the Association of Widows and Orphans and the Boutique des Femmes Sinignesigi.

Bogolanfini and its modern derivative are not the only textile design types of Mande culture. Other groups within it, also using narrow strip weaving, create "textiles in vibrant colours, enlivened by rich and vivid suspensions of the expected placement of weft-blocks, designs virtually to be scanned metrically, in visual resonance with the famed off-beat phrasing of melodic accents in African and Afro-American music ... [there is] is a vibrant propensity for off-beat phrasing in the unfolding of overall design. As multiple strips are sewn together by their edges, the major accents of one strip may be staggered in relation to those of an adjoining strip". This can be done in two ways: a deliberate clash between patterned and unpatterned strips, some white with patterning, some pure indigo without a trace of pattern; or the cutting of broadloom cotton to narrow-loom strip size to complete a multistrip, multidecorative composition. This Mande 'country cloth' spread down into Ghana, Niger, Togo, Dahomey and was internationalised much earlier than the recent Bogolan fashion. African slaves bound for America all shared knowledge of Mande-influenced textiles. These were then reinstated in different forms in Brazil, USA and Suriname.

In asking why a successful modern-day hand-printed textile co-op in India should be seen as odd in comparison with a computer software company, Nidhi Srinivan notes that "Paradoxically the demand for the traditional is precisely due to the rise of the modern, but in a context where it is hard to know if the modern is particularly new, and the traditional is old."

1981

At this time over 240,000 people worked in the textile mills of the Girangaon area located in central Mumbai – an area which dated back to 1851. It has now become hot real estate property, while the mills and the people who worked there have almost all disappeared. In the early 80s, however, housing conditions were terrible – beds used in rotation by workers doing shifts, 20 to a room – but there was an active popular culture and the district had a history of conflict with factory owners both in independent India and under British colonialism. In 1928, faced with a wage cut, the textile workers rejected an arbitration call from Mahatma Gandhi on the grounds that "he is careless about workmen and always lives near capitalists"; they enjoyed considerable success in having the decrease annulled. Soon after, however, with the connivance of the nationalist Congress Party, there took place a concerted attack on communists and union leaders, culminating in the Meerut conspiracy frame-up, and sectarianism began to be encouraged by employers, who made use of Muslim counter-pickets. Not long after Independence the Bombay Industrial Disputes Acts were passed, which made strikes almost impossible legally and gave the Congress Party's RMMS union a monopoly.

Mexico's 'maquiladora' labour system keeps workers in poverty and the state does all it can to ensure that workers don't unionise, or if they do that they join so-called "protection unions" designed to assure the interests of plant owners and keep wages low. Employees work the production line at a factory in Ciudad Acuna, Mexico.

On September 27, 1981, a one-day strike took place demanding higher bonus Payments,a crucial part of the wage, and improvements in working conditions. The accident rate was higher than in other sectors, and in particular respiratory disease from cotton dust and illness from high temperatures in the mills was rife. The RMMS made a deal with the Bombay Mill Owners Association on October 20th. Workers at some mills rejected the deal and staged a sit-down. On the 23rd those from the Standard Mill marched to the house of Dr Dattar Samant, a known militant trade unionist, who had recently won serious gains for workers at the Empire Dyeing company, and asked him to be their representative. He was initially reluctant, but in 1982, having set up the independent MGKU union, he called for an all-out strike for a 30% rise in wages and the demand that the RMMS lose its monopoly of worker representation. Nevertheless, he warned the workers that it might take months to win. Objective conditions were not favourable: there were huge piles of unsold stock; there had been a marked concentration of mill ownership; and, despite rhetorical opposition, the same owners were very much involved in the shift to power looms and the development of synthetic cotton mixes. In spite of this, and employer predictions that it would last just a few weeks, what became a city-wide strike went on for 18 months, during which time amazingly few workers broke the strike. But over time, with the open backing of the Congress Party government and its talk of the 'Samant menace', the mill owners began to see the strike as an opportunity – first to get rid of stocks and then of 'surplus' workers, to whom it could also rid itself of the obligation to pay any compensation.

Activists from the Indian Workers Union march to parliament in New Delhi on November 23, 2011. "They are working for a labour aristocracy, because their interests are tied to them", Rajiv Kumar, secretary general of the Federation of Indian Chambers of Commerce and Industry said, articulating pure capitalist class interest: "The real poor in this country cannot afford to be unionised."

This is what in fact happened. In most accounts Samant himself is blamed for not accepting that victory was impossible and calling off the strike. What he seems not to have understood is the implacable opposition of the government to what he represented. When in March 1983, after 15 months of strike, there was an offer of talks with the Minister of Commerce, Samant was persuaded to dropthe RMMS demand. He found however that the millowners were convinced that the strike was petering out – many workers were returning to the villages from which they had migrated, and operations were shifting to low-wage rural areas outside Bombay – and had persuaded Prime Minister Indira Gandhi to overrule the minister, with the result that there were no negotiations. Arguments as to why the strike turned out tobe so disastrous still continue. Though other union leaders blamed Samant, the evidence is that he was originally reluctant to take on the role of leader, and others say he was the only union leader to put the workers before politics. It was said that his own 'outrageous irresponsibility' was a reflection of the aspirations and feelings of the workers. The other main accusations were that he operated as a one-man band, even though

a high degree of self-organisation developed among the strikers in the form of mill and then zone committees, which took a pride in their non-hierarchical functioning; that while encouraging their development he did not listen to them at crucial moments; and that he refused co-ordinated actions with other trade unionists. It should be said however that the committees were under attack from a variety of forces. First from the imposition of section 144, which initially allowed the police to attack striking workers when they had established effective pickets of mills. Later it was extended to the entire mill area, prohibiting gatherings of five or more people. 119 strike activists were arrested under this legislation, as were Samant and his brothers at regular intervals. Underground meetings were then raided and many activists stopped sleeping at home for fear of arrest. In addition to the police, the struggle was undermined by the RMMS union itself, which encouraged strike-breakers and used village hierarchies to exert pressure on workers, forcing them to return to work; and by the growth of the Shiv Sena, which began as a regional movement for local Marathi interests, but became a sectarian party of violent Hinduism. There is a strong suspicion that it was used by more established political power in this role, since the organisation specifically aligned itself against the strike in the middle of 1982. The outcome though was unequivocal, and by July 1983 the strike was defeated. In consequence of the disappearance of the mills, thousands of people were pushed down the production chain into makeshift sewing factories, which in turn fed the 'gentrification' of this part of central Mumbai, the real estate value of which has gone through the roof. Samant himself was assassinated in 1997.

Hedwig Saxenhuber

Ecstatic religious rites were celebrated in Peru before the Egyptians even began to build their pyramids. A carnival coat bought in Lima, dating from the early 20th century, is interwoven with oscillating gold threads, embroidered ornamentation including beetles and flowers – complete with receptacles, petals, stamina, and pistils – that resemble suns. The Inca saw themselves as the descendants of the great sun god Inti. In the middle of the back of the coat is evidence of

the enforced christianisation and colonisation of the Inca empire at the hands of the Spanish: the letters "IHS" in the halo of the Eucharist. The abbreviation of the name of Christ.
This costume, which I had mentally filed under "baroque coat", was hanging in front of my bookshelves for a while. I looked at it from time to time, feeling at once fascinated and lost. Who wore this coat? Did its wearer actually take part in these legendary carnival processions? Did the wearer, while wearing the coat in the procession, symbolise the god-king Momo? What do the Christian symbols imply? Seeking ideas and points of reference, I followed up on all the associations that occurred to me; I searched in the fields of botany, coleopterology (the scientific study of beetles), colonial history, even the iconography of liturgical textiles. Eventually the coat was reclaimed and I tried to forget that I had promised to write this text about it.
Some time later, during a Skype conversation with a Ukrainian curator and music promoter,

I 'fell for' his on-screen avatar and at that moment I knew: this is the counterpart of the carnival coat. Researching the character led me to the Leningrad micro-scene of theatre, fashion, art, and music influenced by Glasnost and Perestroika. The avatar depicts as a stage character Lucius, the protagonist of the first novel of antiquity, the "Metamorphoses" of Apuleius (commonly known as "Asinus aureus", the Golden Ass). In the course of 11 episodes the first-person narrator describes the world of magic and the mishap that turned him into an animal with the human faculty of reason fully intact. As an ass he is able to see the abyssal dimensions of the ordinary world: class antagonism, slavery and also sexual adventures and excesses. Frivolous stories, burlesque and crudely erotic in parts. In the final episode, the ass Lucius dreams of the Goddess Isis. The next day he eats a rose from the hand of a priest of Isis and is made human again.
Isis, the Egyptian goddess of love and magic, mother of a god and of the sun, queen of the western heaven, was considered an omnipotent sorceress, the undisputed 'super-goddess'. Inscriptions call her "wiser than all the Gods combined". Her symbol was Sirius, the only fixed star regularly worshipped in rituals. Cow horns with sun disks and the wings of the black kite were used as symbols in representations of Isis.
What might it have meant to stage this play in the late 1980s in the disintegrating Soviet Union, when Russia was free of gods and religions by official order? Was the theatrical narrative one of class struggle? Or did Lucius as he is here gendered indicate the place claimed by the emerging Queer scene of St Petersburg? The coat from the Andes, which fulfilled its representational purpose in the carnival, may additionally have served as a late index of colonial transformation, in which the letters "IHS" would appear as in an incunabulum, recording the violence to which missionaries were driven by their desire to convert the heathen. In Peru at the turn of the last century – when Bakhtin was still alive – carnival, theatre and magic, gods and religious symbols formed a pillar of colonial history. In Russia at the century's end, decades after Bakhtin's death, these things were signs of a time when collective utopias were turned private.

Note Head / Mummy Mask with Wig

15

By the time the Spanish arrived in Peru at the beginning of the 16th century the Chachapoya people had already been subsumed into the great Inca Empire. Although they had resisted the Incas fiercely, the lands of these Warriors of the Clouds had been annexed and forced to adopt the customs and culture of their conquerors. Yet they left one thing behind – the sarcophagi in which they would bury their dead.

Probably Late Intermediate Period, approx. 1000–1450 CE; Chanchay; material: wood, human hair, alpaca, wool, cotton; height: 30.5 cm, width: 20.3 cm, depth: 4.8 cm; acquired in Cuzco, 1979, private collection, loan to the archive. The mummy mask was often painted in red, representing the face of someone deceased, who was wrapped in many textile layers, resulting in a bulky bundle. The note head was placed on top of it. Its wrappings are likely to be the textile scraps of Chancay culture. There are 5000 known burial sites in the coastal valleys and many have been looted for the international antiquities market. An under-resourced Peruvian state, corruption and the lax attitude of customs control in the rich world have made this possible. There are also by-products on which ethical judgments should be made with caution. Fragments are usually discarded by the grave robbers and the women of the local impoverished communities have re-used such scraps both for mummy mask layers and to make imitation pre-Colombian dolls with authentic materials. Even though these sell for just a few dollars in Lima they form significant local income and also make a real link between the area's past – its sophisticated textile culture – and the present in which its people survive, in part, by using its leftovers.

Until 1925, a common shade of brown was made from the flesh of Egyptian mummies, both human and feline. Even the mummies of French kings dug up from Saint-Denis in Paris were used. Mummy was first used as a medicinal substance as early as 1300, and the practice came to an end only in the early 20th century, when finally the supply of available mummy remains was exhausted. Virtually all the pigments that were known to painters from the Middle Ages to the Renaissance were also medicines, including lead white, minium, vermilion, chalk, orpiment, sepia, ultramarine ... and mummy. These medicines were supplied by apothecaries, who were the main sources of supplies for painters. Eventually, in 1712, an artist supply shop was opened in Paris called *À la Momie*. But now mummy brown is gone altogether. Geoffrey Roberson-Park, Managing Director of London's venerable C. Roberson colour makers, regretfully admitted in 1964 that the firm had run out of mummies. "We might have a few odd limbs lying around somewhere", he apologised, "but not enough to make any more paint".

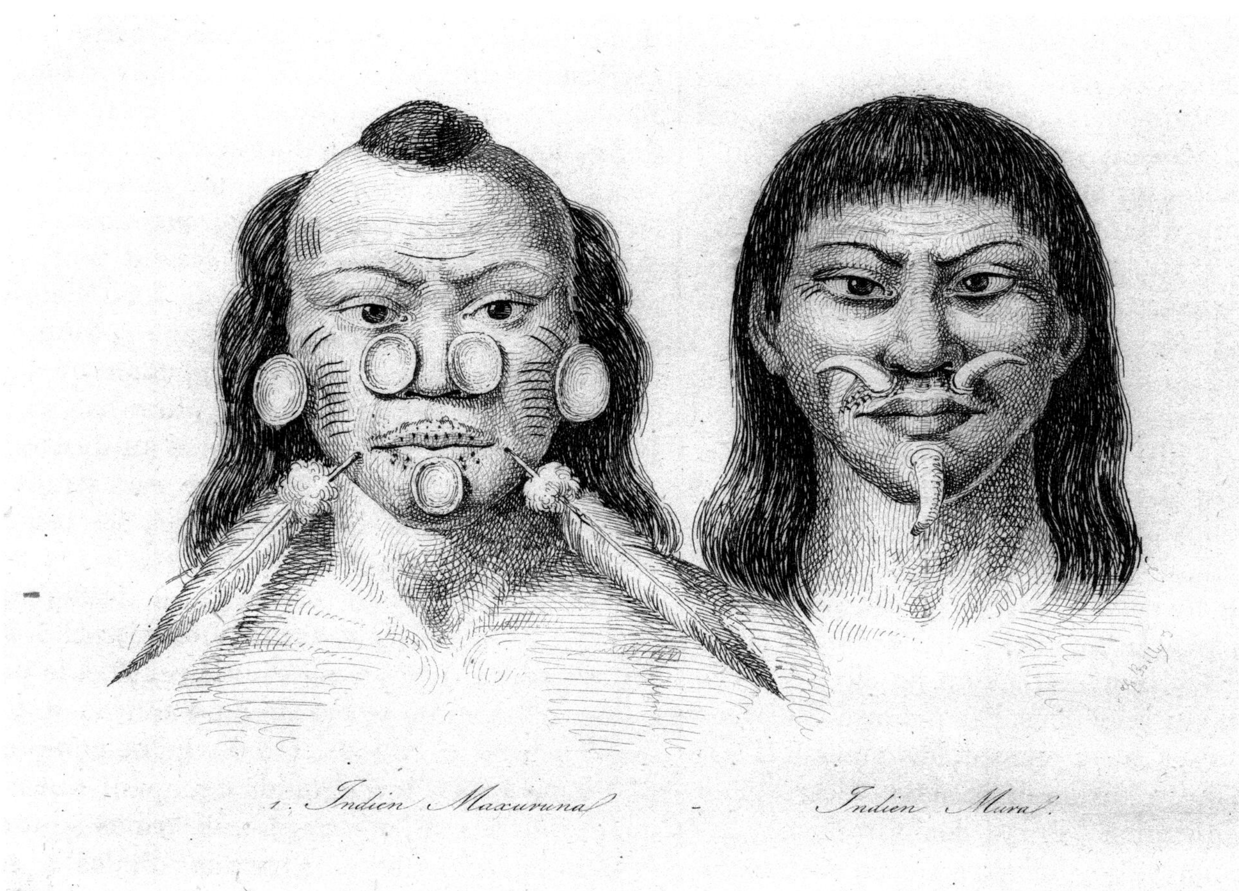

Skins

"Possibly in no other place in the world is there so much variety in complexion and physiognomy as in Lima. From the delicately fair Creole daughter of European parents to the jet black Congo Negro, people of every gradation of colour are seen living in intimate relation one with another ... The designation Creole properly belongs to all the natives of America born of parents who have emigrated from the Old World, be those parents Europeans or Africans. There are, therefore, white as well as black Creoles ...", wrote Johann Jakob von Tschudi in *Travels in Peru, During the Years 1838–1842*, and he gives us this list of varieties of 'half-castes':

Parents	Children
White father and Negro mother	Mulatto
White father and Indian mother	Mestizo
Indian father and Negro mother	Chino
White father and Mulatto mother	Cuarteron
White father and Mestizo mother	Creole (only distinguished from the White by a palish brown complexion)
White father and China mother	Chino-Blanco
White father and Cuarteron mother	Quintero
White father and Quintera mother	White
Negro father and Mulatta mother	Zambo-Negro
Negro father and Mestiza mother	Mulatto-Oscuro
Negro father and China mother	Zambo-Chino
Negro father and Zamba mother	Zambo-Negro (perfectly black)
Negro father and Cuarterona or Quinterona mother	Mulatto (rather dark)
Indian father and Mulatta mother	Chino-Oscuro
Indian father and Mestiza mother	Mestizo-Claro (frequently very beautiful)
Indian father and China mother	Chino-Cholo
Indian father and Zamba mother	Zambo-Claro
Indian father and China-Chola mother	Indian (with short frizzy hair)
Indian father and Cuarterona or Quinterona mother	Mestizo (rather brown)
Mulatto father and Zamba mother	Zambo (a miserable race)
Mulatto father and Mestiza mother	Chino (of rather clear complexion)

Adrian Piper took an outfit of hers and covered it in white paint. She then put a sign across her shirt that said "WET PAINT" and walked down busy streets.

In her 1990 *Colored People* series the artist Carrie Mae Weems has her own version of black skin hues: Deep Black, Ashy Black, Pale Black, Jet Black, Pitch Black, Dead Black, Blue Black, Purple Black, Chocolate-Brown, Coffee, Sealskin-Brown, Deep Brown, Honey Brown, Red Brown, Deep Yella Brown, Chocolate, High-Brown, Low-Brown, Velvet Brown, Bronze, Gingerbread, Light Brown, Tan, Olive, Copper, Pink, Banana, Cream, Orange, High Yella, Lemon, Oh, and yeah, Caramel.

1680

The Navajo Indians believe that the weaving loom was created by Spider Man and its use taught by Spider Woman. "The loom's crosspoles were made of sky and earth cords, the warp stocks of sun rays, the *healds* (heddles) of rock crystal and sheet lightning. The batten was a sun halo, white shell made the comb. There were four spindles: one a stick of zig-zag lightning with a whorl of cannel coal; one a stick of flash lightning with a whorl of turquoise; a third had a stock of sheet lightning with a whorl of abalone; a rain streamer formed the stick of the south, and its whorl was white shell."

The Law of Unintended Consequences may also have been at work, arising from Spanish religious intolerance and a taste for violent repression of the Pueblo people of what is now New Mexico. This caused some of them to seek refuge with the Navajo, previously seen as enemy raiders on them, and that it was these refugees who either taught weaving to the Navajo, or improved their technique. The Spanish repression of Pueblo at a time of famine and disease began with Franciscan missionaries forbidding Kachina dances in which masks were worn representing the polymorphous Kachina spirit. Missionaries were ordered to seize every mask, prayer stick and effigy and burn them. This caused the first wave of Pueblo émigrés in 1675 when four medicine men were arrested and three executed. Some were later released, amongst them Popé who is credited with organising the successful uprising of 1680, the timing of which was coordinated by the use of knotted cords. A second rebellion in 1696 led to a prolonged and brutal repression organised by Diego de Vargas, appointed as Spanish Governor for this very purpose. This caused

Boasting about her weaving skills, the shepherd's daughter Arachne infuriated the godess Athena. In a challenge Athena weaved four scenes in which the gods punished those humans that considered themselves equal to gods and committed hubris. Arachne weaved scenes in which gods abused humans, and as her work was superior to that of Athena's, the goddess transformed her into a spider, condemned to weave for eternity.

a bigger wave of Pueblo seeking refuge with the Navajo. The earliest Navajo weaving shows the same horizontal striping as that of Pueblo, but was developed by their own innovation of breaking up the stripes into terraced geometric shapes that they had made with baskets long before blankets were ever woven. Their finest quality serapes are now described as equalling "the delicacy and sophistication of any pre-mechanical loom-woven textile". Inconsistent areas in certain large woven Navajo blankets often mistaken as mends are more often deliberate incorporations of various substances and objects. "When you weave a blanket in a certain way, harm cannot befall you. There are things that go in a rug that are aligned with wildlife. Objects are woven in to seek an alliance with certain creatures." In one blanket, a patch area examined closely with magnification contained hairs from a bobcat, a goat, and a bear, shavings of a bear claw, and granules of corn. One of the ironies of colonialism is that none of this would have happened without the introduction of the Spanish *churro* sheep, a hardy desert variety that ate less and was disease-resistant. The next colonial wave, that of the United States after the ceding of New Mexico by Mexico, led to the sheep being destroyed as part of a scorched earth policy to remove the Navajo from their land.

Lukas Pusch

Since the 'War on Drugs' in Mexico started in 2006, 45,000 deaths have occurred involving gangs, the army, and a variety of special squads. These figures are far higher than those in the occupation of Afghanistan. Federal statistics have shown that nearly 2000 people were killed in the first month of 2017.

opposite page

A load carrier is on hire in the non-stop Dongdaemun textile market area of Seoul. He shifts cloth and haberdashery in various states of completion from one workshop to another or loads onto or from vans and pick-ups. He uses the wooden stand-up trolley of his trade for a secure nap.

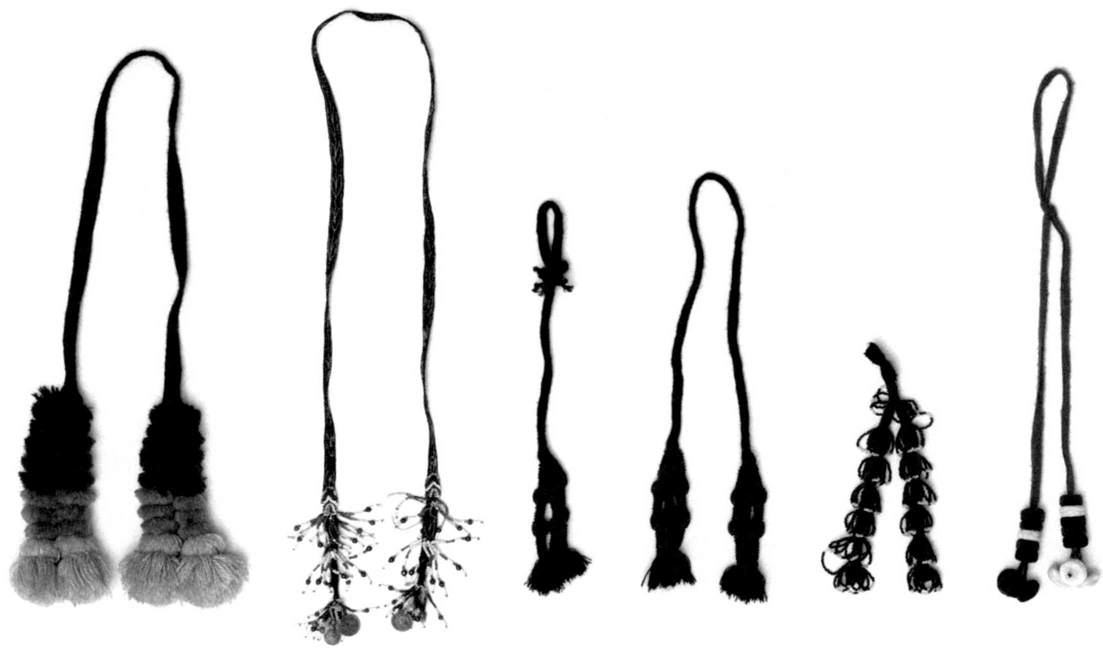

Manufactured and hand-made; sheepwool, synthetic yarns, chemical dyes, beads, coins; late 20th century; acquired from street vendors in Ollantaytambo, Cuzco, La Paz, 2009.

The *Cholitas* of La Paz wear quadruple-layered underskirts called *centros*, bright *polleras* (a big one-piece skirt), fringed *mantas* neatly folded and worn across their backs, and small felt bowler hats balanced on top of their heads. In the chilly winter or rainy summer they put on a pair of alpaca or acrylic leg-warmers and sometimes wrap their hats in plastic bags, but still manage the muddy streets in their patent-leather or clear plastic slip-on shoes without socks. There is a slight change every two or three months in *Cholita* style: for example, hat height can vary by centimetres.

The making of the braids describes their social status. *Cholitas* wear their braids 'normal' and women *de vestido*, those who don't wear *polleras*, braid in reverse. One will not be considered well-dressed if the hair slips over the face.

In the 1940s, as an effect of the Chaco War between Bolivia and Paraguay, multi-coloured synthetically dyed wools appeared, whereas before only natural dyes were used and intermingled with the hair of native women of Cochabamba and Chuquisaca. Today the *Cholas* of La Paz prefer moderate hues like maroons and blacks because they combine well with their hair colour. In the area of Lake Titicaca the hair ties include cascades of pompoms; in the north of Potosi, there are, in addition to the spherical pompoms, *tik'itas*, which have a glass in the centre surrounded by tissue which looks like leaves. In the valley the *tullmas* are made from sequins and tubes. The hairstyle in Tarabuco has the charm of its owners' identity. The braids are long and heavy and on them porcelain pearls of opaque whiteness are placed. Nowadays in the stylised outfits for the fiestas big and colourful *tullmas* enhance female coquetry. The hair is like the branches of trees which give fruits. The braids are the trees and the *tullmas* produce the fruits. Red apples, green limes, orange peaches.

Cochineal

Cloth with bright colours was the prerogative of elites in a wide range of societies, highly desirable in a generally colourless European world. For the Inca aristocracy of the 15th century red was associated with their mythical origins and a symbol of royalty and nobility. European reds at this time came in weak form from madder, but for a deeper red from a group of scaley insects, the most local being kermes from evergreen oak trees. The Incas were at an advantage however, their far stronger dye coming from the insect *dactylopius coccus* – cochineal – living on an *Opuntia*-type cactus which had been used by much earlier Andean societies – the Nazca, Moche and Wari – and which was perfect for dyeing animal fibres like the wool of alpacas. The wheel has since turned full circle because after the collapse of the colonial cochineal business in the face of 19th-century chemical dyes, it has re-emerged on a smaller scale from a taste for natural dyes and as a food colourant, with the Arequipa region of Peru producing 80% of world supply. There is evidence of shipments from Lima in the early colonial period, but it was in and around Oaxaca, Mexico that the Spanish crown and merchant houses centred what was to be a very profitable business for them with what they called grana (grain). In Mexico too it had been highly treasured by the Aztec aristocracy, with Moctezuma I and II receiving large quantities of the dye in powdered cake form as tribute: 40 sacks per year from the Mixtec and 20 bags every 80 days from the Zapotec, in whose languages the word for red was the same as that for colour as such. The invader Cortez immediately alerted King Charles V of Spain as to its likely value, and from then on cochineal became a Spanish monopoly with the first shipment from Veracruz to Seville in 1526. It was highly sought after in Europe because of its brightness and strength of colour that far exceeded that of kermes. As a consequence it was so profitable as to become Mexico's second-highest value export after silver, with draconian punishments in place for giving away the secret of its origin, and a campaign of misinformation which implied that it came from seed or grain with the continuous use of the word *grana*. For the next 300 years there is a whole story of attempted espionage, piracy and great profit. In Oaxaca, unlike the systematic brutality of Spanish occupation elsewhere, the Crown simply took over the Aztec tribute system with pro-

The annual tribute, *Matrícul de tributes*, paid from the Ciaixtahuacan region of northern Oxaca to the Atzec Empire, included 40 bags of *grana cochinilla*, which are indicated by two spotted bags.

duction left to Indian smallholding cactus farms with no forced labour or haciendas. This may in part be because it was so labour-intensive. It took 100,000 insects to make one kilo of the dye, and the insects had to be carefully brushed off the cactus leaves so as not to damage them. Like all Empires however they imposed a royal bureaucracy on the business, the *jueces de grana*, with regulations as to how the insect should be killed, and with weighing stations that checked for quality and adulterants. They were then packed into leather bags, each holding 120 pounds and called *zurron de grana*, for shipping to Spain. Despite the activities of pirates, spies, the seizure of a flotilla of ships with cochineal in the cargo by a Dutch naval force in 1628, and microscopic examination of the insect, the monopoly held so that in 1714 an English dyer was complaining, "Cochineal is no where to be found but in Mexico." The French naturalist Nicholas de Menonville did finally smuggle out samples of both insect and cactus, but the attempt to start the business in the then-French colony of Haiti failed. What did change the situation was oversupply: the Mexican War of Independence and the pre-emptive move to establish plantations in Guatemala and the Canary Islands at the beginning of the 19th century; soon followed, as with other natural dyes, by the development of a chemical dye that isolated alizarin. But this was only after 300 years during which something like 300,000 pounds of cochineal were exported every year, overland to New Mexico and with shipments to China and the Philippines as well as Europe, and though Oaxaca Indian farmers did better than others in the rest of the continent, the vast majority of the profits went to the Spanish crown and the merchant houses of Cinco Gremios Meyores and Casa de Uztáriz.

Cochineal *macnu* pressed into the traditional cakelike form, as described in 16th-century Spanish chronicles.

1738

Trowbridge and Melkshaw, Wiltshire, England. Wool weavers riot over payment in truck (a version of the Company store) by the clothier merchants, unfair pay deductions for what the clothier decided was imperfect work, and a cut in what they were paid. The weavers were organised in clubs with a secretary and a 'king'. After a failure by the clothiers to negotiate, the most detested of them, Henry Coulthurst, has his mansion, workshops and cottages trashed. At the workshops yarn was ripped up and thrown into the river, Coulthurst's account books stamped on and left unreadable. His mansion was destroyed starting with the removal of tiles from its roof, expressing a desire to demolish his pretensions, and that in hard times the clothiers too should share them. The town council were so alarmed that they told the Town crier to announce that the weavers should have "full wages and no truck". This implied that they had not in fact been paid the wages as laid down by the Privy Council, a state institution, in 1726. But at the same time the council called in troops. Several weavers were shot dead and in a subsequent trial three were executed. There was some sympathy for them from local gentry, but the clothiers themselves launched a fierce propaganda campaign in the local newspaper, blaming everything on the weavers themselves. Their leading propagandist William Temple wrote: "The cause of the poor is popular and apt to bypass many thinking and judicious persons who have not had much to do with them. The World would have quite a different opinion of the Manufacturing populace if they were acquainted with their Insolence, Idleness, Debauchery and Dishonesty, so well as the clothiers. It was beyond all contradiction that the poor have such High Wages, as furnish them with the Means and instruments of Luxury and Idleness. So that by reducing wages you would not only make the poor more laborious, more diligent, more virtuous, and not at all lessen the consumption of provisions and necessaries. The reduction of wages in the woollen manufacture would be a national blessing, and no real injury to the poor." He concludes, in a smug voice familiar in today's world, that English clothiers face competition from the Chinese, where workers are treated in an inhumane manner which he himself as a good Christian would not contemplate.

Eighteen years later, in nearby Stroud, came "the autumn of '56", as recalled by the fictionalised surveyor Mason: General Wolfe, "with six companies of Infantry, occupied that unhappy town after wages were cut in half". Mason goes on to comment, in an argument about forms of labour coercion, that "Masters presume themselves better than any who, at their bidding, must contend with the real forces and distances of the World ... When Weavers try to remedy the inequality by forming Associations, the Clothiers bring in Infantry, to kill, disable, or deliver up to Transportation any who be troublesome, these then being replaced, and even more cheaply by others quite happy to labour in silence."

Edgar *Huracán* Ramírez

"So you are going to make an archive you say, starting with textiles made here in the Andes. What a textile history we have, but we want to tell you about another Bolivian history, mining, and the Mining Corporation of Bolivia (COMIBOL) archive we are making here in El Alto, La Paz, which we as volunteers started from scratch with documents that had all been dumped. Let us show you around, what they call a guided tour. Over there, where the street is, there was a shed with a roof made of corrugated iron, which hardly protected from the rain. The whole 500-year history of the mines, thrown out like rubbish. We'd always thought God made miracles individually, but this archive is a collective miracle. In Bolivia mining from the invaders onwards has always been the money-maker. When America was discovered and the spices, cinnamon, clove, etc. etc. were exchanged for gold and for silver, everyone asked for mines separately. Gonzalo Pizarro, he was the owner of Porco mine. He asked for Porco for himself, with all the Indians on it. The hill of Potosí was requested by Juan de Villarruel, the Northern area of Potosí, around Chayanta, by Juan del Valle, and in this way everyone asked for different areas. But as time went by, these give-aways started to concentrate in a few hands. In the 19th century, the period of the Silver Patriarchs, the vast majority of mines was concentrated in no more than 5, 6 or 7 companies. And in the 20th century, these same mining sites, after the silver crisis, were acquired by three other, more powerful industrialists, Patiño, Jochil and Armayo. This period in Bolivia is known as "The Men of Tin". So then, in 1952, the three companies were nationalised and not just the mines themselves but also, and we can't find any other examples of this in the Americas, the archives. They are in the public domain and cannot be privatised. But what a state they were in! Paper everywhere, like the property titles of the mines, just dumped. So some of us ex-miners, we started to rescue them ourselves and now all kinds of people are working together here, that is, here it is proven that this work can be done, not by those who have studied, but by those who love information, research. Workers right from the base. But then there's a university student who, for financial reasons, had to stop. He is still studying systems engineering by himself, and is entering the information into the computer for us. This guy here is a history graduate. So you see, not only have we gathered the records of all times, but we have also gathered human beings from all backgrounds. When we started to store the documents we had to fight for this space, which was a warehouse of the COMIBOL, holding car spare parts, there was nothing, no work clothes, no computer. Around 2003 we convinced them to let us use it and store the records here. These shelves now are already made up, they are like movie actresses; they have put their make-up on. But there are others, in their natural state. And we say, 'we shouldn't have painted anything, we should have left all of them like that, because it is the testimony of how it was made', which was from packing boxes for the engines, and the nails we used were from the boxes too, we would pull them out, straighten and re-sharpen them, so we could use them for the shelves because no one gave

us anything. And we had to fight the pigeons, the mice, and we couldn't kill the mice. Because if you kill a mouse, it stains the paper, with the blood, so we had to catch them alive, and then drown them in water. But then the worst enemy of the documents is neither the mouse, pigeon or the water, it is men always trying to make the evidence disappear.

We have learned as we went that archives are not collected in a single heap, all together. They have to be organised according to their vital cycle, like human beings. We could not put babies in an old people's home. So, for us, the young documents, those that are being born, they are in the office. But after five years of being in the office, they are moved to the central archive. Here they stay until they turn 15. After 15 years, they are transferred to the intermediate archive. They stay there until they turn 35, and then they are transferred to the historic archive. So when we teach archival studies to new colleagues, because we have courses here every week, we tell them, 'they are like a human being; they are born, they are babies and eat from a bottle, they become teenagers, they come here, then they go to the intermediate archive when they are adults, and in the historic archive they are venerable old people'.

Here, our colleagues have the task of classifying the documentation. They analyse archive by archive, because the documents are complete records. Then, the document, this document, for example, is only useful when taken together with the other documents. If you separate it from the others, it is as if you were taking out an eye. It's not worth anything anymore. Now here we do the work of preventive conservation. First the document must be cleaned, sheet by sheet, and all the iron objects must be removed and discarded. All the metallic objects, everything metallic, is thrown away; clips, pins, paper fasteners, all of that has to be removed and discarded. Once that's done, it goes in these envelopes. Right here. Now for the work of conservation and restoration. These books, for example, are ill, they are patients, so with these books we have to remove the cover, and we have to remove all the binding, and then remove all the mould. They have to be cleaned and put in their place. Here this one is half finished, only half of the work is done. This one has its cover already, it is getting another cover fitted. So it has been cleaned of its binding, and all its things have been replaced. But after the cleaning, a clinical history is made in which it says the date that the patient was treated. Then what kind of document, the size, the type of paper, and the kind of treatment it has been exposed to. For example, cleaning: dry, with a vacuum, or cleaning with brushes: 'task completed by Ernesto Copa'. Then we know what kind of treatment was given to this one. If it deteriorates again, then we have to investigate why it is happening, work wasn't done well perhaps. Then we have to do the work again. Because removing the fungus and the other mites, the bugs – this treatment can be given today, but if the work isn't done well, they come back, and the second ones are stronger than the first. So, this one has its life sheet here. This is going to be part of a hospital. There has also been map restoration and the damaged have been repaired.

Before we started working, the solution was to cut what was damaged. Of course, it needed to be repaired differently, but we are going to be able to fill it out with cellulose, and with the information that we have in its record as a basis we will be able to fill it out. This archive, it is a complex, that's why it is called a system. Apart from the fact that there are documents in the central archive, in the office archive, in the intermediate archive, and historical archive, it's also a library, a museum, and, as part of it, the brushes are going to stay, the hammers, the nails, and part of the documentation is going to stay the way it is, in order to show how it was. What we have here is a massive history, 25,000 metres of history, but it's not just history, it has strategic value for the country, for its development. Simon Patiño, who was called the King of Tin, controlling 70% of the world's tin, extracted rich mineral and left behind 'tails' which we can identify, and the oldest 'tails' have a purity level far, far higher than, say, in Japan. And then, some years ago when there was a conflict in the Puerto Suárez area in the east of Bolivia, a Brazilian company was ready to invest $80 million in a mining site, but that meant no money for the community. So they kidnapped some politicians there and the order came to renegotiate the deal, that it should be doubled to 200 million. Now even though international mining companies are always haggling over price, we were able to show from old records of geological surveys we'd preserved and catalogued that the site was worth at least $3 billion and on that basis the Brazilians were pushed to increase the investment to 210 million. I think that helped us to be taken seriously though as I said we started from scratch."

Indian Yellow

Acryl
1377

Ultramarine
2011
Größe
Gobeline
Größe 150×
per Stück S 22—

Wax Print

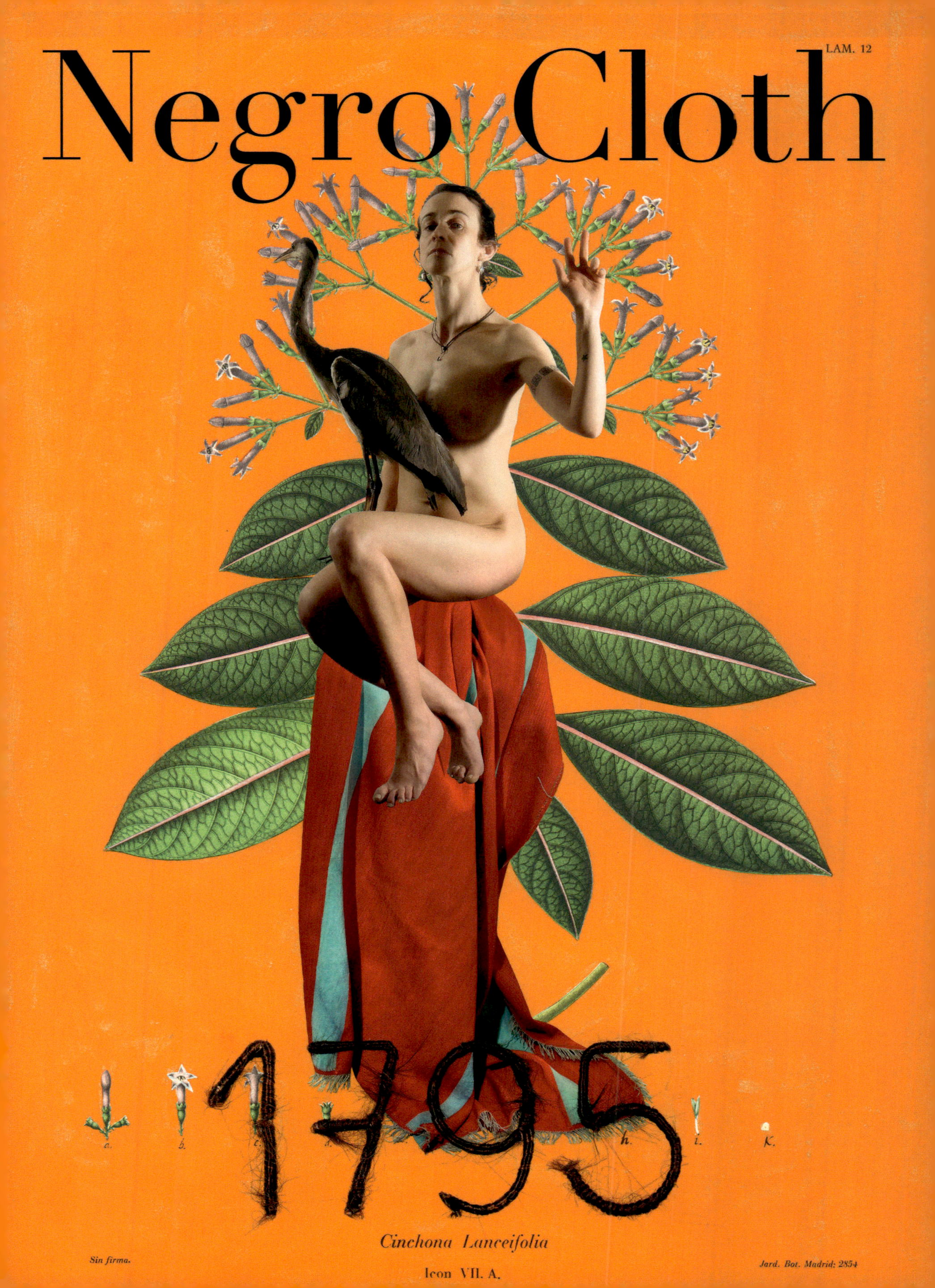
LAM. 12
Negro Cloth
1795
a.
b.
c.
d.
h.
i.
K.
Cinchona Lanceifolia
Sin firma.
Icon VII. A.
Jard. Bot. Madrid: 2854

King Cotton

Turkey Red
1967

Feathers
1904

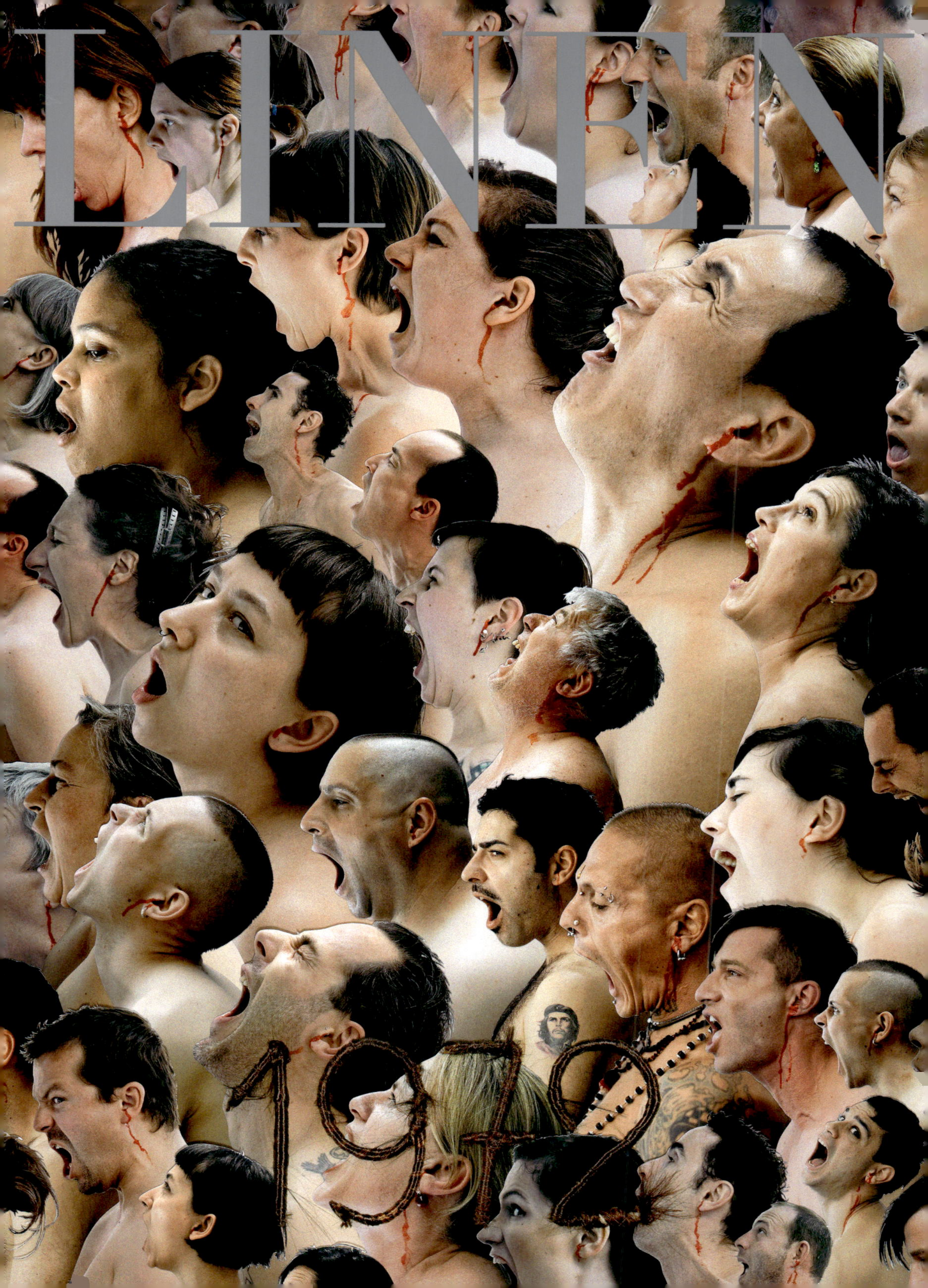
LINEN
1949

AACA
1903

Paisley
2007

1859

HATS
1862

Crinoline
1851

K'eperina / Manta / Carrier Cloth 17

Wool, acrylic; acquired in a shop, La Paz, 2008. The broad definition of writing for Andean peoples would include the pattern they make by throwing coca leaves, the images inscribed by lightning upon rock, their designs in ceramics, the tracings left by dancers or animals upon earth, the historical ritual sites organised by a pattern of pathways, their gestures made by "writing in the air", glyphs upon hide, and also writing on paper. A vital part of the development of every new textile 'being' is its emergent ability to speak. The combined motion of weft and heddles is considered to introduce breath, light, and food into the textile, and also speech. The movement of the weft is the breathing effect. Each face of the different coloured sets of threads has the power of speech, having been nourished with the veinlike threads at each passing of the weft. Respiration and colour, the play of the colours, are women's. A man is just white and tan, otherwise he would be able to weave. Among Aymará people, a woman is considered a fine weaver when she is able to display the rainbow in her weavings. "My Mum used to say 'those are *k'isas*, they are sweet, because they are so nice'. My godmother when she saw a weaving well done used to shout '*hay mama jiwaki! Jiwaki!*' which means it's so pretty that just by looking at it you may die. People say that grandmothers used to weave quite pretty. After the rain passed, they used to look at the *kürmi* (rainbow) without pointing at it though, because if you do, people say your finger may rot. They used to imitate the colours, by looking; people say the best weaver was the one able to catch the *kürmi* in her weaving" (Maríana Quispe, Aymará culture, Ch'issi community, Department of La Paz). Andean myth establishes that sacred mountains such as the Akhamani possess human attributes like eyes and hair. "... when I was little, my grandpa used to say that mountains were sacred by pointing to the Akhamani. He used to say that mountains were alive and took care of the community. He called them *achachilas*, the elders. Then he would point at the animals and say that llama wool and alpaca wool are the hair of the mountains, and the little lagoons were their eyes. He looked at us, and said that women used mountains' hair to weave and the lagoons were those little figures – rhombuses – weavers included in the piece. They were eyes, which took care of the weaving and the weaver. People also say that these eyes have to be included to ask for enough water for our crops" (Felipa Vargas, Kallawaya culture, Kañizaya community, Department of La Paz). Depending on the day on which the women of the Bolivian Qaqachaka weave, their prayers will differ. They may pray to a dead ancestress who was a good weaver on a Monday, the day when the dead are remembered; they may not weave on a Tuesday, which is a devilish day. They may pray to one of the *mamitas* when they weave on a Wednesday or a Saturday, or to a male godsaint, *Killak Tatala* or *Panakach Tatala*, when they weave on a Thursday; but they may not weave on a Friday, another devilish day. Sunday is a day of rest. The strongest desire to weave is felt during the entire period of the rainy season, from the Feast of the Dead in November until the following Carnival, and if a weaving is not finished before Carnival it is believed that it will never be: The weaver will become lethargic, and will finally be grasped by the earth.

Indian Yellow

The pigment enjoyed great popularity in 19th-century Europe among painters, particularly in Britain, where it represented a breakthrough in conveying "a wider range of flesh tones, especially at the darker end of the spectrum". In this it was far superior to British-produced ochre or a previous yellow coming from India and further east called *gamboge*, a resin-based pigment. Its popularity coincided with varieties of racism that proclaimed themselves as 'scientific', for which racial identity in a painting had to use prescribed colour combinations, as well as demanding stereotyped faces. It was a time when British art teachers were preoccupied with the standardisation of colour vocabulary with words like 'dusky' and 'swarthy'. Its disappearance from the palette early in the 20th century is a story of the shifting priorities and reactions of British colonialism in India. Indian yellow or *purree* was produced from the urine of cows fed exclusively on mango leaves, mainly in Bengal. The profits were enormous.
The market price in Calcutta would be 100 to 200 times that given to the farmer. But towards the end of the century some reports suggested that cows fed in this way suffered malnutrition and died early. This might concern animal welfare groups in Britain, but what really concerned the British was the development of Indigenous Hindu Indian cow protection societies in the 1880s. These early public expressions of shared religious precepts evolved into larger ideological statements about imagined communities. The very ambiguity of meaning in the heterogeneous localised worship of 'Mother Cow' allowed activists to link local identities and values to a broader ideological movement. The figure of the sacred cow could "... unite popular and high culture; it could serve reformist and traditional ends; it could reach the heart of townsmen and peasants alike". Lord Landsdowne referred to them as the greatest threat to the British government since the "Indian Mutiny". The fact was that in the Indian Penal Code of 1860 drawn up by the British, the cow was not a sacred object and this was reasserted in 1888. It was to pre-empt further development of this organising that, without specific legislation, they placed a ban on Indian yellow and went out of their way to make it known that this was what they were doing. It was a case where, as Jordanna Bailkin makes so clear, "the desire to paint or visually represent colonized people came to clash directly with the mission to rule them." The replaced *gamboges* remained in use, for instance as a dye for the robes of Buddhist monks, and, as produced in Cambodia, acquired a rather macabre reputation as it progressed from the 19th century into the 20th. As Radiolab reported in *The Perfect Yellow*, during the wars fought over the country, unspent bullets and mud from battlefields were getting mixed into the *gamboge* resin.

Drinking the urine of cows, claimed by some Hindu groups to be healthy for humans and by others to be a cure for cancer.

1917

As he freely admitted, Mahatma Gandhi – who had been consciously experimenting with different kinds of Western and Indian costume for himself – had never seen a spinning wheel (*charka*) in his life when he returned to India in 1915, even though he had chosen it as a symbol of the Indian independence movement. Then on arrival he could not find one. But from as early as 1908 he was advocating homespun weaving as both practical and political at a time when hand spindling had almost disappeared. Indeed, he confused the *charka* with the *kharga* (handloom). But what might otherwise be a cautionary tale of the dangers of using abstract ideological symbols, was offset by its particular relevance. For several hundred years India had been the great maker and worldwide exporter of cotton cloth. The loss of much its export market and the penetration into India itself of English cotton cloth was considerable. It was then not strange that it should be so important in anti-colonial politics and at the end of the 19th century "handloom weaving had been transformed from an endangered rural craft to a powerful symbol of the moral and spiritual regeneration of India". This also keyed into the symbolic power of cloth, unlike most societies it wasn't just an indicator of status, "it could change the moral and physical substance of the individual ... able to absorb and retain spirit/substance for many years". The Swadeshi movement in Bengal pulled these threads together to make a practical political campaign to boycott British goods. By making a virtue of the 'homespun' (as opposed to the machine-made) as practically realisable, Gandhi more pragmatically went further, taking into account the large numbers of unemployed women of all castes who had once spun the yarn to be woven. In his book *Young India* he reprinted a letter written by a widow in the 1820s who had brought up three daughters and seen them married with "no one looking down on them" or on her income as a spinner. It had appeared in the Bengali paper *Samachar Darpan* and described a drastic change in her situation. "Now for three years we are in want of food. The weavers do not call at the house for yarn as they did. Not only this, if the yarn is sent to market it is sold at not even a fourth of the price." She understands this is because of foreign (*bilati*) yarn and, in what sounds like irony to modern ears, she is sympathetic to the foreign women spinners who must be so very poor for their prices to be so low. The women of his own time, Gandhi argued, should once again be "brought into the labour process and augment India's productive power but at the same time the ancient status would be reaffirmed" with reference to the legendary figure of *Manu*, author of an important Sanskrit code of law, the *Dharma Shastra* (Law Book), dated between 200 BCE and 200 CE. It covers all aspects of life and the afterlife, as well as 'norms of practical morality' for Hindu society including some concerning dress codes. At the same time he had a 'Keynesian' understanding of the multiplier effect of income generation and employment to be applied locally and especially for women. It was then a woman naturally enough, 'an enterprising widow', Gangaben Mujmuder, who was to make his ideas work. In 1917, after much searching she found spinning wheels in Vijapur, Baroda state, and went on to organise a spinning centre there. Though it was another follower, Maganhal Gandhi, who made mechanical improvements to the wheel, it was Mujmuder that then found a Muslim weaver who could train other weavers – that had until then woven only mill yarn – to weave the homespun and make the *khadi* cloth that became a symbol of self-sufficiency. That they should be Muslims was ironic in that Hinduism and the Sanskrit Code of Law were essential components of this particular nationalism and the traditions of uncut cloth it had recourse to. It was she again who organised a solution to making *khadi* of greater width, so that Gandhi himself was not "forced to wear a short, coarse *dhoti*". The *dhoti* (wrap-around cloth) and the cap made from *khadi* cloth were articulated as anti-colonial dress and recognised by the British as such. Soon afterwards another woman, Gangbehn Ramji, became an expert teacher in the weaving of *khadi dhotis*. Meanwhile Gandhi himself, contra his stereotyping, insisted on "untiring research on the spinning wheel ... . We have manufactured scores of them, but now we have to produce an expert who is well-versed in the manufacture of machines."

Simon Sheikh

On Object Communication: What makes an object speak to me? In the daily use of language, we talk of something, usually an aesthetic object or cultural artefact, as something that does or does not speak to me, meaning that this thing may very well be interesting or brilliant, but not so to me as a recipient, or, moreover that it does not intend to speak to me, that it does not speak my language. This is no simple transmission of meaning or affect, however, since the

language through which this object supposedly communicates cannot be so easily identified or classified, nor even its very status as intentional, as having an agency and authorial voice – that a thing could 'speak' to you, circumvents the very relation between subject and object. The core of this enigma is thus twofold: that an object can be active towards the gaze of the subject, that it is at all capable of communicating, and, secondly, that such a communication constitutes some sort of language, whether familiar or alien, and as such decipherable and translatable.
In the first instance, the status of the object as intended would seem to have to with its origin, whether a natural or cultural object, where the latter would always be representation, as well as having potential use and exchange value. However, objects found in nature also have shapes, sounds and colours that render them more or less aesthetically pleasing (depending on cultural contexts and readings, of course), more or less alluring or indistinguishable, more or less visible or readable. But does this visual appearance or identity, whether it makes the object stand out or blend into the background, mean that the object is intentional?

Afghan rug depicting a Kalasnikov Rifle, allegedly made by Afghani children, purchased in Bahrain. Courtesy the collection of Dr Anthony Downey

Interestingly, this is not only a religious question, ranging from pagan beliefs in the magic of certain objects to the Christian notion of pantheism and beyond, but also a modernist conundrum. Again, this may appear surprising: whereas the modernist tactic of a universal language of abstraction for the cultural production of objects is well known, we also find a theorising of intending objects outside this authored policy, at the very margins of modernist thought, and sometimes it is as if one can only see the whole field precisely from the margins, at the very edge, which is perhaps why it is precisely these obscure texts that have found a resonance with contemporary writers. Here I am thinking of the work on the subject by such writers as Walter Benjamin and Roger Caillois, who, albeit with different approaches and intentions, were both concerned with what has been termed the language of things. Indeed, Kaja Silverman has employed the term 'the language of things' in a book with the programmatic title *World Spectators*, drawing exactly on Caillois' theories of intentional objects and insects in an elaboration of how things communicate and desire the gaze of the other, and Benjamin has written a text of the idea of object communication, recently revisited by Hito Steyerl in an essay entitled exactly "The Language of Things".
Silverman reads Caillois' texts on insects and rocks as aesthetic – such as his tellingly named "The Writing of Stones" – as drawing attention to themselves through their beautific appearance, and thus as communicating, in the establishment of a specific aesthetic subjecthood, a desirous exchange that is nonetheless initiated by the objects of the world rather than the (human) subject, thus creating a language of things in the forms, shapes, contours, colours, and so on. In other words, a communication of form that is primarily corporeal, and not semantic, even if structured like a language. Benjamin's text, on the other hand, posits and contrasts two actual, if separate languages, the language of things and the language of men, the first one mute, the second one fully immersed in institutionalised practices. As Steyerl – who accurately describes it as the weirdest of all Benjamin's texts! – points out, Benjamin does not describe human languages in terms of nations and peoples, but as institutional practices, and thus as discourse, which would also lead to another understanding of the concept of translation. For Steyerl, crucially, such a translation is made within the assemblage of images in artistic practice, translating, if you will, from one organisational form to another.
This language of things can provide us with the possible coordinates for looking at objects that have, perhaps, been falsely institutionally described, such as Ines Doujak's eccentric collection of textiles from the Andes, whether in their 'original' form and context, or as translated assemblages in Doujak's modifications of them. Rather than interpreting them, giving immediate and obvious meanings to the images of, in this case, the map of Bolivia, or the sign of the eagle, or of the machine gun or the peace pipe, or speaking about the brightness of the colours or the architectonics of the weavings, we must try to think of the thing as a thing, and ask ourselves, how does it speak to me?

Walter Benjamin, 'Goethe's Elective Affinities', *Selected Writings 1913–1926*, Harvard University Press (Bellknap): Cambridge, Mass., 1996, pp. 297–360. Roger Caillois, *The Edge of Surrealism*, Duke University Press: Durham & London, 2003. Roger Caillois, *The Writing of Stones*, University Press of Virginia: Charlottesville, 1985. Kaja Silverman, *World Spectators*, Stanford University Press: Stanford, CA, 2000. Hito Steyerl, "The Language of Things", http://eipcp.net/transversal/0606/steyerl/en

Gauze Cloth Composed of Feline Heads

18

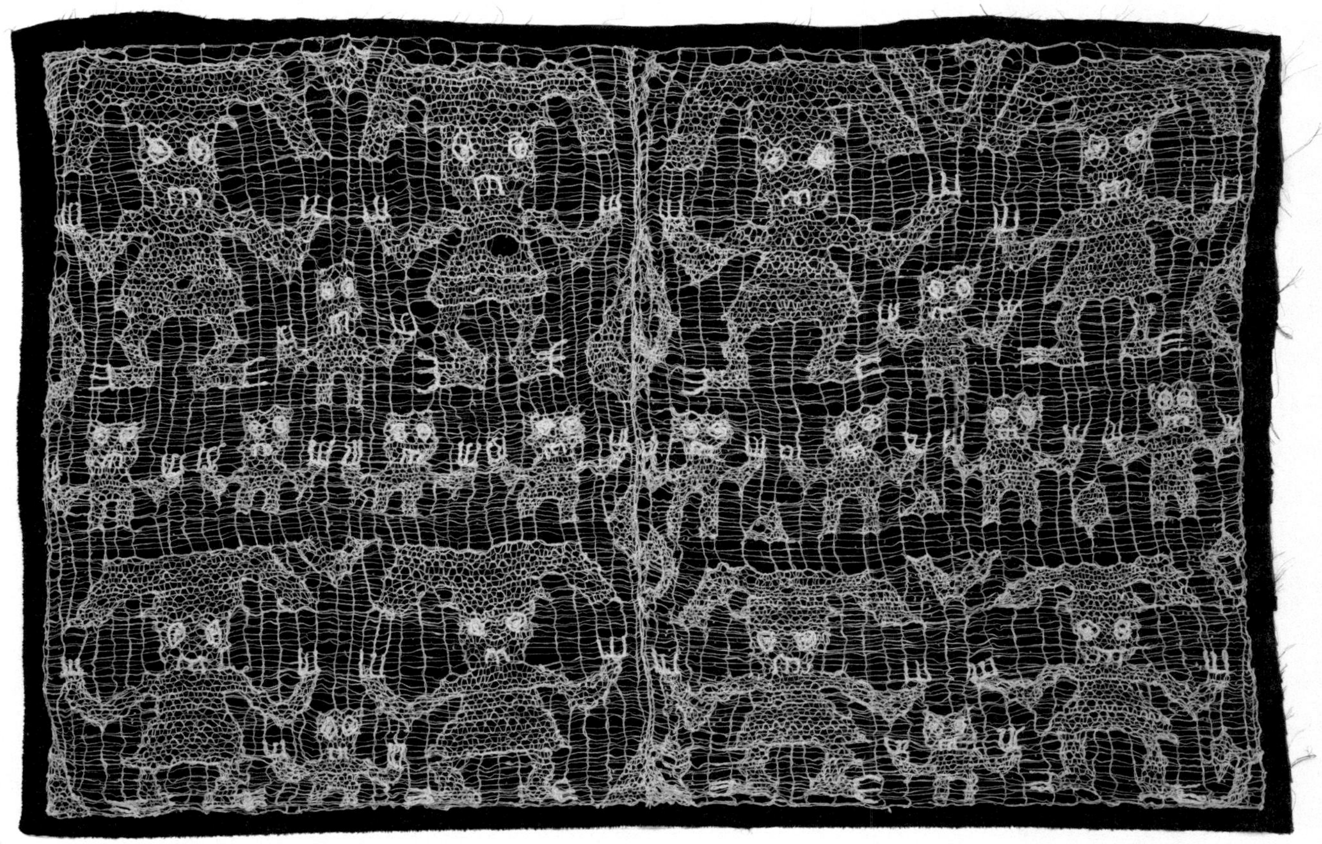

Chancay; cotton; probably 1200 to 1450 CE; Central Coast, Peru; acquired in Ollantaytambo, 1998, private collection, loan to the archive. Gauze has two meanings, the most common a general one for 'flimsy' or 'transparent' cloth. The second sense of the word can refer to such material but specifically means a 'crossed-warp' structure. It is widely accepted to describe a weave made with two different kinds of warp. Such warp threads are "made to intertwist more or less among themselves". It is not the same as twining. It seems likely that the word derives not specifically from Palestinian Gaza, but from the Arabic word *gazz*, meaning floss silk. The gauze was worn on the head in ritual contexts and the feline iconography might have enhanced the power of its owner, considering the significance that Andean people assigned to transformed states of being. The influence of fishing is evident on this type of Chancay open-work fabric. As a coastal culture of central Peru, Chancay people survived on both ocean and river valley fishing. Net-making practices developed into superb cotton open-weave textiles with intricate patterns. Initially wild cotton was used, but later the cotton plant was domesticated. The term gauze is often applied to open-work textiles whose warp threads do not cross, and to lacy cloths despite their weave structure. Gauze weaving requires a special technique, in which the weaver forces some warp threads to cross over or under other warp threads. These gauze crosses are held in place by the insertion of weft threads. This method of warp-crossing contrasts with standard back-strap weaving, where the warp threads do not interact with each other but remain in a fixed position. Different types of gauze weave are classified by the various interactions of the warp threads. The simplest structure is that of plain gauze weave, in which the same warp threads pass over or under each other. More complex gauze weaves are created when variation is introduced into the interworking of warps and interlacing of wefts. The process of gauze weaving on a back-strap loom demanded a highly sophisticated and laborious loom set-up; the correct ordering of warp threads through the string heddles demanded foresight in order to create a textile with crossed warps.

A textile's weave structure, in the case of the gauze a surface area which is composed around *irregularly* shaped negative spaces, forms an integral part of its symbolic content. According to Mary Frame, "the grids and symmetries of fabric structures operate as a construct for the conceptualization of space, giving it form, division, direction, and unity".

Acryl

Of the variety of basic synthetic textiles that were developed in the last century, this yarn, first produced by Du Pont in 1950, is most akin to wool. In the Western world of knitters there are 'yarn snobs', for whom acryl is cheap and nasty, scratchy and sweaty. Naturally enough an anti-snobbery discourse develops in tandem, one which might admit to the sweaty quality of its warmth, but praises precisely its cheapness, washability, and for how well it holds a particularly bright range of dyes. In between there are not only a variety of mixes, especially with wool, but divergences of quality even among 100% acrylic yarn. "Caron One Pound" for instance, is highly rated for its worsted-type weight and for the particularly saturated and exciting colour it is dyed. This snobbery also reflects periodic Western hysteria about what is 'authentic', prevalent since large-scale industrialisation, mixed in with notions of the 'natural' in relation to textile fibres; a case of looking somewhere else for its lost origins. This produces a veritable torrent of ironies, starting with the very idea of a natural fibre when the reality, in the case of cotton, say, is a saturation with synthetic chemicals used both in its growing and in the various treatments applied to its transformation into cloth.
More telling is the variety of pressures and desires that make it more likely that people like the highland Sakaka of Bolivia have "come to rely on acrylic yarn while elite cosmopolitans use natural fibre." What is 'modern', 'civilised or uncivilised', smart or not, remains determined by the powerful. This is how it is, while at the same time there is an "international market for antique Andean cloth" as part of a worldwide demand for the authentic as both hand-woven and 'ethnic'. Some Sakaka people sold their weavings for money, others exchanged them for "factory-spun synthetic fibre yarns in fashionable colours". Their own dress-style refuses essentialisation, likely to be a mixture of new and traditional styles, perhaps a traditional natural-fibre skirt and a synthetic wool sweater. The mix and style might depend on whether worn in a town or the countryside in a country where until recently, 'authentic' dress classified one as both Indigenous and inferior. The demand for synthetic yarn is a consequence of desire – a love of its bright colours – combined with pressures which make the 'authentic' impossible. Wool is harder to get as local sheep pasture is degraded and the trains of alpaca and llama that once passed through the area no longer do so, a tradition that has become 'uneconomic'. Natural dyes too are harder to find because of that loss of accumulated knowledge of technique. Other 'modern' changes in the regional economy have meant men having to go to work in cities like Buenos Aires. A consequence is that women are having to do more agricultural work, leaving less time for the time-intensive business of spinning and weaving. One innovative way out of these externally imposed contradictions has been shown by the handloom weavers around Apu Ausengate near Cuzco, Peru, who have another kind of 'yarn snobbery': they like the colour of acrylic yarns, but don't like the way it is spun.
Acrylic fibres are either dissolved polymers which are extruded into warm air where the fibres solidify by evaporation; or are dissolved and extruded into a bath and then dried. Either way the manufactured yarn is perceived to be poor quality in local Quechua aesthetics. So the women re-spin the manufactured synthetic yarn on drop spindles before use. Properly spun yarn is needed to satisfy both these aesthetics, and ancestral rules for highly valued textiles that are for use rather than for sale to the outside world. It also makes the yarn finer. The skill in re-spinning involves keeping up a constant rate of twist on the spindle, waiting till the moment it kinks back on itself and becomes smooth, and then holding it under tension until it is on the loom bars. For young people in the Cuzco area, synthetic clothing and textiles represent honour, prestige, modernity, and youth. 70-year-old weaver Martina Cachin commented, "Even my husband wants me to weave his *poncho* out of synthetic fibre as if he was still young."

1377

Brushes, cloth, spices, and hats are on offer, 15th century. Rouen, Municipal Library. Cloth was by far the leading article in imports, both of German towns and of Eastern countries. Cloth was bought by Hanseatic merchants and produced in Ghent, Ypres, Tournai, Malines and, later, in Antwerp and Bergen-op-Zoom. In the 13th century and in the first half of the 14th the Hanseatic bought their suites in Bruges. The Flemish materials were of almost infinite variety and prices; profits were up to 30%.

Exchange of gifts, including Ypres cloth, which was referred to in a Novograd charter of the 1130s. Ypres was at that time what it remained in the 13th and 14th centuries: the most complete type that had ever existed of a Middle Ages export centre.

The wool weavers of Ypres, Flanders, launched an uprising to protest against their conditions, marking close to 100 years of contesting the power of cloth merchants that were backed by the military arm of the Flanders aristocracy, and sometimes by the French state. From as early as 1245 there are reports of workers' associations, strikes and machine-breaking. During all this time the town was an internationally famous centre of cloth production for export, highly prized from Russia to North Africa. It was also a time when "weavers did not become heretics, heretics became weavers". This was officially recognised: The council of Reims in 1148 had prescribed imprisonment and branding and exile "for the most wicked sects of the Manchichees who hide among the poor and under the veil of religion labour to undermine the faith of the simple, spread by wicked weavers who move from place to place, often changing their names and accompanied by women sunk in sin". The first revolt took place in 1280 and was aimed at the guild and jury power of the merchants, which had allowed them public control by means of inspectors from whom weavers and their helpers were never safe in their own homes. As in both England and India centuries later, they had the power to decide which cloth they would reject, a potentially arbitrary power. In nearby Douai in the same year laws proclaiming that "no one should be so arrogant as to go on strike" were renewed and three striking weavers – Hanton Lauwer, Jehan Boucey and Collaty Caullet – were decapitated for injuries they "visited on an alderman", while others were banished forever on pain of such punishment, because "they prevented and disrupted work in the city, violating the laws and customs of this city". The following year similar laws were enacted against strikes for higher pay in nearby Clermon-en-Beauvais. To modern ears their tone is more familiar still: "Conspiracy against the common good is when workers contract that they will not work for as low wages as they used to, but they increase the price on their own authority and agree they will not work for less, and impose threats and punishments on their fellows who will not join the conspiracy." The business was highly profi table but there was little 'trickledown' to those who made the cloth, who might own their looms – though some of these were in hock – but were wholly dependent on the merchants for both wool and dye. These merchants had no commitment to any weaver beyond the job in hand; they had the power that goes with arbitrarily cutting off an income. It was an export-oriented business with no interest in domestic consumption and so no desire to pay proper rates for the cloth, a familiar situation in most export-oriented economies, and one which was exacerbated in the course of the 14th century. Some idea of the scale of its exports can be seen in the volume of Flemish cloth imported through the port of Lubeck in 1368: it accounted for more than half of all other commodities put together, supplying North Germany and the Baltic towns and also being re-exported to Russia.

The 1280 revolt did break guild power but the merchants became more enmeshed instead with the Count of Flanders and the local aristocracy. This did not stop the weavers of nearby Saint Omer joining with the fullers – those who cleaned and thickened the wool – in burning their tools. This prompted the Count's government to play off weavers against the fullers, but in 1360 they succeeded in creating a united front against the government. This was both in Ypres and Bruges, which by this time had become, through its commercial and financial sector, dominant in creating a new model of cloth production. It undermined weaver independence and focused on the marketing of high quality cloth for export.

In Ypres itself it led to the authority of the Count's chief officer being overthrown "without anyone paying for this act of treason", a propagandist wrote. The same author went on to describe how the Count had been preparing a wedding and had asked for a few days grace before investigating the chief officer. However, "The beastly and arrogant ones amongst those tradesmen dismissed the Count's plea contemptuously and with shame and spite suspended his effigy from the window of his palace."

The power of the weavers over the town did not last long, and further revolts took place in 1367, 1370–71 and again in 1377. Fifty years later this cycle of struggles in Flanders as a whole was still ongoing. In Tournai in 1424, weavers and fullers joined with blacksmiths to overthrow the city council.

Cordula Daus

Of Gods, Textiles, and Politics. A Web of Threads and Imagination. Transparent, it hovers at the threshold of the material. A fragile veil of cotton, also called gauze. Exact origins and history unknown. Presumably it is worn on the head, a utilitarian object whose permeability somehow refers to transcendence.

The artful weaving techniques for creating ornamental gauze are considered a special characteristic of Chancay culture, a civilisation that flourished on the coast of central Peru from approximately 1200 to 1470 CE. Overtwisted, usually naturally coloured cotton yarn is held in place on a frame of structural threads that are later removed. Horizontal and vertical threads cross over each other, form irregular little loops, a series of gaps, absences and presences. Like net, gauze belongs to the class of openwork textiles, and as such the weaving technique itself and its fundamental elements are visible: the movement and texture of weft and warp threads, and the way their regular course is interrupted by the introduction of knotted-in patterns.

A piece of fabric is not an image, but a textured assemblage. When the veils are worn, the figures woven into them are barely visible. They are simply present in an imperceptible way. They accompany the wearer, cover her head and hair. It takes an appropriate background to make a legible pattern emerge. In the top and bottom rows, the contours of figures emerge that are reminiscent of the central figure in Chancay textile art: a deity with human-like features, depicted from the front, in a proud posture, legs wide apart, arms raised up, with a crescent-shaped headdress. The figure is accompanied by a number of small animal-like beings in anthropomorphic postures. The identity and names of the divine beings cannot be determined precisely, and yet they clearly belong to the Andean vision of the cosmos and the Andean representational scheme. Claws and fangs stitched in after completion incorporate the supernatural attributes of the feline deity that already appears on the earliest textiles of ancient Peru. Even though they do not touch each other, the figures are penetrated by the same plant fibres and lines, clawing into the fabric that they seem to be bringing into being with their presence. Their expressions are defined by the same features and postures that typify them as hybrid being – various degrees removed in their similarity with the other extreme of divine, human, or animal nature. Abstract forms float between them – triangles pointing upward and sickles pointing downward. Structure and decor, space and figures form a unit, and yet the matrix of the thread grid predominates: the image of an animistic cosmos in which the worlds of material and spirit, profane and sacred are joined by the gossamer thread of delicate fibers.

Oil drum, April 24, 1996, archives of Ingrid Wiener.

Who created these textiles, and for what purpose? How much creative freedom did they have in the process of making them? The weavers from Chancay mastered nearly every technique known at the time, and yet the iconography of their textiles is astonishingly repetitive. For centuries, certain religious motifs, images of the same divine figures and animals, were replicated over and over. This fact gives rise to speculations about the extent that in this culture, too, as in the case of the Incas, the weaving of textiles and the symbols woven into them were defined by a priestly bureaucracy and used for government-determined purposes.

Around 1000 to 800 BCE, writes anthropologist Prada Ramírez, "a string of circumstances evolved in the Andes along with the development of the loom (...) that allowed for the production of difficult patterns and the transmission of complex iconographies". This put an ideographical means of communication into the hands of the ruling priestly class, making it possible to transcend the physical realm and its concomitant requirement for an oral tradition and thus extend their power into distant regions. Prada Ramírez underscores that the same period around 1000 BCE, cited by archeologists as the time when woven textiles first emerged, was the moment when the first "imperial" cultures like the Chavín, Moche, Tiahuanaco, and Huari appeared. These are the cultures that historians associate with the birth of government in the Andes. A hole gapes in the woven bodies on the upper left – a tiny tear in the thread, a stretched loop – creating the impression that you could look into the heart or stomach of the deities. The tale of the fabric, the access it might provide to history and its subjects, remains opaque. What is left is a web, the stylistic construct of that dominant cultural technique of weaving that not only speaks of a vanished culture and its myths, but that in and of itself was the materialised form of a myth that bound together the earthly and the supernatural, the individual and the government body.

Manta / Carrier Cloth

19

Ausangate; early 20th century; alpaca; acquired in Cuzco, 2010. For much of its long history, Andean weaving has created textiles that were the same on both sides, described as cloth of two faces, a quality uncommon in European textiles. "They work two faces all of the work they want, so that you do not see a thread nor an end of it in the entire piece" (Acosta, 1590, book 4, chapter 42). Without stains or faults, an object was considered beautiful when it was well made. The fineness of these *cumbi* textiles is comparable only to the *kesi* tapestry of China or to the work of the Fatimid *tiraz* workshops of 13th-century Islamic Egypt (both examples of weaving with the fine fibre of silk and not emphasising a perfect finish). Even the world-famous examples of weaving from 16th-century Northern Europe achieved warp and weft counts only one-quarter of that found in Inca *cumbi* weaving, which generally has 35 warps and more than 200 wefts per inch. They were made by the *cumbimayos*, who were described not only as master-weavers, but as "possessors of a specific force or energy (*camay*)". *Camay* was also translated as: "to charge with being", "to give form and force", or "to animate" (Huarochiri Manuscript 1991, p. 45). The *cumbi* weaver could, in Inca perception, vivify the textile or imbue it with animated properties. Even nowadays textiles are perceived as living beings (see Cereceda, 1978 for the naming of textile parts with human anatomical references – body, mouth, heart, etc., or Desrosiers, 1997). Soon after the invasion the Spanish Crown discouraged the production of luxury textiles in the colonies, eager to stanch competition with Spanish textile industry and to promote exports to the New World. The textile workshops already installed in 1545 by the invaders, the *obrajes*, only produced low quality cloth, intended primarily for garments given in lieu of payment to tributary and forced labourers in the silver mines.

Ultramarine

"And if ye find ... ah God I know not ... if / Bedded in store of rotten fig leaves soft / Some lump of lapis lazuli / Big as a Jew's head cut off at the nape / Blue as vein o'er the virgin's breast ..." This is the 19th-century poet Robert Browning's Bishop, obsessed with the grandeur of his burial arrangements and keen for the lump of lapis lazuli he has buried years before to be recognised and preserved as a posthumous status symbol. And treasured stuff it was, the blue crystal rock from the mines of Badakhshan in Afghanistan where it had first appeared on frescoes around the Buddhist sculpture in Bamiyan. The colour caused a sensation when it arrived in Europe. Writing in his 1464 *Trattato dell' Architettura* A. Fialarete described a "Fine blue is derived from a stone and comes from across the seas and so is called ultramarine".

There was a time in the early Renaissance when the cost of the colour was as crucial as the hue itself, especially when it became the prescribed colour for the Virgin Mary's cloak. Negotiations were carried out and contracts agreed between patron and painter on this specific issue. In 1514 the commission for the Madonna of the Harpies by Andrea del Sarto stipulated that her robe be coloured with ultramarine costing "at least five good florins an ounce." At around the same time Albrecht Dürer was paying "41 grams of gold for 30 grams" of the pigment. though the poet Kaspar Scheit suggested that the artist might have used a pigment from azurite that was available in Europe: "After a few days they/Crossed the river Saar/Close to this place is sited a blue-colour mountain/Where the colour for Dürer's panel/Was taken before he died." There was some material basis to the price of the real thing: It was "the fully justified belief in the durability of this pigment in contrast to azurite (basic copper carbonate), which turned too readily to green on exposure to damp. A stable blue was thus a costly blue." Even the ancient Egyptians had found it expensive and developed an 'Egyptian blue' by applying heat to a mix of silica, copper and lime. Naturally enough a great deal of effort was put into finding substitutes in later periods. In more recent times it was in the Netherlands that new techniques of the preparation of colours – "coating each particle in a film of oil" – were developed. This reduced the likelihood of changes in the colours and therefore, in the case of ultramarine, meant less lapis lazuli could be used.

Then in 1826 a sulphate ultramarine pigment was invented in response to a prize competition in France, but its inventor "refused to reveal its formula". Two years later however a Chemistry professor at the University of Tübingen found a similar process whose formula he did publish. Michael Taussig dismissively compares the subsequent factory-produced ultramarine of the 19th century to fast food in relation to the original colour. It was, he says, 'homogeneous', whereas that from lapis lazuli has irregular crystals which, quoting Anita Albus, "sparkle like stars within the deep blue". A more general critique comes from Alexander Theroux: "A colour may be too pure. Modern shades and colours often appear hideous, ironically, *because* of their extreme purity ... . Old-fashioned blue, which had a dash of yellow in it ... now seems often incongruous against newer, staring, overly luminous eye-killing shades." But Taussig is an enthusiast of IKB (International Klein Blue), patented by the artist Yves Klein, who – with the help of the Parisian paint dealer Edouard Adam – used an ultramarine pigment suspended in the synthetic resin 'Rhodopas', which unlike linseed oil kept its brightness and lived up to the sound of the word, Ultramarine! Meanwhile, the best non-synthetic Lapis, the magnificent 'Fra Angelico' now costs $157 for 5 grams.

2011

Six of seven leading members of a new independent Haitian Trade Union in the textile sector – SOTA – are sacked on October 27th, even though it has been recognised both by the Haitian government and the Trade Union federation. Workers perceive it as an attack on their attempts to organise. Industry owners Charles Baker – a former Presidential candidate – and George Sassine of the Employers lobby justify the instant sackings by saying the Union wants to shut down all the factories rather than just organising. Such a statement is in a long line of familiar rationalisations for keeping wages at a level that workers, doing long hours at the sewing machine with impossible quotas, can barely live on. At the end of 1999, Union activist workers making clothes for the Disney Corporation – the Mickey Mouse conglomerate – were dismissed when organising to improve 30 cent an hour wages, and after the company refused independent wage monitoring. Then, in 2009, the Haitian Parliament voted to increase the minimum wage to $5 a day, following demonstrations by workers. As shown in cables released by WikiLeaks,

US diplomats lobbied by companies like Levi Strauss and Fruit of the Loom immediately put pressure on the government, which with similar promptness reversed its decision down to $3 a day. Could it be that Haiti has never been forgiven for having made a uniquely successful slave revolt against colonial masters at the end of the 18th century? The fact that the country had to pay reparations on account of this 'outrage' to France, the colonisers of that time, for 120 years, and the negligence of the world and its institutions in response to the massive earthquake of 2010 suggest that this is the case. But the country is also subject to the same narrative used against workers in the clothing industry everywhere: that a wage increase would mean production would be 'uncompetitive', 'unviable', causing factories to close. Such was the case in Haiti in 2009 when USAID the official development aid arm of the USA government, and the Employers' Association – headed by the same George Sassine – produced self-interested reports aimed at showing this 'uncompetitiveness'. Since the 2010 earthquake the cost of living has increased drastically, as detailed in a report by the AFL-CIO (USA Federation of Trade Unions) report of March 3rd 2011, but the minimum wage did not change. This is despite a post-earthquake deal – with the grotesque title "HOPE" – whereby all clothing, like that produced for GAP, could enter the USA duty-free, a deal which made no reference to working conditions except for the US Department of Labor's equally perversely titled "Better Luck Haiti", set up to regulate and in effect stifle labour representation. Equally, international donor contributions to the industry's development are not conditional on unionisation. The UN, too, got in on the act with a report which argued for the removal of 'restrictive' labour laws on the grounds that wages must be kept low, despite the fact that they had in fact increased in the nearest competitor countries, the Dominican Republic and Nicaragua.
Since then, in the fast expanding textile industry – the industry has grown by 45% since the earthquake, aided by a tax-free regime for foreign investors, and accounts for 91% of Haiti's National export earnings – workers continue to receive poverty wage and likely as not wear second-hand T-shirts with slogans like "We're the 2% Who Don't Care" or alternatively "Save Darfur". Employers take advantage of a two-tiered wage system that allows them to pay a "piece rate" and often set unattainable quotas to payworkers less than the minimum wage. In 2013 this was increased from 200 to 225 gourds (approx $4). The demand for 500 a day, what was then a liveable wage, was rejected by the state and employers with the slogan "Keep Haiti Competitive", despite an inflation rate of around 120%. In 2014 it was set at close to 300 gourds. In Haiti, it's Groundhog Day. In May 2017, with inflation still rampant, the state Wages Council set its sights on a 400-a-day minimum, but its report was not released. In the face of this, trade unions (including SOTA) called a strike and for street demonstrations for a liveable 800 gourds a day and for protection against continued quota increases. They have been attacked by the police; the Wages Council chief and government minister Herivaux talks of "those who in the shadows, manipulate the most radical fringe of the trade union sector for high-risk events that can seriously affect employment in Haiti"; and the Korean and American employers write identical letters to the government telling them how it is: "Total cost competitiveness, quality production and the proximity (to) the US were the reasons we selected Haiti while betting on major improvements on salary predictability and political stability. ... If those benefits no longer exist, we will have to make other strategic arrangements to move from Haiti to other places."

Liz Conor

MOVEABLE PARTS. From earliest exploratory encounters the "native" body was a revelation to Europeans. They were struck foremost by colour, sometimes querying how much of it could be attributed to dirt.
Captain James Cook remarked, "They were quite naked, and wore no ornaments, unless we consider as such, and as proof of their love of finery, some large punctures or ridges raised on different parts of their bodies, some in straight and others in curved lines" (1955, 55).
Here "love of finery" unambiguously references the feminine – and right at this time even the "gilt cage" of beauty in which Wollstonecraft placed women's enforced irrationality (Wollstonecraft 1982, 131). This feminising of the "native" was part of the ambiguous gender status of Aboriginal men. But it was the beauty of the naked male "native" body, its whole form uninterrupted by the partitions of clothing, that Europeans couldn't quite reconcile to their notions of masculinity.

KERMAN
UNITE
UNITE
Fighting for
at Peerless Clothing
Hold Retailers Responsible!

RESPEKTE
DWA MOUN
KAP TRAVAY
FEHATRAP. SE-ONA

After all, as European men settled the new colony they were undergoing the "great masculine renunciation" following the French and American revolutions, wherein dress stated respectability, and utility – at most elegance, but certainly not beauty (Ross 2008, 59). The three-piece lounge suit would soon bisect the mature male body, the legs would become less defined, the shoulders more accentuated and the arms tailored close to the body. Cook, still in his stockings and wig, made another aside to the feminine, referring to "native" cicatrices as "embroidery of their persons" (Cook 1792, 69).

In an early encounter in Van Diemen's Land the woman Arra-Maïda screamed when one of the Frenchmen removed his glove. Arra-Maïda later insulted the zoologist François Péron in an exchange described by Shino Konishi (2009), wherein he believed the women criticised his parties' appearance and laughed "heartily at their expense". Arra-Maïda approached Péron, crushed charcoal between her palms and applied it to his face, much pleased at the result. We can only hazard a guess that the pale skin of Europeans was deemed in need of correction, or that perhaps charcoal instated a particular relation or identity. Quite possible she stopped at his face because his clothing rendered the rest of his body inaccessible to her powdering. This is not to suggest that Aborigines made less distinction between parts of their bodies. The documentation of ceremonial patterns and body paint, the boring of septums, the ornamenting of hair, tooth avulsion, the donning of decorated possum cloaks assembled from numerous skins and the manner in which children, dilly bags and coolamons were carried, imply otherwise. Yet consider how worlds apart are the customs of European men powdering their wigs white, while Aboriginal women powdered their faces black. R.E. Johns in his 19th-century *Scrapbooks* indexed under "Women" Alaskans pasting their faces black.

For the botanist Joseph Banks it was a contradiction that the "Indians" (as he called the people of New Holland) "seem to be fond of ornament, though they are absolutely without apparel" (Banks 1896, 190). Even less explicable was that modesty seemed to play no part in the rationale for what covering there was.

Commodore Phillips wrote in his dispatches to the Admiralty, "It was a practice with the seamen in these intercourses to dress up the inhabitants with shreds of cloth, and tags of coloured paper; and when they surveyed each other, they would burst into loud laughter, and run howling to the woods" (*London Chronicle*, 1789). A number of explorers and colonials commented on "native" curiosity for clothing, with their reactions ranging from hilarity to fright over articles removed. Perhaps these settlers appeared to have removable as well as moveable body parts. Textile production was foremost in Britain's industrialisation, with ensuing shifts in labour relations and urbanisation. But clothes did not merely maketh the man, they made colonial men bent on the trade expansion that underpinned imperial ambition. Having typed the custodians of New Holland as Native through their nakedness, the typology of Indigeneity was appended by the surgeon, Peter Cunningham, who wrote in his traveller's journal of "dingy dandies" parading with "consequential swagger" in "natural costume" in public "without betraying the least shame". He was just as affronted by men pacing "lordly up our streets" with "a pair of breeches probably dangling round their necks" and "a waddie twirling in their black paws". These states of undress and incongruous apparel were particularly distasteful given that white women were exposed, some of whom conversed with "native" men "carelessly face to face, as if unconscious of their nudity", while still "modest" newer arrivals, "giggle, blush, cover their eyes with their fingers, and hurry confusedly by" (Cunningham 1827, 20). Self-mastery through dress was not only insignia for settler identity. It enshrined the civility and decency which were central to gender relations. The offence at exposure across race and gender compacted. Robert Mudie later wrote of the "seaming of their bodies" in his travelogue. He thought it tended to "deform" the "natives" of "rude nations" (Mudie 1829, 231). Mudie claimed the "natives" wore everything given to them as head ornaments. By 1830, in defence of the "well meaning ladies of Port Jackson", "natives" were not permitted to enter the town unless clothed (Breton 1970, 169). Margaret Maynard has detailed early official regulation of clothing in response to convicts going naked like "savages" and thereby transgressing the boundaries of racial and class identification, or perhaps exposing the skin-like peel of social distinctions (Maynard 1994, 63).

The meanings settlers contrived from textile were plainly gendered. Dorothy Jones has written of the interweave of letters and sewing by colonial women and their importance for "the performance of socially approved femininity and indicating women's complex role both as colonisers and colonial subjects" (Jones 2001, 376). The skills of Indigenous women in fibrecraft, net and basket-making and making skin cloaks were often noted by observers as part of ethnographic detail. Yet the labour demanded of Aboriginal women in the imposition and adoption of European clothing was only either acknowledged in disparaging terms or as proof of assimilation. Understood as a sort of moral skin that was both too permeable but nevertheless the best defence against contamination, dress was thought to effect profound changes in Aboriginal men. "In lieu of broadcloth, white cambric, patent leather, and Delcroix, or Rimmell, he provides an abundant supply of pipeclay, red ochre, and grease, and happy indeed is he if to these he can add a necklace of native dog, or kangaroo teeth, some feathers, and the blubber of a whale that has been stranded for some weeks."

In the 1863 shipwreck narrative of James Murrell, captured white men were subject to "minute examination of our persons" by tribesmen to ascertain their sex, "on account of our being clothed". The local people then appropriated clothing from the wreck, creating a "ludicrous scene" with solitary sleeves, legless pants and the leaves of books fastened to their hair (Gregory 1896, 20). Again, this primitiveness is inscribed by mismatching body parts to pieces of clothing. In a reversal of colonial spectacle the shipwrecked survivors were exhibited "night after night to ever increasing crowds", despite their refusal.

"Native" nakedness was "the unadorned ugliness of nature", said Melbourne town councillor and newspaper editor Thomas McCombie (1840, 96). But there was also undoubtedly an element of transgression and the erotic frisson, the "fancy" of nudity. It was quite another thing to publicise, either in literary or graphic form, accounts of European undress. Specifically, from the mid-18th century, it was pornography (Hunt 1993, 13; Weeks 1981, 84). The publication of accounts and images of "native" undress, though they may have scandalised evangelical opinion, became permissible with the added legitimacy from the 1860s of ethnographic observation.

Clothing was a prime means to articulate and assign racial categories. These were grounded in an overarching belief in material progress and the readiness to crush resistance to land deprivation associated with industrialisation, as already tested on the Swing Rioters and Luddites (Hobsbawm, Rudé 1968).

The nakedness of the New Hollander, as is well established, was a key descriptor for their ranking as primitive and as living in a "state of nature". To settlers this was in turns confronting, repulsive, picturesque and noble. As clothes became part of the banal and everyday exchange on the colonial frontier their very visible wear and tear on the bodies of Aborigines – who were provided no means to maintain them – seemed an almost intolerable display of unassimilable European values, and the attrition of both those social rudiments as well as of Aborigines themselves, when clad in this "thin veneer of civilisation" (Frazer 1890; Burroughs 1912).

As Comaroff has argued, colonial subjects were fashioned as much by "the circulation of stylised objects as from brute force or bureaucratic fiat".

An extended version can be found at http://www.tandfonline.com/loi/riij20

Costal / Large Food Sack

20

Early 20th century, plainweave technique; simple warp-faced structure, warped in one layer; acquired in Cuzco, 2010. Most herders used to weave large sacks to transport goods on the backs of llamas, and these are similar all over the highlands. The sacks are made to carry maize and potatoes or to haul dung down from the corrals to the fields, where it can be used as a fertiliser. They are woven in stripes of natural colours of llama hair and are sewn closed with a heavy piece of twine which is later removed, but never cut, to open the sacks. Sometimes they are used as a ground cloth on which to lay out items for rituals.

In *talegas*, the woven bags made in a traditional Aymará community in Isluga, difference is conveyed by the elaboration of broken symmetries. The design of the *talegas* is formed with elongated, coloured stripes. These bands of colour repeat and have a counterpart on the opposite side of the bag. Since the number of stripes is always uneven, each is unique. This ambivalent stripe, a suspicious axis in a world of complementary pairs, is referred to as the *chhima*, the heart. Translated from Aymará, the word signifies consciousness, memory, insight, understanding, and intelligence. Tantamount to a kind of magic centre, it defines everything that is part of its inner nature, regardless of whether this represents virtue or vice. *Chhima* is both uniting and separating, the meeting point and dividing line between the two sides of woven space. It creates these two halves and at the same time serves as their central connecting link. In other words, the arrangement of the colour stripes on the bags made by these Aymará people is a text that attempts to describe a third space, a space between, one between maximum darkness and daylight.

When the Inca Huayna Capac moved his court from Cuzco to what is today Quito, Ecuador, more than a thousand miles of steep, rugged mountains separated the two capitals. He ordered hundreds of villages to dispatch all their able-bodied men to build a highway. The finished roadway was completely straight and flat, lined with guesthouses for travellers, and so a second, this one along the coast, was built. The Inca highway network – the two main arteries and the mass of secondary courses that joined them – was arguably the biggest, most complex construction project ever undertaken. Running for 3,700 miles between Chile and Ecuador, about the distance from New York to Paris, the backbone of the system cut through every imaginable landscape, from icy mountain peaks to tropical lowlands, from the world's driest desert to one of its wettest forests. Civilisation has four ancient origin places: Mesopotamia, Egypt, the Indus Valley and China's Yellow River. In the past 20 years researchers have added a fifth: the central Andes, which includes southern Ecuador, northwestern Bolivia and most of Peru. Here were pyramids and temples as old as or older than those in Egypt, vast irrigation networks that rivalled those in ancient Sumer, and artworks that would endure for centuries, even millennia. Just as in India and China, rulers built walled fortresses, religions flourished and armies clashed.

Wax Print

A great variety of brilliantly coloured and designed cloths have been, and are, produced in all areas of Africa, but some of the most popular and celebrated are wax-printed cottons, which are an import. West Africa had been involved in the textile trade world since the 16th century, both the importing and exporting of cloth. The story of wax-print is one of a globalised world transacted by colonialism, which begins in Indonesia where there was a long tradition of handmade batiks using wax as the dye resist. Dutch colonisers were impressed and The Haarlem Cotton Company made the first attempt at imitation following the Napoleonic Wars which ended in 1815. The Javanese were unimpressed with their product so the Company sold their prints to a Glasgow merchant, Ebenezer Brown Fleming, who shipped them to West Africa. Then, in the 1850s, the Dutch firm Vlisco copied the technique and produced their own version using engraved roller print machines, and resin on either side of the cloth rather than wax. They then began to export to Indonesia where they again failed to impress the local market, but in the 1870s they too found a market in West Africa. There are different versions of how this happened. One is that Dutch freighters, on their way to Indonesia with such a cargo, stopped at various African ports and developed a client base there.

Since early in the 20th century, the Dutch company Vlisco has controlled the African market by smartly presenting the cloth as an African symbol of power, beauty and wealth and by using local businesswomen to market the product. As a result, some of these women have become exorbitantly wealthy, and when one is seen riding around in her Mercedes Benz, she is known as Mama Benz.

It may also be that they sold them on the way back because they were seen as inferior to the domestic product in Indonesia. So much so, that by 1900 competition in the Asian colony was so fierce that the market was in effect lost. Within this timeframe there was a yet more entangled story of colonialisms. After the Java War of 1825–30, the Dutch experienced a chronic shortage of military manpower in Indonesia, and began a programme of recruiting in West Africa. Their Department of Colonies remembered that there were Dutch possessions on the Guinea coast where commercial activity had fallen away following the official abolition of the slave trade.

In 1837 the Dutch king signed a deal with the king of the Ashanti whereby recruits would be supplied. If they had begun as slaves the guarantee was that recruitment would make them into free men. One thought had been that in the Asian colony the Africans would be less vulnerable to disease, which accounted for more military deaths than actual fighting. This was not the case, many West Africans died. Some however did return to what is now Ghana and may well have brought the cloths with them.

The Dutch may also have had a head start in Africa because their colonial history was nothing like as bad as the grim British story, but by 1909 the Manchester firm ABC were also in the wax-print cloth business alongside Vlisco. The cloth has remained a status item till today with labels to match. Apart from that of Holland there are Real English Wax; Veritable Java Print; Guaranteed Dutch Java; and Veritable Dutch Hollandaise. These prestigious labels ironically have 'mistakes' in the cloth, but these, it turns out, are part of the attraction; during the 'wax' printing the resin is liable to crack giving the textile its 'cracked' look admired in the West African aesthetic. The manufacturers have also become pragmatic. "Earlier design motifs used plants and animals believed to be universal to all cultures. From the middle of the 20th century, however, more effort has been made in creating authentic design by using Indigenous African textiles to create similar motifs." Pragmatic enough also to impose very tight security on their design departments, to put a grip on their intellectual property rights by use of patent, and for both companies to have opened manufacturing subsidiaries in Ghana. In a twist common to contemporary globalisation these companies are now being challenged by Chinese producers. The British ABC and its ATL Ghanaian subsidiary have in fact been bought by a Chinese company initially attracted to the business by African traders going to China to reproduce wax-print cloth cheaper. Rather like those of the 19th-century Dutch, the first Chinese cloths were low quality, but this is said to be "changing rapidly" and they too are claiming patents on designs originating in Africa, which is creating unemployment in Ghana itself.

1819

"The history of the weavers in the 19th century is haunted by the legend of better days." The best days for the independent weaver had gone by 1819, but in August they came together with factory-based spinners for the first time, some 60,000 to 100,000 of them with their children, to Peterloo Fields in Manchester, to demonstrate for the political rights which they believed were needed to improve their much worsened living conditions, and necessary to their dignity. The city was the centre of Lancashire cotton manufacture, "where both the lack of guild control and the proximity to Liverpool as slaver port became key to producers supplying the African trade in slaves and plantations in the Americas". Power looms did exist, but in small number, and were not the reason for the hardship of hand-loom weavers at a time when so much yarn was being produced to be woven. Rather, it resulted from a capitalist strategy – aided by the British state when it removed craft status – of driving down the price paid to weavers during recessions, and keeping it low when demand for cloth returned. It was deliberate and full of unambiguous class hatred for weavers who had at least the freedom to start work as and when they wanted. This hatred is clear in the voice of a magistrate in 1818. For him, the weavers had some years before been extravagantly paid and could maintain themselves in a state of luxury by working only 3 or 4 days a week. In a 'state of luxury' is an exaggeration to say the least, but the cloth merchants, mill-owners and the rest were determined that weavers would never have anything like it again. They had already shown this with a series of executions of men accused of being machine-breaking Luddites between 1812 and 1817, and in the shooting of workers by armed guards employed by mill-owners and by what was, in effect, a military occupation of Yorkshire and Lancashire.

Troops against strikers, USA, 1912.

To the 1819 demonstration came the Lees and Saddleworth Weavers Union with a pitch-black flag, lettered in white paint with LOVE, two hands joined and a heart. One observer talked "of never having seen a gayer spectacle. There were haggard looking men certainly, but the majority were young persons, in their best Sunday suits, and the light-coloured dresses of the cheerful tidy-looking women relieved the effect of the dark fustians worn by the men". The 'marching order', of which so much was said afterwards, was what we often see now in the processions of Sunday-school children and temperance societies. It was this, and the very discipline of the crowd, which so panicked the gentry, who liked, indeed *needed*, to consider them as a rabble. "The peaceable demeanour of so many thousand Unemployed Men is not natural", commented one General Byng. This very peacefulness and the nature of the flag were interpreted as threatening. Thereupon they were attacked by both the regular Hussars of the British army and the Manchester Yeomanry, the armed bourgeoisie, both on horseback and armed with sabres. Eleven were killed and over 400 injured, mostly with sabre wounds. More than a hundred of the injured were women or girls. There is no evidence that the British state organised the attack, but they were not slow to congratulate those who had done so, even in the face of truthful reporting – including that of a journalist from *The Times* who had been arrested on the spot, and renamed the field Peterloo, mimicking the battle of Waterloo. Government minister Canning knew that both magistrates and Yeomanry could not be criticised, though "It is to be sure, very provoking that the magistrates, right as they were in principle, and nearly right in practice, should have spoilt the completeness of their case by half an hour's precipitation." Government policy was then to put on trial some of the victims of whom the judge commented, with undisguised class hatred: "I believe you are a downright blackguard reformer. Some of you reformers ought to be hanged, and some of you are sure to be hanged – the rope is already round your neck." They followed

opposite page

A Chinese pattern book from 1957 converting a traditional gown, *changshan*, into a *Zhongshan zhuang*, a Mao suit.

this with a new set of repressive laws, and yet despite all this attack and the repressive laws that followed, weavers were very significant in the national Chartist movement for political rights that followed in the 1830s, when their material conditions were worse still.

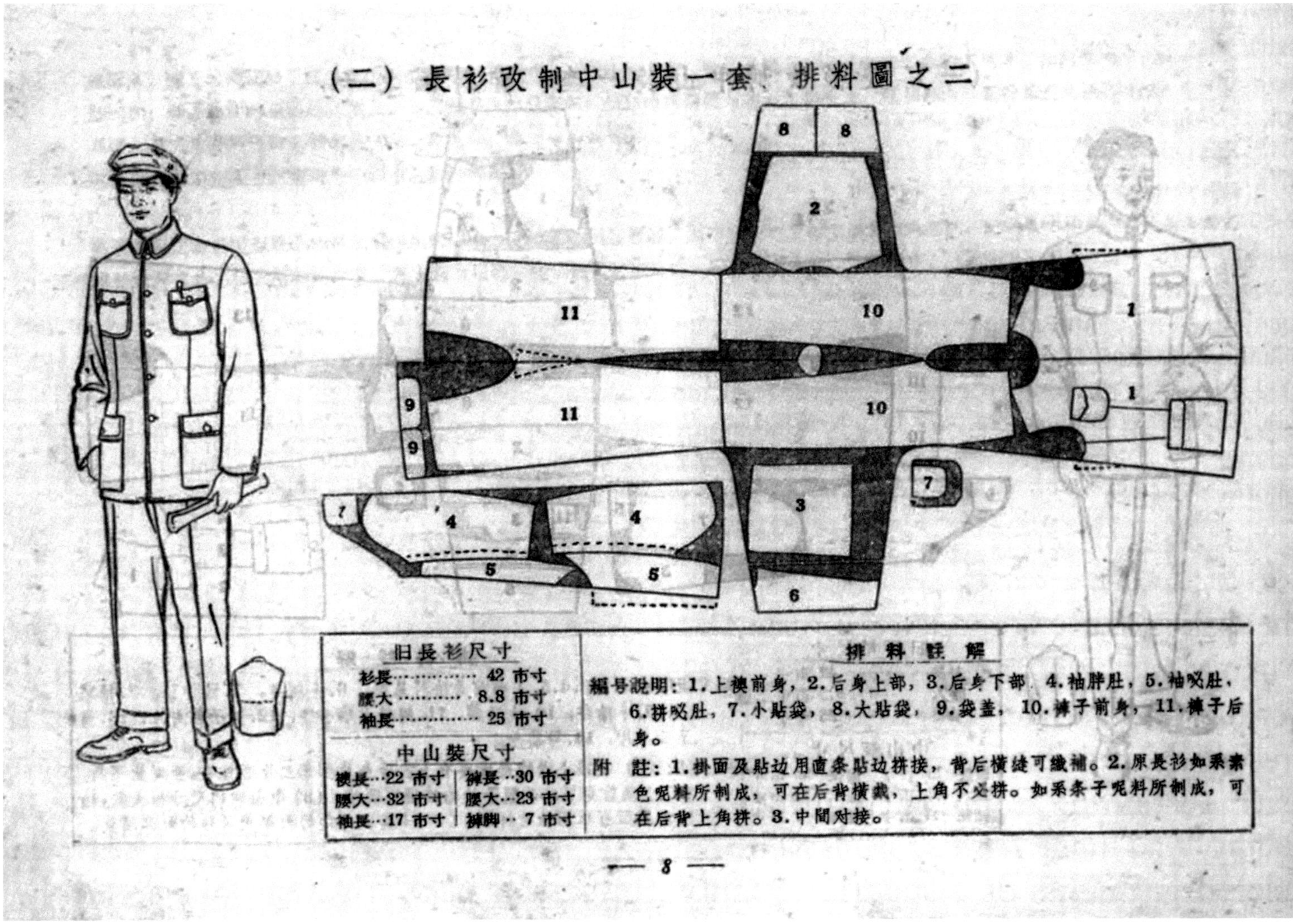

Alice Creischer
Andreas Siekmann

In May 2011, Ines brought this bag to Berlin so we could write about it. When we asked about its origins and the circumstances surrounding the purchase, she said she first saw this kind of bag in a textile museum in Cuzco and later bought this particular one from a textile dealer because it had more patches than the others. It is made of alpaca wool and she estimates that it's about one hundred years old. These bags were made in various sizes, depending whether they were to be carried by a donkey or a mule and depending what kind of crops were meant to be transported in them. People stopped making these bags about forty years ago. They used to be woven by the women in the family, but because the men have gone to the cities to work, the women have to cultivate the fields by themselves and have no time to weave bags. A number of factors have contributed to the more than sixty-year duration of the flight from the land in Peru: the unequal distribution of property ownership, the failure of agrarian reform, the civil war, poor harvests and the impossibility of selling crops, and unemployment, including in the cities. In 2006, 72.2% of Peru's population lived in the cities and 27.8% in the country.
The areas with the highest migration rates have been the same for fifty years: Huancavelica, Ayacucho, and Cuzco. The flight from the land continued with waves of migration to Spain, Italy, Japan, and especially the USA. In 2007, it was estimated that three hundred thousand Peruvians migrate each year. Most of them are young women who get jobs taking care of the elderly or working in the households of people who may very well happen to work in the offices of the same banks, chemical companies, seed corporations, and government departments whose

decisions are partly responsible for the land flight in Peru. The young women are often illegal and have no rights. In fact, that's what distinguishes them from office workers. It's like the difference between seed corporations and farmers. Ines thinks this bag was carried by a lama and was used to transport corn.[1]

Felipe Guamán Poma de Ayala. *El primer nueva cronica y buen gobierno*, 1615. Chapter: Rites, Ceremonies, Customs, Traditions and Administration at the Inca Kingdom.

If it were used for hay, fabric, or larger fruits it would not have been necessary to mend the many holes so carefully. Andreas thinks that if you lay the bag flat, it tells a tale of parceled fields or freshly turned potato beds, of the sky above, and of the clouds, which are bigger there than anywhere. It could be that the bag had a signalling effect. Maybe the stripes were like a code that said exactly what was in the bag. He's thinking of the economic circuit in which these bags were involved: from the country to the city, to the mines, quarries, or factories. There's nothing romantic about it; the mended holes show how precious each grain of corn was, how hard to come by.

Alice remembers a story from the Ingeniero White district in the town of Bahia Blanca on the Atlantic coast of Argentina. Ingeniero White is a big port for shipping grain to Europe. Along the roads, the locals sweep up the grains that fall from the trucks and feed their chickens with it. When money wasn't worth anything in the crisis of 2001, the chickens became currency.

We remember seeing similar sacks in one special drawing of Poma de Ayala's chronicle where he was describing the life of the Incas before the Spanish invasion.

HATVN CVSQVI (month of the big fallow), *AYMORAY QUILLA* (month of harvest).

They are carrying the harvest into the store.

Aymoray Quilla: In that month they sacrifice one more big mottled cow of all colours. In that *Aymoray* there are other smaller feasts; it is said, if they find a maize cob where two are joined together, or potatoes grown in the same way, and when they gather the fruits of the field and store them at their home in the *Cullunas* (granaries), *Chauays* (barns), *Pirua* (stores) ... they celebrate with a big feast and carousal.

They sing:

Harauayo, harauayo	*Harauayo, harauayo,*
Ylla sara camauay.	Keep me, preserve me, lucky maize.
Mana tucocta surcoscayqui	If you don't do so, I will pull you out,
Ylla mama, a Coya!	lucky mother, *o Coya!*

In that month the communities and *Sapci* (the communal land) will be visited because of their maize and their potatoes and the whole food and the common *Sapci* cattle. And they are punished if they don't give a good account. Everything is checked: Charqui (dried meat), wool, *Misquillicoy* (sweet plants), *Pezaca* (big pheasant), *Uicona, Uanaco, Quiuyo, Chalua* (fish), *Cuchucho* (roots); *Ujuta* (sandals), *Uasca* (rope), *Apa* (blanket), *Maytocuna* (bundle), *Cancaua* (plant with eatable root), *Lullocha*. And if they give good account, they sing the *Llamamiches* (song of the llama herders): *Llamaya, llamaya, yalla, llamaya* (my llama, my llama, my good llama), and they entertain themselves.

In that month you have a lot of food; all stores and the houses of the poor fill up, and the *Yuyos*, which they have dried and worked to get it stored, are inspected so that there is enough to eat for the whole year and the poor do not go hungry in the whole kingdom. This account was done in the month of May, *Aymoray Quilla*.

[1] Cf. Aída García Naranjo Morales: "The Peruvian Migration Phenomenon", Centro de Asesoría Laboral del Perú, September, 2007.

Poncho Huayruru

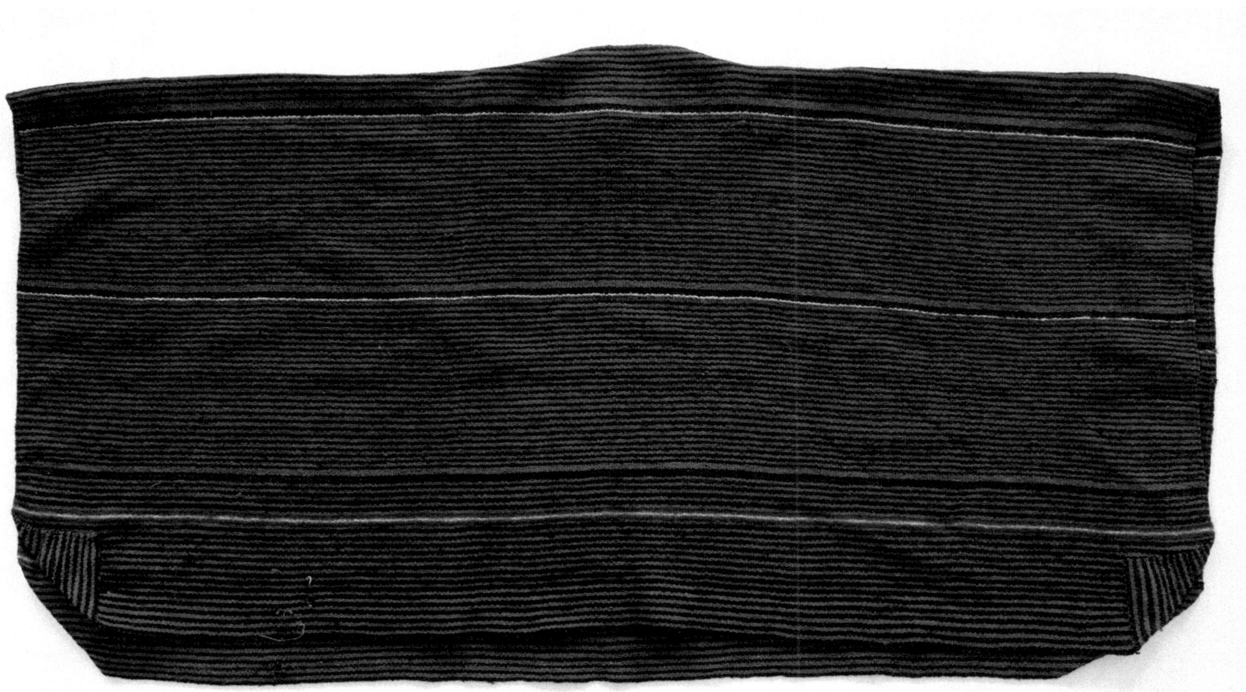

"The reliance of fashion on cutting and tailoring challenges the idea that continuous weaving transmits a spiritual force. In relatively uncommercialised areas of the world taboos on cutting cloth still make this point. Some Indonesians, for example, continue to distinguish between cloth for wearing and cloth for bridewealth, the former being cut and sewn, the latter's endless warp representing the 'continuous thread of kinship and descent'."

Wool, late 20th century; acquired in La Paz, 2010. The *Ponchos Rojos*, always known as fierce warriors, became a symbol of a new 'Indian era' in Bolivia, representing the increasing confidence of the Indigenous population since 2006, when the country's first president to come from the Aymarán majority population was elected. On the webpage of Achacachi, Bolivia, the *Ponchos Rojos* describe themselves as follows: "After the installation of Evo Morales Ayma as Bolivian President, the Bolivian army reserve was turned into a militia to secure and guard the process of inclusion of Indigenous nations as a part of the power of the new Bolivian plurinational State." *Ponchos Rojos* aim to guard against the reassembly of the old racist colonial Bolivian republic, an army reserve to face the separatist and secessionist manoeuvres of the Santa Cruz Department landowner. The red *poncho* is sacred to the utmost degree. It is only used in the ultimate emergency. "Only men over 50 who have served the community and are appreciated are allowed to wear a red *poncho*. If they stand out with special maturity and wisdom, their *ponchos* are refined with black stripes, the *poncho huayruru*."

The *Ponchos Rojos* polarise Bolivian society. Rumours that the people of Achacachi, one of their main bases, literally eat their enemies seemed to be confirmed when, during an assembly in 2007 called "The Great Barrack of Wala Chaka", they tortured and beheaded two dogs as a warning to all those who oppose the government. Their threats are aimed at the 'half moon' (*Media Luna*) Departments of Santa Cruz, Beni, Pando, and Tarija – those that objected to the nationalisation and redistribution of the natural gas that is a major natural resource in the region, and to the policy of land reform announced by the National government.

Historically, the poncho as an item of dress was in use by the Spanish in the 17th century, although the older Andean tunic continued to be worn underneath. The poncho's origin is usually attributed to the Mapuche, who are said to have invented it after the introduction of the horse. Each *poncho* takes six months to weave, and there are several types: the *huayruro* (red and black) *poncho* is used for commemorative and religious acts, such as the solstices, parades, official acts, elections, etc.; the pink one is used for festivities such as Carnival; the orange is for internal acts in the community; the green is used to announce the seed time; and the *noval* (soil colour) *poncho* is used in the winter season.

Dapper Dan in his Harlem store with Gucci raincoat and rainhat, custom made jackets in the back.

Negro Cloth

"I know that many Negroes have died from exposure to weather. They are clad in a flimsy fabric that will turn neither wind nor water." Hon T.T. Bouldin, slaveholder, US Congress, Feb. 16th 1835.

This 'flimsy fabric' was called Negro Cloth, produced by the very few textile mills in the South of the USA. It was a coarse, unbleached or brown-coloured cotton, or blend of wool and cotton, and used for slave and prisoner clothing. It had been mentioned in the Negro Act of 1735 as one of the cheapest fabrics that slaves were allowed to wear. The question of whether they could wear the cast-offs of their masters was hotly debated and a prohibitive measure was carried in South Carolina. It was considered to be of great importance that clothing was used to reinforce the distinction between slave and master. John Woolman observed in his 18th-century journal, "A plantation Negro man receives a bad coat and long pants out of 5 yards of white or blue Negro cloth. Men and women have many times scarce clothes enough to hide their nakedness, and boys and girls, ten and twelve years old are often quite naked among their masters' children." On many plantations slaves were issued once a year with just the cloth itself, and would have to sew clothes for themselves in the little non-working time they had, mostly working on picking the cotton that produced the cloth. If they wore out they had to do without until the next year. And this did happen. "In every slaveholding State many slaves suffer extremely, both while they labour and when they sleep, for want of clothing to keep them warm", wrote the Rev. John Rankin. In the early 19th century the demand for dull and cheap cloth for slaves helped kickstart the first Northern USA mills at Lowell, Massachusetts, to such an extent that Lowell became a generic term used by slaves to refer to coarse cloth.

And yet, a sense of style could not be repressed. Indigo dye was used secretly by the slaves who made the dye for their own clothes, so that as early as 1744 a grand jury in South Carolina complained, "Negro women in particular do not restrain themselves in their Cloathing as the Law requires but dress in Apparel quite gay and beyond their condition." This was a constant colonial complaint: in 17th-century Brazil colonial authorities were concerned with the "superfluity of elegance used in the dress of female slaves of the state." In Arundel County, USA, in 1777, the runaway slave 'Dick' had the cheek to be dressed in a green cloth coat, a red plush cape with blue cuffs and a deep blue jacket with gold lace on the sleeves. One response from whites was scorn, so that the actress Fanny Kemble, even though an abolitionist, could write how on Sundays slaves "dressed in the most ludicrous incongruities you can conceive – frills, flounces, ribbons, combs stuck in their woolly heads".

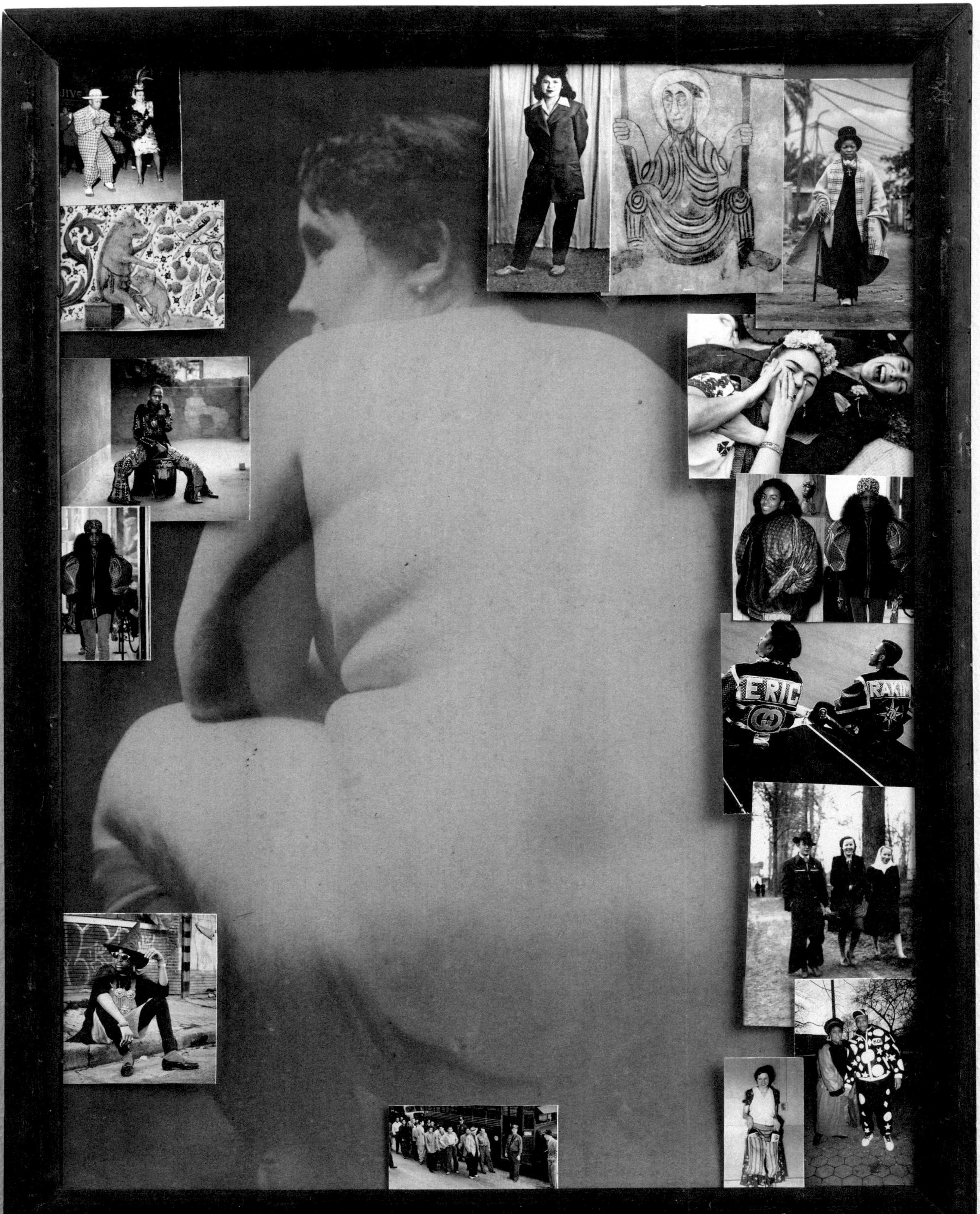
ERIC
RAKIM

In the 1940s, like a storm, fashion made by young black Americans and *pachuchos*, young second-generation Mexicans in the southern USA, became the Zoot Suit. "... walking slowly, their shoulders swaying, their legs swinging from their hips in trousers that ballooned upwards from cuffs fitting snug about their ankles; their coats long and hip-tight with shoulders far too broad to be those of natural western man." Or, in the language of Harlem nightlife, "a killer-diller coat with a drapeshape, real pleats and shoulders padded like a lunatic's cell".
The usual exclusive versions of how and where the style had come from competed with each other, but very quickly, in the middle of World War II and cloth rationing, it became racially defined as 'delinquent' and as the clothing of 'gangs'. The War Production Board produced regulations that effectively banned them, but bootleg tailors kept making them. Instead Zoot-Suiters, who were keeping out of the war, were attacked by the police and by white soldiers. In 1943 this created race riots in Los Angeles and Detroit. The Zoot Suit was just too cool to be tolerated, too openly an act of rebellion. As were the 're-appropriations' of high fashion by Dapper Dan (Daniel Day) in the Harlem, New York, of the 1980s. There, as the man says, "you'll see many older gents still immaculately decked out, heavily co-ordinated and fully passionate about their look". His store and designs were then famous, with a clientele of sports stars, hustlers and hip-hop artists. He used mink, ostrich and crocodile to create what he called "a macho type of ethnic ghetto clothing" to "Africanize Haute Couture".
That the designs were so shameless in copying clothes and accessories from Gucci, Louis Vuitton and so forth brought legal actions down on him and he went underground. In a twist full of ironies, the 2017 Cruise collection of Gucci included a number of Dapper Dan designs, including a jacket originally made in 1989 for the Olympic sprinter Diane Dixon. The New York Museum of Modern Art included some his work in their autumn 2017 exhibition *Items*.

1795

Four weavers in the area of Cuddalore on the east coast of Tamil Nadu, India, construct a straw effigy of a British East India Company agent, Davie Veerpah Chetty, and burn it. Normally such straw figures were burned only in rituals associated with 'bad deaths', either of those who had lived 'sinful lives' or had died violently. This was one incident in a struggle of over 30 years against the Company for whom "privatised violence was one of their core competencies", and which was a pioneer in imposing capitalist discipline on many hundreds of independent weavers. Previously the weavers had dealt with Indian merchants and the French and Dutch East India Companies as well as the British. Despite the French company, who Chetty's father had worked for before deciding the British were a better bet, keeping hold of Pondicherry and its hinterland, it was not a bad move on his part. In the grab for territory in the wake of the decline and break up of the Mughal Empire, The British EIC, had gained revenue collection rights in modern day Chingleput in 1763 and continually expanded the territory it controlled of Madras and Cuddalore, reducing the French to an enclave. It recruited its own armed force from the infantry of declining Indian states, sepoys, as well as company agents like Chetty, to fight colonial opponents and to enforce its power over the weavers of the area, initially to stop them selling to those colonial rivals as in 1771. "It brought to the region a conception of state power and authority unlike anything known in pre-colonial India. ... It gave them an unprecedented position of advantage over weavers". Despite initial plentiful advances to weavers it soon turned the screw in ways familiar to the Flanders weavers of the 14th century and sweatshops today. First it changed the composition of the advances so that it comprised more yarn than money; then the Company reversed the situation, having got near monopoly power, so that it was they who could now break contracts with weavers; it increased intensity of labour by demanding two longcloths per month which weavers said was 'impossible and oppressive'; imposed strict quality control as determined by themselves, again a reversal of the pre-colonial situation, whereby cloth could be rejected at will; and to enforce its monopoly aim, created a tax on non-Company weavers. This was backed up in the areas it controlled by exemplary violence as when it was found that a weaver was working illegally for a private merchant "Company's Gumashta seized him and his son, flogged him severely, painted his face black and white, tied his hands behind his back and marched him through the town escorted by Sepoys announcing that 'any weaver found working for private merchants should receive the same punishment'". Already by in 1779 weavers had reported that despite a high level of demand in the 1770s (which only fell early in the 19th century) their incomes had fallen by 35% since 1768. In response the weavers orchestrated work stoppages and desertion. In the North Sarkars in 1775 it ran for 4 months; three years later 1000 were mobilised in Cuddalore and held up Company investment for 7 months. In 1789 in Arni, weavers flogged its agents who in violation of custom demanded balances on cloth lost to plundering armies. A frequent tactic to avoid its demands or the taxes imposed on non-Company weavers, was to pick up their looms and move elsewhere while the East India Company used *sepoys* as debt collectors and trackers aiming to force them back or prevent escape. While the Company wanted to see the weavers in caste terms, a typical colonial strategy of categorising and division, and to see their complaints as strictly economic, they developed their own identity as weavers and in many instances fought against what they perceived as attacks on their pride, at being also labelled and defined as 'coolies'. "What emerges ... is not the rigidity of the weavers social world, as primordialism implies, but its plasticity. The ties of solidarity the weavers created were not fixed, but continually made and remade ... and demonstrated extraordinary inventiveness, resourcefulness and creativity. In fact, the act of protest itself and the demands of mobilising for protest, lead weavers to create new forms of solidarity."

John Barker

Poncho. Folded inside you, the world of time outside your weave, comfort me this night. Oh Tomás, Tomás Catari, you who did everything the way they say it must be done, who could write their language, who told them so that their King might hear. But they are deaf in Buenos Aires or their voices are not so loud that the white men and their mestizos who rob us, who insult us here in Chayanta province cannot hear them. You told them the truth, how they robbed us, so they killed you, just today when the sun was high in the sky, they killed you. Just for this night keep me warm head-to-foot so that, like a miracle of our saint, sleep may come and I can awake ready to fight again, me, Micaela and the others united again to fight. Your red and blue weave, thick and fast, take me to sleep. I watched Micaela weave it when she was big with our first-born, happy together until the priest ordered that we must be married, that it was a sin how we were. Sin? Not for us. What, do they take marriage so lightly that they do not think we should know each other over time, in the bed, with our work, lived together one day after another before we marry?! Mateo Choque, her father, he complained that the priest was wrong, that we have our way to live, that marriage is too serious, and for this he was punished, so that he must be dragged through the streets and must say that it was right that he, a stupid Indian, be punished for complaining to the priest. I heard him, saw Mateo's suffering and there was anger in my heart. There is anger in my heart and I, who knew nothing of killing, have killed again, just as they killed Tomás, so that life will never be the same from this day. Life will never be the same, and the best of us is dead, but tonight, weave tight around me and give me sleep.

There was anger in Tomás's heart also, how we were robbed in every way by Blas Bernal, made cacique by his friend the Spanish dog Alos who himself paid to be lord over us. Cacique who was not worthy of the name, used it only to rob us and respected nothing. How they forced on us the rubbish they could not sell. Those rich men who would kill for a Peso.

So Tomás wrote. He could write in their language and explained how it was wrong, that we knew our obligations but would not be robbed and abused. That our crops and our animals should not be taxed. He wrote and for this, for saying it was wrong, just like Mateo Choque, he must be punished. Those who cannot hear what is said in Buenos Aires put him in prison where there is no sun, no moon, no light of day and there was more anger in his heart, but he said we should not fight them because, he said, whoever won the fighting, we would lose. No, he would write again because in Buenos Aires where he had been, they had said he was right, that they knew what he said was right.

Too late now, nothing will ever be the same again. But we are not stupid Indians as they call us, we know nothing is ever certain. We plant the crops when we know the time is right. We know from our ancestors exactly when it is right. There is no certainty in the crops coming good, but how and when we sowed, it must be done right and in good time.

And this we did when they had put Tomás in the prison again, it was right that we should say No, he is a good man who tells the truth. It was right and in good time that we should go to Pocoata town and bring him back to be with us, to live our lives in Chayanta. It should not have been that Alos, who would be our lord and master because he had to pay to be what he is, should set soldiers against us, but this is what he did, and to save myself I, who have never killed, killed a soldier. And then we saw that Alos was just a man and we took him and we said we will hold you while you hold Tomás even if that is not a good trade when he is such a better man than you. Yes, we took Tomás home with us and he thought that now we could live as life should be lived for in Buenos Aires they knew the truth.

Fold your warmth around me, make a miracle to my mind that will not stop running as I ran today and let me sleep so that I can fight tomorrow for they cannot be trusted, never Tomás, who died today to know this, these white men, and their mestizos with their mines and the money they have stolen from us as if the whole world is theirs. I will find your brothers Damaso and Nicolas, for they are ready, and Micaela is ready, and we will go to La Plata and we will kill them all, we who have never killed, never thought to kill.

After Pocoata Tomás believed that we could live life as it should be lived, the law was on our side. But the law has no voice here, not for us. He said not to kill, for those who have abused us are experienced in killing and once they have started will not stop, but now I know they understand only fear. That is what happened, Alos was frightened when we took him, that is why he wrote and told them not to send more soldiers. But I did not want to know this then, that they must all be frightened forever. I also wanted to believe that we could live life as it should be lived, that we would not be pressed again.

But they came for him again, imprisoned him again. As if we had not spoken. Even if in Buenos Aires they did not speak loud enough, we had spoken. Alos was afraid but there are always more of them, white men, priests, and those who would live as white men, who would tax our crops, tax our animals, who tell us what we must do and would kill for a Peso. Like today. We came to take Tomás home with us and they killed him, the magistrate and his men, Alvaro the mine-owner and his men, they killed him. We were mad with rage killed some and the others they were afraid and they ran for it is only fear they understand.

There is no peace in my heart, nor my head, nor my blood that will itch until we have killed them all, or they have run away. But for this night fold me in your weave, warm me, make me a potato in the soil and bring me sleep before I join the others that I had to leave when I saw Alvaro slip away to his mine to dig more thousands of pesos from our earth. There was anger in my heart and I followed. He thought he was safe there, that no stupid Indian would follow. From outside I called to him, words using Tomás had taught me, that the Indians had run away and I had brought his reward from La Plata. He came out for he is one who would kill for a Peso and I brought the rock down on his head. I heard it crack and smashed it again, I who had known nothing of killing.

The night thoughts of this anonymous Indigenous Andean man took place early in January 1781 on the night of Tomás Catari's death in what is now Bolivia, but then governed from Buenos Aires. Caciques or Kurakas were intermediaries between Indigenous communities and the Spanish crown (and its intermediaries). Tomás should have been one, but at this time they were being imposed by colonial power factions. Instead he tried to use existing colonial law to protect his own community.

In all probability this anonymous man did join up with Catari's brothers to attack the town of La Plata, modern day Sucre. The brothers were betrayed and executed in the most gruesome fashion. The fate of this man is unknown but he may well have joined up with other Indigenous resistance fighters in the siege of La Paz led by Bartolina Sisa and her partner Julian Apaza who styled himself Tupac Catari in honour of the Catari brothers and the Tupac Amaru uprising in Peru. The city was saved by the Spanish at the very last minute.

22

Wool, beads, tassels, acrylic threads, sequins, horse-hair, ribbons, embroidery, wire mesh, painting; acquired in La Paz, 2010. Carnival is when the *ch'utas* dance. The word *ch'uta* refers to an Indian of provincial origin born and raised in the city of La Paz and the dance represents members of this social group. The mask of the *ch'uta* mimics the white man and is made of wire mesh and has a beard and moustache of twisted horse-hair. Originally this mask was made of thick, gummed gauze, painted with the features of blond, white men. The *ch'uta* has a predecessor, the *pongo*, and a successor, the *cholo*. While the *cholo* dresses in European clothes, the *pongo* was an Indian dressed in native clothes who went to serve in his master's house in the city. He slept beside the door and was subjected to the worst treatment. The *ch'uta* is also known as *aljiris*. *Aljata* means 'to sell' in Aymará, especially in reference to produce. An *aljiri* is a vendor and during the Spanish-imposed *haciendero* system Indians were basically 'for sale'. *Chutas* only communicate in high-pitched voices that probably also relate to their servile role, which dates back to when they lived almost like slaves on Spanish haciendas. The Agrarian Reform of 1952 abolished the *pongo* system and Indians were free to take up different occupations and they became artisans or small-scale traders. Without denying that the *ch'uta* is an Indian who is mocking the 'white man', he also displays a certain social well-being in a racist society.

King Cotton

In 1858 when the US Civil War is becoming a possibility, Senator James Henry Hammond of South Carolina says an attack on the South would bring down Western civilisation. "No you dare not make war on cotton. No power on earth dares make war on cotton. Cotton is King." There was a real basis to such confidence: industrial Europe depended on its export of raw cotton, and was becoming painfully aware of it. Its uncertainty about the continued viability of the slavery system encouraged it to contemplate its own empires as an alternative source for the product. The Confederate point of view, however, was that for the "blessing to mankind" of cotton to continue, "slave labour must also continue, for it is idle to talk of producing cotton for the world's supply with free labour. It has never been grown by voluntary labour". A view supported by the British economist John T. Danson in 1857: "There is not, and never has been" a free labour force in cotton production, "excepting the East Indies, which is not obviously and exclusively maintained by slave labour." It was a kingdom that demanded slavery and pain, as recorded by Solomon Northrop: "It was work hard, git beatins and half fed ... The times I hated most was pickin' cotton when the frost was on the bolls, my hands git sore and crack open and bleed."

"Amor Divinus (My humbleness and slavery, and forgive all my sins)."

Generally speaking, "Cotton, a plant that grew just tall enough to inflict paralyzing backaches from bending and stooping ... and you had to do battle with the thick vegeative fingers that held the lint and seeds firmly in place, and there were dozens of bolls per plant. Slaves picked up to one thousand pounds of lint six days a week in sweltering heat. ... No matter how fatigued and weary a slave may be, a slave never approaches the gin house with his basket of cotton but with fear. If he falls short in weight, he knows that he must suffer. And if he has exceeded it, in all probability his master will measure the next days task accordingly."

The slave was also painfully aware of just how much the intensity of his or her labour was linked to shifts in global capitalist demand for the raw stuff. As John Brown remembered in 1854, "When the price [of cotton] rises in the English market the poor slaves immediately feel the effects for they are driven harder, and the whip is more constantly going." In 1865, at the end of the Civil War and the nominal defeat of the Confederacy, the question for capital was articulated by Lee Higginson, a wealthy Bostonian who was contemplating investing in a cotton plantation: "Making money there is simply a question of being able to make the darkies work." The New York financial paper of November 11, 1865 was clear about the solution: the "pinchings of want" would "correct" the "prevailing indolence of the coloured people" and force them back into the cotton fields. The "pinchings" were duly created with the lever of debt, 'rented' convict labour, and the support of Southern state legislatures. These created vagrancy laws aimed at "driving negro loafers to the field", and gave an amber light to lynching.

The capital accumulated from slave and sharecropped cotton finance has enabled the modern US farmer to buy a John Deere 7760 Cotton Picker, which boasts the ability to pick virtually non-stop, and yet modern day US cotton production is massively subsidised.

In some places now, like Uzbekistan, the fourth largest cotton exporter in the world cotton, harvesting remains arduous physical work. Young children are required to stoop over to pick cotton buds from low stems, carrying kilos of cotton in sacks slung around their backs. The harvest begins in the heat of late summer and ends with the onset of winter, but children are not given any special protective clothing or footwear whilst working. Cotton quotas are given to each child according to their age and the area they are working in. In 2008, some reports suggested that quotas were higher than in previous years, with threats or beatings ensuing if children failed to meet their targets. Students in Ferghana claimed that their daily quota of 80 kilos was twice the amount that they could reasonably pick. Children may be paid a few US cents for each kilo. Since 2012 when child labour became a publicised issue, shaming a set of Western retailers whose products included Uzbek cotton, there has been an increase in the forced labour imposed on 15- to 18-year-olds and adults. New quotas from workers in the public sector including nurses, teachers and office workers have been imposed with the threat of dismissal if they are not met. Shops have been ordered not to open until 7pm to discourage shopping during the "cotton harvest". The beatings continue, now they are for those who protest or publicise the realities of such forced labour while the Tashkent cotton fair attracts large-scale buyers like from the Bangladeshi factories making clothes for the Western market. As against such a labour-intensive regime between 2001 and 2011 US cotton farmers have taken $24 billion in Federal government subsidies, mostly to those operating the most land. A portion of this enables them to have air-conditioned tractor cabs with computerised spraying, sowing and picking facilities as well as GPS guidance. These spindle pickers can consume enough cotton in a day to produce 150 bales. Hand picked cotton, however, is used for luxury fabrics. In recent years the US Cotton lobby has run a PR campaign emphasising the 'naturalness' of cotton against the threat of synthetic fabrics, in spite of the many chemical processes cotton fabric goes through. For the campaign they had Leona Lewis sing this schmalz: *See where you want to be / Imagine All Your Dreams and Plant the Seed / Let the Rivers of your Heart and Mind Collide / And Close Your Eyes / The Touch the Feel / The Fabric of Our Lives / The Touch The Feel of Cotton / The Fabric of My Life.*

1796 Britain declares war on Spain and blockades the River Plate and thus the docks of Buenos Aires through which Catalan cloth had entered for the South American market of the Viceroyalty of Rio de la Plata, originally that of Peru. Spanish production of cloth, and therefore what could be exported, had increased three times in the ten years after the Bourbon 'free trade' reforms and large state subsidies to the textile sector. That it should be dominated by Catalans was an irony that proved the saying that they could make bread from stones: they bitterly resented their domination by Bourbon Spain dating to early in the century, but as a result gained access to Latin American markets through their rule, while in true colonial style the state encouraged the exportation of 'New World' raw cotton to Barcelona. It began with access to the port of Cadiz followed by the creation of the Royal Company of Barcelona and the removal of all trade restrictions. In 1774 the textile industry introduced the first mechanical 'spinning jennies' and imposed modern features of management hierarchy and a division of labour that made for a high intensity of labour. This sector boosted by Bourbon protectionism, experienced an increase of some 400% in its exports in less than ten years, from 1784. Indeed, by the end of the century the cotton mills of Catalonia were second in importance only to the English mills, and Latin America a key export market. Thus in the Viceroyality the British blockade caused a shortage of cloth and an upsurge in regional demand for the homespun cloth, *tocuyo*, produced as a cottage industry around Cochabamba in modern day Bolivia and in normal times for local consumption only, uncompetitive with the Catalan on a bigger scale. This new situation however encouraged the development of an urban artisan weaver class, though these weavers drew little benefit from the *tocuyo* price increase. For one thing the supply of cotton from the Peruvian coast was not just erratic, its price also went up as demand for the raw material increased, while despite local colonial demands it was against the interests of the Spanish state that cotton cultivation be started in the Santa Cruz area of Bolivia. In effect the Catalan industry was protected even during the blockade. This was in keeping with Spain's policy, which was consistent across the continent. Already King Philip II expressed concern about the development of a textile industry in New Spain, "in such a state of growth as to supply it and a greater part of Peru with cloth". And at the end of the 18th century the Viceroy of New Spain commented that a colony whose manufactures displaced the manufactures of the mother country would eventually find political subordination unnecessary. The merchants in Bolivia and Peru involved in cloth, however had no interest in developing a manufacturing business; their profit came from their control of transport, their investment aimed at monopolising the limited number of pack animals essential to the transporting of cloth. Besides, they could take a good guess that the blockade would not last forever, and so it was. The peace of Amiens in 1802 saw the end of the blockade, and the merchants resumed the business of selling imported cloth. *Tocuyo* weaving continued as a cottage industry, but many artisan weavers who had gained little of the profit in the good times were left high and dry by the back-and forth shifts of colonial power. In the post-colonial period, despite the protectionist policy of independent Bolivia's Santa Cruz government, *tocuyo* cloth production declined to one quarter of colonial levels, and finally import prohibitions were lifted under the banner of Free Trade. By 1846 the number of workshops had fallen from a turn of the century high of several hundreds to just one hundred.

“FASHION TORY FASHION WORK” Plastic bags collected from Chinese fashion retailers in Athens between 2011 and 2016.

Chuspa / Coca Bag

23

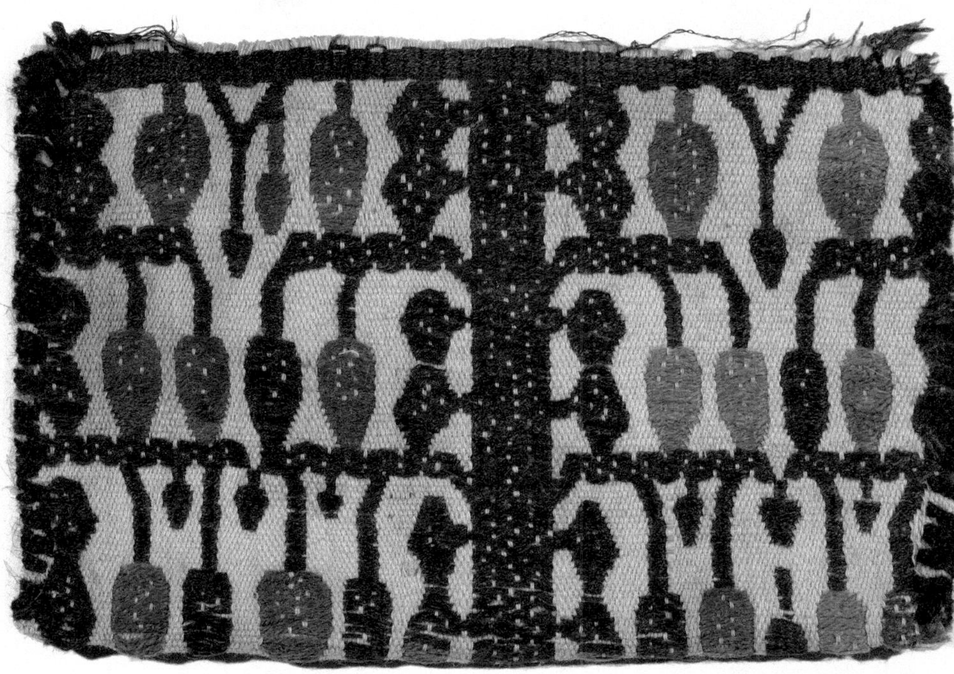

Located in the north of Bolivia, the *Kallawaya*, literally meaning "drug carriers", are itinerant healers who have travelled the Andean lands for over 1600 years. The *Kallawaya* performed brain surgery as early as 700 years CE and knew how to effectively prevent and treat malaria with quinine before the Europeans made the same discovery. They also helped to save thousands of lives during the construction of the Panama Canal, travelling there to heal workers.

Cotton; Pachacámac, central coast, probably Early Intermediate Period, approx. 400–700 CE; acquired in Lima, 1978, loan to the archive. Embroidered onto the natural *Gossypium barbadense* cotton of the Pacific coast in its five natural colours, the bag is a highly unusual example of a textile illustrating the various types of plants, seeds, trees, and roots, which played a vital role in ancient Peruvian agriculture. It is of particular graphic interest because of its visual inversion. The root motifs, when turned upside down, are transformed into prancing figures with waving arms. The flora of Peru, with a few exceptions, did not inspire textile artists. In an account of a procession in Potosí in 1555, Bartolomé de Arzáns de Orsúa y Vela tells us, "The whole part of the floor where the procession was going to pass was covered with rich woollen and cotton mantles that the Indians gave affectionately, and from more than 30 and 40 leagues they brought, in their devotion, in a few days, an infinite variety of fragrant flowers and herbs to cover these carpets so that the natural beauty of the fields substitute for the defects of their hand-made works."

Turkey Red

The aesthetic and commercial importance to Europe of bright and lustrous colours that dyed well, before the development of synthetics in the late 19th century, is made clear by laws of secrecy, and by the attempts made by individual countries to acquire the secrets of other nations. Thus Spain's tight control of information about cochineal and, equally, the instructions of the chauvinist English explorer Richard Hakluyt, issued to the master dyer Hubblethorne on the occasion of his voyage to Persia: "You must have great care to have knowledge of the materials of all countries that you shall passe through that may be used in dyeing, be they herbes, weedes, barkes, gummes, earthes of whatsoever ... in Persia they have great colouring skills with dyed cloth as neither raine, wine nor yet vinegar can staine." In the 18th century this serious concern involved an interplay between scientists, philosophers, dye and paint makers, and artistic practitioners. It also caused the colonial plunder of what might be called Intellectual Property Rights, focused on India's skill in the painting and printing of cloth, featuring bright coloured dyes that held fast in cotton. 'Spies', in the form of French navy men and Jesuit priests in the

Drawing of a healing plant by Maestro Juan Salazar Flores, 2004.

enclave of Pondicherry on the Coromandel coast of India, revealed the techniques of the Indian master dyers in a series of letters and samples, fully conscious of what they were about and acting in spite of a prohibition on cotton printing in France at the time. The naval officer Beaulieu had been asked for information by M. Dufay de Cisternay, a colour chemist and also governmental Inspector of Dye Works and Mines and a director of the Botanical Gardens of Paris, which, like London's Kew, was a storehouse of the plants and botanical knowledge of other nations. Beaulieu observed each of the eleven stages of production and "after each stage of the proceedings cut off a piece of cloth which he brought back to France with him together with samples of all the materials used in the process". Back in France he went through all the stages he had seen from the preparation of the cloth onwards. His work was followed by a French Jesuit priest Father Courdeux, "versed in Tamil and Telegu". Though he makes no reference to Beaulieu, Courdeux was equally conscious of what he was doing, as his letters to his Jesuit superiors in France attest. The first, written in 1742, makes this clear: "I have not forgotten that in several of your letters you have urged me to acquaint you with the discoveries I might make in this part of India, since you are persuaded that knowledge is to be acquired here which, if transmitted to Europe, would possibly contribute to the progress of science, or to the perfection of art." He goes on to modestly boast of how he obtained his knowledge from "various neophytes skilful in this sort of work on whom I recently conferred baptism", their low caste status making them susceptible to conversion. The modesty vanishes in the second letter of 1747, in which he mentions that there may have been others before him but that "as they would not be conversant with the native tongue, indispensable for dealing with the painters nor accustomed to their ways, and since their very condition must give rise to a certain mistrust on these timid natives, I doubt whether they could have successfully carried out the orders imparted in these matters." He repeats that "the aim he had in mind" was to perfect the art of dyeing in Europe, but adds, to make sure that there can be no question as to European superiority, "it's not because Europe doesn't have the skill but India has advantage of certain ingredients and above all, certain waters".

One of the colours of which new knowledge was gained was called Turkey Red (rouge de Turc) or, revealingly, rouge des Indies, and was "closer to carmine than to the dark scarlet or brick reds of the European madder-dyeing process". There were Ottoman dyers who were brought to Europe for their knowledge of dyeing processes, but it is to the tireless Dr Edward Bancroft – whose work on this issue demonstrates that the dye must have been something of a holy grail – that we owe the knowledge that a red from India was the same hue. The disclosure is made during a discussion of the works of those who followed up on the 'discoveries' of Courdeux and Beaulieu – people like Jacques Savary and the Abbé Mazeas. Of another French account, Bancroft stressed the significance of cow dung in the process; and of yet another, that the cotton after being dyed was "soaked in either oil of sesamum or in melted hog's lard". All writers seem to have agreed that the use of the chay root rather than madder was crucial in acquiring the deepness of the red. Bancroft was also much exercised by the employment of alum in the process of dyeing cotton, and wondered whether the French correspondents had missed it, or whether there had been 'studied concealment' by Indian dyers, before finally concluding that it must have been in the water, thus giving some credence to Courdeux's claim. Given this evidence of French knowledge, it is not surprising that for the first extensive dye-house for Turkey Red in Britain, which opened near Glasgow in 1785, a Monsieur Papillon – an eminent Turkey Red dyer – was brought over from Rouen. That the colour really was a dyer's holy grail is further evidenced by the 18 submissions to the Society of Arts concerning Turkey Red, and the significant number of awards offered for a useable manufacturing process.

1967

On February 22nd, mass picketing surrounded the Stockport, Lancashire factory of textile machinery-maker Roberts Arundel, to such effect that police chiefs threatened to impose the Riot Act. Newspapers had first reported it as "A Strike Against Women", though it was soon apparent that it was about trade union rights. The Arundel company, which had been making looms and accessories since the early 20th century, had been recently taken over by the USA-based Roberts company, which had an anti-union history. In November 1966 the company began hiring women as cheap labour, refusing to discuss their pay and conditions with the union, while 51 workers were made redundant and an unofficial strike began. The company responded by sending out sacking letters to the strikers and advertising for 235 men and women in different categories, with the preamble addressed to "those individuals who appreciate working in a free atmosphere rather than the bureaucratic environment of a Union shop"; this in turn prompted an official strike. The company as pioneer of neoliberal ideology and management practice was defeated by tactics its followers have since made illegal: the active support of other workers in refusing to handle the company's work; and picketing against strike-breakers. The company itself was forced to close after over a year of the strike.

The assumption by managements that women should be seen as cheap and less skilled labour has a long and still-present history, but in the following year, 1968, women sewing machinists at the Ford Motor Company's plant at Dagenham, London, go on strike with the demand: End Sex Discrimination In Pay Grading. They wanted recognition of the skill level involved in assembling and sewing car seats and trim that often involved several pieces of material. This meant an upgrading of their skill level to those of men doing jobs with a similar level, though they did not demand equal pay if this required that they do shift work, which would have been incompatible with their domestic life and their unpaid role in "the reproduction of labour-power". They did not win the upgrading demand, but did get their wages lifted to 90% of men at the existing skill level. It was not till 16 years later, at another Ford plant, Halewood, Liverpool, that women did get recognition and upgrading of their skills. But the Dagenham strike broke barriers as well as winning the pay rise. Working class women grew in confidence as they took on the Company and their own union. Some of the male workers, who included their own husbands and sons, turned against them when the lack of the car seats they would normally have sewn brought production to a halt, while others supported them. In the process, the idea that only men were 'breadwinners' and that women worked only for 'pin money' was broken.

Women workers at Ford Dagenham make it clear exactly what they are fighting for.

Although the women at Ford had a particular power because of their position in a complex, high investment production process, 'the breadwinner' ideology had the longest history as a rationalisation for unequal pay between men and women, rooted in patriarchal household textile production and a gendered division of labour. Such household work continued and still continues in the industrialised era, as does the ideology that went and goes with it. This has been the case despite the existence of women-headed households and technological changes that have at times 're-feminised' the workforce, as with the introduction of ring and throstle spinning but which did not change the hierarchy of labour. In the Lancashire 19th-century template of the cotton cloth industry, men continued to operate the weaving machines and as self-actor spinners, were paid more, and it was this model that was exported along with both the cloth and the machinery itself. Even when women also became weavers in Lancashire and "in theory received equal rates, males were assigned cloth types that brought higher rates of pay". In Russia in the 1880s mechanisation changed nothing, nor did the fact that some of the work done by women was the most physically demanding, like wool cleaning and skillful, like warping. "It was a given in Russian culture ... that women should always receive less pay, and employers took advantage of new technologies to switch from male to lower paid female labour." The institutionalising of piece rates made it easier to manipulate rates of pay there and in China where, in the 1930s, it was applied only to women workers while men were paid on an hourly basis. Most of all women workers "were paid less because they were supposed to be low-skilled, but at the same time work could be considered low-skilled and thus low-paid simply because it was performed by women". This is not a Catch-22 of the past, in the same era as the Ford strike the Danish textiles trade paper *Stofog Saks* could declare that women were paid less because less qualified which can be "attributed to a general lack of interest in technical matters among women".

In the clothing industry the same hierarchies apply. The cutting of cloth is a male preserve (though increasingly automated) as are the disciplining role of the foreman. Their power, bullying and favouratism, in this crucial sector of the Korean 'economic miracle' announced in this same year of 1967 by the dictator Park Chung-hee's Five Year Plan was instrumental in having young women working full speed 12–16 hour days.

Sonia Abian

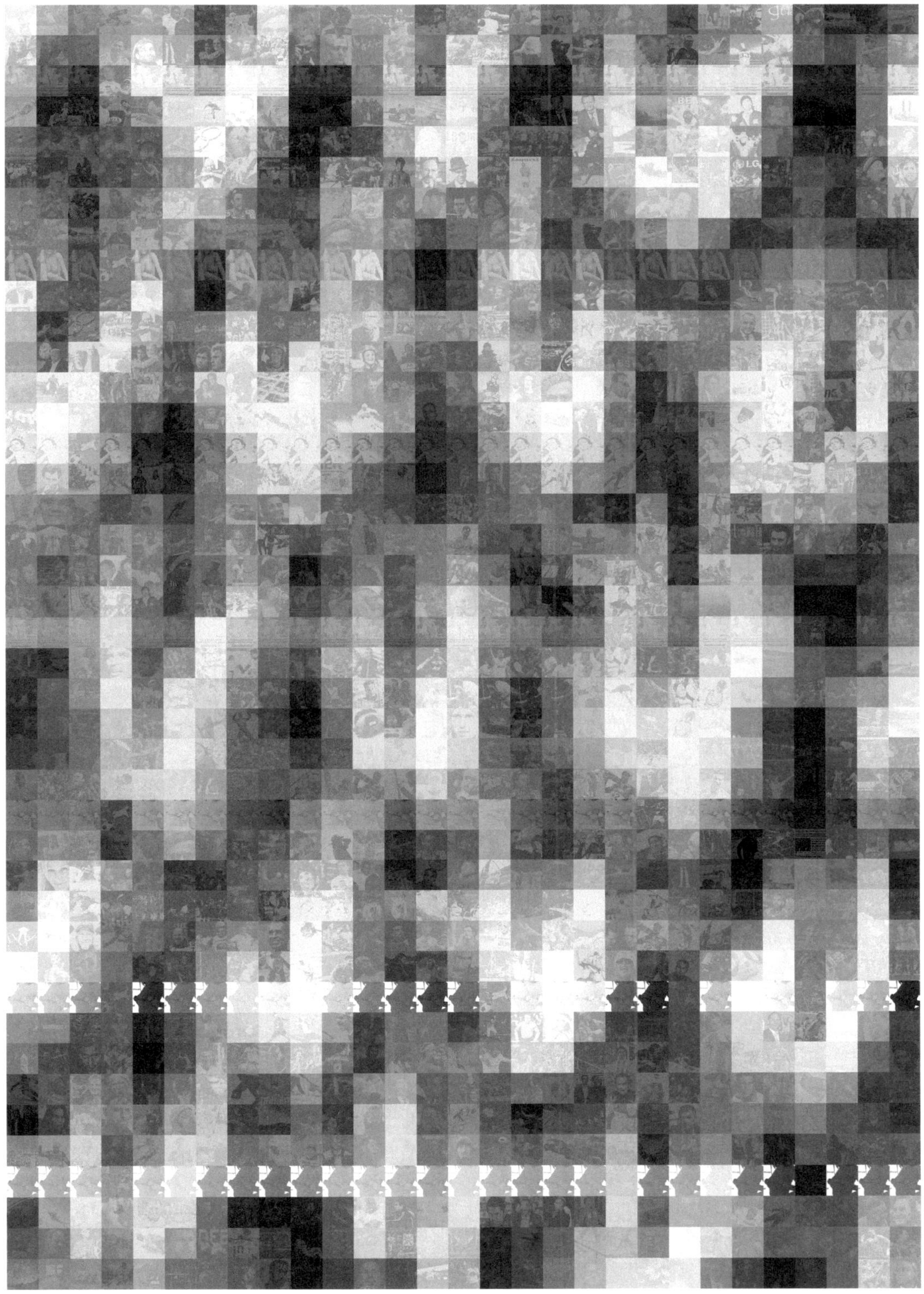

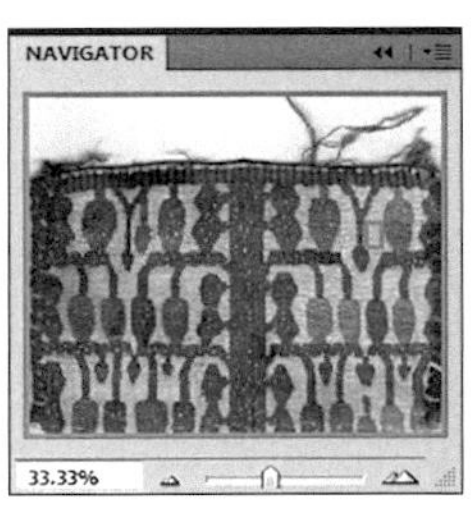

Zwei Muster / Digitalarbeit, 2012
Muster #1: Baum mit symmetrischen Ästen, an denen Figuren, Früchte oder Blätter je nach Sichtweise hängen oder stehen. Gewebter Baumwollstoff in Ocker, Rotbraun und Gelb, der als kleine Tasche zusammen genäht ist, Peru. Stark vergrößerte Sicht auf einen Bereich des Gewebes.
Muster #2: Sich in Streifen aufbauendes Motiv, mit ab- und zunehmenden Spielräumen, die den LeserInnen als Vorbild zur Verfügung stehen. Ausschnitt. Gewebter Medienstoff. 1269 Fotos erschienen in den Sportabteilungen der Zeitungen *Kurier*, *Krone* und *Der Standard*. Wird sichtbar bei Vergrößerung ab 8,33% Zoom. Online-Ausgaben: 10.01/ 12.01/ 23.01/ 28.01/ 09.02/ 10.02/ 13.02/ 15.02/ 16.02/ 18.02.
Die kleinen Ikonen am Rand setzen den Rythmus des Titels fort (*Webschiffe, Kriegspfade*) und beziehen sich auf das Spinnen vor dem Weben und Fotografieren, vor der Bearbeitung der Ausgaben. Das Spinnrad stammt aus dem Bild von Velázquez *Las Hilanderas*. Der Fotoapparat ist aus dem Netz, leider ist es aber ein alter Apparat.

Wichuna / Llama-Bone Pick Tool

24

Acquired in Cuzco, 1978, private collection, loan to the archive. Finger puppet, *loan to the archive by Max Jorge Hinderer Cruz.* For weaving a level of technical skill is necessary, such as the basics of how to warp the loom and how to keep an even tension on it by adjusting the pressure of the back against the backstrap in order to keep the edges even. Indigenous American weaving differs from that of European treadle looms, whose mechanism normally creates the designs, in that the warp yarns must be carefully counted as to number and colour, a skill learned from older women. As weavers work to remember the designs, they carefully select individual warp yarns by lifting them up with a *wichuna* pick tool made from a llama bone. Held above the basic structure of the weaving, these extra yarns float across the surface and become the design in an intricate process requiring precision skills. The weaver calculates by counting exactly where yarns need to be picked up to make additions and reductions, or be able to 'see' the design form without counting. It is more time-consuming, but a relatively complex pattern can be produced on simple equipment and the weaver also has the option of varying the designs as she/he goes along. The weaving has 'one or two faces', depending on whether the designs are created simultaneously during the weaving process on both sides of the textile or have only one good side. Through the reports of those who took it upon themselves to burn idols, we know a little about local belief systems starting around the early 17th century. At that time, the Catholic Church commenced its large-scale campaign against traditional Indigenous beliefs. The Spaniards prohibited ancestor worship, and *huacas* (sacred shrines) were largely destroyed. The shrine of an ancestor contained objects such as a spindle, a loom, a pick tool, and a handful of cotton. These implements had to be protected in the event of a lunar eclipse, because at such times when the moon – viewed as a woman – was threatened by a comet the spindle could be transformed into poisonous snakes and the loom into bears and tigers. Not only the textiles were viewed as receptacles of *sami* (life force), but also the weaving utensils themselves, and as such, both had the capacity to transfer their powers.

Feathers

On the ridge of the upper mandible a broad stripe of most lovely yellow extends from the head to the point; a stripe of the same breadth, though somewhat deeper yellow, falls from it at right angles next the head down to the edge of the mandible; then follows a black stripe, half as broad, falling at right angles from the ridge and running narrower along the edge to within half an inch of the point. The rest of the mandible is bright red. The lower mandible has no yellow: its black and red are distributed in the same manner as on the upper one, with this difference, that there is black about an inch from the point. The stripe corresponding to the deep yellow stripe on the upper mandible is sky-blue. It is worthy of remark that all these brilliant colours of the bill are to be found in the plumage of the body and the bare skin round the eye. All these colours, except the blue, are inherent in the horn: that part which appears blue is in reality transparent white, and receives its colour from a thin piece of blue skin inside. This superb bill fades in death, and in three or four days' time has quite lost its original colours.

A Spanish monk reported that the Incas were able to "fly like birds" over the jungle and the Spanish religious authorities were so worried about the shamanistic powers of feather textiles that they ordered them to be destroyed. In an Inca military camp near Cuzco the Spanish discovered more than 100,000 dried birds. The feathers were stored for uniforms, and soldiers were being paid in them.

Feather art was used in many ancient societies in South America, but most of what has survived originates in pre-Columbian Peru and nowadays Mexico. From the early Maya to the ill-fated Aztecs, nobles, priests and warriors literally worshipped feathers and delighted in arraying themselves in cloaks, headdresses, ear spools, necklaces, bracelets and arm bands of brilliant feathers. Moctezuma possessed his own aviary of exotic species, so large that it required 300 attendants to care for the birds, and also maintained his own group of feather artists. There are only eight of the countless pieces of pre-Columbian feather work still in existence, the piece known as Moctezuma's headdress being the most striking. It is quite large, 166 cm tall and 177 cm wide, and is composed of 500 green-gold *quetzal* tail plumes and trimmed with white, blue and red feather bands and small gold rosettes. After the slaying of Moctezuma during the Spanish invasion of Hernando Cortéz, the crown (*penacho*) was confiscated by the Spaniards. It was found again in the 18th century in a storage chest at Ambras Castle in Tyrol, from where it was brought to the Museum of Ethnology in Vienna. By 1566, when the headdress was listed in an inventory of the castle, its Pre-Columbian origin had been lost and it was called "a moorish hat".

Since 1986, descendants of the Aztec Nation and the Mexican government have been asking the Austrian government to return the feathercrown, even though it is not established to be Moctezuma's or that all the feathers are the originals. In the course of demands for restitution of the crown, Oliver Paget, former director of the Natural History Museum in Vienna, argued that Austria being one of the few European countries without colonies had "therefore" acquired almost all objects in "totally legal" fashion. Currently, a replica of the headpiece created as a National symbol at the time of the Mexican Revolution can be found in the Anthropological National Museum of Mexico City, which is built over the remains of Moctezuma's residence. Since 2011 a temporary loan is being considered by the Museum of Ethnology in Vienna.

The transport issue, concerns of conservation, and political and legal questions still have to be clarified. Negotiations are continuing.

When the Ayoreode chiefs of Paraguay were defeated and taken into the missions they left their furs and feathers behind; they had lost their pride and the right to wear them.

1904

John W. Robinson, a graduate of the all-black Tuskegee state school in Alabama, USA opens a cotton-growing school and experimental farm in German-colonised Togo. Tuskegee was the main power base of Booker T. Washington, who had been born in slavery and was the dominant figure in the African American world at the turn of the last century. In a speech at Atlanta in 1895 he had laid out a programme of black self-improvement while accepting the Jim Crow laws of racial discrimination. He also proclaimed the virtues of a 'New South' built on cotton, which depended on the picking skills of African Americans, a workforce highly disciplined by the sharecropping system that had replaced slavery.

Meanwhile in Africa, in southern Togo, the Ewe people were already growing cotton of their own and the regional markets offered "very durable cotton cloth", but the fibre price was too high for an export business. Only women grew cotton, which they ginned and spun themselves, selling the yarn to weavers of all whom were men. In non-monogamous relationships it meant women had independent incomes. In the eyes of German colonialists women in female-domi-

Ô Caput elle-
AMERICA
Stulto

واستعمار جاودانه خواهد ماند
quis
boro dignum
infinitus
MONDVM COGNITA

nated households had too much power. From the very start colonialists, backed by the racist intellectuals of the *Verein für Sozialpolitik* think-tank, wanted to change cotton agriculture. As with other Europeans they wanted to break the USA's monopoly on cotton fibre calling for a "cotton *Kulturkampf* against America". It was serious business: Germany by 1900 was the world's third largest cotton cloth producer with 400,000 working in the industry, but it was faced with fast-rising prices for raw cotton. Only colonial production, argued Karl Helfferich, could break the "economic rule of America over the European cotton industry". Experience in German East Africa with the plantation system indicated widespread resistance to wage labour and hence labour shortages. Instead in Togo they aimed to create a *Volkskultur* in which nominally free farmers would produce cotton for the world market of their own free will, but would be forced to if they didn't. Modern methods of the plough and labour discipline would make for internationally competitive cotton. At the same time the shift to the plough and the physical strength it required it would weaken women's power and lay the basis for the colonial-patriarchal dream of the bourgeois family as the norm.

Through links made by members of the *Verein* organisation with the group around Tuskegee and Booker T. Washington, the idea came that the expert American 'Negro' would be the perfect role model for the people of south Togo to become world market cotton producers, though he offered the following warning to the Germans: "I hope that you will not make the same mistake that has been made in the South amongst our people, that is teach them to raise nothing but cotton." The Tuskegee graduates were expected to be respectful to the colonial authorities and would bring both seeds and expertise, and set up as farmers themselves. Four of them arrived in 1901 and also brought ploughs to replace the hoes that women had used. They were fanatical about ploughs but the various draught animals tried were all killed by the tsetse fly so that one of the 'experts', Calloway, had them drawn by men acting as animals and this became a norm, a vicious irony of colonial progress. There was an increase in the export of cotton, and women's power was weakened, but by 1904 the colonial power abandoned the exemplary 'Negro' farmers' approach and instead one of the original four, John Robinson, set up a cotton school in Togo at Nosté. It was to be a three-year course for rational cotton farming and every district in the colony had to send students to it. They were forced to go in order to be 'free' farmers. But unlike the Tuskegee Institute, the colonial authorities insisted they were not to learn anything that would give them academic qualifications. The students used a variety of informal resistance strategies, which the colonisers put down to an inherent tendency to "laziness", while at the same time they lost prestige among their own people. This loss of prestige also undermined the colonial aim of producing model patriarchal households. The programme often produced "lonely and miserable young men, unable to attract spouses to a life on an exemplary farm under German oversight". Initially using a price guarantee system, the specialised seeds developed by the Tuskegee farmers, and the building of a railway, cotton exports increased exponentially till 1909 and then tailed off. Robinson was side-lined by the colonial regime because of his saying, in line with what Washington had declared from the very beginning, that cotton would make people richer, but that "the people cannot live by cotton alone ... They should be taught to grow cotton and Yams better". In fact, the farmers of Togo did not need to be told; railways, markets and price guarantees (which were too low) were not sufficient to persuade growers to abandon subsistence agriculture for mono-cultural production, which was more effort-intensive and no more rewarding. Resistance to the global marketplace had staying power because unlike the British in India, the German colonists were unable to institutionalise coercion through exploitative systems of taxation and credit.

Baumwoll-Ernte einer deutschen Versuchs-Station Aufnahme: F.Thorbecke

A Cotton collecting station in German colonial Togo.

Max Jorge Hinderer Cruz

All the Names in History. *Chaka Nayra*, the "weaving bone with the big, beautiful eyes," is a tool made from bone of unspecified origin that appears to have been used for weaving before ending up as a curiosity alongside the other wares spread on the street seller's blanket in Lima's old town. And so, through a different, informal, form of circulation, it has become part of the country's National growth. By now, if not earlier, it knows that "at bottom, every name in history is I."[1] As a tool, *Chaka Nayra* primarily fulfills the function of a weaving comb. In other words, its purpose is to tighten the crisscrossing threads that form geometric axes in relation to each other, pushing together the various directions defined by the threads to create a dense plane, a unified body. But *Chaka Nayra* is a very slender weaving bone, a very, very slender comb for long weaves, belts, or bands, or for detail work, for instance to embellish or finish a valuable, more coarsely textured weaving.

The elongated bone is decorated with various animal-shaped engravings, some mirroring the contours of the object itself and hence creating additional figures. If we turn *Chaka Nayra*, both on its longitudinal axis and sideways, one figure emerges from the other: here, the head of a turtle appears, there maybe a llama, a crocodile, or a heron, even a decorated elephant head with a lifelike trunk. The menagerie of figures and spirits animating this tool is brought to life by

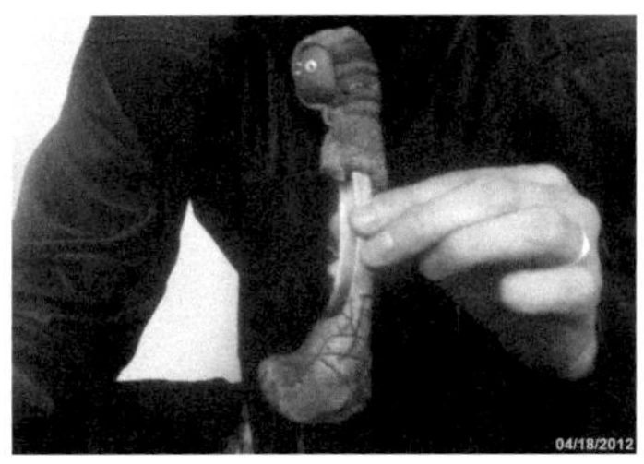

round, white recessed elements and perforations that stare at us as eyes and pairs of eyes. The body is made of a single piece, an elongated bone, with an epiphysis (the capitellum or "little head" of the bone) about the size of an apricot. It fits nicely in the hand and serves as the handle from which protrudes the roughly 11 centimetres long, slender, you could say elegantly, curved neck (or trunk). The piece is a total of 16 centimetres long. It could be made from the hollowed bone of a sheep or llama, cut and filed down to size, then polished, or it could be made from the thighbone of a child of about two years. The bone substance appears to be too heavy to be the bone of a condor, and it's too big to be the ulnar bone of a full-grown Catholic priest.

But we cannot rule out the possibility that different weaving bones were made and/or used for certain work on specific textiles or for representational purposes. They can be characterised according to features like the size, origin, and density of the bone as well as the number of teeth on the comb.

But we are not interested here in the biological being for whose orthopedics *Chaka Nayra* was once significant as a bone, nor in the textile for whose woven form it was used. Rather, we are interested in the fact that *Chaka Nayra* wandered through multiple bodies, necessities, and production-related extensions and circulations, and that as a being, prosthesis, tool, or ethnographic artifact it represents precisely an articulation of mental and formal structures. *Chaka Nayra*, then, speaks to us much more as a plurality and out of the circular dance from which it springs, than about its objectuality. In brief, *Chaka Nayra* always describes a relationship. It speaks to us of concrete constellations, of many different individuals, of the strength and warmth of their bodies, of their relationships between each other, of specific cultural products, and, not least, of the unmistakable fabrics that in turn become skin again, offer protection, or serve as means of labour themselves.

From a Western perspective in the twentieth and twenty-first century, *Chaka Nayra*'s transformation may well describe the relationship between pre-Columbian forms of production and subsistence and the forms of violence of the colonial division of labour and exploitation. Conversely, *Chaka Nayra* attests to the fact that every prematurely aged llama, every unexpected death of a child, and every devoured priest obeys a historic or cosmic necessity, and that by recalling them we can bring them back to life as embodied labour in an attempt to pacify the justified fury of the gods. We do not know how old *Chaka Nayra* is, but we do know that if we turn it once around its axis and inside out, all names of history speak to us from its living eyes.

[1] Here we need to listen to the narrative of our little finger puppet from the Witches Market in La Paz. The finger puppet at once dresses our weaving bone, doubles it, mirrors it, and helps it speak. One of the names of history is supplied by none other than Friedrich Nietzsche himself. In his last letter to the famous Swiss cultural historian Jacob Burckhardt on January 5, 1889, Nietzsche wrote, "The unpleasant thing, and one that nags my modesty, is that at bottom every name in history is I." Historians tend to refer to Nietzsche's last letters as *Wahnbriefe* ("madness letters"). As the finger puppet relates, the word combination *Chaka Nayra* sounds nice as a name, but has no exact meaning in Aymará. *Chaka* means bone and nayra means eyes or big eyes. But *nayra* can also be understood as an extension of the eyes, or as gaze or gaze into the distance. *Chaka Nayra*, then, could just as well be translated as "bone with the big/beautiful eyes" or "bony gaze into the distance".

Acrylic, embroidery; acquired in La Paz, 2009. This was bought in La Paz in 2009 at the time of Bolivia's revolutionary constitution. The iconic image of Che Guevara with beret, as embroidered on the jacket, can be found on clothes all over the world: the face of a communist hero made into what has been called "a commodified expression of nostalgia". It was in Bolivia that Che was liquidated by a CIA-backed hit squad on the 9th of October 1967, during one of Bolivia's many 20th-century dictatorships – nearly all of which were tacitly or openly backed by the USA. Between the 1960s and early 1990s, repression, massacres and torture in Latin America were ubiquitous and involved US training and varieties of support.
In this context, the election of Evo Morales was groundbreaking, as was the Constitution of the country his government put in place in February 2009. A large majority of Bolivian citizens had voted for it in a referendum a month earlier. The Constitution has a claim to be the most humane and progressive in the world, and in its preamble there is recognition of all past struggles, including the water wars, and also of the martyrs of the past. Che is not mentioned by name, but the proliferation of his image at this time makes it clear that he was regarded as one of the martyrs. The Constitution emphasises full recognition both of the plurinational nature of the Bolivian state and of its ecological responsibility. It proclaims political, legal, economic, cultural and linguistic pluralism, making this a reality by being drafted in three languages – Aymará, Quechua and Spanish – while listing all the many other languages used in the country and in doing so giving them recognition. The Constitution also outraged the capitalist world by insisting on the right of nature not to be "affected by mega-infrastructure and development projects that affect the balance of eco-systems and local inhabitants' communities".

Linen

"The Irish wore linen shirts of great length for wantonnesse and braverye." Flax as a source of yarn and linen as the cloth woven from it are the oldest known textiles in Northern Europe; fragments dating back to 8000 BCE have been found in modern-day Switzerland. For thousands of years it was part of a self-sufficient 'peasant' economy, a system called *Kauf*, which was productive enough that its 'Osnabrück' cloth could be exported to dress the slaves in the 'New World'. A 'putting out' system, *Verlag*, along with the division of labour this created, undermined that relative autonomy over time and was systematically developed to become thorough-going capitalist discipline. Ireland, which especially in its northern provinces became the biggest linen producer in the world, was a laboratory for this enforced transformation, which began before the technological developments and factory system of the 19th century. An English traveller there at the end of the 16th century described Indigenous abundance thus: "the native Irish wore shirts of thirty of forty yells dyed with saffron"; a yell being just over a yard. By the middle of the 18th century, 'entrepreneurial' colonial landlords like Sir Richard Cox were fine-tuning systems of social control to make linen a business in which the notion of an abundance for the producers disappeared along with an attack on the Indigenous calendar, its rituals and feast days. For one, May Day became a 'prize' day in which a system of rewards and shame was carried out in public. It made the rural population "into actors 'naturally' distinguishable by their 'unequal skills' and industriousness," while at the same time having to guard against the machinations of some being too successful and becoming rich, which, Cox wrote, would be like a cheesemonger "rearing and cherishing Rats in his shop." This colonial mentality was backed up by the use of credit and how it was advanced against flax or linen in relation to the "dedication to work" of possible recipients.The pieces were in place for this to happen. The English colonial land-grab created a more dependent Irish rural population which was still able to grow, in large part because of the introduction of the 'New World' potato. In 1662 the land-grab was furthered by the confiscation of flax and cloth from the un-co-operative, the legal privileges granted to Protestant immigrants from England, the destruction of the woollen industry by the imposition of massive export taxes on Irish wool, and tariff protection given to linen. All this happened before the arrival of the famous Huguenot exile and linen expert, Louis Crommelin, who supposedly 'created' the Irish linen industry. And what came out of it was that vicious mindset whereby welfare (charity) for the landless vagrant was described as pernicious, and for which linen production would sort out the deserving from the undeserving poor. It also involved gender engineering in relation to production.

The Spinning Room was an important centre for yarn production in German villages from the 15th century through to the late 17th. Sexual promiscuity and disorder are rampant in a world where women were perceived to have the upper hand.

Spinning was seen as a bottleneck: it took 8 spinners to keep one weaver in work, and proto-capitalists like Sir Richard Cox singled out women and children as the best for this work, just as for the final step of flax production when impurities had to removed without shredding the long fibres. For this it was objected that such work for men would require them to "learn an artificial weakness". In the case of spinning it was a question of where women's labour could best be controlled. Not so easy, there were contradictions involved. Visual representations in Holland had the woman at home spinning as the epitome of tranquil virtue, whereas women in groups were too sexy and wild, devilish. In Ireland young women in the home were seen as 'unruly', their idleness leading to "tearing hedges, robbing orchards or beggaring their fathers". On the other hand spinning 'bees', where neighbours assembled in one place to save on light and fuel, might involve too much merriment and because of a lack of chaperoning were seen by both the Protestant and Catholic hierarchy as dens of vice. The ideal solution lay in spinning institutions where, in sight of each other, the women strove to excel. The workhouses and orphanages, where the intensity of labour of each woman could be measured, were the most extreme cases. This was factory discipline before the factory and it was so effective that still in 1811 it meant that linen yarn could be hand-spun in Ireland and sold in the north of the country cheaper than the same material manufactured by machinery in England.

1972

The Self-Employed Women's Association (SEWA) of India was founded as a trade union.
It grew out of the Textile Labour Union, which had been founded in 1920 by a woman, Anasuya Sarabhai, who in turn had been inspired by a textile workers' strike led by Ghandi in 1917. In 1954 a women's wing of the union was formed, focusing on training for the wives and daughters of mill workers, though this expanded into representing self-employed 'homeworker' women tailors, some of the most exploited in the whole clothes production process. However it was another group of women in the business who kick-started the union, migrant women working as cart-pullers in Ahmedabad's cloth market – who were then living on the streets – and 'head-loaders', women carrying loads of clothes between the wholesale and retail markets. Their success in shaming the cloth merchants attracted women working as used garment merchants, and the novel idea of the self-employed having a Trade Union of their own was fought for and finally recognised as such.

In India as elsewhere, textiles and clothing, new and used – Kandla is a major transhipment entrepot for second-hand items – come in and out in standardised metal containers carried by ships. The containers carry RFID tags which means their whereabouts both on the ocean or in a port and in the ship itself can be instantly accessed. In many ports they are lifted on and off, directed by computerised information on which are to be taken off where, by cranes that act on what they are told either with or without human assistance. Their movements are synchronised with flat-bed lorries that arrive in sequence, matching the order in which the containers are lifted off. Robotised logistics are the order of the day and have been instrumental in the development of global production chains and fast fashion. Close to the world where cloth and clothes are actually sold, whole-sale retail markets like Dondaemun, Seoul and down town São Paulo, logistics continue to depend on human load carriers either with their own trolleys, 50cc bikes or on their own shoulders. In La Paz, Bolivia the human load carriers, *aparapitas*, transport far beyond the confines of market areas. In these cases even if there is no official union there is ad hoc organisation based on an informally held etiquette. This is not so for the competitive world of those working in the institutionalised 'smuggling' in and out of the Spanish enclaves of Seuta and Mellia to Morocco and back. Here women are carrying loads of up to 100 kilos through the tight corridor across borders. When one woman was asked what was her dream by a documentary crew, she replied how can I have dreams when I have no future. In this context the existence and longevity of the SEWA is something special.

Beatriz Canedo Patiño

"I am Bolivian, but for many, many years I was a fashion designer in New York, which is the fashion capital of the world – not Paris or Milan – because of the volume that it moves. Now I have my own company here in Bolivia, me designing and the seamstresses under the same roof, and I'm proud that the clothes made here go out with a Made-in-Bolivia label. But my coming back was not an emotional decision. I'll never forget this *Financial Times* journalist interviewing me along the lines of, "What's a nice girl like this doing in La Paz". Like, why after New York? Well the nitty gritty of it is competitive pricing. I'm a designer, not someone with an MBA, but I sat down and did the figures when I had an order for 500 garments from Toronto. And then, of course, even though the seamstresses here have no formal training, they do exquisite work, and the joke is that this tradition of good tailoring, it was the British who brought it when they were building our railways. So some English tailors, came and that's how it started. So this fits well because I am a technical designer, which is maybe why I was always getting mail addressed to Mr Canedo. And who is he, may I ask? They just think there is no such thing as a woman behind a garment business.
Anyway, when I was back in the country I got a visit from the team of Mr Evo Morales, our President, wanting me to design the clothes for his inauguration as President. Well obviously they knew my reputation, I mean, I don't want to brag, but I've dressed a lot of famous people. Maybe also, they knew I'd done a lot of my work with alpaca yarn even though Bolivians themselves, the upper class, so to speak, they wouldn't wear it; for them it was for their maid or their butler to wear alpaca. So when they asked me, well it was an honour for me, the first Indigenous

President in 500 years, and I wanted him to look really good, though I had very little time to do it because – real Bolivian style – they left it very late. They gave me a free hand, and all they said was that he didn't want to wear a tie, which was fine with me, and he wanted to be identified with his own culture, which is Aymará; not Quechua, but Aymará. I liked that, because he could easily just have chosen an Armani suit or something like that. Well, at the time, the President-elect was very busy travelling but the Vice President himself, Álvaro, came to tell me all this, and then he came to look at the drawings I'd made. That the suit would be made from alpaca was without question, but he agreed with me that the colours should be subtle because our flag is loud enough, red, yellow and green. And it would be embroidered with an Aymará motif. I took it very seriously and so did they, them coming here or making phone calls. With just ten days before the inauguration, I did all the research for those motifs myself because that's how I am. They call me exacting, but better that than mediocre. Anyway, they'd also asked me not to reveal that it was me who was doing the clothes for him, and of course I didn't though the press were ringing from all over the world, and here they were insulting, offering me money to reveal that I was the one, and they wanted to bring cameras. Unbelievable, they were climbing the trees outside to try and get a picture. After the inauguration of course I couldn't lie. But I had serious work to get on with.

For one thing I'm involved with work on all camelid fibres, and involved with international experts on the subject with symposia and so on, as well as using them in my designs. The super-luxury fibre, the thinnest, is the *vicuña*, which is way finer than cashmere, and besides it's much prettier, it has such an elegant neck whereas the cashmere goat is so ugly. And I'm the first designer in Latin America to use it. I've been pushing for its use here against some stupid restrictions. I mean I would never have a camelid killed but the *vicuña* can be sheared, and this would be good for *campesinos* who could make a living from this. So now there is such a project in Bolivia and I'm proud to say that at the last symposium in Chile they said that I and my company, we're the only one that could design and manufacture it. This is serious work; it is a sacred cloth.

The cloth is made by a female cooperative in the region around Jatiwangij, Indonesia and shows the area's traditional manufactured roof tiles. Women earn more than men as they do the precision work, everyone looks after the kids, and the mining of the clay goes hand in hand with rice cultivation. Even though *batik* is not a traditional craft in this area, literally everyone is wearing such cloth.

But then you're not allowed to be serious by the press. I mean I was interviewed recently and asked how I'd advise Mrs Obama on what to wear for her husband's inauguration. I and some other designers were asked, but here, this so-called quality newspaper in Santa Cruz made a drawing from what I'd said and I'm furious. It's not my drawing, the head is too big, and of course we know poor Mrs Obama has big hips, but you never show it on the day. And the way they did it! I mean, the coat should be the same length as the dress, and how is she going to be carrying a purse outdoors in the snow. She'll freeze, and besides, everyone knows, queens and princesses, they never carry purses because they have people behind to pay. I was furious, but you can't afford to fight with the Santa Cruz press. And the interviewer was pretty stupid. I said I didn't want her with a scarf because she needs to look chic and elegant, so he asks, what about jewellery. Because they are considered to be a bit like in Caracas, they overdo it with everything: skin, skin, skin; jewellery, jewellery, jewellery. So the first thing I said was "very, very little jewellery", especially now, because it would be very ostentatious with the world economic crisis for the First Lady to come out looking like a Christmas tree."

Ujutas, Ajotas / Sandals

26

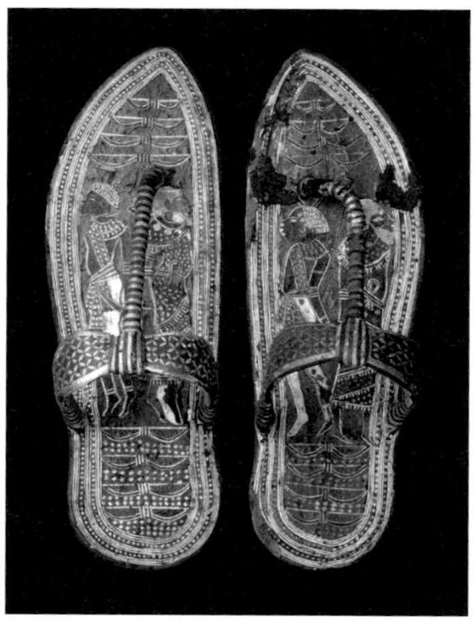

Sandals from the grave of Tutanchanun. Worked in are images of Nubian and Assyrian prisoners in chains. Also 8 arches which represent the traditional enemies of Egypt. This allows him to tread on his enemies continuously.
In 18th-century Brazil, free black people wore shoes as they walked about city streets so that they would not be mistaken for slaves. In one instance a woman who might have been eligible for the labour draft was saved by an official on the grounds that she was "treated as some-one who wears shoes".

Made from recycled truck tyres; acquired at the weekly market of Tarabuco, Bolivia, 2009.
In 1927 the richest man in the world bought land in the Brazilian Amazon to grow rubber. Henry Ford was bringing "white man's magic to the wilderness", wrote the *Washington Post*. He planned to cultivate not only "rubber but the rubber gatherers as well". In 1888, Brazil was the last country in the world to abandon slavery. By this time an estimated four million slaves had been 'imported' from Africa to Brazil, 40% of the total number of slaves brought to the Americas. In the Brazilian colonies, shoes, or the lack thereof, indicated legal status. They protected the feet and distinguished free man from slave; Indians, blacks and mestizos generally went without shoes. A British visitor in the mid-19th century described the sound of the city of Salvador, Bahia, as that of "the nearly noiseless tread of the unshod black population".
Free blacks did wear shoes as they walked about city streets so that they would not be mistaken for slaves; the process was called *calzarse* (to shoe oneself). This recalls the pejorative term 'the barefeet' for everyone south of central Europe. In one instance a woman who might have been eligible for the labour draft was saved by an official on the grounds that she was "treated as

someone who wears shoes". Indian leaders in the Amazon would be given shoes by the royal treasury of colonial Brazil to enhance their position on political occasions, but would be forced to take them off as a punishment for not fulfilling colonial obligations. In Mexico City tanners and leather merchants brought shoes for the creoles and those mestizos able or wanting to adopt Western styles. Sandals were strictly for country hicks. As recently as 1923 a ban existed on *huaraches* (sandals) being worn in the city's downtown, even though out of a population of 400,000 only 50,000 wore shoes. The 6th national census in 1943 collected data on who wore shoes, who sandals and who went barefoot. The question in the census was only dropped in 1980. In 2012 European consumer protection organisations published a report on slavery and cruelty to animals involved in the production of leather shoes in Brazil. They discovered catastrophic quasi-slavery conditions among the workers. *Ujutas*, made from rubber tyres and worn by peasants all over the world who cannot afford leather boots, have recently become high eco-fashion in the US.

An alpaca herder mixing the old and the new. He is using a drop spindle like those that have been used for thousands of years in the Andes, but wearing a suit of Western style that would have been woven with a Spanish-introduced upright treadle loom.

Green

Despite several efforts to re-categorise the colour and its predominance in the natural world, Green has never made it as a Primary Colour, always stuck as one version or another of a mix of Yellow and Blue. Until the early 18th century it was not promoted due to a taboo against mixing. It benefitted as much as blue from the importing of indigo in quantity. Later in the century Scheele's Green was created using arsenic, at a time when it became *the* colour for bedrooms, and there is evidence that its 'restfulness' came at the cost of its poisonousness. It was lethal to those handling it, most of whom were female, and the side effects of working with this colour ranged from sores to convulsions to, in many cases, death.

That it is not a primary colour is true also of animals using it as camouflage. Reptiles, fish, amphibians, and birds appear green, but this is because a reflection of blue lights coming through an over-layer of yellow pigment. At the same time, some languages like Vietnamese, Bantu and Korean do not distinguish between green and blue, but in plants there is not this confusion, it is chlorophyll that is responsible for green and green alone. Its virtues however have never been in doubt. Aristotle saw it as a happy medium between light and dark. Goethe, too, called it the most *balanced* hue and best for easing body and mind. As did Christians, like the 4th-century Basil of Caesarea (St Basil), who perceived it as a specifically restful colour; the view was the same some 900 years later.

"Thanne grene colour is mene bytwene rede and black, and drawe and conforteth the yhen (eyes) to byholde and loke thereonne, and restoreth and conforteth the sight. Therefore hertes and othere wilde bestes loveth and haunteth grene place, and ought oonliche for mete but also for liking and for sight," says Bartholomeus Anglicus, a 13th-century English monk. Here he goes beyond restfulness, writing in English, aware that the colour word came from Old English for 'grow', and in a world that has not been deforested, green is established as the colour of nature just as in ancient Egypt Osiris, worshipped as an agent of crop regeneration, was pictured as green-skinned. It is also not surprising that it is in the most forested area of the world, the Amazon, that there are the most sophisticated vocabularies of the colour. Green is the most venerated colour in Islamic culture, but this too is because paradise is conceived as being full of lush vegetation. More recently it has, for essentially the same reason, become emblematic of an 'environmental' politics concerned with deforestation, climate change and the limited nature of natural resources in need of preservation. In the 20th century Wassily Kandinsky is more sceptical about the colour and its restfulness. For him the association with a radical politics would have been absurd. "Green is the most restful colour that exists. On exhausted men this restfulness has a beneficial effect, but after a time it becomes wearisome. ... in the hierarchy of colours, green is the bourgeoisie, self-satisfied, immovable, narrow." Immovable? Really? As if to disprove him, Edward Lear, James Joyce and Friedrich Schiller allowed green its freedom: "And off they sailed in a pea-green boat" "into the snot-green sea", "dressed in goose-shit green".

And the wise-after-the-eventers asked of the arsenic green gown wearer, Was it really worth it? "The Arsenic Waltz: The New Dance of Death."

2011

"We are our own leaders." In the spring of 2009, Zoran Bulatovic, one of the chairmen of the independent Textile Workers Union in Novi Pazar, Serbia, cut off his little finger and put it in his mouth in front of running TV cameras to draw attention to the catastrophic conditions of the workers in a local textile factory called RASKA. The Serbian media subsequently referred to him as a "finger eater", equating self-mutilation and labour disputes with psychopathic acts. The leftist German newspaper *taz* reported that the laid-off textile workers had had to resort to drastic measures like self-mutilation because no one is impressed by hunger strikes anymore, starving to death is simply not enough. The article's title, "When Workers Become Cannibals", evokes similarly colonial images. This link has a long history, early engravings of the 'savages' of the New World were closely modelled on those of the European poor's celebrations. The protests became increasingly radical when Zoran joined up with several former colleagues and started a hunger-strike, but with each participant vowing to chop off one finger a day until the Belgrade government paid the workers' back wages. Whenever the strikers came to the negotiation table they arrived with chainsaws. On one occasion they choked the director of RASKA until he gave them access to the accounting records.

Among the 125,000 inhabitants of Novi Pazar, the most ethnically diverse area of Serbia and once the centre of Yugoslavia's textile industry, some 33% live below the poverty line and 55% are unemployed. The RASKA textile factory started operation in 1956 and was the heart of Yugoslavia's "Jeans Valley". In the 1990s the plant had as many as 4000 employees. Only one hundred of them, mostly directors and technicians, remained in 2009. The battle for wages and compensation was led by 1523 workers who had been put on forced leave, eighty percent of them single mothers. By law the government, as the owner of such operations, has to continue to pay wages in cases of forced leave, but it had failed to do so since 1993. The protests sought the introduction of pension insurance in the case of unemployment, at least thirty-six months of back pay and the cancellation of the factory's debt. Militant, ineffective hunger strikes had already been held at the factory in 2006 and 2008. When a renewed hunger strike in April 2009 failed to attract the necessary attention, the workers took the dramatic step of self-mutilation. After 110 days of the strike they managed to extract a one-off payment of approximately 300. Tellingly, one of the slogans of striking textile workers in Kragujevac (southern Serbia) is: "We can move Serbia with our little finger!" On June 6, 2010, Zoran Bulatovic was beaten up in the office of the board of directors after exposing the fraudulent activities at the RASKA textile factory during the course of the organisation's privatisation. Notice of the public sale of the company had to be retracted after the intervention of the Textile Workers Union, which

revealed that the former management wanted to participate in the bidding process as part of a consortium. The Serbian government aimed to privatise all public or employee-run operations by the end of 2009 as a result of IMF pressure, which made the repayment of another multi-billion-dollar loan dependent on the reduction of public spending. Since August 2011, the employees have been striking again. Within a couple hours of the announcement that RASKA would have to file for bankruptcy, about 1,500 of the former workers gathered in front of the factory, giving the government an ultimatum to withdraw the insolvency decision, which it did, and to declare its willingness to take over the factory's debt. What happened to the RASKA factory also took place in other areas of former Yugoslavia. In Dalmatia in 2004 the privatised Dalmatinka spinning mill, which in the 1980s had employed 2000 and exported yarn all over the world, was to be relaunched. In fact workers were not paid for months and the mill was asset-stripped before finally being bankrupted in 2008. For the women who had worked there, the loss, in spite of the intensity of piece-rate production, was devastating: "We are the generation whose grandmothers provided for our future through the factory. And we thought we would be able to build an even better future for our children and grandchildren."
In Serbia itself, 2016–17 has seen a burst of foreign investment in the textile sector: German, Italian (led by Benetton), Bulgarian, Romanian, and especially Turkish companies are present. That this is due to the cheapness of a scarred labour force – wages at East Asian levels – is shown by the fact that there is a Bangladeshi company ready to start production in Sombar. Workers say that "employers spend a lot on video surveillance, but not so much on improving ventilation".

B. Traven

ASSEMBLY LINE [Abridged]. The Indian was busy making little baskets from bast and from all kinds of fibres gathered by him in the immense tropical bush which surrounded the village on all sides. The material used had not only been well prepared for its purpose but was also richly coloured with dyes that the basket-maker himself extracted from various native plants, barks, roots and from certain insects by a process known only to him and the members of his family. His principal business, however, was not producing baskets. He was a peasant who lived on the small property he possessed. Baskets he made when there was nothing else for him to do in the fields, because he was unable to dawdle. After all the sale of his baskets, though to a rather limited degree only, added to the small income he received from his little farm.
In spite of being by profession just a plain peasant, it was clearly seen from the small baskets he made that at heart he was an artist, a true and accomplished artist. Each basket looked as if covered all over with the most beautiful and sometimes fantastic ornaments, flowers, butterflies, birds, squirrels, antelopes, tigers and a score of other animals of the wilds. Yet, the most amazing thing was that these decorations, all of them symphonies of colour, were not painted on the baskets but were instead actually part of the baskets themselves. Bast and fibres dyed in dozens of different colours were so cleverly, one must actually say intrinsically, interwoven that those attractive designs appeared on the inner part of the basket as well as on the outside. This performance he accomplished without ever looking at any sketch or pattern.
Mr E.L. Winthrop of New York was on vacation in the Republic of Mexico. "How much for that little basket, friend?" he asked. "Fifty centavos, patroncito, my good little lordy", the Indian answered politely. "All right, sold."
He had expected to hear a price of three or even four pesos, saw right away what great business possibilities this miserable Indian village might offer to a dynamic promoter like himself.
After returning from the USA with a profitable contract for such baskets to be mass produced ...
"I've got big business for you, my friend", Mr Winthrop began. "Suppose I order you to make ten thousand of these baskets, how much time do you think you would need to deliver them?"
After a few minutes the Indian, without interrupting his work, said in a slow voice, "It will take a good long time to make so many baskets, patroncito. You see, the bast and the fibres must be very dry before they can be used properly. Then all during the time they are slowly drying they must be worked and handled in a very special way so that while drying they won't lose their softness and their flexibility and their natural brilliance. Even when dry they must look fresh. They must never lose their natural properties or they will look just as lifeless and dull as straw. Then while they are drying I got to get the plants and roots and barks and insects from which

I brew the dyes. That takes much time also, believe me. The plants must be gathered when the moon is just right or they won't give the right colour. The insects I pick from the plants must also be gathered at the right time and under the right conditions or else they produce no rich colours and are just like dust. But of course, jefecito, I can make as many of these canastitas as you wish, even as many as three dozens if you want them. Only give me time."

"Three dozens? Three dozens?" Mr Winthrop yelled, and threw up both arms in desperation. "Three dozens!" he repeated as if he had to say it many times in his own voice so as to understand the real meaning of it. He had expected the Indian to go crazy on hearing that he was to sell ten thousand of his baskets without having to peddle them from door to door and be treated like a dog with a skin disease. So the American took up the question of price again, by which he hoped to activate the Indian's ambition.

"Si, patroncito, I have the price ready, it is well calculated now without any mistake on my side. If I got to make one thousand canastitas, each will be three pesos. If I must make five thousand, each will cost nine pesos. And if I have to make ten thousand, in such a case I can't make them for less than fifteen pesos each". Immediately he returned to his work as if he were afraid of losing too much time with such idle talk.

Mr Winthrop thought it was perhaps his faulty knowledge of this foreign language that had played a trick on him. "Did I hear you say fifteen pesos each if I eventually would buy ten thousand?" "That's exactly and without any mistake what I've said, patroncito", the Indian answered in his soft and courteous voice.

Mr Winthrop felt as if he would go insane any minute now. "Yes, so you said. Only what I can't comprehend is why you cannot sell at the same price if you make me ten thousand. I certainly don't want to chisel on the price. I am not that kind. Only, well, let's see now if you can sell for forty centavos at all, be it for twenty or fifty or a hundred, I can't quite get the idea why the price has to jump that high if I buy more than a hundred."

"Bueno, patroncito, what is there so difficult to understand? It's all very simple. One thousand canastitas cost me a hundred times more work than a dozen. Ten thousand cost me so much time and labour that I could never finish them, not even in a hundred years. For a thousand canastitas I need more bast than for a hundred, and I need more little red beetles and more plants and roots for the dyes. It isn't that you can just walk into the bush and pick all the things you need at your heart's desire. One root with the true violet blue may cost me four or five days until I can find one in the jungle. And have you thought how much time it takes and how much hard work to prepare the bast and fibres? What is more if I must make so many baskets, who will then look after my corn and my beans and my goats and chase for me occasionally a rabbit for meat on Sunday? If I have no corn then I have no tortillas to eat, and if I grow no beans, where do I get my frijoles from?"

"But since you'll get so much money from me for your baskets you can buy all the corn and beans in the world and more than you need."

"That's what you think, little lordy. But you see it is only the corn I grow for myself that I am sure of. Of the corn which others may or may not grow, I cannot be sure to feast upon."

"Haven't you got some relatives here in this village who might help you to make baskets for me?" Mr Winthrop asked hopefully. "Practically the whole village is related to me somehow or other." "Why then can't they cultivate your fields and look after your goats while you make baskets for me? Not only this, they might gather for you the fibres and the colours in the bush and lend you a hand here and there in preparing the material you need for the baskets."

"They might, patroncito, yes, they might. Possible. But then you see who would take care of their fields and cattle if they work for me? And if they help me with the baskets it turns out the same. No one would any longer work in his fields properly. In such a case corn and beans would get up so high in price that none of us could buy any and we would all starve to death. Now you'll understand, highly estimated caballero and jefecito, why I can't make the baskets any cheaper than fifteen pesos each if I got to make that many."

Lliclla / Woman's Ceremonial Mantle

27

Alpaca; acquired in Lima, 2010. The rectangular black ceremonial mantle is a handwoven alpaca cloth used in funeral or healing rituals. It is a warp faced plain weave with back warp and weft. The plain warp weave is woven of alternating three mm strips of right- and left-spun thread herringbone (*pana* and *lloq'e* in Quechua), a characteristic of magico-religious weavings. There are bands of *lloq'e* at either outside warp edge and black tubular edging is woven onto outer edges. The cloth comes with four selvage edges. The weft yarns were dyed with cochineal and the yarn hand-spun using a drop spindle.

It was in the early part of the 20th century that pre-Colonial and pre-Inca Andean woven textiles began to appear in European museums, especially those in Germany. The largest collection was amassed by one collector, Christian Theodor Wilhelm Gretzer, between 1872 and 1904. Two purchases in 1899 and 1907 account for 44,600 of the 70,000 artefacts that make up the collection of the Völkerkundemuseum in Berlin. He had arrived in Lima in 1876 and as an importer of European textiles was dependent on the Peruvian incomes generated by the *guano* and wool booms of the time. The wealth they generated does not compare to that produced by the silver of Potosí or the sheer scale of human misery that entailed, but the taste for imported luxuries, with textiles a major item, was similar. At the same time such imports were perceived by the Peruvian elite as both civilising and symbolic of modernity. More instrumentally, the local elite believed that a desire for such imports among Indigenous people would induce them to work harder. In Peru in the mid-19th century the British consul was confident that imports, mostly textiles, would increase "as civilisation advances and the needs of the population increase". "Outside urban centres", however, "Indians continued to wear their own textiles and

In a custom dating back to slavery, Indigenous Bolivians pinch passing Afro-Bolivians to grab some of the luck the slaves are said to have brought to the native people, as their arrival meant they were no longer at the bottom of Bolivia's racial hierarchy.

opposite page

Circle of James Pollard: Queen Victoria, Prince Albert, and Victoria, princess royal in Windsor Great Park, Oil on board, 1792–1867.

seemed 'indifferent consumers of manufactures'. From cotton they made their own tunics, dresses and skirts and did not wear what Criollos and Spaniards wore".

The Andean textiles Gretzer sold to German museums excited enthusiasm amongst avant-garde artists. They also provoked a bout of theorising, which involved notions of authenticity, abstract representation, the primitive and tradition. Gottfried Semper argued for a version of technical determinism whereby the 'art' he was prepared to recognise in the weavings was a result of the very technique of weaving: patterns were simply a matter of crossing warp and weft rather than any creative drive. This would later be opposed by the Obrist-Debschitz school, which was determined to break this elitist view by recognising the creativity of art produced by artisans. On a theoretical level Semper's viewpoint was opposed by Alois Riegel, whose universalism saw decorating and arranging as an inherent human need. Another argument was that the abstract and geometrical nature of the weavings were a way in which 'primitive' people gave order to a world they perceived as chaotic. The industrialised brutality of the First World War gave strength to this view. But all such theorising involved bogus universalisms, exhibiting a profound disrespect, as if there was nothing special about particular places and their cultures.

Such disrespect was of a part with the way the weavings had arrived in the museums. Gretzer's collection derived from commissioned graverobbers and provided far more artefacts than official archaeologists like Max Uhle were able to, drawing from a wider area within the region. Worse, the collection in Berlin was determined by Gretzer's personal taste; and in the case of a funeral cloth from Pachacamac dating from between 900 and 1200 CE, which showed both historical and mythical narratives, he cut it into two pieces, selling one to the Berlin Ethnographic Museum and the other to Hannover. He was well attuned, however, to the cultural politics of the time, so that his collection was all safely in Europe and ready for sale before a ban on the export of antiquities came into force in 1905 as a consequence of a first wave of 'regenerative' Peruvian nationalism.

This did not prevent this collection from being used as source material for artistic investigations by members of Bauhaus, who not only borrowed the formal motifs from Andean textiles but also integrated the structural process of weaving into geometric designs.

Alpaca

When the Inca had conquered the peoples around Lake Titicaca – which stretches across modern-day Peru and Bolivia – in the 15th century, they appreciated the value of their alpaca and the cloth they produced. This appreciation lead to them organising 'seed-herds' into other areas and

Representation of America performed at the French court during the 1626 carnival

made herders into highly regarded specialists with a sophisticated knowledge of breeding and pasture. Yet according to the Peruvian social anthropologist Jorge Flores Ochoa, by 1651 – some 115 years after the Spanish invasion – alpaca and llamas had disappeared from many regions, while in others like the Central Highlands they were on the point of extinction.

How had this happened? True, there had been massive human depopulation caused by civil wars and diseases brought from Europe by the Spanish, and this contributed to the neglect of the sophisticated agricultural infrastructure of the Inca and the reduction in herder numbers, but for one thing, the wars themselves contributed to the decline of alpaca numbers as they were

used indiscriminately for meat by the warring parties. They were killed for fun in hunts; sales of them as cheap meat were enforced by the introduction of monetary taxes; and there was an outbreak of scabies in 1544 as a result of a lack of skilled herders. This was not just strategic neglect, there was an attitude of mind whereby even when the camelids, guanaco, vicuña, llamas and alpaca, were known to be specific species with known Indigenous language names, the colonialists continue to call them 'sheep of the Indies'. This mentality had practical consequences, as Ochoa says of the situation of camelid loss, which "... paved the way for the introduction of sheep. Forced sales were frequent and the Indians were obliged to dispose of their animals to buy 'the sheep of Castille'. In 1572 in the *altiplano*, a Father Formizedo jailed the herdsmen who refused to sell their alpaca or llama to buy the sheep they were offered."
And despite the unsuitability of sheep above the 3000-metre line, their depredation of pasture by their ripping it rather than the cutting by the teeth of the alpaca, the colonial attitude was: "There Will be Sheep regardless". As in the Scottish highlands of the 19th century, and after attacks on the Indigenous people of Australia, sheep replaced men in many areas. The still largely unwritten story is that of the survival of both the alpaca and herders pushed into the higher regions of the Peruvian *altiplano*. It is only because they had survived that in the 1830s alpaca wool enters the world of global trade. A combination of free trade policies and a shortage of the sheep wool demanded for European manufacturing capacity made alpaca wool an attractive proposition in the south of Peru. English-dominated trading houses develop in Arequipa and in 1833 someone, probably the firm of Mohens and Company, included a bale of alpaca wool in a consignment to Liverpool. The well known story, gently mocked by Charles Dickens in his piece "The Great Yorkshire Llama", is that the woollen manufacturer Titus Salt of Bradford comes across this bale while in a Liverpool warehouse; that he is curious; takes a piece to a dyer friend who 'discovers' that it dyes well; works out himself how it can be spun, that is on an industrial basis, and hey presto there is an alpaca cloth industry that really takes off when Queen Victoria uses it. From the Arequipa point of view, the alpaca export figures are staggering, a 300-times increase between 1834 and 1840.
If there is irony in the story it's that the fibre spun in the hell-hole of 19th-century Bradford woollen mills – where life expectancy was between 20 and 30 years, as poor as that in the colonial workshops – was inferior to what was being spun and woven in pre-Columbian times. The archaeological evidence described by Jane Wheeler in her ongoing research shows that fleeces were finer then than now, closer in diameter to cashmere. This regression she attributes to the collapse of skilled herder breeding knowledge, and how it ended up with traditional sheep-rearing practices being applied to camelids. Poetic justice perhaps, but at the cost to producers, since the quality could no longer match cashmere. Besides, most of the profit from the alpaca boom went to Yorkshire, where Salt and two other companies set up an alpaca cartel, and to those Arequipa merchant houses. Worse, the boom caused concerted land-grabbing and land-grabbing attempts by haciendas owned by the old and new merchant elites. This often involved violence using a "Law of Terror" when the strategy of creating herder indebtedness with the selling of imported goods at inflated prices did not work.

1903 THE HONOURABLE MUNICIPAL COUNCIL OF THE DEPARTMENT OF LA PAZ Considering: That in our time, culture and proper rules of hygiene establish the convenience of raising the moral and material level of the population. That the municipalities, by virtue of the powers conferred to them by the fundamental law of the sector, have the duty to watch over the adornment and comfort of the community and consequently also over the proper dress of its inhabitants.
DECREES: *1st Article.* – The dress that the Indigenous class in our towns persists in wearing, with bare feet, short, torn trousers on their lower extremities, and long hair, is retrograde and counter to the principles of morality, which therefore condemns and forbids it. *2nd Article.* – We appeal to the diligence and civic spirit of the district's residents, in particular to the authorities, municipal councils and cantonal agents, parish priests and landowners, to encourage the Indigenous population to modify their dress and adopt the usual dress of the civilised mestizo class of the land. *3rd Article.* – It is forbidden, under penalty of fine, for special dress-makers and master tailors to make or use the abolished dress. *4th Article.* – Indigenous

individuals who appear in public wearing the mentioned dress and barefoot on public holidays or on local Patron Saint festivities, will be fined and forced to leave the town. This penalty will not be enforced outside of these days. (Signed)
And back in 1804 (did it ever change?) "The Attorney General of the Council of the Indies in Madrid advises against overdoing the sale of whiteness certificates, to the end that persons of colour should not seek to generalise these favours believing that these make them equal to whites with no difference but the accident of colour, and believing themselves able to obtain all destinies and employments and to form links with any legitimate and mixture-free family ... consequences which it is fitting to avoid in a monarchy, where the classification of classes contributes to better order, security, and good government ... Coloured or brown persons stemming from infected mixtures constitute a very inferior species which, due to its vitiated nature, its arrogance and inclination for freedom, has been and is little attached to our government and nation."

T.J. Clark

A Piece of Cloth. I have been living with a square of deep purple cloth – the purple threaded through with black, so that the whole thing, depending on the light, seems on the verge of disappearing into darkness – for several months now. Most of the time it has been pinned across bookshelves facing me as I sit at my desk. Just to the left of it are Delacroix's *Journals*, just to the right Pizarro's *Letters to Lucien*. Sacred texts. Somewhere near the start of my time with the cloth I got sent (just occasionally the e-world throws up things you're glad to receive) a mysterious photograph with another square of dark colour in it, over to the left in the mid-distance; and the two squares have ended up coexisting in my mind.
I tried to find out more about the photograph after it reached me, but nobody seemed to have a clue. It is certainly of the Soviet army, and the best guess is that it was taken during the Polish campaign in 1920. We know that Kazimir Malevich and his young followers had seized control of the art school in Vitebsk at the time, and that the Black Square (or less often a Red Square) was their emblem – of world revolution and Nothingness. Did they make a few banners for the Red Army to carry through the woods to Warsaw? Maybe – the architect Lubetkin remembered Malevich's abstract 'anti-paintings' being hoisted on poles in processions. I wish I could see more clearly how the soldiers round the flagpole are looking. A bit sheepish? Or a bit ironical about the young lads back in town, with their dreams of the final Void? "Then raise the scarlet standard high/ Beneath its shade we'll live or die." Easy for *them* to sing. Deep purple is an imperial colour. The square pinned on my bookshelves looks properly regal. The word 'perse', I am told, started off meaning blue or bluish-grey, but then drifted towards purplish black. Some say it derives from 'Persia' – from a deep past of Asiatic pomp. Thomas Kenneally, very much not a pompous writer, still uses the word, and knows how closely it is connected with death. "He noticed the perse under each lid, and the blue, death-struck lips." (*Bring Larks and Heroes*, 1967)

I do not imagine, or want, my mid-size square of perse to be up on a pole above a new Red Army, or draped on an emperor's coffin. But these bits of the past do cling to it. Coriolanus says – it's one of the few thoughts of his that I find sympathetic – that if we went on doing things, and thinking of things, according to 'Custom', "The dust on antique time would lie unswept, / And mountainous error be too highly heaped / For truth to o'er-peer." The purple of the past is one thing, that of the present another. The truth of the deathly, majestic, nothing-filled square of colour I have been living with does peer out, I think – occasionally, fitfully – from behind its history. And Kenneally is right: the truth is funereal but lovely: perse is a mourning colour, a formal colour, always with the sound of muffled drums as accompaniment; but maybe still fit to put error in its place.

Winchucas / 3 Pairs of Leggings

28

Acrylic wool, handknitted; Potosí; acquired at the market in El Alto, 2010. Jula Jula is a serious dance that probably originated in pre-colonial times. It is the dance and music that precedes the famous and dangerous *tinku* battles, fought annually between Andean *ayllus*, or family territories. *Tinku* battles are fierce and bloody encounters that terminate in ceremonial gestures of respect, forgiveness and sometimes alliances that are maintained until the battles are repeated a year later. The men's heads are covered with thick bull hide helmets resembling those of the Spanish invaders. Lined on the inside with metal plate, these helmets protect the wearer from potentially lethal projectiles thrown from their opponents' slings during the *tinku* battles. Thick wool leggings decorated with magical lightning strikes protect the lower legs and long, colourful wool scarves sway to the melody of cane wind instruments. Long, painted Andean ostrich or *suri*, feathers planted on top of the helmets, remind one of gallant medieval knights. Young women wear heavy, hand-woven wool dresses, or *almillas*, elaborately embroidered along the lower hems and accompanied by fine, hand-woven textiles with intricate designs wrapped around one side of the body and the shoulders. A white wool hat adorned with flowers and colourful pins covers the head, and streamers of a leguminous plant called *molle* hide the face. The leaves of the plant never lose their colour and represent the youth and vitality of young women. The costumes also include small mirrors attached to the hat and dress. The dance is relatively simple in its steps and movement. A procession of dancers, separated but close together, begins a serpentine rhythmic movement in a counterclockwise direction and forms a large circle. The circle expands and contracts, usually in a spiral march. The soldier-like steps and swaying of the upper body follow the rhythm of a variety of wind instruments made from hollow canes.

Paisley

By 1870 Paisley, an industrial town in Scotland, was "not only synonymous with shawls but even – in a shameless misappropriation of Intellectual Property – with the quintessential motif of shawl design, the *buteh*, developed thousands of miles away in the ateliers of the Kashmiri designers" of the authentic 'cashmere' shawls. *Buteh*, with its origins in Mughal-style flowering plant motifs that had developed into a flowing, abstract scroll, was appropriated after technological developments in Europe could make use of production process information provided by European travellers in Kashmir. These developments made it possible to make 'cashmere' shawls using both merino sheep wool and cotton rather than cashmere itself and, as scarf or shawl, it became a mass-market item. As early as 1832 the fashion-conscious in Kandahar were wearing British imitation shawls as sashes.

Paisley designs in Britain were one of the first examples of copyright protection in the creative fields and date back to the 1840s. The teardrop design was meant to represent the cypress tree or mango tree, symbols of eternal life and prosperity.

The technological developments that made this possible were the Jacquard loom and also methods of dyeing and the large-scale printing of cloth. Both originated in France and the combination continued to set the pace in design. The Jacquard loom with its set of punched cards allowed for the weaver to be his own designer, though designers as such also existed, but also changed the production equation because a simple set of cards "reflecting the design of one quarter of the shawl could be flipped horizontally and vertically to produce mirror-images of the design on the other three parts". At the start of the 19th century and also in France, Daniel Coechlin of the company Nicolas Coechlin et Frères had worked out how to use chrome yellow (lead chromate) to etch madder-dyed cloth for the first Cashmere shawl and scarf imitations called merinos, or yellow-red merinos. He also got the designer L.J. Malaine to create many versions of the basic *buteh* pattern.

Paisley itself got on the bandwagon relatively late, in the early part of the 19th century, after its silk-weaving industry went into crisis when the Napoleonic wars cut off supplies of silk, and then only as a result of the outsourcing of production by shawl makers in Edinburgh. The adoption of the Jacquard loom saw the creation of larger mills and by 1850 there were some 7000 weavers in the town, but the secret of Paisley's success was the same as the accusation thrown at East Asian countries in our own times, they copied and took none of the risk that creating new designs might involve. They copied from Kashmir itself but most of all from Paris to which they sent representatives every year to buy new designs or sent their own artists to do apprenticeships there. The decline of the business occurred around 1880 at the same time demand for the authentic shawl from Kashmir collapsed, and, in a not unfamiliar quirk, only became synonymous with the *buteh* pattern after this decline in shawls was underway. In the late 1960s the pattern re-emerged as a characteristic of psychedelic visuals associated with LSD use. 'Trippers' frequently talked of their experience of Paisley fractals, while fabrics and clothes, badges, colouring books and wallpapers were produced with the pattern. When 20 years later, in 1980s Los Angeles, a music scene emerged that went back to the music of the period and recycled some of its central characteristics, it became known as the Paisley Underground.

2007

The USA Senate ratifies a free-trade agreement with Peru, negotiations for which had been started in 2005. Warnings were made that this would have a devastating impact on Peruvian cotton farmers, whose pima cotton had a long history as among the very best, and whose genetic make-up had been copied at the start of the 20th century by the USA's agricultural service at its experimental farm in Sacaton, Arizona and become the standard luxury cotton grown there whereas the Peruvian state repressed rather than developed other special varieties. Beginning in 1931 it implemented a series of laws and decrees aimed at destroying perennial pigmented forms of native cotton, in an effort to protect the all-white varieties that it perceived to be commercially viable. Nowadays there is a significant premium for coloured cottons.

China has set out a vision to revive the famous overland trade route to Europe that was first formed more than 2000 years ago, but instead of camels and caravans hauling spices and textiles, the route would now consist of trains hauling people and modern freight. Anchoring the plan is a 6000-km high-speed link from the western Xinjiang Province that passes through Kyrgyzstan, Tajikistan, Uzbekistan, Turkmenistan, Iran and Turkey to Bulgaria and, from there, straight into the heart of Western Europe.

As the Free Trade deal was being negotiated it was pointed out that the 25,000 US cotton farmers received approximately $3.5 billion in subsidies after a further increase in the 2002 Farm Bill, while 28,000 Peruvian farmers receive no subsidies. Further, that under a trade preference deal tied to coca eradication (despite its being legal within the country), although Andean textiles could enter US markets, this was only if they were made mainly from US cotton. The warnings that the trade deal would decimate Peruvian cotton farming were not taken into account, and the results were predictable. Annual production of Peruvian cotton had been around 90,000 metric tonnes in 2007. By 2010 it had fallen to 22,000, that is, to a quarter of what it had been. In 2011 there was talk of it rising again to 38,000 tonnes, but this was only because the rainy season was late and farmers have switched to it temporarily from rice and corn. The usual rationalisations for this devastation have been made, the small size of farms, 'inefficiency', and so forth, with no mention of those US subsidies.

The Alan Garcia neoliberal government, very keen on such Free Trade deals, and made a similar one with China that came onto effect in 2010. All this to the benefit of mineral exports and the signing of mining deals with China that are opposed by local Indigenous people. Already in 2004 there was a political battle between pro-safeguard groups, especially in the clothing and textiles sector, and anti-safeguard mineral exporters. When the China deal was first proposed in 2007, *The National Institute for the Defence of Competition and Intellectual Property Rights* ruled that "no harm was being done to local industry from Chinese textile imports". That in fact quite the reverse, an increase in tax revenue as well as local employment was the consequence. Another official report from the Peruvian Customs authority however showed that between 2005–2013 237 million items of locally produced textile items from the Gamarra textile district of Lima had been replaced by Chinese imports and that 30,000 jobs were lost, Chinese products being 40% cheaper. When the Free Trade deal was signed it was said to exclude textiles after lobbying from the Gamarra district, but an anti-dumping rule was abolished in 2012.

Luis Jacobs

The tattoos are a manifestation of the Shipibos' central myth of the world as infinite pattern. Rather differently in the 16th century the Spanish bishop in Mexico, Vasco de Quiroga, wrote to the Council of the Indies about slaves taken from Africa: "They are branded with iron on their face and the initials of their successive owner are oriented on their skin; they are passed from one owner to another, and some bear three or four names, so that the face of these human beings who were created with God's image has, through our sins, been transformed into writing paper."

Commercial plain weave cotton called tocuyo, with embroidery; technique: plain woven/warp; acquired from the producer in Pucallpa, 1978. The Shipibo designs are traditionally applied to natural un-dyed cotton (which the designers often grow themselves) or on cotton dyed in mahogany bark (usually three or four times), which gives the distinctive brown colour. The producers paint using either a pointed piece of *chonta* (bamboo) or an iron nail with the juice of crushed *huito* (*Genipa americana*) berry fruits, which becomes a blue-brown-black dye once exposed to air. For the Amazonian Shipibo all designs are visual music. They are representations of the creator of the universe called *Ronin Kené*, whose skin has a radiating, electrifying vibration of light, colour, sound, and movement and is the embodiment of all possible patterns and designs past, present, and future. Each pattern is a visual code which can be transformed into music. One can "listen" to a song or chant by looking at the designs; likewise one can paint a pattern by listening to a song or music. Although in our cultural paradigm we perceive that the geometric patterns are bound within the border of the textile, for the Shipibo the patterns extend far beyond these borders and permeate the entire world. By re-creating these patterns in their art, the Shipibo reconnect themselves to this original code. Drops from *piripiri* (a species of *Cyperus SP*) berries are squeezed into the eyes of girls to give them the vision for the designs; this is only done once and lasts a lifetime. Shaman-led ceremonies of healing, self-knowledge and religion use the hallucinogenic herb *ayahuasca* as a means of access to cosmic visions. The patterns of *kené* are part of the heavenly world that becomes visible through the handwork of women. "The shaman tells us that the whole visible world is covered with invisible patterns." It is the responsibility of the shaman to rescue the designs of the heavenly world and transmit them to the women. The production of these designs on all the objects of material culture gives power and protection to the home, to individuals, and to the whole group. Through *kené* designs, the culture of the Shipibo is at once defined, decorated, and owned both by individuals and by the group.

Gold

A llama wished to have / golden hair, / brilliant as the sun, strong as love / and soft as the mist / that the dawn dissolves, / to weave a braid / on which to mark, / knot by knot, the moon that pass, / the flowers that die. 'All that glistens is not gold.' The phrase is steeped in a European moralism, both wary of beauty and thoroughly hypocritical. It was not a view shared by Andean societies from long before the Incas and far into those territories they did not conquer. Gold and silver were valued for their colour and craftwork, metallurgy was both colour- and surface-oriented, so that sophisticated methods of the gilding all kinds of metal were common. For them, surface was not a deception, but the visible manifestation of an inner state. This was of no interest to the Spanish invaders, mostly adventurers, for whom gold meant money, the ability to buy anything, and thereby to raise their social status. Their own aristocracies, it is true, liked the appearance of gold thread woven into their velvet clothing, indeed in Europe there were two separate guilds for gold thread craftsmen, beaters and pullers – though in sophisticated India there were seven separate crafts – but for them it was precisely the appearance of such thread that did matter as a signifier of power. For the invaders themselves however, it meant that they too could live like lords, and thus it provoked a greed that saw them ripping off the gold sheathing from the Coricancha sun temple in Cuzco with crowbars, fighting each other, and getting hooked on a childish and cruel fantasy of such greed, El Dorado. Gold was crucial to Inca imperial ideology, according to which they were directly descended from the sun, by saying that the sun talked directly to them through the medium of gold. El Dorado itself, based on shadowy directions to its location left by on a drawing later in the 16th century, is a story that has run and run right up to the present day.

Baron Jean-Frédérik Waldeck, 1766–1875; The artist carried in a *sillero* over the Chiapas from Palenque to Ocosingo, Mexico.

The reality is more brutal and sordid. The story is that a chief of Muisca people around the Lake Guatavita in what is now Colombia was covered with gold dust at the moment of his initiation and either dived in or went out and threw gold pieces into the lake. For these people gold represented the energy that existed in "the trinity of Chiminigagua which constitutes the creative power of everything that exists". They were expert goldsmiths but had to trade outside of their region for the gold itself. However, when a Spanish expedition eventually conquered the area in 1537–38, they got a huge hoard of gold but, still not satisfied, burned off the feet of one leader to find out where there was more, and found none. This kind of cruelty was common to what happened in Latin America. The gold rush kings of 18th-century Brazil were able to "execute violence without any fear of the law", and set new standards in nouveau-riche vulgarity. Anxiety that at some point currencies will not be worth the paper they are written on has pushed the price of the metal to unprecedented levels and this has prompted a new Gold Rush. Impunity this time is for hedge fund managers; devastation reaped on the Amazonian Madre de Dios region and Congolese civilians. The former, an area of Peru, is the source of the river's upper watershed and subject to 'illegal' gold mining, mercury poisoning, deforestation, child prostitution, and the deaths of desperate miners in landslides. Government controls are weak as gold is such an important export for Peru. In the Democratic Republic of Congo 100,000 miners and their families depend on the gold trade that involves it being smuggled to Doha, but it also finances military corruption and heavily armed 'rebel' groups in the east of the country. Its victims, other civilians, wounded, raped, killed, or in constant flight from their homes.

1859

A campaign was begun by Muslim tenant farmers in Bengal against being forced to continually grow indigo as a cash crop for British planters, who were making fortunes from its large-scale export following their arrival from their West Indies plantations in 1788. By 1815, with an increasingly monopolistic position, Bengal was already exporting 3500 tonnes of the dye. During the 19th century it came to be the British Empire's most lucrative activity in Europe: the dye was used in vast quantities in military uniforms and also as the staple textile colourant in China. Any threat to the business was of the gravest concern to its administrators. The price paid to the farmers had been fixed in 1800 and not increased, while the price of rice had increased sevenfold. The situation had been worsened by five years of bad weather and low yields so that the peasants couldn't recoup their advances. Their grievances, anticipating those of so many cash-crop farmers, were expressed in a satirical play, *Nil Darpan*, created in support of the struggle: "Then, if we are to give sixty bighar for the cultivation of indigo, we cannot engage in any other cultivation whatever, then we shall die without rice crops." The planters themselves had formed their own association and blamed the Lieutenant Governor of Bengal, J.P. Grant, for giving the green light to peasant resistance when he advised magistrates to protect the rights of farmers and made a circular curbing excessive demands on them. He was forced to resign before the end of his term. Early in 1860 all the cultivators of the Barasal refused to sow any indigo. Their refusal soon spread across Bengal. In the same year, as the peasant farmers grew in confidence, factories were burned and indigo plants destroyed. The British, worried by the scale and level of self-organisation involved in these attacks, did not send in troops but established a Commission of Inquiry, which was somewhat critical of the indigo business. The disturbances however had longer-term consequences, they "first taught the natives the value of combination" as one observer said. It created a precedent for the Indian Independence movement. At the same time in another empire, the Ottoman Pasha of Sudan was pushing peasants there to produce only indigo at little profit to themselves and to the exclusion of food crops, which was also to create a revolt culminating in 1882. What radically changed the business itself in both places, virtually destroying natural indigo dye as a profitable concern, was the creation of industrial-scale chemical indigo dye, a process which began in this same year of 1859. It was when the German chemist August Wilhelm Hofmann obtained the first synthetic purple dye from coal tar, having worked out how to transform benzene into dye. German and Swiss chemists had a strong motive to break Britain's dominance of the global indigo business. Finally, in 1897, BASF was able to manufacture a synthetic version at a competitive price. The formula was especially hard to crack, but such was its importance that its investors were willing to dedicate to it 17 years of work and 18 million Goldmarks. As soon as the synthetic product was marketed, the local economies of India that had been made dependent on the crop were ruthlessly abandoned. In a British Report that appeared in the *Journal of the Society of Dyers and Colourists* in 1899, one C. Rawson wrote that, "From a scientific point of view, the production of artificial indigo is undoubtedly a great achievement, but if it can be produced in large quantities as to render indigo planting unprofitable it can only be regarded as a national calamity."

Catherine Lord

1 'A bunch of 4 ribbons narrow–Yellow, Blue, Green & Pink'. Foundling 170, a girl. © Coram

December 31, 2011. It's a length of white cotton, loosely woven on a backstrap loom. On it has been stitched a pattern – an Ariadne's maze in black, green, orange, magenta, yellow, teal, crimson, turquoise and black. Or if not a maze, a circuit board. Such metaphors are my translation. The fabric came from Peru. Its pattern was dictated by vibrations that a Shipibo woman heard during a dream induced by Ayahuasca, a psychotropic brew made by fermenting a certain kind of vine and a certain kind of shrub. The fabric is that woman's translation of her dream. As no two dreams are the same, no two weavings are the same. Thirtyfour years ago, when Ines bought the fabric in Peru, she decided to use the fabric as a skirt. Skirt is the translation Ines laid over her body. The elements in this chain are not decoration, but language. But what language? The language of fabric against skin? The language of ornament? Of the bodies of women? Of the dialect Ines and I use between us? Of the peregrinations of objects made for the tourist trade? The text you are reading is my translation of Ines's dream. If you are reading my words in Spanish, you are reading a translation of my translation of her translation of her translation. We skirt the issue. Fabric is delicate. The idea of a dream rendered in thread that travelled from Peru to Vienna to Los Angeles protects each translation from the next. In return for the skirt, I offer an extended metaphor. Historians of the 18th century, particularly those interested in the lives of women, know that the largest collection of textiles used by ordinary people in ordinary life is held by the Foundling Museum in London. Located in Brunswick Square, the museum houses the remains of the Foundling Hospital, an institution created in 1740 to remove from the streets of London the children of women who could not care for their offspring, either because of extreme poverty or because of their unwed status, both conditions

Girls exercising at the front of the London Foundling Hospital school.

being the consequence of 'moral laxity'. (Georg Friedrich Händel and William Hogarth were among those involved.)

By 1760, that is, in a mere twenty years, the hospital had admitted 16,282 children. No records were kept that would identify the child or the parents. Upon admission, the child was given a number and a new name. Parents who hoped to reclaim their child one day left a small piece of fabric which hospital officials pinned to the ledger page that recorded the date of the child's acquisition, along with her weight, hair colour, physical condition, marks on the body and so forth. The scrap of fabric was the translation of a child. An accurate description of the scrap, or the woman's offering of a matching piece of the same fabric, were the only way to reclaim a child. The museum retains about 5000 scraps of linen, muslin, calico, gingham, satin, susy, calimanco, linsey, worsted, and flannels, a world of names for touch against the skin covered with dots, stripes, checks, plaids, flowers, butterflies, birds, and abstract patterns, something like a circuit board. Reds and blues predominate, though rose, pale blue, and lime green are also to be found. Only 152 children were successfully retrieved by this system, something like a coat check applied to infants.

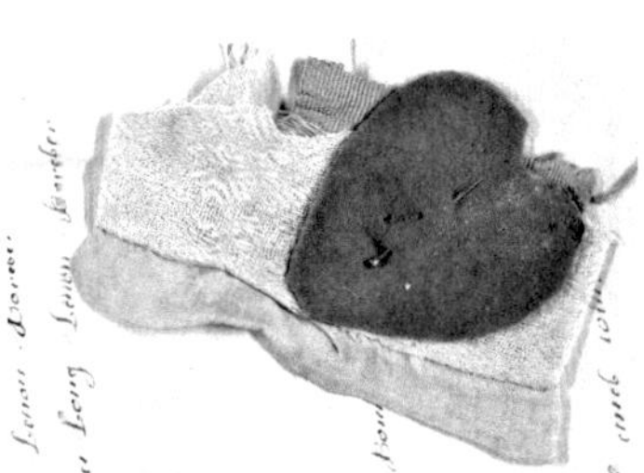

A heart cut from red woollen cloth, a ribbon of blue paduasoy silk and a piece of linen diaper. Foundling 10563, a girl, 1758. © Coram

Q'ero mestanas; wool; 62 x 70 cm, bought in Chinchero, 2010. The two carrying cloths were made in the Quechua-speaking Q'ero community in the Andean Cuzco region of Peru. These people consider themselves to be the last descendants of the Inca. The cloth is used to carry lunch to the fields. The food is placed in the centre, two diagonal corners are folded in, and the final two corners are tied to keep the contents secure. They are highly sophisticated single-loom panels, woven with undyed alpaca yarn and with a few narrow red, pink and black stripes along the edges. The undyed areas have 'spin stripes', created by alternating the spin direction of the yarn. To spin, the fibre is first teased apart with the fingers and then loosely rolled so that the roll can be wound round the left wrist. The newly spun thread is attached to the top of a spindle with a top knot. Depending on the spinners' movement, the result is a Z or S spin. While the spindle is twirling, the spinner draws out the real fibres with her hands to form the thread.
In order to create the four colour blocks, the weaver used a discontinuous warp. Instead of running the entire length of the textile, the warp yarns of each colour turn around a single weft in the centre, creating the dovetailed warp join in the middle of the textile. In their contemporary textiles a key motif is the *ch'uncho* or wild man of the jungle north and east of Cuzco. This symbolic figure dates back to Inca concepts of insider vs outsider, and is closely related to pre-contact, culture-hero mythology. It reflects the insistent survival of a pre-invasion worldview. The masculine-feminine notions of *hanan* and *hurin* are also present here. In ritualised mock battles between the *ch'uncho* and llama herders the former wins, but there is a constantly changing relationship between the *hanan* and *hurin* aspects of the figure.
The religion of the Q'eros is syncretic, mixing European Christianity with elements of precolonial Andean beliefs and rituals, worshipping *pachamama* (Mother Nature) and various mountain spirits, the *apus*. At Easter the importance of woven textiles to life and culture is shown when, during intervals of music, dance and drinking, the finest textiles are displayed high up on the crossbar of a three-poled structure. This is neither competitive nor sanctimonious: there is laughter when a person leaving throws an old rag on as his contribution.

Wool

Until the end of the 19th century wool was the most important textile fibre in the world. Only then was it overtaken by cotton. Wool was the basis of commerce and the accumulation of capital in the European Middle Ages especially in England, the Lowlands, France and Italy where the Medici and other Florence houses built their banking business on the back of it. Its importance can be measured by the number and complexity of tariffs and prohibitions involved in its trading. Most of the raw material came originally from England and the English state depended on taxes on wool exports. Periodically, however, from the 13th to 17th centuries it banned such exports because too much woven wool cloth was being imported (with only the rich exempted), and to develop its own textile industry with tax advantages for broadcloth production. At one point smuggling out wool could be punished by cutting off a hand. The commercial treaties extracted by the English could even lead to war, as in the Anglo-Burgundian war of 1436. It was a very profitable business. Sir Edward Coke, writing in the early 17th century, had it that "nine parts in ten of our Exported Commodities doth come from the Sheep's Back and from thence alone is the Spring of our Riches". The resultant greed provoked the first wave of enclosures of land in England.

"The intent of Spanish acculturation was to rupture the nexus between the objects, their designs and the cultural arena in which they operated. The signifying unity in Andean art was under siege by the late 16th century."

Sir Thomas More wrote of how sheep replaced people, "The increase of pasture, by which your sheep, which are naturally mild, and easily kept in order, may be said now to devour men and people, not only villages, but towns; for wherever it is found that the sheep of any soil yield a softer and richer wool than ordinary, there the nobility and gentry, and even those holy men, the abbots not contented with the old rents which their farms yielded, nor thinking it enough that they, living at their ease, do no good to the public, resolve to do it hurt instead of good."

It is estimated that 3000 medieval villages disappeared between the 11th and 18th centuries. There was a sting in the tail for the greedy – a contemporary text complains that the grazing patterns of the sheep had been altered by these enclosures so that "the gift of fynne wolle is yerly lost." The coarse wool meant a greater emphasis on producing worsteds, while developing cross-breeding with the Spanish merino sheep which at this time were also being introduced to the Americas by Spanish invaders. In Mexico their numbers increased exponentially, replacing humans already decimated by European diseases. The Spaniards made choices based on production levels current at the time of the invasion rather than on the capacity of the land to support new and different regimes. "A densely populated agricultural mosaic was transformed into a sparsely populated mesquite desert; and the Indigenous people marginalised while land and regional production passed into the hands of large landowners. It meant the conquest and domination of the Indigenous societies and their physical world."

Some 250 years later fresh land-grabbing to remove people to make way for sheep began in two places far apart. In Scotland the notorious Highland Clearances that provoked Marx into his angriest writing in *Das Kapital*, were systematic acts of betrayal by the leaders of its clans. They ditched tradition for the money that could buy them grand town houses, art collections and social status in London and Edinburgh. Their clan tenants, living a life of poor-man self-sufficiency, did not pay enough rent compared with what sheep magnates were prepared to pay. With the usual talk of progress, a reign of terror followed well into the second half of the 19th century, the homes of existing tenants burned down in front of their eyes; imprisoned or killed if they resisted. It brought this curse from the Gaelic bard of the Chisholm clan, Donnachadh Buidhe: "Destruction to the sheep from all corners of Europe! Scab, wasting, pining, tumours on the stomach and on the hide. Foxes and eagles for the lambs! Nothing more to be seen of them but fleshless hides and the grey shepherds leaving the country without laces in their shoes."

At the very same time Europe was being supplanted as a wool producer by British-colonised Australia. Unlike the usual sequence whereby colonial policy was later applied to the countries of the coloniser, with enclosure and sheep, the process was copied from what had already happened in Britain. We have no record of the curses of the Aboriginal people of the continent but they must surely have been many. The British government granted Aboriginal land to big pastoral companies. White settlers here poisoned and hunted Aboriginal people and abused and exploited Aboriginal women and children and, where lands were sought for more sheep, they were pushed deeper and deeper into the more desert-like interior where there was less to hunt. With less food, in addition to terror tactics against them, their numbers fell. In Tasmania it was a case of genocide. Breeding experiments improved the merino sheep for Australian conditions and the population increased 13 times over in just the 30 years up to 1850. Despite some brilliant guerrilla warfare by the Eora people and their strategist Pemulwuy, settler revenge attacks like the Risdon and Ryall Creek massacres and then a coordinated 'pacification by force' meant that by 1860 Europeans occupied over 400 million hectares of Aboriginal land and from the 24,000 sheep in 1830, by 1860 there were 20 million.

Even though woollen cloth was produced and consumed in volumes equal to that of cotton until the beginning of the 20th century, it is now a minority fibre, representing 6% of global cloth production as opposed to cotton's 50%. This is partly because it is not favoured for its feel, especially in warmer climates. In the late 17th century the East India Company soon discovered that in India, to their chagrin, the finest wool broadcloth "is so little regarded by the people of this country that they use it seldom". In addition, it requires the labour-time-consuming methods of weaving, knitting and embroidery in order to introduce coloured patterns. In the late 16th century the promoter of English industrial espionage, Richard Hakluyt, understood the importance of pattern and colour: "Fir that England hath the best wool and cloth of the world, and for that the cloths of the Realme have no good vent if good dyeing not be added: therefore it is much to be wished, that the dyeing of forren Coinyeries were seene, to the end that the art of dyeing may be brought into the Realme in greatest excellence." But, unlike cotton, wool has never been good for coloured printing and painting.

In the contemporary world it has become more of a luxury fibre, though the association with land-grabbing has not changed. In the contemporary world of the Americas, Benetton – the biggest consumer of virgin wool in the world – has become the largest landowner in Patagonia, with a 2.3 million acre estate for sheep. Despite the right-on image, Benetton has shown no shame in asserting the rights of private property against attempts by Indigenous Mapuche people around Leleque to assert their traditional, communal rights.

1580

When Montaigne stopped in a little French town in September 1580, he heard an unusual story that he recorded in his travel diary. It was about seven or eight girls who agreed to "dress up as males and thus continue their life in the world. One of them set up as a weaver ... fell in love with a woman, courted her, and married. The couple lived together for four or five months, to the wife's satisfaction," Montaigne reported. But then the transvestite was recognised. "The matter was brought to justice, and she was condemned to be hanged, which she said she would rather undergo than return to a girl's status; and she was hanged for using *illicit devices* to supply her *defect* in sex." What Montaigne does not tell us is that contrary to what is assumed, tapestry weaving was men's work and exclusively so, using both low-warp and high warp looms. The pre-industrial division gendered division of labour meant "weaving was a predominantly male occupation, a pattern that characterised nor merely much of pre-modern Europe but also Egypt, India and the non-Indigenous production of Mexico". Given also the dominance of household production of textiles, the man as family head was at the top of the labour hierarchy and this was reproduced in the labour process: women serviced the male weaver by spinning the yarn he would use. In most parts of the world, spinning was women's work. An estimate for Holland at this time was that up to 90% of spinners were women and their 'over-supply' kept wages low. At the same time, from the Middle Ages onwards, "most women were excluded from vocational training and from guild-regulated jobs, which made it difficult for them to acquire the necessary skills forwell paid jobs". Hardly surprising that Montaigne's victim/heroine should be fatally unwilling to accept her given role. Opposition from patriarchal society to women working in textiles continued into modern times. When in 1951 "poor village girls" started work at the Dalmatinka

Designer Karl Lagerfeld walks the runway during the finale of the Chanel show, which was staging a 'feminist' protest, 2015.

Womer of Naples in a brothel in 1945.

spinning mill in Croatia, they were labelled as prostitutes and the factory a whorehouse. The night shift especially caused a moral panic. As there was no bus service, the women had to cycle to work from their villages. Old women crossed themselves when they passed and respectable families kept their daughters away from the factory and its workers. In present day Bangladesh, despite the primary importance of the industry, women workers have been denounced by Islamists in similar terms.

Ferdinand Schmatz

Das Öffnen der Schachtel von Ines
bringt etwas vor den Schein.

Das Muster:
Kein Brettchen, kein Bändchen.
Ein Flirren.
So ein Stoff!
Sichtbar und greifbar.
Noch:
ohne Begriff
Doch:
etwas wirkt.
Wirkt auf den Gedanken ein.
Etwas.
Der Stoff.

Der Stoff
webt sich in mich und mich in sich
hinein wie hinaus:
Ohne Brettchen ohne Bändchen –
mein Verlangen, nicht endlich auf ein Ende hin,
sondern, endlich! zu sein:

JETZT

Das Wort "endlich" doppeldeutig.
Ein Wort, mehrere Bedeutungen:
"Endlich" und "endlich".
Zwei gleiche Wörter stricken verschiedene Muster.
Buchstäblich ist das eine das Andere.
Bildlich nicht.

Das Wort "unendlich" meint "ewig", "ohne Ende".
Eine Bedeutung, mehrere Wörter.
Ein Wort strickt verschiedene Muster.
Buchstäblich ist das eine nicht das andere.
Bildlich schon.

Die Schachtel der Wörter ist endlich.
Die Bildung zu Worten unendlich.
Es kommt auf die Muster an. die hervorkommen.
Auf die Verbindungen, auf die Bande,
wie sie geknüpft werden, die Bändchen auch.

Manchmal kann die Bande auch eine Gruppe sein.
Sie webt ihren Stoff.
Es ist der Stoff, der sich vom Mantel der Macht abhebt.
Unter dem Grund.
Löst er sich.
Oben.

Er verknüpft "endlich" mit "unendlich":
Des unendlichen Lebens endliches Tuch.

Das alles, Buchstaben, Silben, Wörter, den Satz
halte ich in Händen und im Denken, das im Auge sitzt
mit den Fingerspitzen im Verstand.

Gewoben wird mit der Hand.
Das Denken wird ein Schauen.
Gedacht wird auch mit Händen und Wörtern.

Opening the box from Ines
brings something forth, it seems.

The pattern:
No card, no ribbon.
A flutter.
Such a stuff!
To be seen and touched.
Still:
no definition
But:
something works.
Works on the thought.
Something.
The stuff.

The stuff
weaves itself into me and me into it
inward and outward:
With no card, no ribbon –
My longing not for a finite – *endlich* – end,
but *endlich* – finally! – to be:

NOW

The ambivalent word *endlich*.
One word, more meanings:
endlich and *endlich*, final(ly) and finite(ly).
Two same words knit different patterns.
One is literally the other.
Figuratively not.

The word *unendlich* means 'perpetual', 'unending'.
One meaning, more words.
One word knits different patterns.
One is not literally the other.
But figuratively so.

The box of words is finite.
The figuring of words infinite.
Depending on the patterns brought forth.
On the bonds, the bands,
how they are bound, the ribbons too.

Sometimes the band (the gang) can also be a group.
It weaves its stuff.
The stuff that sets itself apart from the robe of power.
Under the ground.
It unravels.
Above.

It binds *endlich* to *unendlich*:
Final cloth of endless life.

All of which – letters, syllables, words, the sentence –
I hold in hand and in thought that sits in the eye, finger-
tips in the mind.

Weaving done by hand.
Thought becomes looking.
Thinking also done by hands and words.

Erkennen ist Tun.

Die Schrift im Denken geschrieben mit der Hand.
Geschrieben. Gezeichnet.
Auf Papier,
Auf dem Tuch,
Im Bewusstsein.

Wörter wie Wolle.

Die Wolle. Das Wollen.

Ich will Wolle weben, wie jene, die den Stoff gewebt haben, den Ines mir geschickt hat.
Die waren und sind sehr geschickt.

Ich wollte schreiben, dass ich auch so geschickt sein will.
Nämlich:
Nicht talentiert, sondern wagend in der Verknüpfung.

Übrigens:
Auch das Wortspiel von "wollen" und "Wolle" ist buchstäblich
nicht übersetzbar.

Dann eben anders.

So – ein Stoff aus dem die Räume sind.
Dort, wo dieser Stoff zu Hause ist.
Die "Räume" spielen auf die Träume an.
Es heißt ja:
Der Stoff, aus dem die Träume sind.

Das ist nicht übersetzbar.

Englisch hieße das "room" und "dream".
Aber es klingt ja ähnlich.
Immerhin.
Wenn wir hören und schauen, ist das Übersetzen eine greifbare Sache, wie ein Gegenstand, der dich umgibt, der aus dir kommt oder den du gereicht bekommst

– ein summendes Ding, schwebt, vibriert, stört die Blüte und erfüllt sie dadurch. Die Bienen tanzen im Gewebe der Waben.

Flechten. Verflochten entsteht das Muster. Mein Text ist keiner aus Textilien, aber ein Wort verflechte sich mit dem anderen zum Gewebe des Sagens,
das gehört hier sehr wohl auch noch hin.

Der Stoff spricht.
Ich höre und schaue in die Hände derer, die ihn gewebt und geschickt haben.

In die Schachtel von Ines hinein gelegt, kommen wir alle zusammen aus ihr.

To acknowledge is to do.

Writing written in thought by hand
Written, drawn.
On paper,
On the cloth,
In consciousness.

Words as wool.

The wool. The willing.

I want to weave wool as they wove the stuff that Ines sent me.
They were and are so able.

I wanted to write that I also want to be so able.
Namely:
Not talented, but bold in binding.

And in passing:
The word-play with 'wool' – *Wolle* – and *wollen* – 'to will' – isn't literally
translatable either.

Another way again, then.

So – a stuff that rooms are made of.
There, where the stuff is at home.
The word *Räume* – 'rooms' – plays on *Träume*, 'dreams'.
It's called:
Such stuff as dreams are made on.

That's not translatable.

But the English 'rooms' and 'dreams'
Ring similar.
All the same.
If we listen and look, the act of translating is a thing to be touched, like something that surrounds you, that comes out of you or that you receive.

– a humming thing that hovers, vibrates, disturbs the bloom and so fulfils it.
Bees dance in the tissue of the combs.

Entwining. The pattern emerges entwined. My text is no text of textiles, but one word shall entwine itself with the other in the tissue of saying: this must be said here too.

The stuff speaks.
I listen and I look into the hands of those who wove and sent it.

Placed in the box by Ines, we all come out of it together.*

Centre cradle with two handles, one with loop; used for herding, dance, festivals; alpaca, wool, acrylic fibre, pompoms; acquired in Lima, 2008. The *waraq'a* was an Inca insignia and one of their chief hunting weapons. The original fist-braided slings were only made in two places worldwide: in Tibet and the Andean highlands. The technique of fist-braiding was done over the fist, sometimes manipulating up to 92 loose strands, without any other tool, and was used to make round, flat, square and rectangular braids. The Incas (1400–1534 CE) made their slings out of plant fibre and alpaca wool, though now they are made mainly out of sheep's wool. Tibetan slings are much coarser and are made out of yak's, goat's or sheep's wool. Nowadays slings are used mainly in herding, to scare off predators and to guide the animals. They can fling stones accurately over long distances. More elaborate slings are made to be worn wrapped diagonally around the body in dances and ritual battles, which are known from ancient times through chroniclers like Bernabé Cobo (1653): *When the moon was new, those who had been knighted came to the plaza with new clothes, black tunics, beige mantles and white plumage, and with their slings in their hands they divided into two bands, one composed of those from Hasan (Upper) Cuzco, and the other from Hurin (Lower) Cuzco. ... they came to prove their strength until the Inca rose and calmed them. ... then they sat down in friendship and offered a sheep to the new moon.*

Hats

"Hats in today's Bolivia are descended from Europe, brought by conquistadors and merchants; but they have been adapted to belong to this land and these people. Originally they were like cattle brands, compulsory disguises that helped each Spanish master to recognise the Indians he owned. As time passed, communities began to deck out their headgear with their own stamps of pride, symbols of joy; stars and little moons of silver, coloured feathers, glass beads, paper flowers, crowns of corn ... Later the English flooded Bolivia with bowlers and top hats: the black stovepipe hat of the Potosí women, the white ones of those of Cochabamba. By some mistake, the borsalino hat arrived from Italy and settled down on the heads of La Paz's Indian women. The Bolivian Indian, man or woman, boy or girl, may go barefoot, but never hatless. The hat prolongs the head it protects; and when the soul falls, the hat picks it up off the ground." The

Dic de Pago

mestizas in colonial towns developed a new-found love for European fashions: among other things, they fell for hats. In pre-columbian times, hats never existed in the Andes; men wore little caps and women folded cloths on top of their heads. Then European women arrived in the wide-brimmed hats fashionable in the 17th century. The colonial workshops were making hats for Europeans and for Indigenous women, particularly the *mestiza* class. These hats are still the same today. British military invaders adopted the topee for themselves in tropical colonies. It was a helmet made of cork or pith, and typically hybrid, merging the German *Pickelhaube* of the Franco-Prussian war with the *salakot*, a traditional Philippine design. It was then taken up by white civilian invaders everywhere as if to mark themselves off comprehensively from the 'natives'. Meanwhile, just as it became so generally adopted in the 1880s, a new vulgarity in hats developed amongst the English rich, beneficiaries of the British Empire."Hats piled high with white wings ripped from innumerable doves could be regarded as 'chaste' symbols of innocence, and the comment 'it would be better taste to wear only two or three as half a dozen', seems tainted with madness. Fifty million humming birds were slaughtered annually to provide an iridescent aura, or to be stuffed and stuck into mountains of false hair from which unfamiliar environs they peered out glassily, their tails raised and studded with diamonds." The same humming birds whose nests receive offerings in Peru because 'only this tiny bird can bathe in the rays of the sun'. Elsewhere headware became a plaything between rhetorics of tradition and modernity defined as Western habits, without the subversive wit of Andean women and men. In the Ottoman Empire the Fez was imposed by Sultan Mahmud II, but Kemal Attaturk banned it in 1925. Instead the fashion was for panama and top hats, within the general rule that all men should wear *brimmed* hats.

Lina Bo Bardi

The Thai dictator of the 1940s, 'Philbun' Plaek Phibunsongkhram constantly issued edicts on clothing in the name of the modern and civilised. The edicts involved an obsession with Western-style hats. "Wear a hat for your country" and "Hats will lead Thailand to Greatness". Free enterprise responded by an hourly hat rental service for when the police might be in the vicinity. But the real thrust of these commands was evident in a state radio program 'Dialogues of Mr Man and Mr Kong' (*mankhong* meaning stability) in which could be heard: *Mr K:* To wear proper dress would show that we do not have barbaric minds as those wild people of Central Africa. *Mr M:* That is right. If we go to Central Africa we will see that those barbarians do not dress themselves orderly and beautiful. On the contrary, if we go to London ... Playing both sides of the rhetoric, president Sukarno of Indonesia, while wearing immaculate European clothes, added to this an Indigenous-style black hat, the *peci*. As if to emphasise the ironies of such 'hybridity', its name derived from the Dutch colonial word 'petje', small hat. Meanwhile in 1953 in what is now Ghana, as stated in the *Accra Evening News*: "In the Gold Coast today, hats have become a rarity. The young men walk through the sun, bareheaded, wearing their hair the Nkrumah way and ladies have taken to the turban and handkerchief. For years Gold Coast citizens spent vast sums in hats & became so used to them that going about in the sun without a hat on became unbearable. Meanwhile the men who had introduced this infirmity were gradually discarding their hats. Eventually they were to become acclimatised to the tropics, while the African became a weakling in his own home. Then came Nkrumah on the scene, He opened the eyes of his people to the danger and off went the hats. Hats off to Nkrumah. He is a dynamic leader."

1862

As the American Civil War was being fought, an effective blockade of the export of the cotton produced in the Southern 'Confederate' States was created by forces loyal to the North. The cotton textile industry of Britain, which then dominated the world market, depended greatly on this American raw material, so that the blockade lead to a 'cotton famine' in Lancashire with devastating effect: full time employment in the industry there fell by over 300,000. A similar effect was felt keenly in the newly established large scale textile factories with their worker accommodation and facilities in Lodz, Poland. The Confederacy had itself first banned the export of cotton, believing that its political allies among the cotton merchants and manufacturers of Liverpool and Manchester would force its recognition by the British government. Liverpool indeed was said to be the most pro-Confederate location outside of the Confederacy itself, and the President of the Manchester Chamber of Commerce proclaimed that the "permanent secession of the Southern states was inevitable". However, the plan had misfired, since it had provided the North with the time in which to organise the blockade. In 1862 Frederick Douglass, the fugitive American slave and abolitionist issued *The Slave's Appeal to Great Britain* in which he recognised the suffering of Lancashire workers but nevertheless asked for their support, declaring that the North was fighting against "slavery and barbarism" and that "humanity could not permit the needs of the British mills to determine the future of millions in slavery". This message, though it went against the self-interest of mill workers, had a "profound effect" in Lancashire, as the abolitionist and working class organiser Alexander Innes told Douglass. There was strong backing by workers, as at a mass meeting at Manchester's Free Trade Hall on December 31st, 1862 which passed a resolution, stating "That this meeting records its detestation of negro slavery in America, and of the attempts of the rebellious Southern slaveholders to organise on the great American continent a nation having slavery as its basis". At another meeting of the "distressed operatives of Blackburn" they "earnestly prayed ... that the Civil war may come to a speedy termination on favour of freedom, regardless of race or colour". When the *George Griswold* reached Liverpool with food and cash donations for Lancashire mill workers from the Union side in America, dockers "refused payment for their services". These actions had a real political impact in Britain: the pressure from working class movements, despite their exclusion from political representation, helped block the plans of the imperialist British Prime Minister Lord Palmerston to intervene militarily in the Civil War on behalf of the South and its plantation owners. The cotton mill workers were celebrated by Karl Marx in his inaugural speech to the international Working Men's Association in 1864, whose creation owed much to the campaign. "It was not," he said, "the wisdom of the ruling classes but the heroic resistance to their criminal folly by the working classes of England, that saved the rest of Europe from plunging headlong into an infamous crusade for the propagation of slavery on the other side of the Atlantic". and this when they had borne "patiently the hardships imposes upon them by the cotton crisis".

Half of Atlanta's black wage earners were women, almost all doing domestic work for white households, many as washerwomen. In 1881, twenty of them met and formed the Washing Society; their ranks swelled to 3000 in three weeks. Strike meetings were held every night, and strikers faced arrests and harassment from police. Eventually, the Society settled for paying an annual licensing fee in exchange for higher rates and more autonomy. What followed was that demands from other domestic workers for higher pay were met.

Peter Linebaugh

"Fortune" or Commons? The sling depicted here is from the Andes, and I have been asked to comment on it. Is the sling a tool or a weapon? Is it both? What is the difference? Is the tool-making animal also a killing animal in which both creation and destruction are outcomes by some kind of twisted psychological subconscious process? I wonder whether it was actually used to propel a stone? I myself do not know how to use one, and I am reluctant to experiment, because I did once with a whip which taught me that clumsy handling results in injury. I have respect for the centrifugal force of the arm which the sling only magnifies. I would not know at which point to release the stone. Or rather, since the stone is not in one's hand, which holds instead the two ends of the sling, the release of the stone is accomplished by the release of one of these ends. The sling was a herder's inexpensive weapon against predators. The stones were not slung to hit the llamas but to make a noise on the ground nearby, catching the animal's attention and persuading it to move away from that point of the stone's impact.

The llama is a friendly and curious animal. The llama hums but it also spits. Its wool is lanolin free. It is a herding animal, 40 million years old. At birth all females gather round to protect it from males and predators. Llamas were essential beasts of burden. They made possible the metallic money of the first centuries of capitalism because three hundred thousand of the animals carried the silver ore down from the famed mountain in the Andes, the Cerro Rico at Potosí. Their dung made possible the transition from pastoral to agricultural life. The sling remains a weapon of the weak, to employ a term of James Scott, for the stone throwers of the Palestinian intifada. Slings were used during the Spanish Civil War to throw grenades.

The sling throwers of the Balearic Islands were famed for their excellence, capable of slinging a stone four hundred metres. The sling had a longer range than the bow. It was the first projectile weapon, part of paleo-technics or stone age ballistics. Incas used them as weapons used against the conquistadors. In Peru the sling is called the huaracas. Perhaps in street fighting they are useful in returning tear-gas canisters. What has been the role of the sling, if any, with recent revolts in the Andes? David used a sling against Goliath. "And there went out a champion out of the camp of the Philistines, named Goliath of Gath, whose height was six cubits and a span. And he had a helmet of brass upon his head, and he was armed with a coat of mail; and the weight of the coat was five thousand shekels of brass. And he had greaves of brass upon his legs, and a target of brass between his shoulders. And the staff of his spear was like a weaver's beam; and his spear's head weighed six hundred shekels of iron ...."

Little youthful David instead of looking after the sheep accepted Goliath's challenge to fight. He convinced Saul that he could be victorious because he had smote a bear and bearded a lion while protecting his herd of sheep. Saul, first king of Israel, fitted him out in a helmet, a coat of mail, and a sword. David rejected these and instead put five smooth stones into his shepherd's bag and drew near the Philistines with a sling in hand. Goliath taunted David and promised to feed him to the birds and beasts.

These events took place sometime between 1050 and 1010 BCE. This was the beginning of he Iron Age when the technologies of mining, smelting, and casting were transmitted from the Hittites into the eastern Mediterranean and Europe. The Bronze Age had commenced two thousand years earlier. Goliath is thus showing off both classic (brass) and the latest (iron) materials of warfare while David sticks to the old ways, the ways of his trade, the ways of his ancestors.

"And David put his hand in his bag, and took thence a stone, and slang it, and smote the Philistine in his forehead, that the stone sunk into his forehead; and he fell upon his face to the earth." This is the part of the story that is often told because it shows the valor of the little, the weak, the marginal. A shepherd boy defeats a giant. Skill is superior to brute force, and lightness of being superior to the heavy laden. The story is told in holy scriptures as a lesson of the power of monotheism of a god named Jahweh.

The story continues, and becomes less palatable. David had no sword so he took Goliath's and chopped off his head. With severed head dripping in hand David returned. The women heaped praise upon him singing "Saul has slain his thousands and David his tens of thousands." Saul grew jealous. He tried to hide it by offering his daughter Michal to David as a wife. The King did not demand a dowry "but an hundred foreskins of the Philistines ...". David went to battle and brought back two hundred foreskins, and they "gave them in full tale to the king, that he might be the king's son-in-law." It is a tale of mutilation and the exchange of body parts for women. It pertains to the barbarian stage of patriarchal history. The mutilation of body parts and their triumphalist display was a form of warfare that corresponded to the territorialisation of land, the formation of nations, the violence of boundaries, and the purchase of women.

The sling was thus a "backwards" technology during the "progressive" Neolithic Revolution which in addition to metals, iron especially, was characterised by urbanisation, agriculture, centralised government, and the separation of people into different economic classes, masters and slaves. David's victory with the sling can thus be interpreted as a victory from an earlier social formation, pastoralism, in which private property, the state, war, and class oppression did not prevail. This is certainly the suggestion of the prophet, Samuel, who anointed Saul, king of Israel.

The pastoralist lives in the high lands. I have only read about them in the Andes though I have seen them at work in the mountains of north Wales where they worked with dogs, by whistling, a sound which carried well in the silences of narrow valleys. I thought again of pastoralism because thinking about 'the commons' brings these examples quickly to the researcher's attention. The pastoralist does not own the high places but uses them in common as the animals roam the grasses. That's the story among the Kurds, in the Alps, and perhaps too in the California Sierras when the Basque people settled there high up. The high places of Ireland likewise were pastoral country.

I imagine that this particular sling is neither a weapon nor a working tool. It's design is intricate, its workmanship skillful. Its beauty of colour and material and its beautiful workmanship suggest to me symbolic purposes. What could these be? It may be a work of art. Certainly it is pretty, from afar it looks like jewelry. I learn from the internet that they are objects of interest to collectors. This sling perhaps was ornamental or ceremonial. They were used as accessories in dances and mock battles.

The axe is part of the fasces, that tied bundle of sticks, used by the ancient Romans as the symbol of force, power, and the sovereignty of taking life by war or capital punishment. You see the fasces in the chambers of power. The warden of Attica prison interviewed me prior to taking up my duties as a teacher in the maximum security prison of New York. He showed me a stick. The stick was used, he said, in the days of the electric chair, by a prison guard to prod or poke the condemned person to make them move smartly from their prison cell to the room with the electric chair. The diameter of the stick may have been two inches. It consisted of some kind of hard wood, and it was carved with the initials of those who had been electrocuted. By the time the warden displayed it to me capital punishment had been abolished in New York state, it was used merely as a fetish of power. The club, the stick, too, had once been both a weapon and a tool.

When contemplating ending his life ("To be or not to be") Hamlet referred to "the slings and arrows of outrageous fortune". Here "fortune" comes from the sky arriving as unpredictable destructive projectiles far from the person projecting them. It is this distance between cause and effect that characterises the drones that are commanded in Utah and do their damage on the other side of the earth, Yemen, Afghanistan, Pakistan. Only in this case it is not "fortune" but the US Pentagon on behalf of the strategic requirements of empire. Samuel was a favourite of republicans because he warned against monarchy. Samuel was a favourite text for democrats in the 17th century (Levellers, Diggers), the 18th century (radical Jacobins), and the 19th century (Chartists). The Jews, not content with spiritual favour, wished to be like other nations. The passage is full of particularity to primitive pastoral society which yet can easily be brought forward down the centuries of war, taxation, and slavery. These, monarchy, the state, was the blasphemous choice.

"He will take your sons and make them serve in his chariots and with his cavalry, and will make them run before his chariot. Some he will appoint officers over units of a thousand and units of fifty. Others will plough his fields and reap his harvest; others again will make weapons of war and equipment for mounted troops. He will take your daughters for perfumers, cooks, and confectioners, and will seize the best of your cornfields, vineyards, and olive-yards, and give them to his lackeys. He will take a tenth of your grain and your vintage to give to his eunuchs and lackeys. Your slaves, both men and women, and the best of your cattle and your asses he will seize and put to his own use. He will take a tenth of your flocks, and you yourselves will become his slaves. When that day comes, you will cry out against the king whom you have chosen; but it will be too late, the Lord will not answer you." 1 Samuel 8:10–20.

Gerrard Winstanley wrote The Law of Freedom in 1651 after Oliver Cromwell had overthrown monarchy in England. His goal was to describe the difference between Kingly government and commonwealth government. Winstanley compared Cromwell to the Biblical David whose law of

war was that its spoils were to be divided between those who went to war and those who stayed at home. Cromwell's weapon was not the sling, he was a horseman and his cavalry was called "Ironsides". They knew why they fought and loved what they knew.
The liberty of a free common wealth is what Winstanley aims at. The earth is a common treasury for all. Winstanley believed in and advocated what we would call economic equality. He himself had once been a cowherd. "There is no pricking briar in all this holy mountain." Nations, he says, are governed by buying and selling. Covetousness and pride brought in the state; war, oppression, and slavery followed. That is his interpretation of history. His evidence was the Hebrew Bible (the Old Testament), first book of Samuel, chapter eight, verses ten through nineteen. It could belong to the anarchist's credo.
The free people of the common wealth of Israel chose to have a centralised monarchy with powers to tax and tithe, conscript soldiers, make war, render judgment, and take land. Theologically speaking, we could, with Samuel, call it a blasphemous choice. Historically speaking, it was a counter-revolutionary victory of the master class installing monotheism, trade, and war. Certainly it was not inevitable, nor was it what Hamlet called "fortune" which is actually human history. Those who know history know it to be many-sided and far from finished.
I doubt the day of the sling is over.

Awajún, painted, using coloured cotton in the weaving, Amazon, Peru, acquired in Lima, 2009. The US-Peru Free Trade Agreement was signed on December 8, 2005, in Washington, DC, by then-presidents George W. Bush and Alán García. In June 2006 the FTA was ratified by Peru, and in December 2007 by the US Congress. On December 19, 2007 Peru's Congress gave the government a six-month mandate to implement FTA-related legislation by unilateral decree. Making full use of these powers, the executive drafted ninety-nine legislative decrees. On February 1, 2009 the agreement went into effect. The many legislative decrees have grave consequences for the Indigenous people living in the Peruvian Amazon. For example, "LD 1083 (Promotion of Efficient Use and Conservation of Hydraulic Resources) favors the privatization of water to large consumers such as mining companies." "It is LD 1090 (Forestry and Woodland Fauna Law), however, that is at the crux of the debate. This decree leaves 45 million hectares out of the forestry framework, that is, 64 percent of the forests of Peru, including their biodiversity in flora and fauna, making it possible to sell this vast commonwealth to transnational corporations." On April 9, 2009 over one thousand Indigenous communities of the jungle regions started demonstrations, which were peaceful attempts to stop oil pipelines and other industrial encroachments on the forest. These were the result of the Free Trade Agreement decrees. On World Environment Day, June 5, 2009, protesting Peruvian Amazon Indians were massacred by the government of Alán García. Three MI-17 helicopters arrived at a section of the Peruvian highway that connects the jungle to the northern coast, which for ten days had been occupied by 5000 Awajún and Wampi people. The helicopters unleashed tear gas and allegedly also machine guns, while a ground force deployed by Alán García's government began to fire off rifle rounds into the crowd. "An estimated five hundred police bore down on the protesters, some of whom were still sleeping, and opened fire." "The government claimed days after the clash that eleven Indigenous people were dead along with twenty-three police agents. The Indigenous organizations reported fifty dead among their ranks and up to four hundred disappeared. According to witnesses, the military burned bodies and threw them into the river to hide the massacre, and also took prisoners from among the wounded in hospitals." Garcia declared the Indigenous elements to be standing in the way of progress; to be blocking the path of National development; wrenches in the gears of modernity; and part of an international conspiracy to keep Peru down. In a troubling statement on the resemblance of the Indigenous protestors to the infamous *Sendero Luminoso* (Shining Path) armed insurrection, Garcia seemed to imply that the Natives were a band of terrorists. He would not allow anything to get in the way of "our development" of the oil and mineral resources the Amazon has to offer, especially a bunch of "confused savages" who are pawns of the international market and of Indian elites, and who therefore have no real reason to be resisting.

Crinoline

Starting in Britain and France in the early 19th century as a fabric with a weft of horse-hair and a warp of cotton or linen, crinoline soon came to mean a stiffened petticoat starched for extra stiffness or a rigid, 'hooped' skirt. It was an excuse to show off as much material as possible, including the new machine-made lace, especially for the new class made rich by a variety of such textile production innovations. "Their wealth and position had to be obviously eye-catchingly displayed so that they could not possibly be overlooked. The swelling hoops of the crinolines were inflations of their egos, and their skirts became ever more ostentatiously enlarged until ladies had to be warned if she suffers much from the comments of vulgar little boys it would be better, in a high wind, to remain at home."

A young women from Otaheite bringing a present.

By the late 1860s it more or less disappears, and one can see this may be on the wane with a 'satirical' piece in the Manchester Guardian of 16th October 1861. Arguing that "it is responsible for more deaths than any other fashion ever caused" a contemporary writes, "During these five years we have done our best to be patient under an evil we had hoped would be short-lived. We had no comfort in social meetings, because no dinner table and no ballroom, no box or stall at the theatre, no carriage and no boat, could accommodate both our families and ourselves ... For five years we have not had room to move in ourselves round in our own homes ... Worse, the craze has spread to servants; what dangers that presents ... The cook could not pursue her business without incessant personal danger; the housemaid may meet the fate of other housemaids and be burned to death upon the hearth; and the nursemaid is more likely than not to push one of the children off the footbridge. Besides deaths by fire, there have been many by crushing under carriage wheels and in machinery ... there have been drownings, wounds, crushings, burning."

The burning was real enough. Two of Oscar Wilde's half-sisters, Emma and Mary, had died from such a fire, and its prevalence had earlier been remarked upon, with a more sober, if heavy-handedly patronising tone by *The New York Times*. In 1858 *The Times* lamented that "an average of three deaths per week from crinolines in conflagration ought to startle the most thoughtless of the privileged sex".

But if the fashion for these hooped skirts with their yards of material in the metropolis was dying out, the fashion reached the colonies always, at this time, behind the fashion curve. This was especially the case when the diamond mines opened in Kimberly, South Africa. For a brief period African miners were paid better than many in Europe and both men and women spent on clothes. This outraged Lutheran missionaries, all for Africans to be dressed rather than naked but not as they wanted, in 'immoderate extravagance', which for women took the form of crinoline. The Rev. Grüneberger in Pretoria preached about the misuses of crinoline in 1875, which he said was unfortunately spreading among black people. One woman, threatened with its prohibition, said she would convert to the English church where they didn't care about such things. This was intolerable and in the gloating voice of a lynch mob the Reverend wrote, "So I had to take tough action. I went with two elders from house to house, starting off with the very reluctant woman and we confiscated all crinoline to burn them to death before their eyes with the others joyfully laughing."

1851

Isaac Singer is granted USA patent 8294 for a sewing machine, which he had developed from an existent Lerow and Blodgett version. This type had been difficult to use and Singer's innovations had been to make the shuttle move in a straight line rather than in a circle, and the use of a straight rather than curved needle. There had been previous attempts starting with Thomas Saint in England, Joseph Hadersperger in Austria in 1814, and Barthélémy Thimonnier in France, who around 1830 had made a machine that could do straight seams with chain stitches. By 1841 Thimonnier had 80 machines working to produce uniforms for the French army, but these were destroyed by rioting tailors seeing themselves put out of work. Meanwhile in the USA, Walter Hunt had invented an eye-pointed needle machine in 1834; he did not apply for a patent as he feared it would create unemployment, but Elias Howe adapted it and did obtain a patent. That was in 1846, and though his machine was different, in that it used a crank rather than a treadle and its needle moved sideways, he was successful in getting royalties from Singer and the 'patent pool' Singer had created with others in 1854. But it was Singer, and the company he created, who made the sewing machine a worldwide tool both for industry and home working. Despite some technical developments it remains the template of the machine which hundreds of thousands of factory workers, with the longest hours and lowest wages worldwide, continue to use and be used by. With further heavy investment, the Singer company introduced a machine for domestic work. This had a massive impact on 'homeworking' by women who, despite owning this 'means of production' have always experienced the highest levels of exploitation in the textile industry.

The success of Singer was partly built on making machines available on an instalment payment plan, and by its concentrating on marketing and support services. Its innovation in this sphere was the creation of a brand identity. By 1913 it was the 7th largest company in the world; it sold 90% of all family machines in Europe, Asia, Africa and Australasia and had sales of two and a half million sewing machines per annum. This success however was also built on an intensity of labour in its factory in Glasgow where 10,000 machines a week were being produced by a workforce of 5000. In 1911, it employed 12,000 and, using Taylorist methods of de-skilling and time-and-motion, along with a ban on Trade Unions, made workers labour still faster. In that year they called a strike when three 'defect repairers' were taken off a team in the cabinet polishing department so that 12 women would have to do the work of 15 with no increase in pay. They walked off the job and by the end of the day nearly the entire workforce had walked out, overcoming divisions of gender, skill and religious sectarianism. The company went on the offensive by closing the works and making the now familiar threat of moving production elsewhere. In the end the strike was defeated and its 'leaders' blacklisted. Things might have been very different if instead of the avant-garde capitalism of Singer, the machine of John Murray Spear had been taken up. Spear was a US American abolitionist, activist against the death penalty, and advocate for women's rights, who during the industrial revolution organised séances with a group of followers with the stated aim of developing a more user-friendly sewing machine. Guided by the channelled spirit of Benjamin Franklin, Spear believed that the invention should be achieved through what he thought of as a trance dance. Already he had developed a widely distributed sewing machine, but the costs of the patents made it too expensive for ordinary people. Though the séances Spear tried to find a blueprint for a new machine, one which would be significantly cheaper to produce and would serve as an alternative to corporate industrial production. Spear was convinced that the drawings for the new sewing machine already existed in immaterial form and that he had found the key to access them. Each participant in the séance was assigned to a role and would become an automated part of the machine, enacting its essential movements. Together they would form a model for its actions as a working whole. The new sewing machine, "embodying and expressing a bisexual nature", would revolutionise the relations between the sexes by giving women an opportunity to earn enough money to take control of their lives. A prototype was made and production started but sales were slow. Franklin also relayed information to assist in the development of new technology, including a

Joseph Cornell addresses "the embodiment of woman as garment and the sewing machine as creative enterprise".

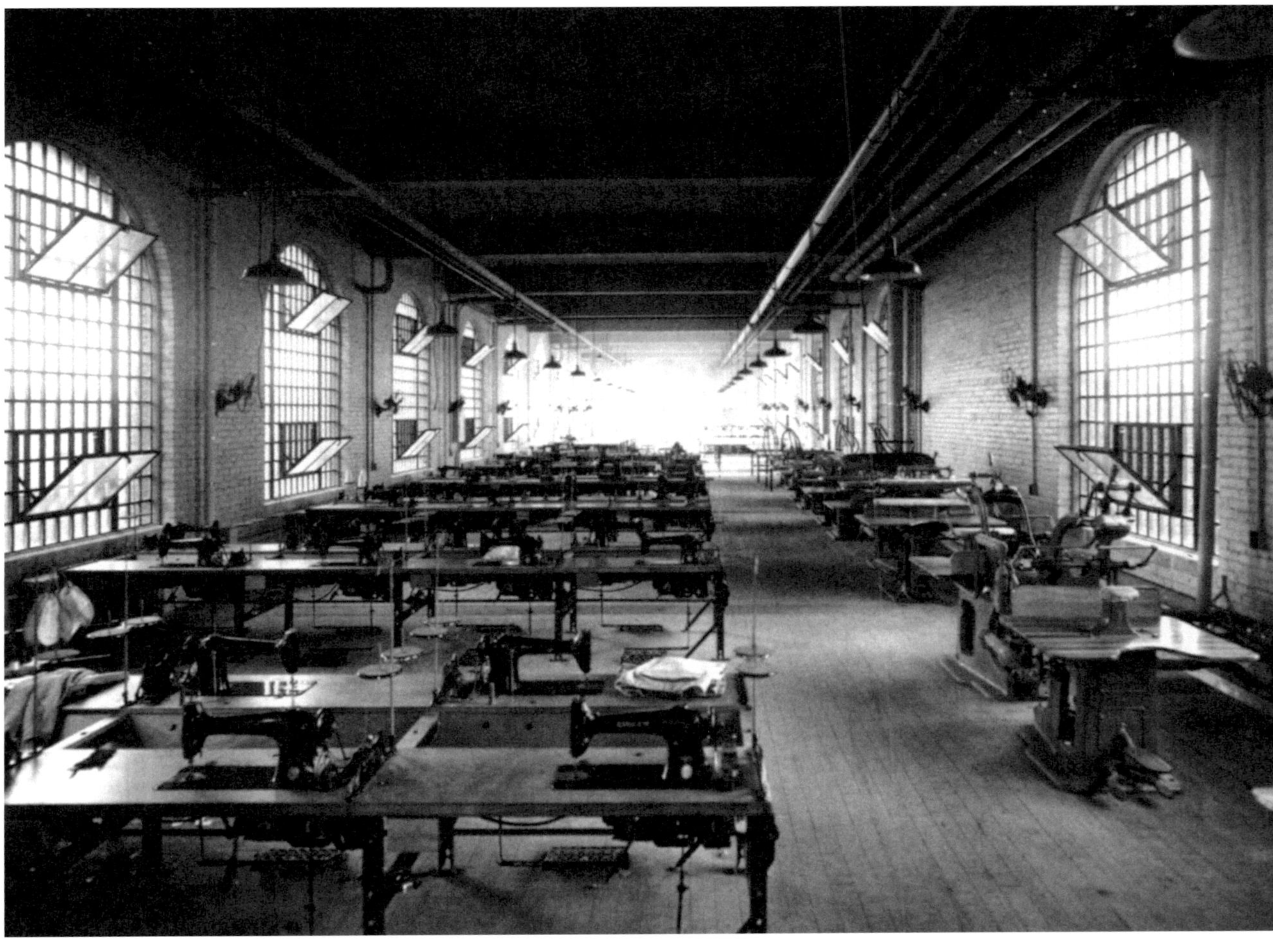

The needle-trades industry was one of more than a dozen occupations for patients at the Narcotics Farm in Lexington, Kentucky, which operated from 1935. Both a prison and a humane hospital until the war on drugs was declared, when the 'humane' went out of the window. The farm was closed in 1975. The machines were all Singer.

perpetual motion machine, an electric thinking machine, an electric ship, and an intercontinental telepathic network. Spear's spiritualism became even more controversial in 1857. Speaking through him, the spirits began to urge free love as a way to regenerate society. His new programme would replace institutionally sanctioned marriage with sexual relations governed entirely by mutual desire and love. He championed the availability of birth control methods and the woman's right to refuse sexual intercourse, even with her husband.

Sewing was already integral to both western and Muslim societies. Girls coming from the Foundling Foundation at Coram Fields were taught to sew there as the only means of making a living in 18th-century London. In this world, the Singer was a "decisively revolutionary machine", as Marx put it, though in his view this revolution was responsible for the de-skilling of workers and "the fearful increase in death from starvation during the last ten years [which] runs parallel with the extension of machine sewing". In the period of its introduction it was crucial in implementing the semi-customisation required to market a mass-produced garment to a growing number of white-collar workers, and it has to be seen in connection with developments in cloth-cutting machinery and mass-produced patterns. Another important development was the shift from the treadle-only machines to stream power, with the latter providing a uniformity of pace and regularity of stitching that the treadle was unable to match. By the end of the 19th century the process of making a jacket in New York had been divided into 37 unskilled sewing tasks. In this sense the sewing machine led not only to de-skilling but also to an increasing 'one-sidedness' in the worker's productive activity. This would be applauded by employers who admired – in the words of the champion of de-skilling, F.W. Taylor – "the unerring accuracy that is gained by years of practice at one thing only".

The effects of the machine have been revolutionary for millions of women and still are, even though there is a world of difference between a Japanese haute couture seamstress; people currently deciding to make their own clothes; a Honduran woman in a clothes factory; and 'homeworkers' in contemporary India.

Boris Ondreička

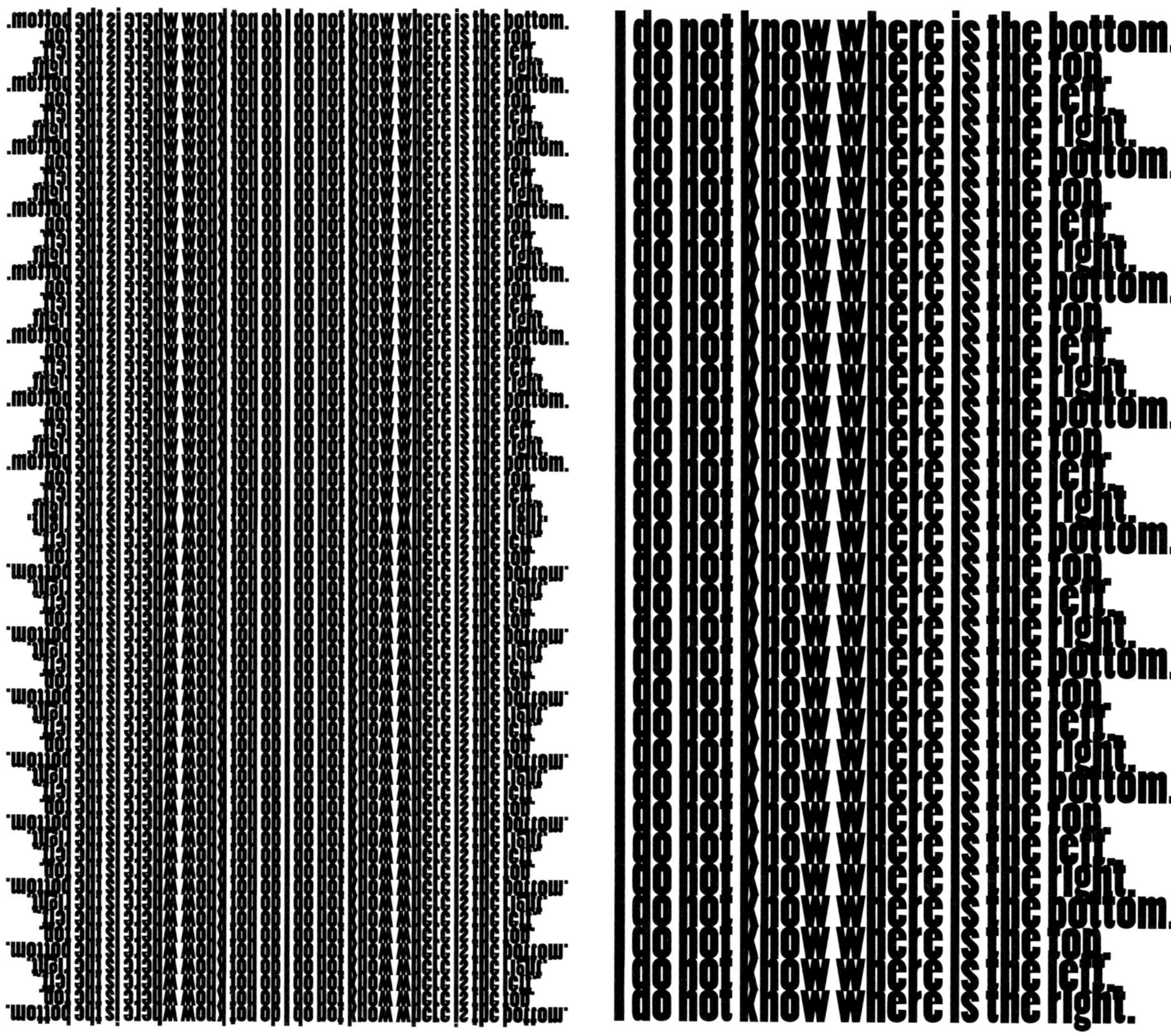

for Ines Doujak, Untitled, September 2011; media and dimensions variable

1831
Camouflage

Devil's Food

Sky and Water
2014

MUSLIN
1907

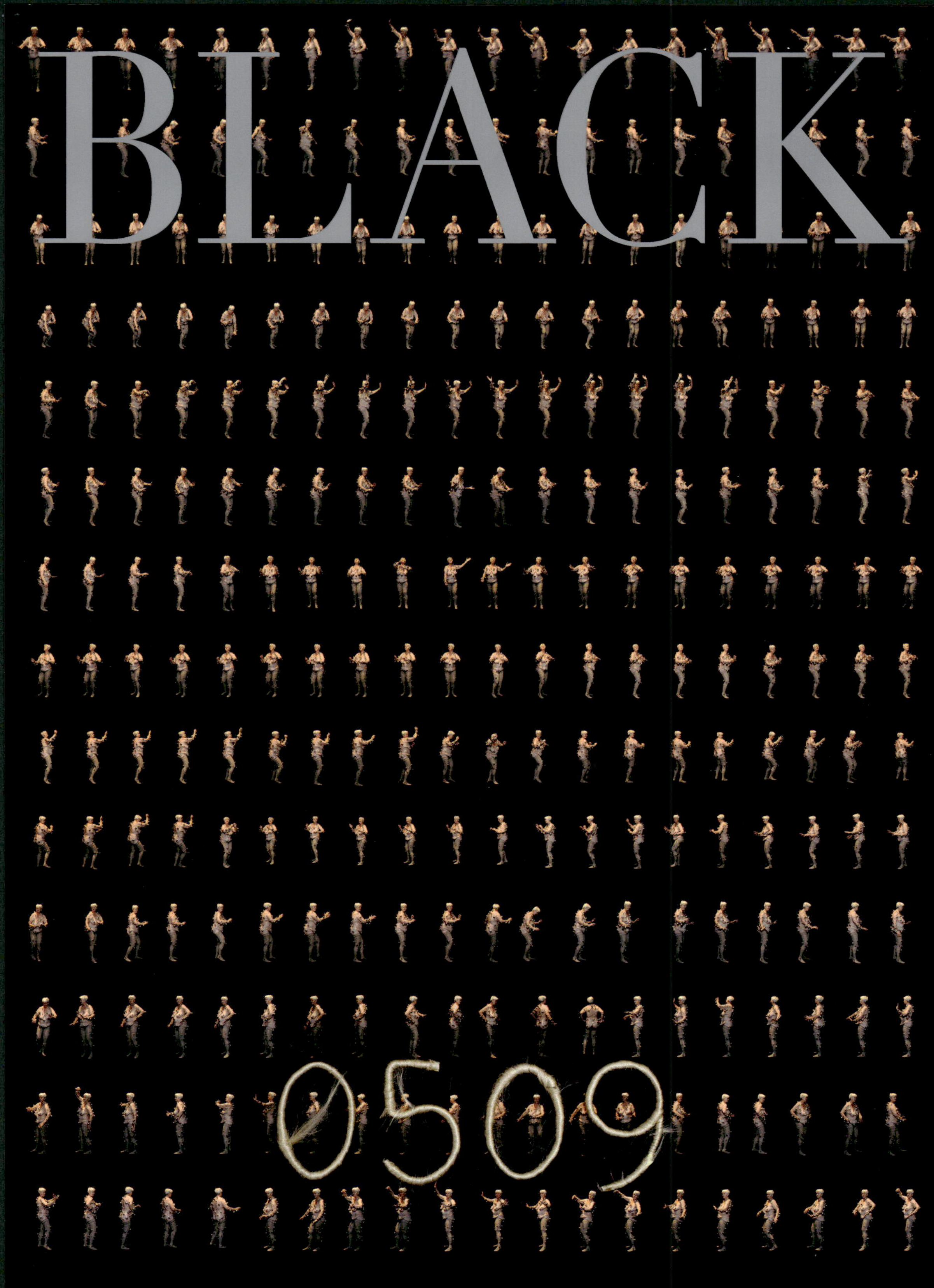
BLACK
0509

SILK
1941

Wood Dyes
2006

Tartan
ASIA
EVROPA
1844

SILVER
1866
PILZE

THE GONADS
Colour Control
2 EFFECTS OF SEX HORMONES ON RABBIT
a. Uterus of immature animal
b. Same after treatment
After treatment
b. Same after treatment
TESTOSTER

Hateful Yellow
2004

Nylon

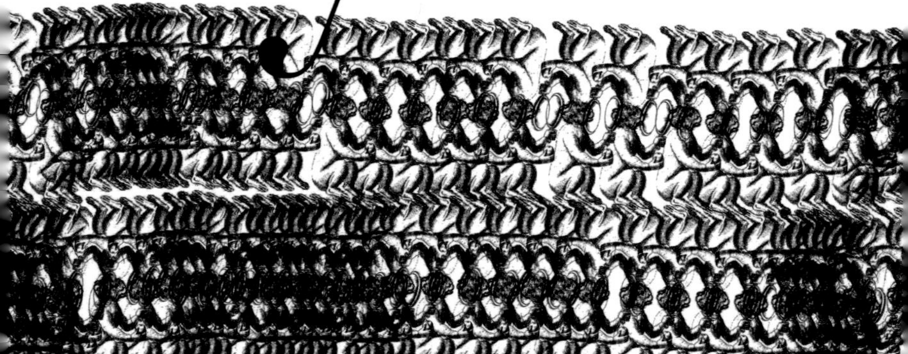

1912

Grey
1780

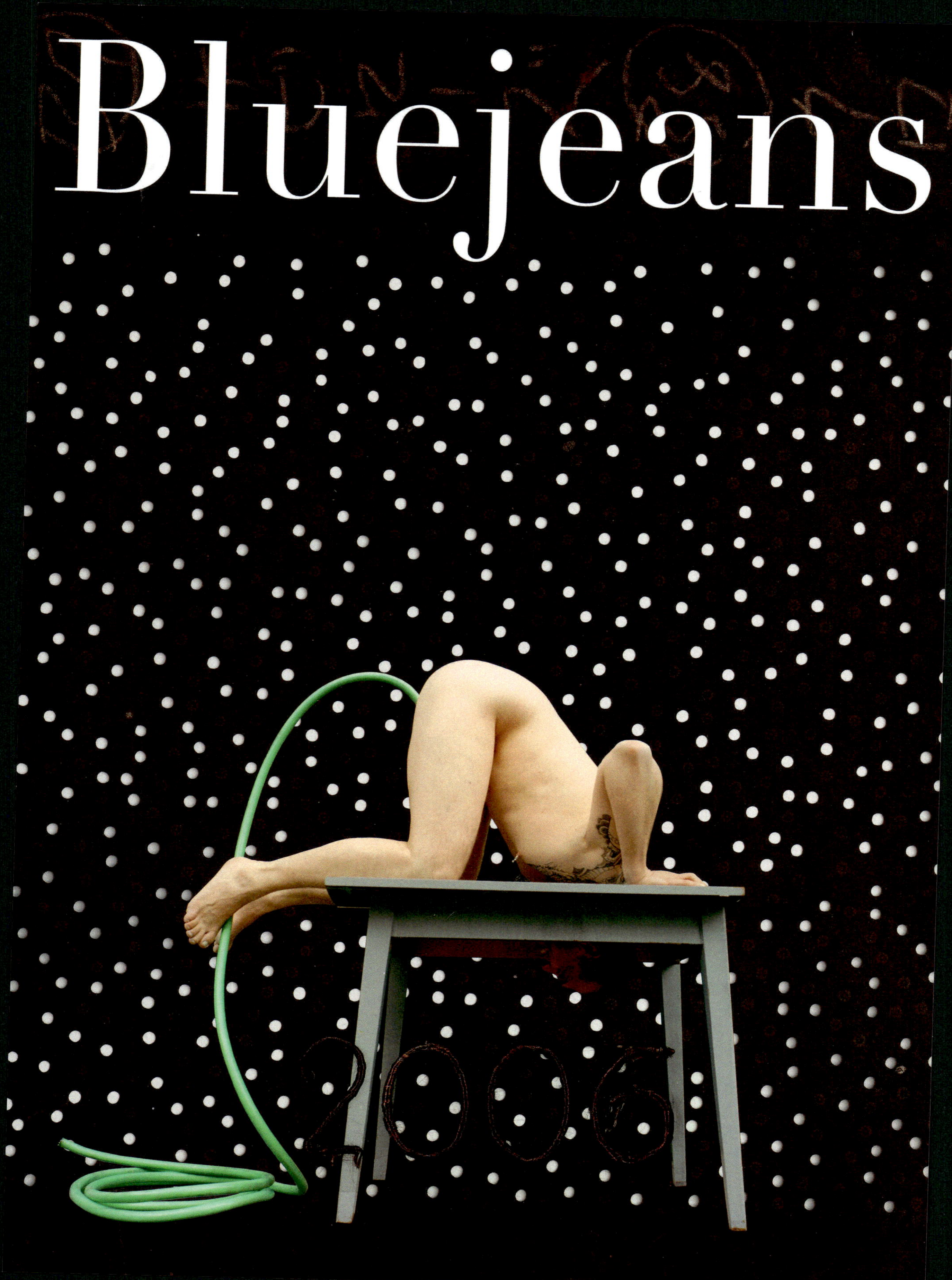
Bluejeans
2006

Pistachio

BLUE
1913

Isoshëta / Monkey-Teeth Bracelet

33

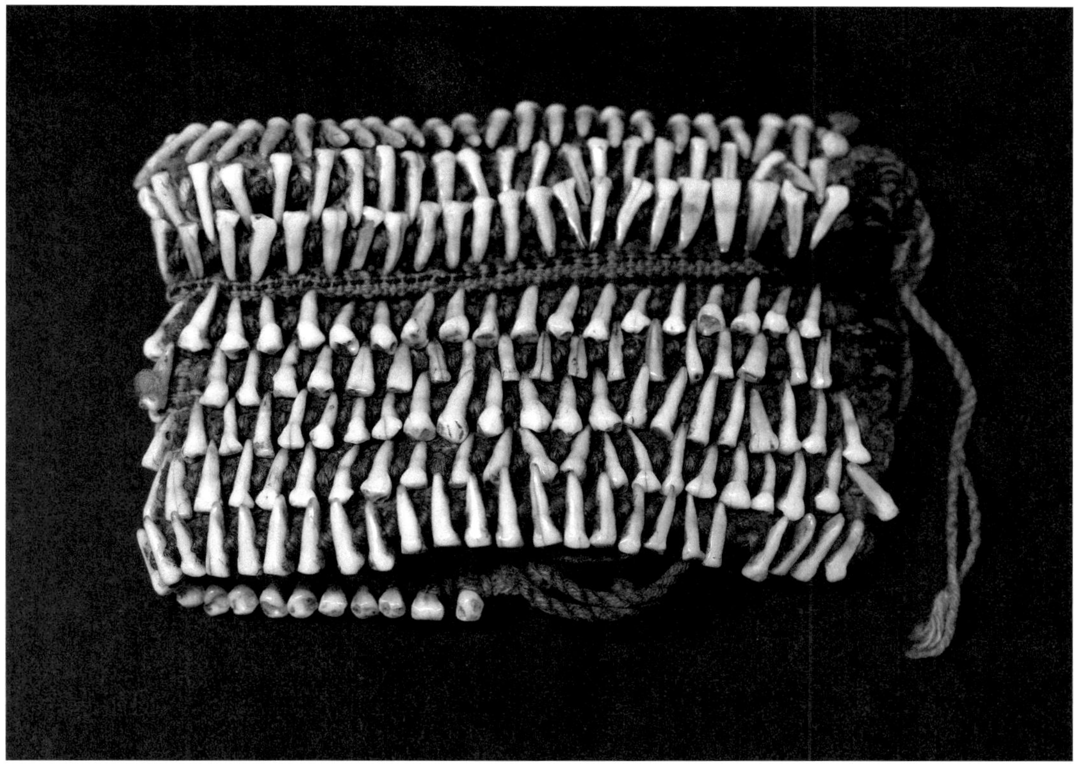

Cotton, monkey teeth; acquired in Pucallpa, 1978, private collection, loan to the archive. "Not only is the monkey, as a kind of Forest Ogre, hairy, humanoid, clever, and oversexed, but he is also dirty, cannibalistic, noisy, laughable, and with underworld affiliations. How can the monkey, with all of its readily perceived similarities to humans, be related both to people and to Forest Ogres? Just as in Western culture, the monkey becomes a burlesque of the human condition, a humanoid buffoon. If one wants to emphasise the petty aspects of human frailties, the Black Jaguar is too awesome a figure to be used, so an allied but considerably less imposing figure must be found: the monkey. Of all the monkeys, the black mantled (*Alouatta palliate*) and red (*Alouatta seniculus*) howler monkeys and related species of varied pelage produce, with the enlarged larynx of the male, the most prodigious output of sound in the forest canopy. Din or random noise is typically aligned with animality, filth and females, in contrast to music, or the ordered tones of male sounds. If the monkey represents the negative qualities of din, the howler monkey is the paragon of monkeys. The noisy aspect of the howler monkey is sometimes further emphasised by aligning him with the noisiest of natural phenomena, thunder. As thunder has an underworld connotation, it is interesting to find that the Barasana see a number of aquatic aspects to the howler monkey. Not only is he identified with the phallic flutes stored underwater and representing male aquatic spirits, he is also identified with the Thunders who dwell beneath waterfalls. Like the similar aquatic-seducer dolphin figure these Thunders put women to sleep through magic for sexual purposes. "The howler monkey ... is a producer of filth: metaphorically, by virtue of the correlation between din and corruption, and literally, since the howler monkey is an incontinent animal which drops its excrement from the tops of trees" and actually uses it as a weapon, whether intentionally or unintentionally, as part of a threat display. The anal continence of the sloth is widely contrasted with the anal incontinence of the howler monkey. To the extent that the retention of excrement can be considered a 'closed' quality, closed orifices being a characteristic of males, whereas the evacuation of excrement is an 'open' and therefore female quality, the sloth is a male-associated figure whereas the howler monkey is a female-associated one. The sloth has a phallic staff, like the sun, and like the sun he uses it to dry up water when in confrontation with the aquatic cayman."

Camouflage

"A chameleon: Its master put it down on a tartan rug and it died of over-exertion." In Tinnis, near Port Said, Egypt, famous throughout the Islamic world for its fabrics, one of the special products made between the 7th and 11th centuries was *bukakalum*. It was a cloth that constantly changed colour and was used for saddle cloths and covering the royal litter. Its name derived from *abu-kalamun*, the chamaeleon. French soldiers wore red trousers well into World War I. In a parliamentary debate before the war it had been deemed un-French and cowardly to make any change. The many thousands of dead and dying soldiers in the mud and trenches of that war finally persuaded them that such honour was of no use to the dead. The blue uniforms of Prussia had changed to 'fieldgrey' before the war, and the British had adopted khaki. The modern-age military use of camouflage began with khaki (Persian for dust) first used by British soldiers in India and Egypt. Originally soldiers applied mud and earth dust to white uniforms. In the dye account books of Henry Day there was a sample of 'one of the first pieces of khaki as used in the South African war' at the start of the 20th century, made by using two natural dyestuffs called Gambier and Cutch. A synthetic khaki was then developed during World War I, a war which provoked a rush of camouflage techniques. "Whether it was the English speaking of 'dazzling', the Germans of '*Tarnung*' (masking and screening), the Americans of 'protective colouration' or the French of 'the art bordering on the miraculous', the catch-cry of camouflage was that it was more important to be unseen or invisible than it was to be protected or invincible." Despite its imaginative use on battlefields, involving much wishful thinking, it did not prevent mass deaths or injuries. Facial injuries instigated another development in camouflage, 'plastic surgery'. The English version of 'dazzle', also called 'razzle dazzle' as applied to ships in the same war was not so much for concealment – or rather of an invisibility made by hyper-visibility – but to make it difficult to estimate a ship's range, speed and direction and thus harder to fire on with any accuracy. It appeared cubist in style but its originator was a far more conventional seascape painter of that time, Norman Wilkinson, but whose experience on military ships during that same period must have focused his visual imagination on not being fired upon. Up to and during the Second World War camouflage patterns emerged. Germany was ahead of the game with uniforms of Leaf, Swamp, Oak Leaf and Pea Patterns. The British employed the artist Roland Penrose and the stage magician Jasper Maskelyne in their Camouflage centre and introduced the Airborne Smock Denison Camouflage in 1942, while the USA, whose uniform had changed in every war from the 18th-century Revolutionary War to the First World War, started to use "frog skin/leopard spot" patterning, with the Leopard Spot still in use for the Bay of Pigs fiasco when, in 1961, an invasion of independent Cuba was easily repelled. Since then a 'lizard pattern' was developed for French troops in which two overlapping prints – usually green and brown – printed with gaps to allow for a third colour, a lighter green or khaki; the British made Disruptive Pattern Material, and now Multi-Terrain Pattern, standard issue. Contemporary development is focused on Digital Camouflage using micro-patterns as being less detectable than larger blocks of colour.

The newest thing in bathing suits on the beach in 1919. The dazzle pattern was designed to confuse enemy ships in World War I.

When they try to catch a chamaeleon / under the mat, / the chameleon takes the colour of the mat / and they can't tell which is which. / When they try to catch a crocodile / the crocodile takes the colour of the water and they can't distinguish him from the current. / When the Wizard tries to catch me / May I take on the agility of the wind / And escape with a puff!

1831

The independent silk weavers of Lyons, France – the *canuts* – begin a cycle of insurrections prompted by a drastic cut in the prices they received from the 'manufacturers without factories', those whose capital gave them control of raw materials and marketing. At the time a quarter of the city's population was dependent on the industry, which had grown from the mid-17th century onwards. Uprisings and repression had taken place before, in 1744 and 1786, but following the introduction of new laws in the first year of the French Revolution of 1791, the 18th century came to be remembered with a certain degree of nostalgia. These laws asserted that in payment disputes the employers' word was to be taken without question, whereas the employee had to prove wrongdoing; banned guilds, unions and the right to strike; and proclaimed free enterprise as the norm. These measures proved more significant in shifting the balance of class power than

the introduction of the Jacquard loom after 1808. Initially opposed by the weavers, the loom was later accepted by them on the grounds that it "had not automated the physical labour of weaving", but rather the "implementing of a design" made by the weavers themselves. What the size of these new looms did effect, along with rent increases in the old city, was an increasing shift of production to the La Croix Rousse area where "one could walk from the base to the top without exposing the cloth one was carrying to the elements". Here, despite the differences between master weavers and apprentices, new forms of solidarity developed, and a new newspaper, *l'Echo se la Fabrique*. To this was allied an awareness and self-determination of beauty in the weavers' own manufactures. Describing the weavers and their work to a British Parliamentary Committee in 1832, John Bowring said that "I was exceedingly surprised at finding

In the Quran the Prophet Joseph is described so beautiful in his brightly coloured *jellabiya* that the women wanted the same fabric. The multi-coloured cloth became prominent in Palestinian dresses, and would change the look of Syrian textiles for generations to come.

among the weavers themselves and among their children, an attention devoted to everything that was in any way connected with beauty, either in arrangement or in colour. I have, again and again, seen weavers walking about gathering flowers, arranging them in the most attractive shapes".

The potential weakness of the weavers' position was the elasticity of demand for their high-quality work. Shifts in the general economic situation could have an immediate effect, and in the lead up to 1831 this was compounded by imports of cheap English silk. The merchant cartel, the *Fabrique*, cut the price that was paid to weavers, to which they responded with the demand that the prefect of Lyon impose a basic minimum price. This was agreed by the prefect on the 25th October, with introduction to take place on November 5th. However, after lobbying by the cartel, which threatened to ignore the tariff, and even went so far as to claim that such an agreement was "against the spirit of the French Revolution", it was watered down, in the now familiar manner, to become 'not legally binding'. On the 21st the weavers retaliated, taking police barracks and raiding the arsenal for weapons. They were assisted in this by the possession of their own contingent of the National Guard – a force open to all respectable citizens – and were able to outsmart the *Fabrique's* contingent. By November 23rd they had control of the whole city. The Parisian government re-took control without bloodshed in December, and abolished the fixed rate, ultimately a victory for the cartel. In 1834 the 'capitalists without factories' again decided to cut what they paid the weavers, whose wages had risen slightly after a renewal of demand – "the orders from America are immense" – and the weavers responded with strikes. Their leaders were promptly arrested. As their trial was about to begin, the weavers, acting in spite of new repressive laws, fought the army and took control of the city. The bourgeois Republican factions of the city tried to co-opt the rebellion, but it was a class issue and was recognised as such by the French state. Led by Interior Minister Thiers, it responded by isolating the city and then attacking with artillery, the strategy later used by the same Thiers against the Paris Commune. This led to many deaths, and in the 1836 trials of 10,000 weavers many more were condemned to deportation or heavy prison sentences.

Anonymous, Horrible Massacre in Lyon, 9th April 1834

Fahim Amir

Like Teeth in Teeth (22610) in reference to Tom Tyler's reading of Georges Bataille's understanding of animality as "water in water".

1. Monkeys have been known as clownish, speedy animals since the Western Middle Ages. When the motorised beasts of the modern day took off – their gait regulated through switches of iron teeth and zags – two German expressions melded into a term for murderous speed: With *einen Affenzahn zulegen* (literally to "put on an ape's tooth") the ape's velocity and the act of shifting gears in an automobile or pursuit plane merged to form the English equivalent of "hitting breakneck speed." In Bahrain, this "ape's tooth" was moistened with the blood of regime-critical protesters. And: Territories laboriously wrested from the Indigenous population in the southern United States should make way for motorised animals – ape's teeth versus the ape's tooth.

2. What does it mean to give the critique of ideology over to the gnawing criticism of animal teeth? For Marx and Engels, it meant evading a public reckoning with their former, philosophical conscience and leaving it over to nature's processes of decay. In vain: the reckoning came anyway, infinitely far away and in an altogether different time, but one that itself felt intimately bound to it. Animal teeth, transpositions, and abandoned theory experience their real birth in the post-present.

3. How to undermine the architecture of the present, to plunge mole tunnels through the colonial character of the notion of contemporality, a contemporality that speaks of human beings who live at the same time, yet are assigned another one? As Brecht put it: the shark, he has teeth, and he wears them in his face. To refuse the meat of this rotting present and fight for the seemingly utopian: the Bengal tiger as a vegetarian.

4. An ape's report to the academy: In the literature of the Moderns, animals are our ontology – they are vivid, graphic description of the irreducible, undivided and eidetic world of the 'other', a world that has been drawn into and pervaded by our own. In the many contemporary Sistine Chapels where animals have replaced God on the ceiling, the desire for contact stubbornly persists.

5. Showing your teeth: The 'West' versus the nuclear program of the peacock's eye, the peacock's eye versus the nationalities in its own territory and versus the entire region and its biters. Who wants to deny to the Other the adornment of teeth that he himself had put in, row by row? Because the wrong person could be bitten, or because the ability to bite precarises the monopoly on biting?

6. The idea of the city as protection from wild animals – in the urban planning concept of the linear city, human beings are to be protected from human beings. If a person's neck has all the charm of a border town, then the band of apes is a meeting of both mimesis and alterity, but also culture and nature, technology and mortality, colonialism and anti-colonialism – and cultural pessimism and "in spite of it all!" Violence is not the bond of all things: the promise is a slip of the tongue.

Phullu / Cloth for Mourning

34

Wool, acquired in Puno, 2008. At four years of age a girl starts on a series of garments of lesser to greater complexity, and with a mixture of designs, including both plain and the more complex 'selected'. At six, she advances to complicated hatbands, at seven to a small food bag, and at eight to her first coca cloth. From ten to twelve she learns warp-faced designs using two or three warp threads and, at thirteen, she starts to make figures with four warps and more. After that she strikes off into creations of her own inspiration. At the same time girls learn the norms of combining colours and the textile configurations that distinguish the weaving of their *ayllu* from those of others. Although the great majority of girls manage to weave figures using up to twenty warps, only the most spirited learn to weave figures using from sixty up to two hundred and more. A weaver increases her repertory by copying small samples and at the same time develops the complexity of her own discourse about textiles in song, narratives, and other oral genres. The action of weaving is like converting something into a person, whereby a defined space is filled in all directions with the things that belong there. Filling the loom means making a person. A weaving is never cut but worn as it is. Cutting a weaving would mean to cut your own hands; it is like killing it.

Many native people in Peru, Brazil, and other South American countries think of the soul as a birdlike entity that can fly from the body at will and often does so during sleep. When the soul returns, the sleeper awakens. Should the soul neglect to return, the sleeper enters the long sleep of death. This cloth was used in the cemetery by friends and relatives, who would place offerings, small piles of grain like corn, quinoa, or barley, or small breads in animal or human shapes, on the tomb. During the night, while all contributors attend a feast at the relative's home, the offerings are taken by spirits.

Devil's Food

Under the influence of the domestic woad lobby and in a pre-colonial mercantilist spirit, European states described indigo as devil's food because it was a far superior dye producing more colourfast blues, but was an import. Perhaps, too, because its earliest production known to Europeans had been by Jews in the Levant. This perception continued until they themselves had either begun to control its production through colonial land-grabs (originally in the Caribbean), or the interests of the dyeing and cloth industries were asserted. Until then dyers had had to take an oath not use the dye. In France a 1609 edict made its use the subject of a death sentence. Its significance there was shown by the way in which indigo made the fortunes of ports like Nantes and Bourdeaux, while ruining the woad centres of Toulouse and Amiens. It had been prohibited in Germany in 1557, and in 1700 magistrates in Nuremberg, a centre of woad production, still enforced a ban. This talk of the devil – in Germany it was the devil's dye – takes place in the latter part of the period of the persecution, torture, and killing of women, mostly older women, as 'witches'.

In the Hausa Kingdoms of Kano, the original indigo dye pits of Kotar Mafa were controlled by women concubines, "raided in acts of war against the west and south". They used indigo cloth as currency, and "became the territorial representatives of the Emir in the areas where they were captured." Their control of the business involved "ancient ideas about indigo dyeing and its mimicking of birth and deep-held taboos about male contact with the dye pot". But at the turn of the 19th century and the establishment of the Kano Empire this power was taken from the women by the Emir and became a large-scale male-dominated business.

English indigo factories in India cornered the world market. The process of turning leaf into dye was unmechanised despite the Industrial Revolution because of the cheapness of colonised labour. It involved the fermentation of the leaf, which was then beaten in vats by workers waist deep in the nauseous liquid. These workers in turn were supervised by white men in pith helmets.

Today the association between the dye and an array of occult knowledge is acknowledged in the case of Dogon women in Africa, and, in another part of the world, on the Indonesian island of Sumba, whose warp ikat cloth has worldwide fame. The women who exclusively make indigo dye are precisely the mature women so persecuted in Europe's witchcraft terror. To be initiated into the secrets of dyeing women need to have had children and ideally will have passed menopause. In practical terms there is a bad smell coming from the dye baths and women who are either pregnant or menstruating are not allowed to go near them. For men it is prohibited, they are never allowed even to observe the process, just as they are not allowed to be present at childbirth. A chicken is sacrificed to a 'witch' from the neighbouring island of Savu, believed to be the originator of the process, but the process is also linked to theories of human conception and the growth of the foetus. Practically, 'the binding mechanisms used in the indigo bath to make the colours fast is also used to stop women bleeding after childbirth.' It is the darkest shade of the dye, a blue-black that is most valued, and this is especially secret knowledge, as is the mix in the baths that involves various plant nutrients and lime. The skill lies in knowing when the almost colourless solube indigo has penetrated the thread enough to be ready for oxidisation, which is when, hung on branches, the pale greenish colour turns to blue. To get the deep blue, further dips are needed but without the lime.

1378

In the city state of Florence, dominated by the wool trade, the *ciompi*, workers without guild status and especially the wool carders, participated in riots in June and July which led to them taking power in the city and, through various shifts in the make-up of the new power structure, holding it until January 1382. The context in which this took place was both political and economic and included a history of attempts by them to organise for status and inclusion in the city's political structure. It was also the period after the Black Death across Europe when there was "a new class confidence that the commoner could change their social, economic and political worlds in practical ways." It is this attitude that is given fictional voice by Machiavelli in his *Florentine Histories*, written some 100 years later, in which someone within the crowd urges it not to be afraid. "Do not let their (politicians') antiquity of blood, with which they reproach us, dismay you; for all men having the same beginning, are equally ancient and have been made by nature in one mode. Strip us all naked, you will see we are alike."

Politically, in a period of war with the Papal states there was a split between the 'aristocratic' ruling group, the *guelphs*, and a merchant class around Salvatore de Medici, who had accused the *guelphs* of fixing elections and of making his faction repurchase their status from magistrates. All this was to be recorded by Machiavelli as a warning that successful republican rule required accommodations. More importantly this split gave space for the disenfranchised *ciompi* to assert their own class power when 14 minor guilds used *ciompi* support against the *guelphs* in a bid for increased government representation. The deal was that in return for this support the *ciompi* would get their own guild status and consuls, and formal separation from the Wool Guild, the *Lana*, under whom their status was one of powerlessness. The deal was betrayed and their demands not fulfilled.

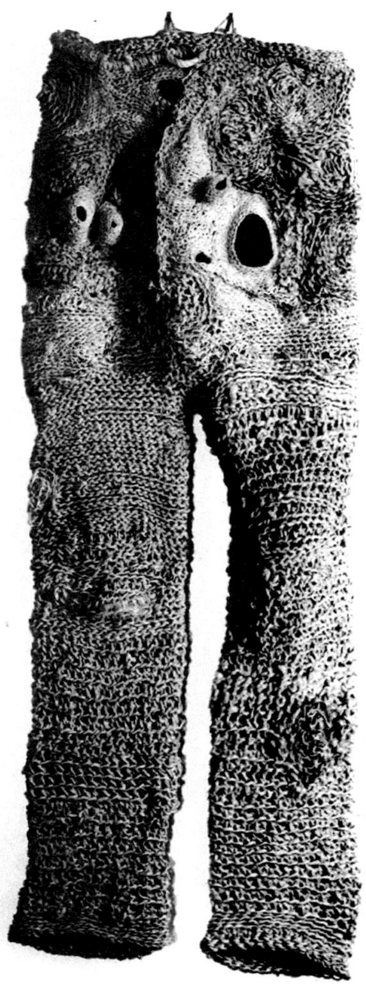

Ewa Jaroszynska, *Trousers*, 1969.

Economically the war meant higher taxes and food shortages while wool workers were also suffering a downturn in work and consequently deterioration of their working conditions, as a result of defaulted loans in England, the source of most of the wool that provided their livelihoods. The gap between rich and poor increased, but what happened was no simple food riot. There was also a history of organising and repression among these workers who were oppressed by the *Lana*, which with its special internal tribunal and its judge, the hated *forestiere*, had the power to remove civic liberties from them. In 1345 the wool carder and labour organiser Cinto Brandini was arrested and executed for forming a fraternity of disenfranchised wool workers. This followed the rescinding by the *Lana* of an earlier agreement whereby the *ciompi* could form their own guild, which prompted a period of rioting. Dyers of wool had also been punished in the 1369–71 period for striking against a lowered rate of pay.

The betrayal of the deal in 1378 led to more demonstrations. On July 20th four of the crowd were arrested and were to be executed. Their release was demanded and gained. The archives of the Justices were burned, as were the records of the Wool Guild. Two days later a rumour spread that a cloth manufacturer, Migliore Guadagni, intended to invade the city with 5000 armed men. This prompted the *ciompi* to seize the palace and take over executive roles. Their policies were the removal of *Lana officials*; for wool carders, beaters and washers to have their own guild and consuls; and no arrests. Banners, crucial to guild organising in Southern Europe, were created. The new *ciompi* banner had arms holding Justice; tailors and shearers had one with Jesus holding an olive branch. What was special was that these new guilds cut across trades and skills.

The accounts of how the new city executive worked and even how long it lasted depend on the class origin of their authors. Machiavelli with his own agenda gives agency to the *ciompi* as a collective force, but then, searching for a 'Prince' figure turns it into the work of the individual, natural political leader, Michele di Lando.

A wool carder himself, he is said to have calmed the crowd by decisively having one of the oppressors executed, before reaching out to make alliances with the old factions. In Machiavelli's version this strategy, which he approved of, brought about di Lando's rapid downfall along with that of the *ciompi* itself who, the author implies, wanted exclusive power, which led to their defeat in a matter of weeks. In fact a city government with strong *ciompi* representation continued for 3 years. Its final loss of power, after a campaign financed by the old Wool Guild, was in large part because it ignored the interests and grievances of those outside the city but in its domain. They were perceived by all city dwellers, regardless of class, to be inferior.

However,this was a re-writing of history, for a government with strong *ciompi* representation continued for three years. It was finally overthrown in 1382 by the *popolano grassi* (fat cats) of Florence, with the help of foreign governments. This new government of oligarchs abolished the two main revolutionary guilds of craftsmen, primarily those in wool. It is true that the radical movement had been weakened by the earlier dissolution of the guild of the unskilled, but a truly non-judgmental assessment of its period of government came from a wool shearer, Pagnolo Ser Guido. Shearers had had no guild recognition before, and Pagnolo Ser Guido was proud to have become part of the Florentine government and confident of its achievements.

Cornelia Klinger

Some time ago, the weaving was ceremoniously delivered. Wrapped in fine tissue paper, placed in a little box as if in a boat, it was sent on its journey to me. I accepted it, brought it home, and laid it on my bed, where it stayed for a few weeks. I looked at it closely every day to find an answer to the question of what the weaving transported: "The weavings may be understood by listening to their memories as a continuing process," said a note accompanying the project.
Now that I am beginning to report about it, I am far from home and am trying to remember what the cloth looks like and what it feels like. It is a rectangular piece, about 40 by 60 centimetres, dark, with a linear pattern that is at once complex and simple in bright, luminescent colours: white, turquoise green, and blue. The pattern is rhythmic, even, and precise. It stands out against a nearly black background, monochromatic, but intricately structured like the night sky. The weaving is not hard or rough, but firm; the cloth curls a little at the corners and edges. This is what I could see and feel in the presence of the cloth. The experience, now a memory, was visually and texturally aesthetic. It is a beautiful cloth.
Nothing less and nothing more. I did not hear a message. I do not recognise a relationship between myself and the ones who spun the yarn and wove the cloth. If the weaving is supposed to speak a language, I do not understand it; if it transports memories, they do not arrive to me. I received only one piece of information along with the weaving. When it was delivered, I was told, verbally, that it is a cloth for the dead, the kind of cloth that is used to wrap up food for the deceased and carry it to the burial ground. I do not know – either I didn't hear or already forgot – what kind of living people used this weaving (or others like it) as a means of transportation to bring what kind of food to what dead people. Still, this message moved me, pleased me even. This kind of thing is just right for me, I thought; I could put it to good use because my dead are buried in places far away from me, places from which I have removed myself, and that I sometimes yearn to return to. I would like to take the cloth, wrap some fruit or flowers in it and visit my dead to bring them offerings that are nothing other than metaphors for love and mourning.
This thought accompanied me and became an occasion to turn my thoughts around and contemplate the things my dead left behind for me. Each day I walk on the rugs that were once in the house of my parents; I wear my mother's jewelry and even a few pieces of her clothing. I like to surround myself with these things and would not like to lose them. And yet, the things themselves are silent, as silent as the cloth for the dead of those foreign, faraway people is for me. My parents did not weave the rugs themselves, my mother did not make her jewelry with her own hands, and she would not have even considered sewing her own clothes. They are "oriental" rugs, the kind of "colonial" goods that were common in European households, and other consumer or luxury goods: not homemade, but bought for money. Would the things be less foreign and silent for me if it were any different? Do those foreign, faraway people have a different, warmer, more intimate relationship to the objects they make by hand? Perhaps …
Perhaps, however, things made, traded, given, borrowed, bought, or stolen are only tools in the essentially helpless confrontation with the past; traces and signs of people and the relationships between them in a world that in the end remains silent.
In my thoughts, I take my mother's ring, wrap it in the cloth that is and isn't comforting, warming, to cry at her cold and faraway grave. Could it be that the people who weave cloths like these make use of them in a way quite similar to what I imagine?

Wood, gilded; probably Baroque, 18th century; acquired in Lima, 2010. When the Spaniards arrived in Peru in 1526 they encountered a total population of 12 million, according to the last census of the Inca Quipucamayoc. Only 45 years later the census counted one million Indigenous people. Nine tenths of the population had been killed in one of the most dramatic genocides in the history of colonialism. By 1564 Indian slaves from all parts of Peru were being marched into the mercury mines of Huancavelica and the Potosi silver mines, where an average of 75 Indians and African slaves were to die every day for over 300 years. Beaten with iron bars, torn by whips, they remained underground for a week at a time, strung together in iron collars, working rock faces to extract the daily quota, twenty-five loads per man, one hundred pounds to the load. To their Spanish overseers they were not people but *little horses*, and when after a few months they stumbled from the pit, chests burning from the toxic dust and vapours, muscles contorted with shakes and tremors, unable to walk, let alone maintain their production, they were simply killed to make room for the next worker. In time mothers began to bury their infant sons alive to save them from the horror of the mines.
López de Quiroga was described as one of the most versatile and capable businessmen during the period of the Spanish Empire in the Americas. Once a week, he organised a large soup kitchen. Afterwards the poor knotted their *ponchos* and Quiroga threw a few coins into them. One time somebody refused to do so and said: "I will only accept money if you wring out your cloak." After hesitating, Quiroga took off his cloak and wrung it out and blood dripped from it.

Sky and Water

"I was walking by the Thames. Half-past morning on an autumn day. Sun in a mist. Like an orange in a fried fish shop. All bright below. Low tide, dusty water and a crooked bar of straw, chicken-boxes, dirt and oil from mud to mud. Like a viper swimming in skim milk ... The sun had crackled into flames at the top; the mist was getting thin in places, you could see crooked lines of grey, like old cracks under spring ice. Tide on the turn. Snake broken up. Emeralds and sapphires. Water like varnish with bits of gold leaf floating thick and heavy. Gold is the metal of intellect. And all at once the sun burned through in a new place, at the side, and shot out a ray that hit the Eagle and Child right on the new signboard.
And through the day. A few small red clouds dawdling up, beige pink ... The powder-puff clouds were getting harder and rounder. The sky was turning green as starboard light ... ... Surrey all in

one blaze, like a forest fire. Great clouds of dirty yellow smoke rolling up. Nine carat gold. Sky water-green to lettuce green. A few top clouds, yellow and solid as lemons ... River disappeared out of its hole. Just a gap full of the same fire, the same smoky gold, the same green ... ... The clouds had turned into old mahogany, heavy and solid. The fire underneath had burned out-nothing left but a yellow streak like a gas flame seen through a kitchen blind. Cabbage-green sky with one star coming through like the tinsel behind gauze. And over on the East the blue rising thick as a forest ... ... On the Surrey side the fire was dead. Clouds all in blue and blue-and-soot. Black smoke drifting up like smoky candles, and a blue sky as blue as blue spectacles with long pieces of sooty cobweb floating high, stars coming up through like needle-points; green-blue and neon-blue; and the river pouring quietly along, as bright as ink out of a bottle ... ... We had turned east along Greenbank. The moon was coming up, as if somebody had flashed a torch under the far edge of the dish-cover. A fog of white light seeping up into the blue air. Overhead the sky was black as Prussian blue. The stars were sparkling like electric cars. And the river crawling along, the colour of pig iron, like a stream of lava going solid ... ... from the side bay-window the moon was making the trees like fossils in a coalfield, and the houses look like fresh-cut blocks of coal, glittering green and blue; and the river banks like two great solid veins of coal left bare, and the river sliding along like heavy oil. It was a working model of the earth before someone thought of dirt, and colours and birds and humans."

2014

The workers of the Cambodian garment industry have been subject to international flim-flam and state violence as the business has become a real 'player' in the international low-wage game. On January 4th five garment workers were shot dead by the Cambodian military police and 20 were wounded at the Canadia industrial park in Phnom Penh, where many factories produce clothes for companies like H&M and Adidas. They were continuing a mass strike that had begun in December 2013, aiming to double the minimum wage to $160 a month after rejecting a government-imposed increase from $80 to 95/100 as an inadequate 'living' wage. The killings are not a new element in the struggle. The industry's rise follows a familiar trajectory of the use of young women workers in which 'overtime' is the norm and the factory owners in the aggressive umbrella of the Garment Manufacturers Association in Cambodia (GMAC) are mostly from Taiwan, Hong Kong and Korea, using capital gained from the overworking of a previous generation of young women in their own countries. In January 2004 Chea Vichea, a Trade Union President, was murdered and the real culprits not apprehended. Since then other union leaders of the FTUWKC union have been murdered: Ros Sovannareth in May 2004 and Hy Vuthy in 2007. Other forms of intimidation have included the beatings of strikers, their dismissal and their imprisonment. In February 2012 three women workers were wounded by gunmen in Svay Rieng province. The strike that ended – perhaps temporarily – with these killings also has a history, and was itself indicative of the courage, persistence and confidence of the some 500,000 workers in the industry. Back in the 2008-11 period following the Western financial crisis, Kin Jae Dong, director of the Korean Sae Han company talked smugly of how the unions had been strong, "but after the economic crisis they became weaker and more cooperative". And, he added, President Hun Sen had 'got tough' with union leaders. Meanwhile, despite the serious whitewash on working conditions supplied by the International Labour Organisation's Better Factories Cambodia 'monitoring' system, Fire Safety standards were getting progressively worse – on May 2 people were killed and 7 injured when the ceiling of a footwear factory collapsed – while short-term contracts had become the norm and wages levels stuck despite inflation. Despite rivalry between different unions, even the ones outside government influence, did not stop the strike wave. In May a strike at Sabrina Garment Manufacturing, which has Nike as a main client, prompted police violence which caused two pregnant women to miscarry. This in turn provoked a statutory period of concern from Nike, which did not extend to the eight union workers imprisoned and hundreds of workers dismissed. Meanwhile the GMAC blamed any violence on workers and demanded punishment in order to "bolster investor confidence in the industry". What stands out, however, was the persistence of mostly women workers demonstrating for the release of those who had been imprisoned. In

Garment workers at a Kandal province factory in Cambodia ended their most recent strike after management agreed to pay out part of their wages for the days they were absent during a previous strike.

November the police, using batons, tear gas and guns, killed one woman worker and wounded eight at the Singapore-owned SL Garment Processing that was making garments for H&M. The killing came after two months of strikes, suspensions and lay-offs. SL Garment itself has a long history of poor conditions and was using armed personnel as a disciplinary force at the factory. Within days of the killings, H&M – perhaps heeding industry consultant David Birnbaum's warning that "If the factory looks like a cross between an orphanage and a prison camp, you have a potential PR problem" – announced that it would 'support' owners at two factories in Bangladesh and one in Cambodia to adopt a "fair living wage" in 2015, to be extended in 2018.

Cambodia Textile workers strike: state intervention.

The mass of workers naturally wanted a fair living wage without waiting, and by this time, late in 2013, two other events had changed the situation and the strike that started in December was unprecedented in its scale and Union unity. Three months earlier workers on even lower wages in Bangladesh had won a significant increase in their minimum wage. At the same time the opposition political party, which promised a $160 minimum wage, had narrowly lost an election to the militarised Hun Sen government and claimed it had been a fraud. How real that promise would be if the opposition were to be in power we cannot know, but the cohesion of strikers and the political opposition triggered the violence of the state's response. The violence, however is also a measure of the victory of workers in almost doubling the minimum wage in a one-year period. Since then the power of worker organisation has been recognised – by Hong Kong investors looking at outsourcing possibilities for one – as a reason for the relatively high wages of Cambodian textile workers in East and Southern Asia, which in 2017 have risen to $153. Relatively high, because the demand was for $177 and annual inflation is over 5%, and because short-term contracts make it risky to refuse overtime. A spate of factory fainting in 2017 revealed not just the level of overtime but also poor ventilation and working temperatures of 37 degrees – direct outcomes of the absence of health and safety regulation.

Elena and Nora Izcue

An imagined conversation between Elena and Nora Izcue in 1997, based on interview with Nora, conducted in 2008.

Dear Elena Izcue, I am Nora, also Izcue, but for many years I knew nothing of you or your achievements. It was my cousin Elba who told me and showed me many of the beautiful things you had made here in Lima, which she had stowed under the bed. They were all hand-made, embroidery, textile prints, linocuts and posters. You have been dead nearly 30 years but I want to make a film about you and your work. It will be called La Armonia Silenciosa. Well, dead though I am, I hope that you will make it clear in your film that all my work was a joint work with my dear sister Victoria. Of course I had the name because of the books, and it is the design rather than the practice which gets the fame. But neither of us was ever interested in fame.

Yes I can understand that, and it must have been hard with our family and society, the way it is that your mother and father were not married. With me it was because of the films I made about the lives of Indigenous peoples. This was new then and all they could say was, "Oh, she became a communist, why doesn't she make something beautiful." Really? A communist. Ah well back in the 1920s I did do some prints as covers for the magazine *Amauta* for poor Mariategui, he called himself a communist though he had terrible trouble with the Russians I believe, because he was all for the Indigenous village, but for me it was the work that counted, as an artist, as a craft. I started working for a living very young but you shouldn't feel sorry for me or Victoria. Our mother was a wonderful woman and because of her I was already confident of the power of art.

You worked as a teacher? Yes, I would have been 19 when I started teaching drawing and it wasn't till I was around 30 that I started to study myself. I was in the first class of the Escuela Nacional de Bellas Artes. The teaching was rather old-fashioned European but it was also the time when the archaeologists were discovering our pre-colonial past and for me especially Nazca culture and its sophisticated designs.

And this coincided with what was the socio-political movement of 'Indigenism' which you articulated in the second Volume of your book El Arte Peruviano en la Escuela. Describing

Living room of Nora Izcue with a photograph of her with Fidel Castro at the first meeting of the Foundation of New Latin American Cinema in Havana and with a drawing by Elena for the *House of Worth*, Paris.

Plate 6 and I quote, "Our object is to show that there are plenty of very beautiful Peruvian designs and that it is not necessary to have recourse to those of other countries which are very monotonous." Did you see yourself as part of a nationalist project? A nationalist project, no dear. For one thing in the end my design books for school had to be printed in Paris, but it is true that what the archaeologists had discovered showed us not just that we had an artistic history, but one with aesthetic values whereas the pre-modernist European art we were importing had very little worth. The fact that I simplified the designs I saw from Moche and Nazca artefacts for those school books was only because it was for children. I used squared paper in the books not to be restrictive but to reflect the geometric nature of the designs. If there was a 'project' as you say, it was of a patron of my work, Rafael Larco Herrera. That would have been around 1923 and Rafael wanted to build a model school on his estate, which would encourage Indigenous children in the arts. It was he who got the two books printed.

There has been an accusation that model schools were part of the paternalism of 'Indigenism', that Indians were still conceived of as children who somehow hadn't lived up to this tradition, this culture of their rich past. Perhaps you are right, it was very difficult to know Indigenous people in any close way then, and in my lifetime it had not changed, and I did find Lima and Peruvian society to be very narrow and that's why me and my sister went to Paris. But before that I want to say that I had my own ideas at this time and a high regard for manual crafts and what came to be called applied arts. The Bellas Artes school had a very low opinion of such work, those Indigenous artefacts were merely decorative, they said. I didn't see it that way.

So how was Paris? You'd never been out of Peru till then? Paris was wonderful. We had such a productive and happy time and modernism gave validity to our own work. I remember the archaeologist Cordova had called pre-colonial design 'naturalist cubism' and it was in textiles, just as it had been for the Incas and their predecessors, that we had real success. Also the art world was then so much more open-minded. So just before we arrived there had been an international Exhibition of Decorative Arts. They were not seen as inferior there, and then soon after, a pre-Colombian exhibition in the Louvre.

You think this made it easier for you. I think so, but it's only work that really makes things easier. We learned new skills and perhaps fortunately the fashion business took an interest in modernist design, which is how I came to do work for Charles Worth and other fashion houses there. I wasn't interested in mass-production, my textiles were all printed manually but we were able to make our living and make wonderful friends and learn from people like Leger. I didn't reject what I'd done in the past but knew somehow I was a better artist.

It's one of the most comforting things isn't it, that one can get better in one's craft? The coming war forced you to leave however, how was it, to return to Peru after twelve years? Yes, in 1938 but one learns to live with loss and work is the great healer so with the support of the government which had just created a National Workshop of Graphic Arts we worked with women engaged with the traditional craft of straw weaving. We introduced new designs and dyeing techniques, and incidentally cut out merchants so that the women weavers got all the money of the selling price. It made a huge difference to them, and we saw it as our job to rescue traditional techniques.

You got better money for the producers Elena, that is political. We only did what was right whereas you, I think you said the family called you a communist. I know the family was narrow-minded but how was that?

It was, well the first time I stepped out of the world I was brought up in, I went to Cuzco and made a film about a unionist and campesino, peasant, about their struggles and uprisings. It helped me discover the reality of my country, but the family were afraid they would lose their farms with agrarian reform. And then I made a film about black women in the coastal village of Chincha. All around the times were very terrible, in Chile, in Bolivia, and film makers were being put in prison, I was involved in those struggles when only Cuba offered hope. We went on to create as movie school there, the Foundation of New Latin American Cinema, it became very prestigious. But I also wanted to say I was the first female director in Peru. Elena, you and Victoria did so much, kept Indigenous techniques alive and produced so much beautiful work. There is no politics without beauty. And most of all because all that has disappeared from the history, what you did and what you made needs recognition. Recognition, it only mattered in that it might help one get on with the next work, financially or as recommendation. It was the work dear, always the work and though we were quiet in our later years, that's what we did.

Kushma Shipibo / Tunic

36

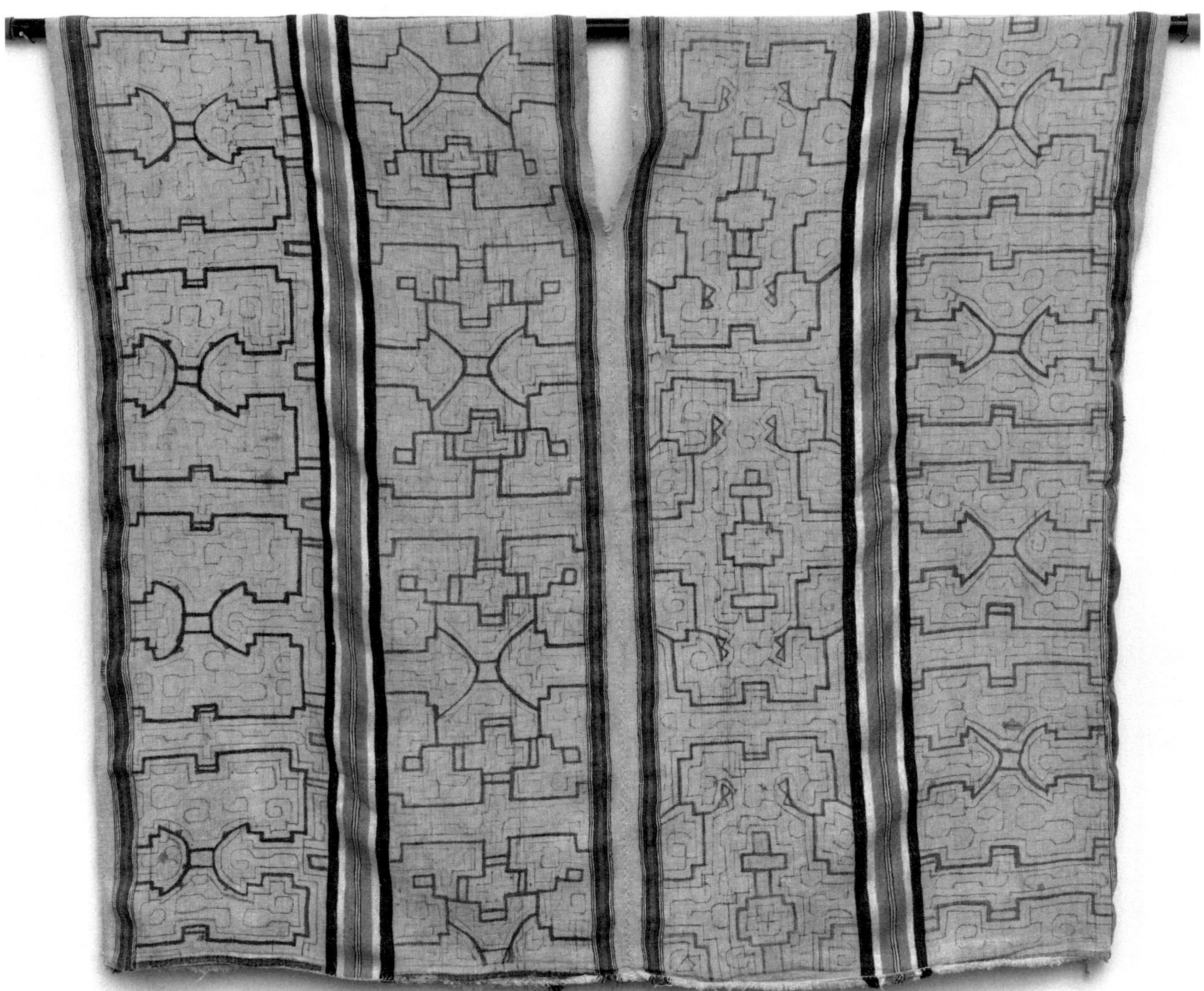

Cotton; dyed with warp-patterned and painted designs, 1960s, acquired in San Francisco de Yarinacocha, 1978. The *kushma* is a full-length cotton tunic of two panels uncut in width, sewn in the centre, leaving a head opening, and sewn on the sides, leaving arm-holes. Traditionally it was woven on a backstrap loom, often with colourful warp stripes, in either one or two separate warp lengths.

Muslin

In 18th-century Brazil an elite voice complained that "even the most wretched black woman wears her underskirt of good embroidered muslin". Meanwhile it is the most frequently mentioned fabric in the early 19th-century English novels of Jane Austen. In *Northanger Abbey* a whole conversation centres around it, with the hero taking what for a man is an "uncommon interest" in cloth. He has just bought some for his sister: a "prodigious bargain ... I gave but five shillings a yard for it, and a true Indian muslin." The emphasis on its origin is important because innovations by James Monteith in Blantyre, Scotland, and then John Heathcote, are about to mass-produce a muslin-type net material and further destroy the craft employment

Late-19th-century drawing of Kabir, a poet and weaver.

centred on Bengal. Bengal cotton fabrics were exported both to the Roman and Chinese empires and are mentioned in Ptolemy's Geography. The Romans had talked of muslin as woven wind and its degrees of delicacy were described variously as spiderwebs and evening dew. Even the hard-nosed English cotton expert of the 18th century, Edward Baines, was moved to say that "... some of the muslins might be thought to be the work of fairies, or insects, rather than of men". The name muslin itself is said to have derived from Mosul in modern day Iraq, but if that is the case it is only because it would have been through the Middle East that the cloth reached Europe and thus was identified by its trade origin. References to its origins in Bengal, however, occur over 2000 years ago, and this was later confirmed by a 9th-century Arab merchant Sulaiman al-Tajir. Traders came also from China and Malaya. Dhaka and its surrounding area was the main centre of production. The cloth connoisseurs of the Mughal Empire institutionalised production, appointing an officer – the Darogh-i-Malbus Khas – to supervise its manufacture for the emperor or for Nawabs. This finest type was called *Malmal* and like all the highest quality muslin it was made of *phuti* cotton grown on the banks of the Brahmaputra river. There were a further 14 types including *Jamdani* in which decorative motifs were woven, by inserting extra weft threads by hand, *Jhuna* used by native dancers, and *Abirawan*, poetically likened to running water. "So fine, indeed, are these muslins that merchants place them in hollow bambus, about two spans long, and, thus secured, carry them through Corazane, Persia, Turkey and many other countries," wrote an early 17th-century traveller. The extent of trading links before the arrival of Europeans in militarised ships was described by another traveller, Ludovico di Verthema, a hundred years earlier in 1508: "Fifty ships are laden every year in this place with cotton and silk stuffs. These same stuffs go through all Turkey, through Syria, through Persia, through Arab Felix, through Ethiopia and all India." This meant a favourable balance of trade with the rest of the world, as is shown by the influx of silver in the period from 1650 to 1750.

As early as the 10th century, one Arab traveller wrote that "these garments ... [are] woven to that degree of fineness that they may be drawn through a ring of a middling size". A Chinese traveller to India around 629–45 CE observed that "The cloth is like the light vapours of dawn".

European settlements – English, Dutch and French – were created in Bengal in the 17th century and the export of Dhaka muslin increased enormously, so much so that the settlers set up their own factories and pressured weavers and spinners to increase the intensity of their labour. The political power situation changed and the production pressure increased again with the victory of the East India Company over the Nawab of Bengal and his French allies in the battle of Palashi in 1757. This gave the Company a monopoly over the trade and reduced the spending capacity of the Mughal elite, thereby reducing domestic demand for the finest muslins. From then on too, the British squeezed out other traders, both European and Asian. Subsequently the industrial developments in Britain – the key invention being the Mule Jenny in 1779, which could make cotton thread fine enough to spin 'muslin' – meant that by the end of the 18th century the export of Dhaka muslin was down to half what it had been in 1747. The English resident of Dhaka John Taylor reported that many were dying of famine and that the "great wealth" of the city was now a "melancholy retrospect". By 1833 E.E. Perkins could list in his Treatise on Haberdashery 25 different kinds of muslin made in Britain and how they dominated the markets of the Americas and the Caribbean. His categories are distinctly unpoetic, instead of 'woven wind', we find 'stiff', 'foundation', 'hard', 'mourning', 'soft', and 'book' muslin. Even though Bengal muslins were still admired at London's Great Exhibition of 1851, the name came to be generic, describing a whole range of net material used for filtering, lining, cheese-making and theatrical sets.

1907

Lizzie Berkley, a suffragette 'fustian-clothing machinist' from the Yorkshire textile town of Hebden Bridge, known as 'Fustianopolis', was arrested as one of the women fighting with 500 police who were preventing them reaching the Parliament building demanding votes for women. The police were far from gentle, carrying the women upside down with their skirts over their heads; they squeezed and pinched their breasts, kicked and punched them in the stomach. Lizzie was one of 75 arrested and served 14 days imprisonment. The suffragette movement which campaigned and fought for the right of women to vote in Britain, has usually been presented as one of middle and upper class women, but as a mass movement its real base was the mill workers in the cotton and woollen towns of Lancashire and Yorkshire. Some, like Selina Cooper, a mill-girl from Nelson, Lancashire (where, some years, later Gandhi received a warm welcome from women workers), were Trade Unionists and suffragettes in an atmosphere where politics was their open university. Class barriers were overturned and bonds forged between women, sometimes across the social divide. "Lavena Saltonstall, a tailoress-turned-weaver-cum-writer, contributed a regular column to *Halifax Labour News* and wrote a series, 'Letters of a Tailoress', for the magazine of the newly founded Workers' Education Association." Edith Key who became president of the Huddersfield, Yorkshire branch of the Women's Social and Political Union was working as a knotter who prepared thread for the looms. Cissy Foley who had worked as a teenager in a Lancashire cotton mill to support her family became a suffragette through being a labour militant.

One of the basic commodities for trade between town and country, textiles are among the first objects from the new culture to reach the backward, outlying areas. [...] textile design has an enormous part to play in changing old tastes, in breaking old aesthetic traditions and habits (along with the ideological ones that are so bound up in them); [...] But it is far too crude and naive a ploy to use textiles merely as bearers of printed pictures, a practice which, unfortunately, continues in this country to this day [...]. Art historian A.A. Fyodorov-Davidov introduces the First Art Exhibition of Soviet Domestic Textiles, in Moscow, 1928.

The Yorkshire women were especially militant. Laura Wilson, a worsted-coating weaver from Halifax, told a newspaper reporter on her release from prison that she had gone in a rebel "but I have come out a regular terror". Prisons themselves were another site of resistance and violence where hunger striker women were force-fed. The campaign also revealed the ignorance of the British establishment about the real conditions in the country's still dominant textile industry. In 1907, after further clashes with the police in London, 16-year-old Dora Thewlis was told by the magistrate that she ought to be in school. In Yorkshire at the time girls went half-time into the weaving shed aged 11, and she herself was already earning a pound a week and saw herself as a worker with rights.

"In June 1911, the last time all the suffrage groups presented a united front, forty thousand women, including seven hundred prisoners or their proxies dressed in white, walked for seven miles of gold and glitter and sparkling pageantry with a panoply of new banners and pennants held aloft. The suffrage societies sold ribbons in their own colours and Oxford Street stores did a nice line in lace blouses with 'Votes for Women' cunningly embroidered into their yokes." Throughout the campaign they had been adept in the use of self-made visual propaganda. While banners had been carried in protests from Peterloo in 1819 onwards and used by Trade

Gandhi visiting textile factory, Darwen, Lancashire.

Unions, most had been made by George Tuthill's banner-making business. Feminist ones were more varied and tended to be individually made, combining embroidery, collage, paint and raised works. On the mass demonstration of 1908, not just banners but also parasols were displayed, embroidered in the colours of purple, green and white. This tactically countered the patriarchal portrayal of feminists as unattractive. Furthermore, in their subversive use of embroidery the suffragettes understood the symbolic content of their materials, as can be seen from their decision to present a militant hammer and horseshoes image flanked by irises – a key symbol of femininity. 20 years later women in the Lancashire cotton mills were again being imprisoned after being violently arrested, during a strikes against sackings and the introduction of a gender-biased 8-loom system and consequent unemployment, for trying to stop strike-breaking 'scab' labour from working.

Grant Watson

BODYMAP. In the late 1960s Michel Foucault participated fully in gay life including the burgeoning San Francisco sex scene, which was then developing into perhaps one of the most experimental and libertarian in recorded history. In his short novel *To the Friend Who Did Not Save My Life*, French writer and friend of Foucault Hervé Guibert explains how Foucault "adored" the "violent orgies" which took place in the city's bathhouses and while "he didn't dare frequent the baths in Paris for fear of being recognised", when "he went off to give his annual seminar near San Francisco he went at it to his heart's content."[1] Apparently it was the Sado-Masochist clubs which most attracted Foucault, and after initially arriving and renting a place in Berkeley he quickly moved to a new apartment across the bay, close to Folsom Street and the heart of the city's leather scene. In his Foucault biography James Miller describes the variety of clubs that sprung up around Folsom Street – and how "each place offered a somewhat different atmosphere, evoking various "fantasy environments" – many simulating settings that, historically, had been dangerous for gay men. "Glory hole" recreated toilet stalls. Mazes allowed players safely to enact furtive assignations in dark places. Welcoming dungeons filled with whips, chains and cells conjured up prison as a cosy habitat of the sexual outlaw and his punishing master."[2] Miller also draws on Larry Townshend's *The Leatherman's Handbook* which describes a list of "ritualised interactions" that occurred in these places and which included a "wide range of possibilities" such as "gagging piercing, cutting, hanging, electric shocking, stretching on racks, imprisoning, branding, blindfolding, mummifying, pissing on, shitting on, shaving, burning, crucifying, suspending, clamping, suffocating, fist fucking."[3] Foucault avoided going into detail about exactly which of these he personally signed up for, but instead marvelled aloud in public about the wonderful potential of these extreme limit experiences to transform the subject, to snap it out of itself as it were. Seeing in this elaborate cocktail of sex and drugs, pleasure and pain, experienced through myriad encounters, an "exceptional possibility" to "desubjectify oneself, to desubjugate oneself, to desexualise oneself by affirming a non identity through a kind of plunge beneath the water."[4] His sexual imagination (and we guess practice) is theorised in a way that also seeks to delocalise the erotic experience away from the genital organs and distribute it in a polymorphic array across the body, and through a fusion of bodies which occurs at multiple points, so that the body becomes map criss-crossed by a range of extreme and prolonged sensations. Taking up the motif of the map, Miller quotes from Geoff Mains's book *Urban Aboriginals* when he writes that in bondage "a man comes to better understand the map of his body" whereas in torture, the "map" of the body is completely "obliterated and redrawn."[5] Foucault's interest in and personal experience of the elaborate sexual practices of gay men in San Francisco in the late 1970s reflects in part his larger interest in the different techniques of subjectivation, practices that took place in different cultures and in different historical periods, which were discussed in his books on sexuality and lectures at the College de France. And Miller points out how the ritualised practices constructed by gay men at this time, which at their limits could produce mind-altering experiences through combinations of sex, drugs, torture and role play, can be compared to those described in "religious societies and religions who use drugs, physical pain, starvation, or other means of altering consciousness." For example, in his anthropological papers for the American Museum of Natural History, published in 1917, J.R. Walker describes at length "The Sun Gaze Dance" that constituted a stage in the "Sun Dance ceremonies" occurring over several days, practiced by the Native American tribes of the Great Plains (including the Arapaho, Arikara, Assiniboine, Bannock, Blackfoot, Blood, Cheyenne, Cree, Crow, Gros Ventre, Hidatsa, Kiowa, Mandan, Ojibway, Omaha, Ponca, Sarasi, Shoshone, Sioux, and the Ut).[6] These rituals could include what we might now describe as torture and role-play, a fact which, despite the criminal brutality that accompanied the colonization of America, shocked the Europeans to the extent that they legislated against such aspects of the ceremony. Walker describes at great length the practices of the Oglala Division of the Teton Dakota (Sioux) that formed a part of the Sun Dance, which included (after several days of preparation) a routine of capture, torture, captivity and release which was played out by the males of the tribe. He recounts how, once the men had established who would play what role, it was designated that – "the captors should come together a short distance from the dancers and feign discovery of the dancers as enemies." Then "they should shout the war cry and rush upon the dancers, each grasp his dancer about the waist, wrestle with him, throw him prone, and loudly announce that he has captured an enemy. When all the dancers are thus made captive, their captors should feign to consult together, and determine to torture the captives." The second act of the "dance" included a variety of different permutations with varying accompanying levels of bravery and pain. Here "the captors should each pierce the flesh of his captive and make wounds sufficient to accomplish the form of the Sun-Gaze Dance he is to dance" including the instructions to turn the "captive's body face down and then grasp the skin and flesh of his back at one side of the spine, draw them out as far as possible, and pierce crosswise through the flesh with a sharp-pointed implement, so as to make a wound that the sharp-pointed stick provided may pass through; then the captor should make a like wound on the other side of the spine." Alternatively the captor should "grasp the skin and flesh of the captive's breast, draw them out as far as possible, and pierce through the flesh, making a wound that will permit the sharp-pointed stick to pass through it; then he should make a like wound through the flesh of the captive's other breast; then he should turn the captive so that he will be face down and make like wounds on the back over each shoulder blade." The captor then variously suspends a number of Buffalo heads to these sticks, or ties the sticks to four poles that surround the prisoner, or "if the dancer is to dance actually suspended, the thongs bound to the sticks should pass through the fork of the Sacred Pole so that the dancer can be drawn from the ground or lowered to it." Subsequently after periods of dancing, singing and drumming interspersed with moments of rest and relief the "captors should feign to discover that the captives are" in fact "buffalo men whom they should befriend. Then they should rush to the captives and protest that they are friends who will help them to escape from captivity. After this they are called friends and each should remain by his dancer while he dances."

1 Hervé Guibert, *To the Friend Who Did Not Save My Life*, Quartet Books, London 1995, p. 21.
2 James Miller, *The Passion of Michel Foucault*, Flamingo, London 1994, p. 260.
3 Ibid, p. 265.
4 Ibid, p. 264.
5 Ibid, p. 268.
6 J.R. Walker, *The Sun Dance and other ceremonies of the Oglala Division of the Teton Dakota*, Anthropological Papers of the American Museum of Natural History, New York, 1917.

37

Wool, cotton, plant fibre; probably Late Intermediate Period, approx. 1000–1450 CE; Chancay; acquired on eBay, 2013. To this day, the existence of many Peruvian and Bolivian highland natives is highly dependent on the llama population. In addition to their significance for economic independence, these camelids play a central role in Indigenous belief systems. In the 16th century, the Spaniards decimated them to ten percent of their precolonial population within a few decades, even though their wool is superior to the wool of the sheep introduced by them. The Andean herders developed a demotic taxonomy capable of describing each individual animal in the herd. This hierarchically disordered system is extremely flexible and offers a broad range of potential uses. Animals are not only classified as male or female, but are also grouped into a number of other gender categories in which, for example, a reproducing animal has a different gender from that of a non-reproducing animal. The age of an animal is not determined by the number of years, but rather according to the quality and altitude of the grazing pastures, the number of offspring, illnesses, the condition of teeth, the quality and quantity of wool, the animal's load-carrying capacity, and other influencing factors. The first part of an animal's name indicates whether it is a llama or an alpaca. The next indicates the distribution of colours or the type of pattern, followed by differences in terms of gender, age, and wool quality. If animals should resemble each other, additional descriptors are added. If light colours predominate in an animal's wool, it is generally called *alqa*. The 53 terms for variations of *alqa* and the four dark base colours result in 212 different combinations. The base colours can have about 19 different shades, resulting in 4028 possible *alqa* varieties. If the gender is added as a reference, the number can be trebled to 12,084 because the animals always have more than two genders. By adding the age factor, we arrive at more than 20,000 descriptive names that herders can use to identify their animals.

Male llamas and alpacas carry loads to and from the fields and sometimes between villages. Alpaca and llama hides are used as mattresses and pillows and their wool for clothing, carrying cloths, blankets, ropes, and slings.

Alpaca hair is spun into wool either in its natural colours of white, brown, gray, or black, or a combination thereof, or it is dyed before being processed into thread. The hair that grows for four or more years on the chest of the alpacas serves to make slings. As meat alpaca is either cooked fresh or it is salted and preserved as *ch'arki*. Each part of the animal is either consumed or used to make things. Various dishes are prepared with blood. The tendons are used for sewing as well as for strings on stringed instruments and to tie musical instruments together. The liver is eaten fried, the lungs with vegetable and chillies, and the head is made into a broth. Out of animal fat, which is a prime ingredient for offerings to major deities, candles are made. Bones serve to make a comb-like tool used for weavings. The dung fertilises the fields and when sun-dried serves as cooking fuel.

Among the herders of Puno, animals that have died by a stroke of lightning receive the same burial rituals as humans, and after eight days the departure of their spirit is acknowledged by means of another ritual.

Black

"'Let us', said one of the natives whose language we could speak, but imperfectly, 'build from the trees a thing we call "ship" – from the wood remaining I will show you how to make "paper" – on this "paper" (once we set sail) I shall show you how to "write" (with a charred twig from the same tree) – and if your grandmother is with you, here's how we suck eggs'."

In modern Greece a widow who stays dressed in black day in and day out, the 'traditional' dress, can be seen as self-denying, repressed by a patriarchal society. The late Steve Jobs, an epitome of modernity as represented by Apple Mac, equally chose black certainly in his public clothes. The earlier pictures show him in a black suit, which changes over time into an ascetic-looking black polo-neck, simplicity itself. He is in a line from the early-15th-century Lucca merchant Giovanni Arnolfini in the painting by Jan van Eyck, in which he wears a black beaver hat and a black dress, stockings and shoes, the sign of dignity and loyalty in merchants. These contextual shifts are not new and can co-exist. Alongside Mr Jobs in the contemporary world, the Gothic sub-culture – black clothes, cosmetics and pale faces – continues as an international phenomenon. It continues a much earlier association with the devil, later refracted through late-18th- and 19th-century Romanticism, and which has made another specific comeback in vampire-genre film and TV. It was not so funny for 16th-century women accused of devil worship. The state's executioners, who normally wore red, had black dress in their cases.

For the ancient Egyptians it had been a positive colour, speaking of the fertility of the earth, all that black silt from the Nile, and ensuring the passage of the dead into the next world. In the Greek world it changes into a negative as the notion of the afterlife also changes. Hades is dull, black without the sun, light and sky of the living sensuous world. From its iconography of the satyr, the Christian notion of the devil is also taken, and from around 1000 CE the devil and the very notion of evil adds black to that picture. Two hundred years later however it became the colour of choice for the clothes of "urban patricians and officeholders or those in authority", symbolising both dignity and integrity. In the middle of the 14th century progress in the technology of dyeing and a shift in public attitudes to dyers themselves who took on the black-skinned Saint Maurice as their patron. "Dyers were proud of him and told his story with paintings, stained glass and performance processions." They also created a narrative of Jesus's boyhood in which he became apprenticed to a dyer in Tiberias and performed miracles to make colours.

The developed techniques, with a greater reliance on mordants, made more properly black tones possible. This, and the sumptuary laws which forbade certain coloured clothing for any but the nobility may have been instrumental in how between 1360 and 1380 merchants, and men of finance also took up black. It may also have been seen by them as adding a necessary austerity to how they looked, as if they were already preparing the way for a Protestant aesthetic, of chromophobia and the trustworthy appearance of self-denial.

Over the centuries it has competed with grey as the colour to express such sobriety. People of refinement Goethe says disliked bright colours, which were for "uncivilised nations and children", instead wearing black for men, and white for women. The judgmental adjective 'garish' perpetuated the notion that brightly coloured clothing was essentially vulgar. Not that they gave a damn in 17th-century Brazil, far from it: British cloth was seen as "too gloomy for people who laugh at themselves: Let us have no drabs, we have no Quakers here. We want no dismal colours for an English November."

拜耳顏料廠
Farbenfabriken
vorm.
FRIEDR. BAYER & Co
拜耳顏料廠
LEVERKUSEN
Katigen Black T N extra 2134
大德顏料廠
Black MO extra strong
I.G.FARBENINDUSTRIE AKTIENGESELLSCHAFT FRANKFURT AM MAIN

At times this inclination could be fetishistic, as with the Protestant capitalist Henry Ford telling his customers that they could have their car in any colour they wanted, "so long as it's black"; or representative of gruesome rituals as when English judges put little black caps on to their wigs to pronounce the death sentence. In the age of the creative professional class and its intelligentsia, for whom Steve Jobs was an iconic figure, it has been given a new lease of life, trans-muted with a notion of 'cool' into the colour of choice for this new priesthood. These are serious people artistic perhaps but clear and uncluttered. Black, far from dirtying, which is how Ludwig Wittgenstein sees it as colour, is sharp and clear-cut. Recently the blackest black ever, one that reflects almost no light at all, called Vantablack, has been created and patented for use on stealth satellites. It follows the example of many of the innovations now coming out of the defence industry. In a mutually satisfactory deal its makers, NanoSystems, have given exclusive rights for its use to the British artist Anish Kapoor, who has a reputation for chromatic effects. Another boost for black as super-cool.

0509

At the Second Meeting of American Organisations and Movements in Tihuanacu, Bolivia, in 1983, September 5th was officially designated International Indigenous Women's Day, in honour of Aymarán Military Leader Bartolina Sisa Vargas.

During the early 1780s, in the highlands of Peru and Alto Peru (present-day Bolivia) armed Quechua and Aymará groups fought their Spanish oppressors. Bartolina Sisa, together with her husband Túpac Catari, led the Indigenous uprising with an army of more than 40,000, which laid siege to the city of La Paz in 1781. Sisa was the commander of the siege, which was maintained for 184 days, and was executed when the insurgency was put down after 11 months.

From the start, Bartolina made a dynamic contribution to the movement, ensuring the concerns of women were addressed in revolutionary councils. The popular uprisings had many similarities to the goals of present-day social movements, a restoration of Indigenous rights and a more equitable redistribution of the Andean region's abundant natural resources.

Bartolina Sisa emerges from the jail naked and bleeding with rope around her neck, tied to the tail of a horse. Her sister-in-law Gregoria Apaza, another notable rebel commander, is brought out on a donkey. Each of them carries a cross of sticks, like a scepter, in the right hand, and has a crown of thorns fastened on her head. Before them, prisoners sweep the ground clear with branches. Bartolina and Gregoria make several turns around the main plaza of La Paz, Bolivia suffering in silence the stones and laughter of those who mock them as Indian queens, until the hour the gallows strikes. Their heads and hands, the sentence reads, will be paraded through the towns of the region.

Bartolina's fate has never been forgotten. September 5th is a day not only to remember her but it honours the indispensable role played by generations of Indigenous women most of whose names have been lost to history in the 500-year struggle for decolonisation, land reform and social justice. Today the Bartolina Sisa National Federation of Bolivian Peasant Women (FNMCB-BS or Bartolinas) has grown into a powerful organisation. In 2010 Bartolina leader Nilda Copa was appointed as Minister of Justice, and the Plurinational Legislative Assembly has a total of 30% female representation. In addition 43% of all the Bolivian council members are women. The present political administration has also implemented various policies designed to improve women's lives: between 2006 and 2008 the government distributed 10,300 property titles to rural women.

Things are very different in Honduras where, since a coup in 2009, which was not condemned by the West, 120 Mayan people protecting their land and 31 trade unionists have been murdered with impunity. The coup was against the government of Manuel Zelaya, which had recently increased the minimum wage, including for the 110,000 women working in the textile and clothes sector, and signed up to – against US 'free trade' interests – the Bolivarian Alternative for the Americas. Unlike Bartolina, Berta Cáceres was an internationally recognised Indigenous environmentalist hero, but this did not prevent her assassination in 2016 or the brazen attempt on her daughter's life in 2017. Despite the regime's strategy of terror and textile companies closing factories rather than negotiating with workers, 9000 women won the right to form a union at the Canadian-owned Gildan factories in 2015 and in 2017, after two years of struggle.

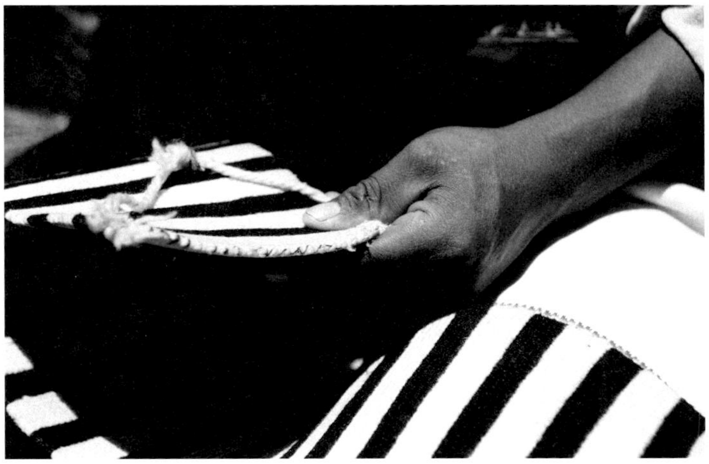

Juan Quispe

Juan showing Maria's hair woven into his belt.
Maria and Juan Quispe gardening.

"My name is Juan Quispe and I live on the island of Taquile in Lake Titicaca and I'd like to tell you about how we live here, what we make and what we wear and especially about the *faja* (wide belt), woven by women and the *ch'ullu* (wool cap), knitted by men. But first let me speak about a cloth whose name would translate as *plate of generosity*. One has to maintain the spirit of it, so that, if I don't have, I have. And if you have, nature has always to provide, I mean, you are never going to lack food, or spirit, and you are never going to lack joy. This cloth is at the edge, so to speak, protecting us from not having. Now with the *faja* and the *chu'llu* the symbols that are used are the same as it was for our parents and grandparents. For example, there is a calendar belt (*chumpi calendario*), and even with the arrival of modern calendars it is very important for those of us who understand it. We see time through the woven patterns of the birds, the blossomings, the crops; we read the season to build houses, and the fishing season; and also some festivities, for example the festivity to the dead, the arrival of new animals, and also the New Year are written there. It is the same cosmological view that our grandparents had, but our textiles have also evolved, nowadays we are using the rainbow colours quite a bit. So I asked my grandfather why, since they could make many colours, why didn't our ancestors use rainbow colours. He said that back then they respected the rainbow, and, using its colours, the rainbow could burn people or take their intestines out.

But nowadays we young people are changing, and we know that when we use rainbow colour we have never been burnt. Maybe our grandparents wanted to protect respect for the rainbow in this way, and even today it is still like a sign, when the rainbow falls in June or May we know that rain will stop. If there is a rainbow at sundown, then it won't rain. If there is a rainbow at sunrise, then it is going to rain. This is the forecast. Maybe our grandparents attitude was to protect themselves, but you can see that in using the colours our textiles have evolved. And another example, one of my sisters had woven a *faja* with a space shuttle. And I asked her why she had woven, what does it mean, and my sister says, I don't know. But that same year the Challenger space shuttle, when it took off and exploded in mid-air, they gave the news on television and my sister had seen the whole tragedy, she was very affected by it, so then she had woven what she had felt.

Anyway, that's why I say that in the *faja* is like a register, through symbols, a person's life, his past, his future, his feelings, his plans, experience of his life. What I understand is that culture belongs to the person who lives it. It doesn't belong to him who stopped living, for example, I see that there are many cultures, or many customs, that have disappeared, but, nevertheless, they say, it is ours but they don't live it anymore. They've changed their ways of celebrating, their clothing, everything has changed. And where they have their past, they only have a museum, a doll dressed up, that is like that. But not in Taquile, it is still alive, it is walking. Well, Taquile in this case would be like a living museum.

The *faja* too is living, it is like a body. There is a heart, and also that which supports the *faja*, that which secures it at the back and is like the arms. The belt, which is not for sale, with a white striped underbelt also supports the wearer's back during heavy agricultural labour. But also, it has a head with its braids, like its hair. Yes, it is alive, it is practically alive. So a knitter or a weaver cannot cut his own textile, it is a sin, he or she simply cannot cut it. Now with the

The south-west coastal France was marsh land of very poor soil supporting one sheep per hectare. Shepherds used stilts to travel long distances each day to find better grazing for their sheep, but also to keep dry feet. They used a stick to form a tripod when they wanted to rest. Perched 3 metres in the air, they knitted woollen garments and scanned the horizon for stray sheep. People who saw them in the distance compared them to tiny steeples and giant spiders.

chu'llu, as a child I would watch my grandfather when he was knitting them, and I found it really absorbing, really beautiful and I wanted to do it. At some point, my grandfather left his knitting, thread, everything, while I was playing and my grandfather said, do you want to knit, and I said yes, I want to knit. Well at that moment, my grandfather was just about to give me his threads, but my grandmother said no, she said to me, you have to go and tend to the sheep.
At that time I didn't understand why my grandmother was telling me first you have to tend to the sheep when all I wanted to do was knit. But anyway, I was little and went with the sheep into the field to run with them, which was also a lot of fun. To go down to the lake with the sheep, go and look for pasture for them was very interesting, but still I wanted to knit. Anyway, several years passed, or several months or years, and for the first time I saw how a little sheep was born, and its wool grew, and then, when it was ready for shearing, my mother sheared the wool and said, here it is, now you have to make your own thread. The next day I tried threading the *apuscan*, the spindle.
It started to move, and I began to make my threads in such a way that maybe my faith or the belief of my grandfather worked. I mean, really it is a medicine that truly cured me, because I felt like spinning, I made my first threads, and when I had just made them, my grandfather was also just preparing his needles and said, there you go, now you are going to knit. Only in the colour white, like the sheep, only in white. And I already wanted to make the little birds, and the symbols, but first I had to finish a complete white cap. Boring.
Luckily my grandfather taught me to be very patient when knitting, patient enough to create my own cap from the sheep wool and I did it and finished the plain white *ch'ullu*. It was badly made, badly shaped but when I'd finished, my grandfather took out his red, blue, green, yellow threads, all his threads, right there; now you can make your *ch'ullu*, he said. Then I started. First I didn't like that colour combination, I'd started to create my own combinations and what I learned but when I finished, ahhh, everyone, older boys would laugh at me.
It was shameful. I liked those colours, but then I understood that the colours that I had used were all wrong because the colours that combine are yellow and green, or with blue. They are the only colours that are always used here. And in some way I learned that I had violated the colour code, because all the colours, they also have a meaning. They would say, for example, if I had used black instead of blue, and instead of red a darker colour, why a *chu'llu* of this colour, darker, you know? Because I like the darker colour, I thought the yellows would reflect too much, but then I realised, when a person would say, you are a widower, where do you come from, you must be from another planet?
So that is a colour code, but the *ch'ullu* is also personal. For someone who doesn't know, they all look all the same, but each Taquileño when he sees a fabric, he recognises it quickly. If you wear this, my *ch'ullu*, and you go and show it to someone and ask them, whose textile is this they will tell you that belongs to Juan. Many of us know each other from our knitting or weaving, they are our colours, but with a naked eye they all look the same.
In some families, when it is about getting together and starting living together, couples have to pass the test of their textiles' skill. Sometimes, the father of the girl has to check the make of the *ch'ullu* that has to be strong, a very strong fabric, it has to hold well and also some families pour water in it. So then, almost the whole family has to see if the young man has the skill to knit well, to knit his textile waterproof. And the family has to see that the water is still in the *ch'ullu*. This is the way one starts performing in society."

Taquile, whose population was estimated at nineteen hundred in the year 2000, is a small island in Lake Titicaca, on the Peruvian side, of the Andean *altiplano* (high plateau) at nearly 13,000 feet (3,815 metres), above sea level. This community's Quechua-speaking inhabitants are renowned worldwide for their dramatically coloured finely handwoven textiles and for their model of community-controlled tourism. In 2005 Taquile and its textile art were recognised by UNESCO as a Masterpiece of the Oral and Intangible Heritage of Humanity.

Man's Scarf / Chalina, CDG Scarf

38

Wool; Charazani, Bolivia; acquired in Copacabana, 2010; alpaca, bought 2016 from a second-hand shop in London. The scarf in the Andes is a Spanish introduction. This one was made in Charazani, which is located in the department of La Paz in the northwest of Bolivia. Charazani weavings almost always use alpaca and llama wool and are characterised by small, finely woven designs, various zoomorphic figures and anthropomorphic images depicting important social events. The delicate scroll motif, or *caracol*, is also often employed in Charazani weavings. During nightly rituals women must wear headbands, for only if they do so are their souls protected from negative influences.

In Amarete, one of the bigger communities of the municipality of Charazani, everything is gendered: men, fields, mountains, things, offices, and rituals. Men and women don't just differ biologically. The Amaretens also know five symbolic genders: male, female–female, female–male, male–female, male–male. Combined with the biological, this results in ten different gender roles, and these occupy a large space in religion, ritual and everyday life. They determine the sitting order, the walking order, the order of procedures, the so-called corner-order, the order of hospitality and above all the complex sacrificial order in rituals. In taking on any formal status someone's symbolic gender may also change, as do space, time and matter.

The second scarf is the last item acquired for the archive. It is *Made in Bolivia* and comes from the 2008 Crystal Journey Collection of Comme des Garçons, with the logo spelled out in Swarovski crystals. CDG "was travelling around the world in search of the good energy of crystals and the treasure of time-honoured tradition".

The debate over cultural appropriation and intellectual property is an ongoing issue in the fashion industry, with numerous instances when Western fashion designers have controversially taken inspiration from cultures around the world. In the autumn 1999 these intellectual property concerns became pressing when the New York City fashion designer Donna Karan sent a buyer to the Western Arctic to collect older traditional Inuit clothing for inspiration for her autumn 2000 fashion line. Pauktuutit people mobilised a media and letter-writing campaign to put a stop to this misappropriation of Inuit culture. The incident stressed the urgent need to explore effective forms of legal protection that respect the nature of traditional knowledge and

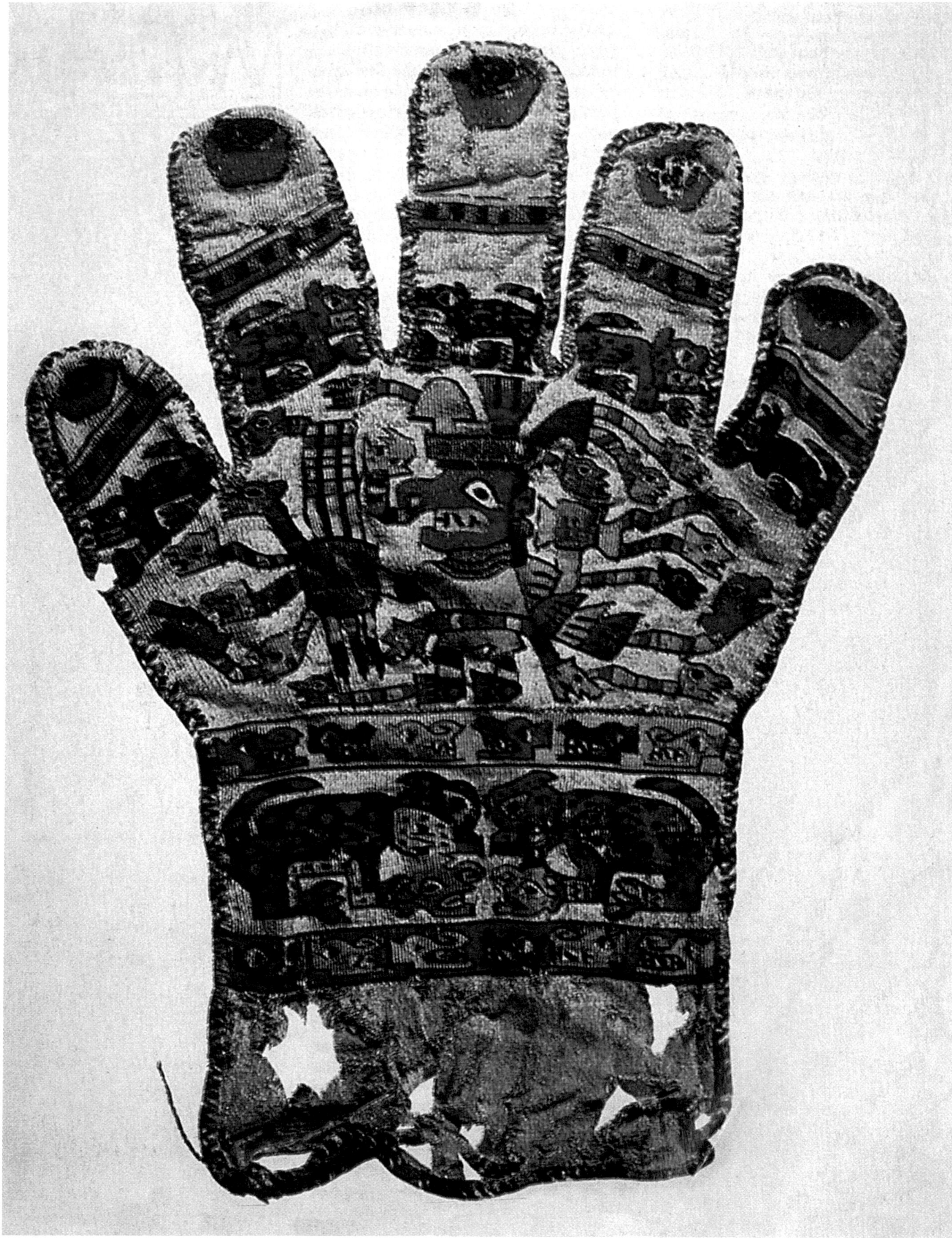

cultural heritage. Victoria's Secret was forced to apologise after a model wore a Native American-inspired feathered headdress and very little else on the catwalk at Paris Fashion Week in 2012. A blog representing the rights of native peoples, Native Appropriations, reacted by saying, "This isn't fun, this isn't a fantasy character. This is about our cultures, our bodies, and our lives." The underwear brand replied in a statement that they "didn't mean to offend anyone".
That same year, the Navajo nation sued Urban Outfitters months after they had sent a letter to the high street brand demanding it remove the Navajo name from items, including a hip flask and hipster pants. In 2015 designer Paul Smith came under scrutiny after modifying a Peshawari *chappal*, a leather sandal worn in parts of Pakistan, naming it Robert and adding a price tag of £ 300 when *chappals* generally cost less than £ 15. After a petition, Paul Smith said the shoe was "inspired by the Peshawari *chappal*" and has removed the name Robert. The scarf from CDG is different in that although it is an appropriation it does, intentionally or otherwise, show the real beauty of Andean cloth aesthetics. Both scarves in the collection were bought second-hand, one for 10 USD, the other for 200 USD.

Silk

One of the thousands of Clérambault photos of draped women. This one is entitled *Winter Palace Niqab*.

Gaétan de Clérimbaut was a polymath, famous for the thousands of photographs he took, and especially the thousands of draped women in Morocco. He was also a psychologist who is said by Jacques Lacan to have inspired him to become one himself. At one time Clérimbaut was employed by the Paris police and in 1908 and 1910 he published case studies, or rather accounts of his interrogations, of four women arrested for stealing pieces of silk. Not those of the middle-class shoplifting epidemic of the time, but those who'd had tough lives as widows or abused women and who stole the silk for sexual pleasure, its touch and sound 'delicious'. Sometimes, just imagining the feel and sound of the silk was enough for arousal. After masturbation they lost interest in the fabric. As one woman described, she liked silk when it was still 'stiff'. He also noted that sexual arousal was likely to be accompanied by the smell of perfume and referred to synesthèsie génitale as if it were a form of 'sexual imbalance'. Like a good bourgeois, he was outraged at their lack of remorse and defined them both as 'hysterical' and 'selfishly' fetishistic since it was a private source of arousal unrelated to men. Given his own obsession with the drapery itself that covered women, this was characteristic of the judgmentalism and hypocrisy of his class. On the other hand, stealing silk was not exclusive to such women. In her *London Journal* first published in 1842, Flora Tristan describes the trade in stolen silk handkerchiefs "in a country where the desire to make money is paramount. ... dealing in stolen goods is tolerated, theft becomes a regular industry; thus a multitude of people make a profession out of stealing silk handkerchiefs, and their harvest is so abundant that the resale of these articles constitutes a special branch of the trade of *honest shopkeepers*. In Field Lane, an alley in Holborn, there is nothing to be seen but dealers in second hand silk handkerchiefs. ... The men and women dealers, whose looks are in perfect harmony with their trade, stand in their doorways and hector the customers who come under cover of night to buy dirt cheap. ... the stolen handkerchiefs have been taken into the back of the shop after price haggling and given to a servant whose sole and constant occupation is to unpick any identifying marks and then to wash them." The actual making of silk is a far more sober story. Silk worms need a careful feeding schedule to produce good fibres and an equal attention given to their ambient temperature, a degree of warmth necessary for their survival. Thus over a few thousand years Chinese women would sometimes sew the tiny eggs into little cotton bags and wear them beneath their own clothing. They would also have made use of the handle-spindle: the oldest known, and described as the outstanding technological achievement of the Neolithic age. The earliest fragments of silk that have been found are from 5000 years ago, and its production has always been taken seriously. In the Shang period some three and half thousand years ago there was an official office of Nu Cang, mistress of the silk worm. Later, institutions were created like the *Dianis* for collecting, testing, storing and distribution of silk; others for controlling the female labour force and for raw materials, and the *Ranren* for the dyeing of silk yarn and fabrics. There was a huge though hierarchical demand for the most complex silk weaves and the technology to make them. Sophisticated damask looms, some with

opposite page:

"In 1492, the natives discovered they were Indians, discovered they lived in America, discovered they were naked, discovered that the Sin existed, discovered they owed allegiance to a King and Kingdom from another world and a God from another sky ... "
Glove from Moche civilisation (about 100 to 700 CE) representing a warrior carrying arrows and decorated with felines and zoomorphes.

50 treadles for 50 shaft looms, existed over 2000 years ago. They were followed by the Zilu patterning loom and the 1-N cord system for patterning, where a single thread can control several cords to form a pattern unit for the warps. And these in turn were synthesised in the drawloom, a combination of pattern programme and 1-N cord system, which was developed around 600 CE. As for the hierarchy it is said that there were 700 weavers devoted entirely to the demands of "Yang the Precious Consort", the concubine of the Emperor Xuanxong, later executed as a scapegoat for military defeats. The demand also led, as in most parts of the world, to sumptuary laws inspired by notions both of exclusiveness and of the Other's decadence. First in 771 and then in 829 it is decreed that on the first day of the New Year "looms and reeds used in the production of gaudy and frivolous textiles be burned". Despite such laws, a new burst of technical advance and advice occurred some 400 years later, prompted by a big increase in demand from the aristocracy, scholar-officials, merchants, and the nouveaux riche as well as an expensive pay-off to the 'barbarians' on the Northern frontier. It led to improvements in worm-breeding, novel grafting techniques for mulberry trees and new techniques of silk-reeling. Shih Nung Pi Yung gave detailed advice on the construction of commercial heating rooms and types of reeling. At the same time Huai Nan Tzu called for restraint, warning that even though two crops of worms a year were possible, it might lead to damaging the trees. In 1313 Wang Chen in his "Treatise on Agriculture" describes a treadle-operated silk-reeling machine with roller-frames and a water-powered machine for hemp-spinning that had been adapted from one for reeling silk. There were also developments in printing techniques on silk which could make delicate patterns highlighted with gold, but not without an accompanying decree to maintain exclusivity, one which forbade common people to dress in finely printed silks. It was not just Chinese technology that was copied and adapted in Italy at around this time, but a stream of such sumptuary laws about who could wear the silks that started to be produced in Lucca and then Venice and Bologna.

1911

The Durbar – a historical Mughal court in India that was also used for a ceremonial gathering under the British Raj – was set up in Delhi in this year for the visit of the British King George V. It was a massive display of British military strength with much pomp and circumstance attached. Indian troops, elephants, and Indian royalty were all dressed in the exotic style, which the British favoured for Indians. "Indians, it was believed, were susceptible to show and drama, and hence the insistence that chiefs and their retinues should appear in their most colourful (if outmoded) clothes." At this same ceremony the king was presented with two 4.6-metre lengths of cloth with superbly crafted tapestry weave using in one silk thread wrapped in silver, and in the other wrapped in gold. These are still in the possession of the British royal family, a fact that came to light when the Queen Elizabeth II lent one to an exhibition of Indian textiles in 2015 at the London museum named after her ancestors, The Victoria and Albert. The Gaekwar of Baroda was one of those presented to George V to whom etiquette demanded that he bow three times. His insult is said to be that he bowed only once in curt fashion, but what was more keenly felt by the British was that he appeared in European clothes with a walking stick. The wearing of the clothes of the oppressor by the Gaekwar was not unique, from at least the 16th century, styles of Jewish men's dress in Eastern Europe were influenced by those of the *szlachta* (Polish nobles). While the nobles abandoned certain types of clothing for newer fashions, Hasidim have preserved some of those older styles to the present day. A more dramatic case is that of another people subjected to genocide, the Herero of modern-day Namibia. In the period of German colonial rule in what was then South West Africa, land grabbing, a failed rebellion and concentration camps lead to the deaths of approximately 80% of the Herero between 1904 and 1907. After the defeat of German forces there in 1915, the Herero men began to wear versions of the oppressor's dress, and women those of the missionary ladies that came with colonialism in the 1890s. This is how it is still is, partly as a living day-to-day reminder of that terrible history. "Wearing the enemy's uniform will diminish their power and transfer some of their strength to the new wearer … part appropriation, a coming-to-terms with and overcoming of history and the colonial experience."

Prabhakar Pachpute

Dancer in Cuzco, Peru.

Wool, acquired in Pisac, 2005. I bought these slings at the market in Pisac, Peru, because of their colours and shapes, and I admired the way Indigenous people adorned their llamas with them. At this time I didn't know about the importance of these animals and that they are considered to be part of the family. In a book I saw images of people dancing with the slings which were described as *flying gardens*, the pompoms being the flowers.

Later, visiting the *pueblo jovenes* (young villages), the slums of Lima, to meet a painter, Elena, from the Amazon, the slings came into my mind again. These *pueblo jovenes* are spreading into the desert surrounding the city and are very densely populated. The people live in small houses of which the richer ones have tin roofs, increasing the already unbearable heat. Everything there is ochre: the walls of the houses, the sandy paths in between, the dried-out rubbish-filled bed of the river Rimac. How painful this must be for the eyes of people like her, who are used to luscious shades of green.

Elena travels back and forth between there and the Amazon. Business can be done in the city but she has to carry to it the ingredients for the natural dyes she uses – barks, leaves, flowers, mud – from the forests far away. In her house these were simmering in huge pots or waiting to be used, covered with a thick layer of mould. She is subject to constraint, and it's the same for the ethnic handicraft market and for her work as an artist; her white clients label her as 'ethnic' and thus expect her to use natural colours and to paint on cotton cloth. In order to sell she also has to limit herself to producing only patterns from her 'tribe' for handicrafts and images from the 'natural world' in her art.

In the *pueblo jovenes* there is no running water. It has to be carried on foot from far away, so wool flowers seemed to be a good option. Later I met the painter again in her house, close to the jungle town of Pucallpa. She was just about to finish a commissioned painting with hundreds of butterflies, and as I was about to indulge in the variety of species and her knowledge of them she showed me torn out pages from a newspaper where butterflies were used in the graphics of an advertisement and which she used as a template.

Wood Dyes

Logwood "is so essentially necessary in dyeing our manufactures that it would be the last and worst consequence to be deprived thereof", wrote Richard Harris in 1714. This English wool merchant recognised the importance for wool of the base for a red, black and grey dye that came from the heartwood of the tree (*haemataxylum campechinaum*). He was worried because too much was going to Holland and Hamburg, carried by the merchant ships of Boston or Jamaica from the Bay of Honduras in what is now Belize.

As was so often the cause with dyes and cloths coming into Europe, this concern followed an earlier period, 1581–1662, when an English parliament had forbidden its use for dyeing because locally produced plant dyes were the norm. The acceleration of its production involved the strategic move by pirates and buccaneers after the 1667 Treaty of Madrid to resort, for the time being, to legitimate work. Many settled in Belize, and having in their previous life seen the value of the then-rare logwood cargoes carried by Spanish ships, started logging in heavily mosquito'd swamps full of crocodiles. Logs were floated towards the coast where they were picked up by merchant ships for re-export to Europe. Demand peaked in the first half of the 18th century as prices rose to a record 25 pounds a ton in 1750. In the 1720s the Baymen (Belize settlers) brought in African slave labour through the Antillean slave markets, though numbers were small. The number of slaves increased rapidly as the logwood boom declined at the end of the 18th century and the logging business shifted to mahogany. The business of logwood did not cause deforestation in Belize itself but when introduced into Jamaica and Haiti in the early 18th century it denuded large areas of tropical vegetation. The European attitude is succinctly put by the English Dr Thomas Preston in 1791: "Countries yet barbarous are the right and proper nurseries" for British timber supplies. It is the colonial right to be omnivorous when it comes to the natural resources of others, and at this time it

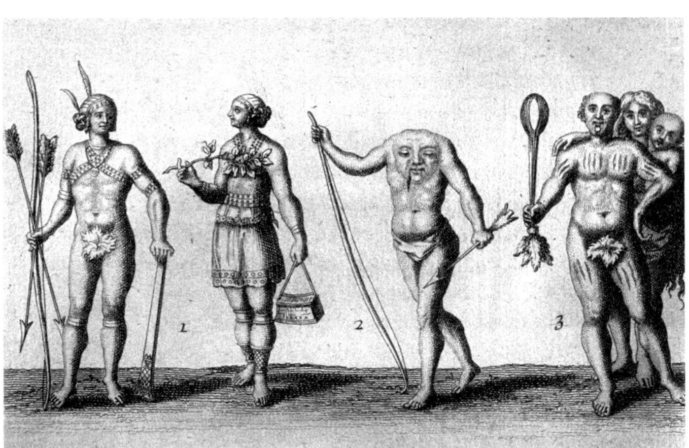

Caribs of the Antilles male & female, Acephali from South America, Brazilians.

applied to all the constituents for the business of the mechanised production of cloth and its colours: biocolonialism. In what is now Brazil, Europeans found out about a tropical tree that provided wood with the same tinctorial properties as *brasileum*, which came from Asian trees to produce a red dye the colour of burning coals. Originally this land of plenty – possessing such trees in abundance far greater than the Asian *caesalpinia* – was called Land of the Holy Cross, but then it was named after the dye colour itself. This was seen as a blasphemy by the 16th-century chronicler and representative of the Portuguese Crown, João de Barros who with reference to the devil writes, "I admonish all of you who read these words in the name of the cross of Jesus Christ to give this land the name which it so solemnly received [Land of the Holy Cross] for fear that same cross, which will be present before us in the final days, accuse you of being more devoted to Brazil wood than to it." Like the cross the name was stained with red but this was not holy blood, but profit. The secret of how to extract the red pigment was stolen from the Indigenous people of the region. This pigment was then used as a dye for high-demand luxury textiles like velvet. The highly profitable monopoly held by the Portuguese crown stimulated other nations to smuggle this prized wood out of Brazil. The unsuccessful attempt in 1555 of a French expedition led by Nicolas Durand de Villegagnon, vice-admiral of Brittany, to establish a colony in present-day Rio de Janeiro was motivated in part by the bounty generated by economic exploitation of brazilwood. Excessive exploitation (it has been estimated that in two centuries, more than 50 million trees were destroyed) finally led to a steep decrease in the number of brazilwood trees in the 18th century, causing the collapse of this economic activity. Emblematic of today's vanishing flora and fauna, the wood, which gave Brazil its name, has disappeared entirely there and has been preserved only in a few botanical gardens in the North. It is now officially listed as an endangered species.

2006

"Is there no-one who might lend a dark suit in a pinch?" asked Antonio Burgos in the Spanish newspaper *ABC* on the occasion of Evo Morales – President-elect of Bolivia – meeting with King Juan Carlos in Madrid. Morales wore a pullover of red, blue and white hoops for the occasion and Burgos went on to write, "Pullovers like that are given as charity by catechism teachers and then thrown back in their faces by the poor." Another professional opinionist, Jose Berlanga in *La Razon*, compared him to children on a UNICEF postcard. Even attempts at irony like Rosa Belmonte comparing him with the *sans-culottes* – the radical militants of the lower classes, urban labourers literally without silk knee-breeches – of the French Revolution, were weighed down with Eurocentrism. In fact the pullover, a *chompa*, is an entirely respectable garment in Bolivia. For the well-to-do it would be woven in alpaca wool, but the President-elect's was acrylic as it would be for ordinary Bolivians. The upset was that with a combination of good taste and political acumen the President-elect simply ignored the obligatory 'serious man' Western suit, and left it to politicians like Presidents Bush and Putin to look ridiculous in *ponchos* at an APEC summit held in Santiago de Chile in November 2004. Their show of 'authenticity' was especially absurd given how much the *poncho* is a legacy of cross-cultural adaptation. The Mapuche of southern Chile were a people the Spanish invaders were never able to entirely subdue, and became expert horsemen, even though the horse had been alien to Latin America, after stealing Spanish horses. During an uprising late in the 18th century, the Spanish noticed something different in the dress of the Mapuche: they had previously worn the pre-Colombian style tunic – a short woven garment with a slit for the head, sewn up the side with small armholes, and the trousers the Spanish had insisted on, but for their horseback attacks had opened up the sides of their tunics for greater freedom for their arms. The colonisers themselves saw the advantages and began to copy this new style for their soldiers and *hacienda* bosses, and had them made in the super-exploited textile workshops they had set up. In a further twist, native Andean men did not want to wear *ponchos*, considering it now to be the dress of the invaders and it was only during the independence movement of the early 19th century, when men like Simón Bolívar were wearing striking looking *ponchos* that they started to wear them themselves.

Bolivian President Evo Morales meets Spain's ex-King Juan Carlos in Madrid, Jan. 4, 2006.

Pedro G. Romero

Bramble found on the way
is split into different heaps
some are for making saints
others for making coals

(Soleares de la Serneta)[1]

The same savage who, apparently in order to kill his enemy, sticks his knife through a picture of him, really does build his hut of wood and cuts his arrow with skill and not in effigy ...

(Ludwig Wittgenstein, *Remarks on Frazer's* Golden Bough, 1930–1936)

Los informantes informes. (Formless Informants.) "We feel incapable of reading. We have lost our ties to any thing that is not a word, writing, alphabets. The world as revealed by signs. Words are read, but rarely understood. That is to say, what they actually express has hardly any relevance. Semiotics has impoverished experience. Is it just about signs?"[2]

2

Bobote listened in astonishment to these words as they came out of the digital recorder. Okay, I had given him a bunch of different colour fabrics, some of them knotted together. Lots of bright colours. On the ends of the fabrics, big fabric tasseling balls seemed to make sense of the thing. If you shook them in the air, the balls on the ends made the whole artefact turn, producing startling bursts of colour which explained the festive nature of the loud hues. Bobote was Gypsy and, used as he was to the ethnographic survey, he assumed that my question was guided by an anthropological intent. The thing is that he found *wichi-wichi*, the artefact's name, incredibly funny. He could not stop laughing every time he uttered the words, over and over again. "This isn't from around here", he said as I looked on in an obvious way. "I know that. But, what do you think it could be?" He put the thing around his neck and started walking back and forth and repeating the words *wichi-wichi*, giving "them a sexual connotation by mimicking the act of fucking with the movement and arch of his fingers. At one point, something lit up his face, he stopped this particular dance and stuttered: "this is something to do with the '*payo-poni*', a gift or an object that is part of their customs that you have bought from them, that's it, yes, I have seen them wearing it in the *Tres Mil Ulea market*". Bobote was referring to the improvised shops that a number of Latin American emigrants set up in the market inside the *Tres Mil Viviendas* neighbourhood, in Seville's south side, a neighbourhood with a high index of Gypsy population, and also at present, with a great number of Ecuadorian, Colombian and especially Peruvian migrants. The pejorative term *payo-poni*, which was hardly made better by the affection with which Bobote had spit out the epithet, actually referred to the latter population. Gypsies call us non-Gypsy *payos*. The origin of the word *payo* is *campesino*, peasant, *payes* in Catalan, and also *paisano*, the native of the land. Interestingly, *payo* ended up integrated in the word *payador*, a payo who sings. This latter linguistic drift is intriguing, given that *payador* is in fact a word of classical origin which refers to the Provençal term *trovar*, singing in verse. We find the same integration of terms in the Quechua language, *paya* refers both to *peasant* and to the "singing in verse" typical of story tellers, the verse improvisers. *Poni* means small, of course, from "pony", the small horse. My friendly advice, "don't call them *payo-poni*, Bobote!", was met with a burst of laughter and a great hug for Rudolph, a small Hungarian Gypsy who was in the room with us, "we are brothers, brothers!", proclaimed Bobote, clutching his friend against his body.[3]

And yet, Rudolph was of another opinion altogether. For many years he had worked in Hungarian folkore dance groups, and during a tour of Bulgaria he had seen cloths, similar to the *wichi-wichi*, embellishing the countrywomen's dresses. Both Bobote and I were looking at him in amazement and with incredulity. The reasons behind our reservations differed however. Bobote regarded Rudolph as a rival fighting for both my attention and that of my recorder. For my part, well, as I already knew something about the origin of the object – Ines had told me that she had got it in Peru – my face combined both surprise and admiration. Rudolph picked up the thing and started playing with it, at the same time as he explained to us how the Bulgarian countrywomen used it. "Some use it as an embellishment, like this, on their heads, and others hang it from their house door on special, festive days." And indeed, Rudolph had first worn the *wichi-wichi* as a hat, and then had stretched it between the lamp and the doorjamb. He continued with his explanations as he skilfully threw the thing up in the air. "These are for embellishment, but there are other less colourful ones, or old ones, that are thrown like this in order to catch hens and geese, which the countrywomen, too fat for running, cannot catch on their own." At this point Rudolph had skilfully thrown the *wichi-wichi* and entangled it between Rambo and Cobra, two huge dogs, feral yet docile, who followed Bobote wherever he went. He insisted to anyone who would listen that they weren't his, that they didn't belong to him. Rudolph had accompanied his explanation about the Bulgarian *wichi-wichi* with Chaplinesque gestures and had littered his speech with words and phrases in Romany, the Gypsy language. Bobote could not understand those bits, even though he bragged about speaking *caló*, the language of the Iberian Gypsies. Truth be told, *caló* and Romany are very different languages when spoken, well, actually, as much or as little as Spanish and Portuguese. The truth is that Bobote was not in the mood for paying attention.[4]

3

4

5

Noam Chomsky had been listening to our conversation from the big arm sofa which presided the old stately room – by now slowly surrendering to the early evening darkness – at House Wittegenstein. Unhurriedly, with his peculiar accent, he addressed us directly. It was as if he was masticating his words, as if he had to stop here and there in order to draw smoke from a pipe or lick the edge of a glass of whiskey. We were indeed aware that at the time he neither drank nor smoked. Every single thing that he slowly told us, felt unquestionable to us. To start with, he began by agreeing with the two Romas, according to each of their positions, as we would learn later on in his speech. At that precise moment, Rambo and Cobra were guarding Chomsky, each at one side of the armchair, conferring his words a regal air, which he delivered with rigour and steadiness. Such was the rigour and steadiness in his speech, that it did not lose a bit of authority and seriousness when, to great comic effect , the philosopher wore the *wichi-wichi* on his head, as a sort of embellishment, laurel or crown. Chomsky started to talk about the *gañacho*, a dancer from the Peruvian Andean plateau, who carries the *wichi-wichi* in his hands, as a tassel whip to assist his dancing. Bobote and Rudolph could not avoid their comedic condition and started performing a swaying walk that was meant to accompany Chomsky's description of the dance. "*Gañanes!*", screamed Bobote, referring to the skilled dancer that the American philosopher had described for us. Not long after, the Chomskian monologue slid down the complex world of the carnival and the implications that a few words have in any description of the things of the world, when those words' main condition is precisely to betray their original meaning. Despite it all, the carnivalesque nature of the *wichi-wichi* was obvious, and when accompanied by *chuspas* and *huaracas*, they were an essential part of the festive celebrations in the Andean world. As it often occurs in buffoonery scenes, I had to interrupt the maestro in order to get Rudolph and Bobote to calm down, as they had embarked on a game of playfully hitting each other. It's true that they seemed to be joking, but I knew very well that that kind of initial silliness did always turn into a rain of blows, during which bad temper was as quick to spring up as jokes and laughter. Chomsky then started to discuss the military origin of the objects, the *wichi-wichi*, which up until then had seemed to us like harmless fun objects. Inca soldiers had used them as offensive weapons. They were a kind of *boleadoras* made up of two or three heavy projectiles joined by ropes that the Inca warriors would spin in the air and hurl at their enemies. These then would either be brought down by the heavy blows to their heads, or they would fall down on the ground at full speed after getting their legs entangled in the *wichi-wichi*. Needless to say, the *wichi-wichi* was also used as a hunting weapon, but its most important and valued function was as a warrior weapon against the human enemy. Antisuyo soldiers would colour in red the tassels already stained by blood. Similarly to the *huaraca*, a kind of sling, *wichi-wichi* had been used mostly in combat and battles previous to the arrival of the Spanish colonisers. Manco Inca already used horses and Uirearms in his fight against the European invaders. *Wichi-wichi boleadoras* were at that time relegated to more domestic tasks. First, cattle breeders used it to capture and tame llamas. Herders walking along the Tahuantinsuyo paths on their way to the Inti Raymi festivities in Cuzco would embellish their llamas with the *wichi-wichi*. The swaying walk, that both Bobote and Rudolph had mimicked, probably originated in the celebrations of these cavalcades. "On the 20th of January, day of Saint Sebastian, the ritual battle between Checca and Langui will take place on the Chiaraje pampas ... Ritual battles foresee better harvests, the expansion of territory and the satisfaction of the *apus*, the guardian deities ... *pinkuyllo*, *coca*, *huaracas* and *wichi-wichis* are the essential elements of the new *pukllay* where warriors of eight different communities will fight against each other in a ritual game, during which blood always runs ... wounded and dead are familiar words devoid of any great emotion, at most that of leaving proof of a new year that has been transcended, renewed and purified, and that can now be confronted ... and so, slowly and gradually, they all arrive, loners, groups of friends, young couples and also entire families, dressed up for the occasion in their party dresses ... it is easy to distinguish the inhabitants of the different Andean communities, known as *ayllus*, in their traditional dress. Among the men, the popular *tablacasaca* stands out, a tight dress coat made of woollen cloth ... those who migrated to urban centres, which make up the largest group, they no longer wear the *tablacasaca* but rather an attire deeply affected by modernity, where trainers and other sports brand items stand out ... especially the young, the older population and the better-off, they wear a leather jacket or a red poncho, locally made hats and riding boots, an undeniable sign of their social status ... this year however, after the battles, there were a number of wounded, but none were dead, and this fact was interpreted as a bad omen, which the locals directly linked to the 'presence' or interference of a foreign TV crew, who were making a documentary – on an international level, they said – about the warrior rituals that continue to be honoured today. The film crew's presence would not have had any significance were it not for the fact that two of the groups filming positioned themselves in the worst possible location, obstructing the customary development of events ... one camera-man, recklessly stood on one of the rocks that was meant to be conquered, hindering said action and irritating the participants, until he literally had to 'run for his life' due to the ferocity that the battle was reaching ... another film crew was flying over the area on board a mosquito helicopter, and on top of the deafening sound it made, it was the low-flying manoeuvres that unsettled and exasperated everyone. The participants, as is well known, are not mere enthusiastic 'actors', they are actual members of ancestral communities celebrating one of the most important rituals of their lives ... during which dying is not just an offering to the earth, but more importantly, an offering to their family and their community ... it is for this reason that they are attentive to everything external that could affect the signs coming from nature, which announce or prophesy the final outcome of the battle ... the rain, for instance, which carries a meaning in the way it falls or in the angle at which it falls, or hailstones, which mean different things depending on whether they are big or small ... or the wind itself, which is considered the major doomsayer, and which is venerated with devotion and intimacy before going into battle, as it is the wind itself who will carry pleas and promises to the mountains, the hills, and the guardian mountaintops, the Uirst and most important witnesses to the battle ..." Chomsky had been reading the last paragraphs, sentences and words from his iPad, and it was clear from the way his voice had become more fatigued. Rudolph and Bobote pretended to be sleeping, one was spread out on the sofa, and the other simulated laying on the table. Needing to overcome this drowsiness, when they perceived that Chomsky's tired silence had taken over, they started to argue with each other about which one of the two had actually hit the target with their interpretation of the word, the *wichi-wichi*, and the thing. It seemed as though they were actually talking to each other, but actually, nothing intelligent was coming out of their mouths. With their hands up in the air, and waving their extended arms, who could say that these were not indeed acts of communication? Well they weren't, they were just clowning around. Words and nonsense, likewise in their meaningless gestures. Nothing rational enough to be of interest for my recorder. Chomsky fell asleep, and for real this time. I opened the door and just left. The scene was all but edifying.[5]

And I started getting further and further away from the house. And I left them there, fighting and arguing. Uchi, Bobote's partner and wife, seemed to be coming from the *qhaswana pata*, the place to sing and dance. She met up with me when I was still in the garden that surrounded the house, still slowly moving away, deep in thought. With a happy curiosity she inquired what was going on, and looking towards the big glass on the house's exterior, she answered herself: "All kinds of dolls of different colours moving inside the window frame, that is what we see, such is the world." These were the last sentences that I felt like transcribing from the events of that day.[6]

6

1 *Soleá* is one of the *palos* (modes, styles) of Ulamenco. [T.N.]
2 *Wichi-wichi* over the lemon tree in House Wittgenstein, Seville, 2015.
3 Bobote in the *San Pablo* neighbourhood. "Flamenco singing children" episode of the series "Rite and Geography of Flamenco", TVE, 1973.
4 Rudolph Rostas in *Utopian Pulse*, Stuttgart, 2015.
5 Noam Chomsky and Michel Foucault in conversation for the *International Philosophers Project*, Amsterdam, 1971.
6 Uchi acting for the advertising campaign of *The Real*. Photograph by Javier Andrada, Seville, 2012.

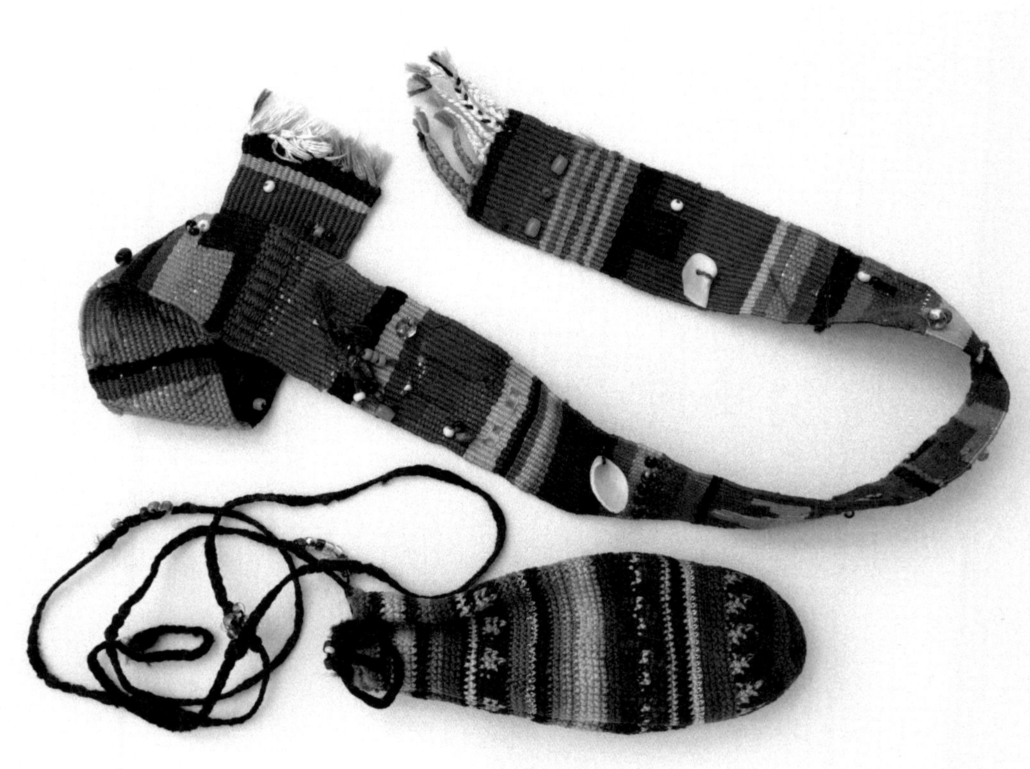

Since its founding in 1988, Maison Martin Margiela has collected used and new clothes, accessories and objects from around the world. Sourced in Cuzco, Peru, cotton and nylon bracelets are assembled to create this classic tailored jacket for the Spring-Summer 2012 "Artisanal Collection".

Made by Ines Doujak, Cuzco, 1978. The Kogi people of the Amazon understand "their place in the cosmos as part of a great weaving: (as they) pass over the earth, they (weave) a sacred cloak over the Great Mother, each journey like a thread ... (Even) a person's thoughts are like threads. The act of spinning is the act of thinking. The cloth they weave and the clothes they wear become their thoughts. Everything they do is conceived of as a fabric, and everything begins and ends with the loom."

Weaving is a primary reference in stories of the origins of the world among the Dogon of Mali. At sunrise on the appointed day the seventh ancestor Spirit spat out eighty threads of cotton; these he distributed between his upper teeth, which acted as the teeth of a weaver's reed. In this way he made the uneven threads of a weaver's warp. He did the same with the lower teeth to make the even threads. By opening and shutting his jaws the Spirit caused the threads of the warp to make the movements required in weaving. His whole face took part in the work, his nose studs serving as a block, while the stud in his lower lip was the shuttle. As the threads crossed and uncrossed, the two tips of the Spirit's forked tongue pushed the thread of the weft to and fro, and the web took shape from his mouth in the breath of the second revealed Word.

Tartan

One of the very first Scottish clan tartans, made by William Wilson and Son of Bannockburn for the Macphersons in the late 18th century, was one the company had ready off the peg because they had previously sold the same cloth to a Mr Kidd to clothe his West Indian slaves. Before that sale it had simply been cloth Number 155. This was appropriate to the whole fraudulent, constructed story according to which tartan and the kilt (or 'philbeg') was the authentic dress of Scottish Highlanders 'since time immemorial'. When a British Royal visit by George IV to Scotland was proposed in 1819, the same company created a 'Key Pattern Book' which was sent to the Highland Society several hundred miles away in London, where the Society duly 'certified' the patterns as belonging to this or that clan. This was at a time when no peasant tenant Highlander was wearing either kilt or tartan unless he was in a British army regiment, and when they were being driven off the land by the greed of their clan chiefs and

The kilt does have a continuing life, worn by Herero people in Namibia who survived their almost complete genocide under German colonialism early in the 20th century. European military clothes are worn both as a reminder and as a giver of power.

sheep colonialism; and when the traditional Highlands were smashed in the name of efficiency, the houses burned to the ground. In modern times the Guatemalan state, while proclaiming Mayan dress and culture as authentically Guatemalan, was in the process of the mass killing of actual Mayan people who were to afraid to wear traditional dress for fear of being marked as 'rebels'. It was only after the distinctive Highland society of Scotland had been broken that its people could be romanticised as an endangered species of 'noble savages', with the novelist Sir Walter Scott providing the romance. As an ordinary non-clan cloth, tartan seems originally to have come from Flanders, whereas Scottish clan distinctions were marked by cockades in the bonnet. The kilt was an invention of an English Quaker from Lancashire, Thomas Rawlinson. He was of a family of iron-masters who needed charcoal, and when the Highland forests were opened up for fuel after the 1717 rebellion he made an agreement with a McDonnell clan chief. He found the traditional cheap belted plaid (usually plain brown unless worn by Chiefs) too cumbersome for efficient workers, and came up with the idea of the kilt. It was bestowed "on the highlanders in order not to preserve their traditional way of life but to ease its transformation: to bring them out of the heather and into the factory."

The British government seems not to have understood any of this when, after a second rebellion in 1745 had been crushed, it banned the wearing of the kilt as if that were the traditional dress of the rebels. So it was that, when the ban was lifted some 40 years later, it became the fashion for "Anglicised Scottish peers, improving gentry, well-educated Edinburgh lawyers and Aberdeen merchants who were not constrained by poverty and who would never have to skip over bogs or lie in heather all night, to exhibit themselves publicly not in the trews, the traditional costume of their class, nor in the cumbrous belted plaid, but in a costly and fanciful version of that recent innovation, the philbeg or small kilt".

1844

Self-employed "Silesian weavers – formally independent but constantly dependent on a few merchant entrepreneurs – in the 'industrial villages' of Peterswalden and Langenbielau, Germany, where 12,000 worked for a few cloth merchant capitalists, attacked the factories and houses of some of these entrepreneurs".

These were not the severely impoverished linen weavers, whose incomes had been in decline from the start of the century and who suffered "terrible destitution", but those who had made the switch to the greater promise of cotton but now had good reason to fear that they too were going to be made poor by the forces of capital and the state. The Prussian state had made the political decision to adopt free trade policies, and the weavers were subject to a raft of taxes. The free trade policy meant the worldwide downward pressure on the price of woven cotton would reach them while at the same time the aristocratic landlord still wanted his ground rent and protection tribute along with school fees for the weavers children. The entrepreneurs themselves paid little in taxes, which meant there was no communal poor relief – a fact which compounded the weavers' fears still further. In 1843, as the prices they were paid by the 'entrepreneurs' were cut, they petitioned various levels of the state, and put emphasis on how the largest companies based in their villages – Zwanziger and F&W Dierig – were employing workers from elsewhere and then cutting wages. These petitions made no difference. Violence was seen to be the only response likely to have any impact.

Weavers with very different income levels – which depended on whether the loom was owned or rented, the quality of the loom and whether they paid for the yarn or had it on credit – all joined in, on a level of organisation shown in how they ripped up account books and destroyed some semi-mechanised looms, along with the houses of the offending merchants. Most of all they destroyed the luxury homes of the two dominant families,who had boasted of how much they had cost, who evaded community taxes and had shown 'scorn and ridicule' towards them. In addition to wage cuts, the weavers had been disrespectedand were not treated as formal equals. An anonymous letter addressed to Zwanziger made the following accusation: "once he has earned his thousands he defies the town and says, 'I am going to close my business ... and do whatever I want'". Others accused the family of living "luxuriously, gluttonously and wastefully".

Artist Illma Gore spent three months making a Lous Vuitton toilet using 24 bags worth $15,000, offering it now for $100,000.

The weavers held off the first attack by soldiers ordered in by the Prussian state, and community support was shown by the laxness of magistrates in arresting rioters. The liberal German press took up the issue and the Prussianstate showed an interest in 'the problem', but only after the troops had killed 12 weavers in a second attack, injured many more and imprisoned a further 120. But in the short term the weavers had been right, violence worked: wages were increased and the Prussian state set up wage-paying public works, even if in the long-term the weavers' formal independence exposed them to competition from mechanised looms. Nevertheless, the Silesian weavers did inspire Heinrich Heine's poem "Germany, We Weave Your Burial Shroud". Into it we weave the threefold curse. God, King and the Fatherland cursed, suggesting that a profound change in Germany was imminent and that the self-confident weavers were not only promoting their interests but working towards a fundamental political change. Karl Marx claimed their actions as a precursor to the 1848 'revolution' and as exhibiting a degree of class-consciousness that overcame different income levels among the weavers themselves, though their uprising was essentially local and not the product of collective organisation. Heine'spoem was banned by the Royal Prussian Supreme Court because of its 'rebellious tone'.

Käthe Kollwitz, *Webe-zug, pl. 4* (from: *Ein Weberaufstand*) 1893–1897.

The combination of a wage cut and a perceived betrayal of acceptable (if still hierarchical) trade relations was and has been a frequent cause of strikes and protest. Some 35 years later, in the Damascus of 1879, conflict started between journeymen and master weavers with workshops of their own. Above them, as in Prussia and Lyon, were non-factory owning merchants who had replaced the master as arbiters of workshop conditions. Over the period since 1820 this change had occurred along with a gradual shift from silk and silk-cotton weaves to mostly cotton. More importantly,despite ups and downs in demand,and even when production was booming again from the 1860s, the journeyman's standard of living was nothing like as good as it had once been, while changes to the structure of the business meant they could no longer realistically aspire to become masters themselves. Up until this point, grievances had been settled individually, and falling real wages had been accepted if it was felt that this was keeping the workshops competitive with some European imports. But when in January 1879 the masters decided to cut the rate for each piece of cloth produced, even though they were taking their cut from the increased profits made by the merchants, it prompted the journeymen to their first collective action. 3000 journeymen went on strike – the most militant cutting threads on the looms – and after four weeks the piece-rate cuts were rescinded. One advantage the weavers had was that, unlike in Europe, where government authorities were quick to intervene, the Ottoman state did not act as a police force for merchants or masters, not believing the business to be of real importance to its power.

Zdenka Silvia Ballon

"I have a history in defending coca fields here in Bolivia dating back to the 1980s when I was an active leftist. At this time US obsessions instigated chemical spraying of the crop to destroy it. The synthesising of cocaine from coca and its abuse are both Western, and yet despite its once having been declared a wonder drug, its abuse was being used to attack Indigenous chewing of coca leaves. In this period I was coming to understand how absolutely central coca leaves are to the culture and cosmology of Indigenous Andean people. To start with its material properties: for one thing, the leaves are very good food, one of the best sources in the world, full of proteins, minerals and with more calcium than in milk or eggs. In fact Bolivia is full of medicinal plants that are used by shamans. People go to shamans when they are sick or have some problem that's eating them, and they use the coca in several ways. The shaman reads them, through the leaves he finds out what's your sickness and how to cure it. Coca is used as a cure for diabetes, as a way of balancing the sugar in the blood, and when you break a bone they wrap coca leaves around it because of their calcium content. In other instances a shaman might use hallucinogens, but coca is not one, coca is for having a clear mind, lucid. It helps if rain is needed or if you want to give thanks to *pachamama* who you can loosely translate as Mother Earth, a feminine spirit. The leaf also acts as an intermediary, or rather a way in which people can know that the ancestors are with them in a particular moment, and which makes that moment sacred, different from other moments. The leaf brings together past, present and future. For old people who believe that when you die you have a long way to go, it acts as a clear-headed guide. Equally with the coca you might 'awaken the space' as they say; that is when you go to the mountain or one of the many scared places, because the sacred is everywhere in sharp contrast to Christianity, and with the leaves, you can become aware of the spirits of that place. This is not all *esoteric* in the Western sense, in the rather vulgar way that appeals to it. Coca is chewed every day by most Indigenous people, and this chewing, which white people do not do, is not greedy consumption. Nor is it just for work, which is what the colonialists saw as its only purpose when they used Indigenous people to exploit and die in the mines, and when they made a double profit by taxing the leaves too. Instead, and this is crucial to understand, there is no division between the normal and the sacred. Coca is used in a variety of situations and has several 'functions'. There is almost nowhere in this country you can't use coca in exchange for something, like money. That's its economic function if you like. And in the *yungas*, these steep tropical valleys near enough to La Paz, the communities have always produced coca. It is not commercial, and if you see the country as a whole it's built on a kind of geographical reciprocity between *pisos ecologicos* (ecological zones). There's always been exchange between say, potatoes and llama in the *altiplano*, and in the *yungas* coca, fruits and coffee.

In the community you might chew it for work in the morning, and later in the day chew another *k'intu* (offering of usually three perfect coca leaves placed green side-up in a bouquet) to meet with friends and then at a another time when you might want to say thanks or hello to *pacha-mama*, or to *apu*, the powerful protector of the little mountains. In Aymarán communities there is always an up and down balance, up is masculine; down, feminine, and there the *apu* embraces both, it's a duality of balance. Whereas the colonial priests were always trying to impose their crude dichotomies of good and bad which are alien to this culture in which the world and its family are one spirit. So in the mines, they have the *tio*, literally meaning uncle, who is in effect neither good nor bad but for whom there should be ceremonies as a form of protection. His dark side embraces the dangers of the mine.

This alien dichotomy is also at odds with the basis of this society, which is reciprocity, which means to give and to receive. I see that as both a social, ecological and feminine concept to which exploitation is alien. In the past and now, the more power people have in an Indian community, they must bring coca leaves to social events. It means prestige and is one aspect of reciprocity that is a cultural reality surviving to this day in the Andean world. From the other side, when there is a new chief of the community the people bring him his stick and coca leaves. If they give a lot they are happy with you; if not they are not very happy. In this, coca is an everyday intermediary, both with others, with ancestors and as an indicator of intentions. With friendship for example; if I am your friend I will invite you to share coca leaves with me. Coca leaves are the beginning of a friendship, the main means of receiving and giving. It's the same with work. Reciprocity is the most important Andean concept and its main principle is *ayni* which implies a conscious and willing acknowledgement of the interconnections between humans and between humans and the natural world. And if you look at all the terraces that have been made here to grow the coca you can see the work of reciprocity materialised. This is an Andean technology, a huge work, but you can see that though they are in disrepair in other parts of the country they are maintained where there is coca growing. In the world of the colonisers I suspect there's a fear of this reciprocity, the feeling that receiving automatically puts you under some kind of obligation, something repellent to individualism. But it's not like that here. It's not judged by quantity, by exchange value; reciprocity is not accountancy. When you work with your heart, like working to keep the terraces good, then a coca plant will last 35–40 years and produce 4 times a year. It's not, 'Oh, I did so many hours so you owe me'. There are women here who may not work in the fields but are experts in drying the leaf after the harvest. No one counts the hours and the drying is a very important process. Do it wrong and you can get a very bad smell, but with experience it can be dried like a mummy, in fact like an ancestor. The attack on coca itself has to be seen in the context of Bolivian racism, which continues now with the hostility of rich people to the election of Evo Morales as President and the abuse of Indigenous people in the Pando and Sucre. It's interesting that in Chile they can be very friendly with Indians, how nice they are, but that is because they don't have them, at least very few. In Bolivia people have been killed demonstrating for their rights, for defending local ecologies and for the wealth coming from the exploitation of natural resources gas, water and proper roads. Perhaps the most important of the self-organisations of this struggle for rights were the coca-growers. Their *sindicatos* work just like the Indigenous community works even when they use words like *el secretario general*, it is truly democratic because the chief decides nothing, it's not him, it's all the community in which every person can be chief at least once in their life. So that when the organisation developed for 3 monthly meetings of the local *sindicatos* in bigger areas, *marcas*, the chiefs go with the decisions of their own communities. And of course coca is chewed in all these meetings, often they go on through the night where most of all a lucid head is required."

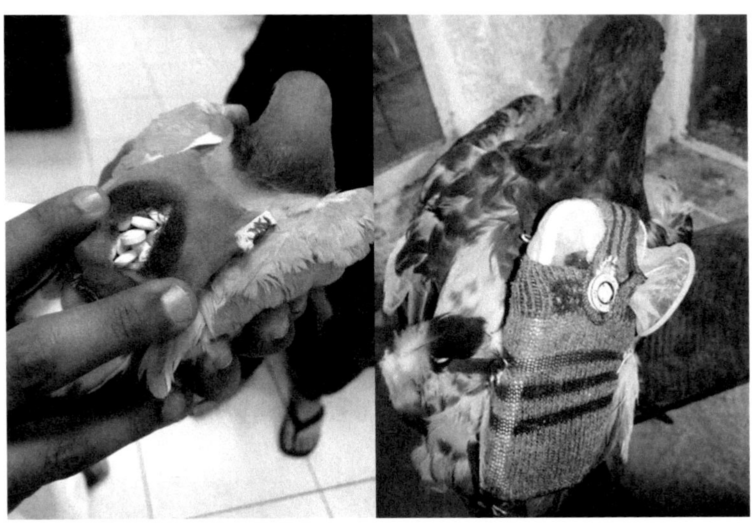

Colombian drug dealers were the first to use pigeons as drug mules in prisons.

Man's Suit

41

Wool with cotton lining made out of a flour sack; acquired from an antique dealer in Puno, 2010. The act of dressing up in Western clothes in present day Peru is called *civilizarse*, 'to civilise oneself', by Indigenous people, who go to special shops to rent these clothes if they are too poor to buy them. The handwoven fabric of this suit mimics English tweed, with the lining cut out of a cotton flour sack.

In 1575 Viceroy Toledo, invoking the authority of King Philip II of Spain, enacted an ordinance that prohibited the wearing of Inca-style garments. Native Andeans were encouraged to "accommodate themselves to our clothing", meaning they were to wear Spanish-style garments: shirts, pants, skirts, blouses. Anything that would not recall the "pain and lamentable memory". For a long time Spanish laws had governed the wearing of luxury fabrics, codifying which social class could wear what, and when. In the Viceroyalty, similar laws regulated dress according to social hierarchies as well as racial distinctions. The amount of silk a native woman could wear, for example, was restricted, as was the number of pieces of lace that could be added to her mantle.

In 1571 women of mixed descent were completely forbidden to wear silk mantles, gold, or pearls. In the 18th century displeasure grew among viceregal authorities over what they perceived as an excess of luxury in the garments worn by native Andeans. As a result, people were then "forbidden to dress themselves like us" (Recopilación de Leyes 1791, p. 403). Around the same time, concern grew among administrators that Inca-style clothing was becoming increasingly politicised as a consequence of the Túpac Amaru rebellion, so that in 1781 these garments were outlawed again in order not to bring back ancient memories and an idealised vision of the former rulers.

Yet in the same period Inca-style garments were incorporated into colonial public displays, as they had been at the Corpus Christi processions of 1555 in Potosí and Cuzco, where the costumes served as a re-enactment of the past and a kind of 'theatre' of Inca heritage. It is likely that many colonial tunics preserved today were made specifically for these public processions. As a result of worries about the 'indecency' of native Andeans' loosely wrapped dresses, laws imposed by the viceregal administrators of the 1570s required the garments to be sewn up. Maybe as an act of resistance or maybe just as a takeover of an aesthetic form, meaningless in its content, in some Inca-period tapestry *lliclla*s an actual false seam was stitched onto the surface of the panel to mimic the joining of the two *callu* in a warp-patterned mantle.

Silver

In the stories of the *Arabian Nights*, composed and collected between the 8th and 13th centuries, stories in which cloth merchants are very present, there are few descriptions of the clothes themselves, but where this is the case, they often contain gold or silver thread. By then the use of these metals had a long history, with references made in Homer's works and Assyrian sculpture. In India too such thread-making was an important art, using a variety of specialised craftsmen. Usually the 'gold' wire was sliver gilt, the silver wire itself being pure silver. The wire would be drawn by means of simple drawer-plates from rounded bars of silver or gold-plated silver and regular beating on a round-topped anvil with a heavy hammer having a slightly convex surface. Threads could also be made by tightly wrapping flattened metal around a core of textile thread like silk or linen. In the Byzantine Empire and later in Europe, such threads were incorporated into the clothes of the rich and powerful. Ostentatious vulgarity could however create the problem of excessive weight, putting too great a strain on the foundation fabrics, so that imitation threads were developed. Referred to as membrane gold or membrane silver, the result was a greater use of metallics in textiles even though less of the precious metals was used per costume.

"For Hegel there is no reciprocity; here the master laughs at the consciousness of the slave. What he wants from the slave is not recognition, but work."

The real significance of silver in the history of cloth, however, is the mining of the metal itself. Already in 1545 what turned out to be nearly an entire mountain of silver (Cerro Rico) was discovered at Potosí, then part of the Viceroyalty of Peru and now in modern-day Bolivia. Its fabulous mine created an stream of wealth: "Caravans of llamas and mules carry to the port of Arica the silver that the Potosí mountain bleeds from each of its mouths. At the end of a long voyage the ingots arrive in Europe to finance war, peace, and progress there." 'Progress' consisted of a kick-start to European capitalism and a transformation of the trading patterns of the world. Silver worth hundreds of millions of pesos was removed, refined, and converted to coins in Potosí's Mint (Casa de la Moneda). To achieve production and export goals, the mine owners needed slave labour (*mita*). The short working lives both of Indigenous people and of the kidnapped African slaves were uniquely brutal. So much so that in 1659 Count Lemos, viceroy of Peru, wrote to the king in Spain, "There is no people in the world so exhausted. I unburden my conscience to inform Your Majesty with due clarity. It is not silver that is brought to Spain but the blood and sweat of Indians." When the reply comes from the Council of the Indies in Madrid it is unequivocal: it declines to suppress forced labour in the mines. It is estimated that eight million people died during the working life of the mine there from 1556 to 1783.

The silver extracted also gave European traders something that the cloth producers of India might actually want. Previously they had had little to offer. Silver was regarded as significantly less pure than gold, but it was used as coinage throughout the Middle East, India and China.

"It is well-known ... that so far as Bengal's international trade was concerned, the huge demand for its commodities in the global markets, especially its textiles and raw silk, attracted buyers from various parts of the world. As Bengal between 1650 and 1757 was self-sufficient and as the market for import commodities was strictly limited, almost all these traders, whether Europeans or Asians, had to bring in precious metals, mostly silver, to Bengal for the procurement of the export commodities. Thus the influx of silver to Bengal in the seventeenth and the early half of the 18th century was because of Bengal's favourable balance of trade with the rest of the world." This contact with the Indian cotton industry, which played a unique role in its trading reach and as an agent of consumer tastes, was then to provoke a European, especially English, drive to copy and then industrialise cotton cloth production while using state-backed naval force and African slavery to make it a global business. Meanwhile the nouveau-riche slave-driving mine controllers of Potosí were importing luxury textiles from the whole world over – the world their oyster – and paving the town literally with silver. What luxury fabrics were made in the region itself were metallic yarns from Spain, made of solid-cut sheets of Andean silver and re-imported as thread. With traditional skill and good taste, wound around silk, linen or cotton core yarns, these were enthusiastically but sparingly used by native weavers who would sometimes alternate yellow and white yarns with them to emphasise the visual impact. With the advent of photography and computers, silver is no longer a metal to be coveted simply for its value and beauty, but has become functional. An excellent conductor of electricity and a principal element in photographic processing, silver is an integral part of computers, electronic equipment and the filmmaking process. A 2003 sports fashion catalogue features lingerie and 'active wear' "with silver ions embedded in the fabric, to help prevent odours and the spread of bacteria on clothing".

1866

A *campesino* (peasant) uprising in the Peruvian province of Huancané, later known as the Bustamente rebellion, began in this year. A new Indian head tax was 'the straw that broke the camel's back'. It added to the burdens and anger of Indian communities of the Peruvian South, already hit by the Civil Code of 1852 (the very year British wool merchant William Ricketts arrived in Peru), which appeared to give Indian limited civic rights but was in reality an attack on their traditional right to a collective existence and made them subject to individualised contracts. The Civil Code was instituted just as the export of wool became the areas most important source of income. As a consequence there was a continuous increase in the size of landholdings and a stark juxtaposition of Hispanised *haciendas* and the Indian peasant *estancias*. The Spanish landholdings expanded by 140 notarised purchases in the 1860s, peaking in 1867. This went with a politico-cultural offensive whereby prestigious Indians who had been treated as equals were now seen as backward.

The two dynamics meant that in addition to military marauding there were "a growing number of merchants scouring the highlands for cheap wool", both sheep and alpaca, now backed by 'contract', however spurious. 'Cheap' does not do justice to the methods that became commonplace, whereby wool merchant agents, *rescatistas*, left either 'loans' or overpriced British goods as advance payment for wool and then claimed that the wool was not enough, or of poor quality, and then, with armed backing, took land and animals in lieu. The higher the price of wool on the world market the more intensive this process became, as the Peruvian elite and British finance capital (which would then 'rescue' Peru from sovereign debt default) both found

It is estimated that six million Peruvians and African slaves died over 230 years while extracting the mountain's silver. They die from exhaustion, respiratory disease and mercury poisoning in the course of the silver's mining, grinding, coining and transportation. The image shows *El Tío* (The Uncle), who is believed to be the "Lord of the Underworld'. He rules over the mines, simultaneously offering protection and destruction.

Raised arch with textiles displayed as part of Andean Easter celebration.

that an export-led economy suited them. "Although the Indian problem had not yet become an urgent national priority, it demanded attention from politicians eager for re-colonisation of the Indian highlands by agrarian capitalists, merchants and 'agents of civilization'". Using a "Law on Terror" the Peruvian state put down the uprising and engineered a state of terror. 'Colonel' Juan Bustamante, an itinerant merchant himself who had set up a *Sociedad Amiga de los Indios* in Lima, became their leader. His Society had been concerned with the 'backwardness' of 'the Indian', but Bustamante opposed the deliberate and material perpetuation of this condition, whereby communities were treated neither as free men nor as citizens: "The persons opposed to the regeneration of the Indian and frustrating every well-intentioned effort ... enrich themselves by abusing the ignorance, humiliation and abandonment of the Indian." His hope was that the "involuntary" uprising would change this, but the insurgents were poorly armed and were defeated by the troops of Puno. Bustamente and sixty Indians were executed and the "insurgent villages of the highlands were uprooted and sent into labour camps in the steamy jungles of Crabaya".

Not many years later better prepared Indians who had fought against Chilean troops in the War of the Pacific of 1881, and not rewarded for their sacrifices, used the situation to their own advantage and began an uprising that lasted from 1882–84 in which hacienda administrators were assassinated and 'collaborator' haciendas occupied. Though guerrilla leaders were finally captured and executed in 1884 the uprising made hacienda owners more cautious in their dealing with Indigenous communities, preventing that avalanche of hacienda expansion that had provoked the Bustamente rebellion.

Antke Engel

I got to know a suit that turned out to be a hybrid – metamorphosing between a business suit and a Sunday best, as comfortable as jogging wear, yet also passing as a designer piece when displayed in the right bar. Its soft alpaca fabric and delicate black-and-white pattern made it a most attractive acquaintance. At first sight the pattern looked like a herringbone but in fact did not resemble any typical suit fabric. Fingertip-sized squares, surrounded by a zigzag, with a small dot in the middle; white on anthracite ground, rough cloth rather than fine fiber. Tweed? Too playful. Cheviot? Much smoother. We met by chance and at first I could not guess anything about its background or its story. Then I learned it came from Bolivia, made it to Europe by coincidence; not that it had been longing for that, but curiosity took over when the opportunity occurred. When we got closer it allowed me to find out that there is a further layer to its *mestiza* existence (*mestiza*, I learned, not hybrid). Its lining is made from flour bags, retired from former duties; now in old age supporting representation rather than reproduction, yet also serving as a reminder of a tough working life in the food industries. No, not subsistence production; visual design and product information printed in red and yellow on the ecru linen indicate a business somehow or other involved in globalised economy. This is, actually, what *mestiza* is all about: Acknowledging that one cannot escape global market economy or the aftermath of colonial history, yet claiming the legacy of heterogeneous histories and social cultures; dwelling in border zones made of imperial violence as much as of Indigenous life, migration, and procreation, and turning the subjectivities and relationalities evolving from those never pure, never coherent bearings into a source of strength. You might find *mestiza* existence on the local markets of some small town in rural Bolivia: a suit on sale, produced by an Indigenous woman, who dares to cut the traditional woven cloth (an act that offends all traditional knowledge, since a cloth is a living being that is not to be injured by cutting) in order to tailor a business suit of classical 'cut' for someone to enter the terrains of capitalist business negotiation, bourgeois politics, christian institutions, or occidentalist knowledge. You can also in the meantime find *mestizaje* claiming a stance in global politics. The new constitutions of Ecuador (2008) and Bolivia (2009) are siblings of the tailor suit I met in Berlin – hybrid beings that secure private property and National sovereignty, while simultaneously submitting capitalist economy and neoliberal nationhood to the principles of *sumak kawsay* (buen vivir, good living) and the indivisible conviviality of all being (pachamama, madre tierra). The constitutions recognise the state as a plurination and a plurality of economic forms (diversidad economia), including various forms of property and of production and reproduction. They declare nature a subject of rights, thus restricting the possibilities of exploiting resources, and restrict the size of large estate property, since the earth cannot be owned. Yet, although the monopoly of capitalist economy as the sole form of organising the economy is broken, the global market, private property and transnational companies are still celebrated as vital moments of maintaining the nation state. The mystery of how to tackle the contradictions between different forms of economy, how to overcome the fact that they compete with each other while highly unequal power relations, domination and exploitation structure their relationships, is not solved on paper. And in practice one is forced to realise that the routes of exchange between market economy and household, subsistence, communal, and solidarity economy are not defined by anti-capitalist redistribution: Asoban (the association of private banks in Bolivia) rejected the request of president Evo Morales for abatement of debt to micro-credit recipients. The campaign of the feminist organisation Mujeres Creandos to hand in a heap of petitions signed by people to gain debt cancellation was not crowned with success. The Ecuadorian initiative in 2009 to save the Yasuní National Park by appealing at the climate conference in Copenhagen to National governments to pay compensation for the country's non-exploitation of its oil resources neither found resonance nor impressed transnational companies or the Ecuadorian shareholders. Thus, how can the *mestiza* suit, lively sibling of the paper constitution and in intimate relationship with local border zone dwellers, become a means of transport that connects between and enables exchange between different economies and ways of good living, but also empowers household and subsistence, communal, collective and solidarity economy to loosen the grip of globalised market economy?

Poncho Capote / Festival Poncho Made into a Cushion; Manta / Carrier Cloth

42

Red, dark maroon and multicoloured sheep wool and multicoloured acrylic, ground- and complementary-warp spin, Z2S; weft Z2S; 1970; Potólo; acquired in 1978. Space in the design of the Jalq'a people can be treated as one grand totality or as a division into three bands: one wide centre and two narrower borders. In these three bands no element separates the borders. These spacious areas without breaks are a creation of present day Jalq'a bands (*pa'lays*). At the turn of the century and afterwards, bands could be clearly distinguished, whereas the increase in the decorated area has since permitted a more precise expression of ideas which were latent in older textiles, such as 'chaos or disorder' and 'filled space'. The idea of disorder is realised through a lack of reference-points to guide the eye, or through a complete absence of symmetry. The selection of tones is intended to produce two effects: darkness, where neither the clear light of day with its luminosity nor the rays of the sun is evoked; and ambiguity between the background and the figures represented.

Chaos, darkness, a profusion of beings and ambiguity are all characteristics developed deliberately. They have continued to develop throughout history, permitting the recreation of an 'atmosphere' in which the content of the *pallay* images is unfolded: a difficult-to-understand world, confused and disordered; a secret world which does not belong to everyday experience. Such are the *khurus*, which are the principle theme of the Jalq'a weavings. These are animals characterised as indomitable, wild, impossible to domesticate. Their depiction converts them into anatomical impossibilities or unreal creatures: their bodies are stretched and lengthened, or they receive some attribute which removes them from the plane of normal experience. Others are represented just as they are, but they belong to faraway ecological zones never inhabited by Jalq'as, like the beautiful lions, which frequently appear, or the monkeys, which are always portrayed with their faces in profile and both eyes facing forward. Finally, there is the characteristic theme of the Jalq'a *pallay*: the imaginary animals, such as birds with four feet or with teeth, hunchbacked creatures with humps not only on their backs but on their heads as well, griffins, characters unfolding themselves into mirror images, or *khurus* with incredible tails, full of eyes. In the course of the last century, the *khurus* have taken possession of the entire space, and today they are the key theme defining Jalq'a identity. *Khurus* belong to a semi-demonic universe called *saxra parti*: the world of the deity *saxra*, who has power over creative acts, ranging from *pallays* and music to the procreation and birth of species. Consequently many *khurus*, though of undefined sex, appear to be pregnant: the small figures inside them are designated as *unas* (their young).

Colour Control

Goethe's *Farbenlehre*, published in 1810, starts or re-starts in modern terms the notion of the psychological effects of different colours. The search for a more instrumentalist approach begins with Charles Féré in the 1880s testing and treating hysterics under various coloured lights in a Chromotherapy programme. His analysis of blue as calming opens the door to colour as a means of control. While this is benign in the hands of W. Kandinsky, talking in 1911 of how "Colour contains within itself a little studied but enormous power which can influence the entire physical body as a physical organism", the dangers of its crude reductionism were already evident in Max Nordau's ironically hysterical book *Degeneration* of 1892.
"Red has another peculiarity, explanatory of the predilection shown for it by the hysterical. The experiments of Binet have established that the impressions conveyed to the brain by the sensory nerves exercise an important influence on the species and strength of the excitation distributed by the brain to the motor nerves. Many sense impressions operate enervatingly and inhibitively on the movements; others on the contrary make these more powerful, rapid and active; they are dynamogenous. As a feeling of pleasure is always connected with dynamogeny, every living thing, therefore, instinctively seeks for dynamogenous sense-impressions and avoids enervating and inhibitive ones ... Hence it is intelligible that hysterical painters revel in red, and that hysterical beholders take special pleasure in pictures operating dynamogenously and producing feelings of pleasure."
In 1943 Fernand Léger was talking in more measured but equally reductionist terms of a polychrome clinic, a colour cure, "beginning to thrill young doctors; some green and blue wards for nervous and sick people, some other painted yellow and red, stimulating and nutritious for depressed and anaemic people". This has since become part of the practice of prison and school architecture. Alexander G. Schauss reports on "a significant use of colour to reduce potential or actual aggression. It has been discovered that the use of a specific shade of pink can have a moderating effect on subjects experiencing feelings of anger or agitation. The calming effect of pink, if appropriately applied, relaxes hostile or agitated behaviour in approximately ten to fifteen minutes. ... The subject experiences a significant loss of muscular strength. In 1978, I demonstrated the Kinesoid experiment, involving pink colour to a series of classes on innovative treatment techniques in corrections. As a result of this provocative demonstration, I had suggested that a pink holding cell might be useful as a 'time-out' room for acting out confines. Two commanding officers at the US Naval Correctional in Seattle, Commander Gene Baker and Captain Ron Miller, decided to try the pink holding cell in early 1979. After 223 days of continuous use as a temporary holding facility for new confines, the results have been impressive ... the new confines only required a maximum of 15 minutes of exposure to ensure that the potential for violent or aggressive behaviour had been reduced."
In at least two Texas jails, penitentiary pink has been used as a means of humiliation. In Mason County jail convicts have refused the option of working outside because they would have to wear pink jumpsuits. In Phoenix this was taken a step further, with prisoners forced to wear pink underwear – a form of non-consensual 'sissification'. The practice came to light when one of the inmates died of a fatal panic attack, after he interpreted the underwear as a prelude to being raped.

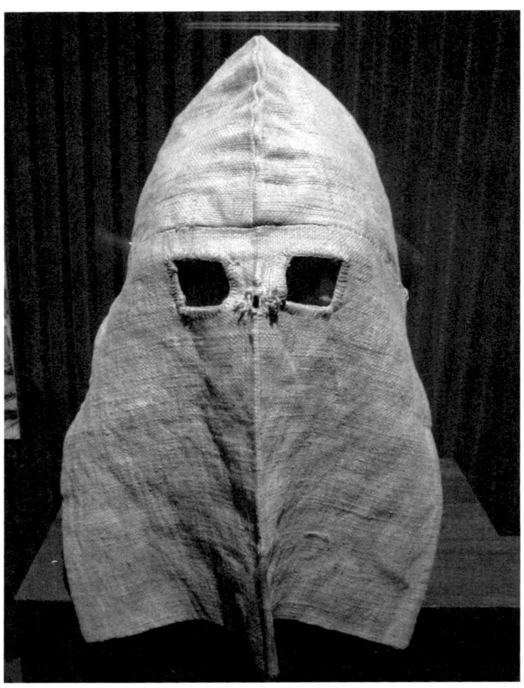

In the Old Melbourne Gaol, Australia, ca. 1875, hoods made of calico were worn by all prisoners in solitary confinement when outside their cells. The Pentonville system of reform tried to isolate prisoners from others in all possible ways.

2009

A demonstration by factory workers from small textile plants took place in Cochabamba, Bolivia, to protest against the importation of second-hand clothing from the USA. The imports massively undercut Bolivian-made clothes on price and many local clothing factories have closed. Almost immediately afterwards a counter-demonstration was then held by an equal number of *rompajeros*, those who sell the imports of things like shirts embossed with the names of long-forgotten US football stars. "It's my job and I will protect my job," says *rompajera* Patricia Patzi. The textile workers' situation is now one of a greater need of domestic sales because exports to the USA have dried up after Bolivia lost duty-free status under the Andean Trade Promotion and Drug Eradication Act. Never mind that coca production was increasing more in US-favoured Colombia and Peru, the government of Evo Morales wasn't playing the Drug War game as laid down in Washington. 2 years later, in 2011, the Morales government, following bans on second-hand clothing imports in many other 'Southern' world countries, especially in Africa, announced that it would clamp down on such imports. In response the *rompajeros*, the second-hand clothes sellers, came out in force in La Paz. This time it was then 5000 textile workers who held their own counter-demonstration in support of the ban. Such a ban is likely to be unsuccessful as most imported clothes are smuggled through Chile, and the poor can only afford the imports, which are liable to be cheaper. The contradictions, the opposing interests of different groups of working people are real just as they are in Ghana or Nigeria. The conflict between domestic manufacture and used clothing occurs all over the 'the South'. And when the second-hand trade is conservatively estimated by the UN at $3.4 billion a year – an estimate which excludes movement of rags – this should come as no surprise. As Marx noted, the used clothes trade was already in full swing in the mid-19th century. At the same time, Charles Dickens's David Copperfield, desperate for money, was trying to get a good price for his waistcoat from a dealer. In 15th-century Florence there had even been a guild of dealers in used luxury clothing. Nowadays the goods travel the world in compressed 45 kg bales, 250–300 items in 20 foot containers or double that in 40 footers. What has made the trade so big in recent years has been the double effect of the charity business and of debt-enforced policies, particularly in Africa. Even the normally unreflective USAID (United States Agency for International Development) stated the obvious about IMF/World Bank approved Mozambique: "Substantial imports of used clothing underscored the limited means of most Mozambican consumers." In its role as a leading charity, the Salvation Army tries to smooth over the contradiction by producing vastly exaggerated figures for those working in the second-hand clothing industry. One such estimate for Ghana suggested that such workers made up 20% of the entire workforce. Even so, even a more realistic estimate says that in Kenya there are 100,000 people employed in the business. And it is against this, with the knowledge that some African countries are serious cotton producers and are failing to get the real value-added that goes with clothes production, that some countries have imposed bans on such imports. Nigeria, trying to diversify from oil, introduced such a ban, but it is now the biggest market in West Africa, with the clothes smuggled in from Benin. South Africa also has such a ban, but the textile industry is nevertheless hit from two sides. On the one handclothes are smuggled in from Mozambique, while on the other its manufacturers are relocating to Lesotho or Botswana, with the aim of undercutting wages. In the second-hand business a familiar hierarchy is at work, all the risk taken by the retailer – say in Xipamine market, Maputo – who must buy a bale on trust, unseen.

Edgar Endress

The response to the *awayo* (cloth) was generated by using found photographs. The photographs are formatted to comply with the requirements to procure a personal legal document in Bolivia, like an identity card. The photographs were found in a cardboard box in La Paz – Bolivia. The response deals with the *awayo* that serves multiple purposes: decorative, utilitarian, and ceremonial. People use them to carry small children or all kinds of items on their backs. The cloth defines a sacred territory; when placed on the floor it can hold offerings to *pachamama*. The *awayo* here is a territory that contains the "legal" photographs with overlapping drawings of various symbolic balaclavas which are used extensively in the Andes to shield from the weather conditions, but are also used ceremonially and in celebrations. Together the balaclava and the *awayo* define a territory of the self and of the collective. Both are forms of identity and a response to the legacy of colonialism.

43

Q'ero; wool, alpaca; acquired in Ollantaytambo, 2010. An *unkuña* is a woven cloth for carrying coca and personal belongings which is sometimes also used as a base to make a *pago* (offering). In Peru *pago* literally means a payment in the form of prayers and material gifts of food and alcohol. The offerings are made to the spirits residing in the highest mountain peaks, known as *apus*, or to *pachamama*, Mother Earth. The ceremony is usually performed by a *misayoq*, who is believed to possess the ability to communicate directly with the mountain spirits and all natural forces and is a specialist in Andean rituals. The ceremony generally takes place outdoors. The *misayoq* lays an *unkuña*, a small rectangular finely woven cloth made from natural alpaca, on the ground, oriented in the direction of the nearest important *apu*. There he places one by one the various elements that make up the offering. The ceremony is conducted with the utmost respect and faith. The particular act of healing intended determines the final shape of the offering and some of its contents. The intent of the ceremony may be to bring harmony and balance to the earth, manifested in abundant crops and fertile animals; to honour a new beginning, such as a new house, business or marriage; to get rid of an illness or negative energy; or to ward off witchcraft and sorcery. Participation in the ceremony can help reinforce spiritual relationships between members of the community and cleanse each participant of negative energy.

Hateful Yellow

The yellow badge: In the early Islamic period both Christians and Jews were required to wear such badges, possibly as early as 9th-century Baghdad, as well as Hindus in Islamic India, but for Jews it has had a longer and more continuous use in Christian Europe. It was made official by the Fourth Lateran Council of 1215 for both Muslims and Jews, but thereafter was used

exclusively for Jewish people. The badges were sometimes in the shape of the Star of David, sometimes as square patches; the rule was reinforced by Popes in 1415 and 1555. Local impositions took place, as in Augsburg in 1434 when Jewish money was no longer needed by the textile bourgeoisie. It was infamously reintroduced in the 20th century by the Nazi regime in Germany and Austria, and then in German-occupied Eastern Europe.
The yellow smock: Victims of the Spanish Inquisition were clothed in such a garment as they were led to where they were to be burned to death. Those who were decreed unrepentant had images of flames pointing upwards painted onto the yellow. Those who had repented in the time immediately before they were to be burned had the flames pointing downwards and for such repentance were granted the mercy of being strangled before being burned. It was the Catholic Church of this time that wielded so much power in the Spanish invasion of the Americas, where it continued practicing its ideology of hatred and violence.
The Yellow Peril: In the late 19th century a fear and the Chinese was manufactured in the Western World and especially in the United States of America. This happened as Chinese migrant labour appeared in many parts of the industrialised world. A series of US government Acts, starting with the Chinese Exclusion Act of 1882, both fed and fed on such strategic paranoia. It was given popular currency by mass-readership fiction, most notably in Jack London's "The Unparalleled Invasion", an apocalyptic version of this fear by a writer whose socialism gave way to unvarnished racism. The series of Fu Manchu novelettes ran in the same vein, re-fuelled by 20th-century Japanese expansionism. There is a grim irony to its original anti-Chinese impetus in that the legendary first Chinese Emperor was the Yellow Emperor at a time when only members of the Chinese Imperial family could wear yellow.
Yellow Press: Again in late 19th-century USA, the newspaper rivalry between the Hearst and Pulitzer newspaper titles took sensationalism and distortion to new levels. It was given impetus by the Spanish-American War of 1898. The term derived from a cartoon strip "The Yellow Kid" that ran in both publishers' newspapers.
Yellow(-bellied): 'Yellow' meaning cowardly had entered American vocabulary in the first half of the 19th century, appearing in P.T. Barnum's *Struggles and Triumphs* in 1856. With the 'bellied' attached it appeared in a book by Percy Marks in 1926, and was all too readily used by British imperialists to describe those of its agents who 'let the side down', when it came to those violent confrontations that are so endemic to Empires.

2004

On the 14th September 6800 workers at the Xianyang Huaran textile factory in China went on strike. It lasted for seven weeks and was groundbreaking in many ways. For one thing, most of the workers were women, casting off the 'docile' image that is often thrust on them. The length of the strike itself marks it as probably the longest recorded industrial action in China's post-1949 history. Equally significant is that it arose from contract negotiation disputes when the factory was switched from public to private ownership, a process common to many enterprises in this period. It was described as a wake-up call to local government and prospective investors that workers would not take just any offer they are given when the factories were up for sale. And it was such an 'offer' by China Resources, a Hong Kong-based mainland conglomerate, that caused the strike. Under its terms the entire workforce would have to accept a one-off severance payment amounting to one month's pay for each year of service. After this an unspecified number of workers would be re-employed on short term contracts which would involve an insulting six-month 'probationary' work period and – most brazen of all – China Resources indicated that it would not be paying their future retirement pension and medical insurance premiums once the new contract was signed. A certain slipperiness as regards pensions is not unique to Chinese companies, and appears in 're-structuring' plans all over the world. In this instance the conflict was sharpened by individual managers getting large compensation packages for loss of the state firm while the workers got none. All production was stopped and workers kept up a 24-hour guard in rotating

Modern Chinese spinning mill.

Intensity of labour is scalec up in China as elsewhere.

shifts of 200 at a time by the factory's main gate. At this time there was no trade union and the decision was taken to form one in accordance with Trade Union Law of 2001, which would give strike leaders some protection. After just a few days a huge body of police with water cannon came to the factory, the demand for an independent union having alarmed the local authority, but withdrew in the face of mass passive resistance. The next response in mid-October was pre-emptive, it imposed a 'trade union organising committee' on the factory without consulting any of the workers or holding elections. They followed this up by televised demands for a return to work. All this enraged workers, who on 24th October staged a railway blockade which, combined with some stones being thrown at management windows, gave the authorities the excuse to break up the blockade with a thousand anti-riot police. Over the next days 20 workers designated as strike leaders were arrested and another 3 put on a wanted list.

Victories are often partial but in this instance, despite the strike ending without agreement and with some workers in prison, concessions were made: workers would be re-hired on longer contracts; the 'probationary' period was dropped and the threatened wage cuts abandoned. Older workers took the severance money while 2000 took on jobs at the privatised company. All the arrested workers, including 5 who had been tried and convicted of offences, were released at the beginning of 2005.

Strikes outside the control of the state-controlled trade union are still attacked. Recent proof was supplied at a garment factory in Shenzhen in December 2014, after nine days of a strike. The demand was for social insurance, a front-line issue for internal migrants without the advantages city residents under the *hukou*, or household registration system. Nevertheless, the struggles of migrant workers for better wages and conditions have been felt in the country's coastal regions. Average wages in the apparel industry are five times higher than those of Bangladesh, and twice those of Vietnam and Cambodia. Manufacturers have been encouraged to relocate to Western and Central areas of the country. Others, following the earlier trajectories of Taiwan and Korea, are relocating production outside the country. Twelve Hong Kong-based manufacturers have opened factories in the Thilawa Special Economic Zone in Myanmar, close to a container port, where there can be found an abundance of workers who are "hard-working and obedient".

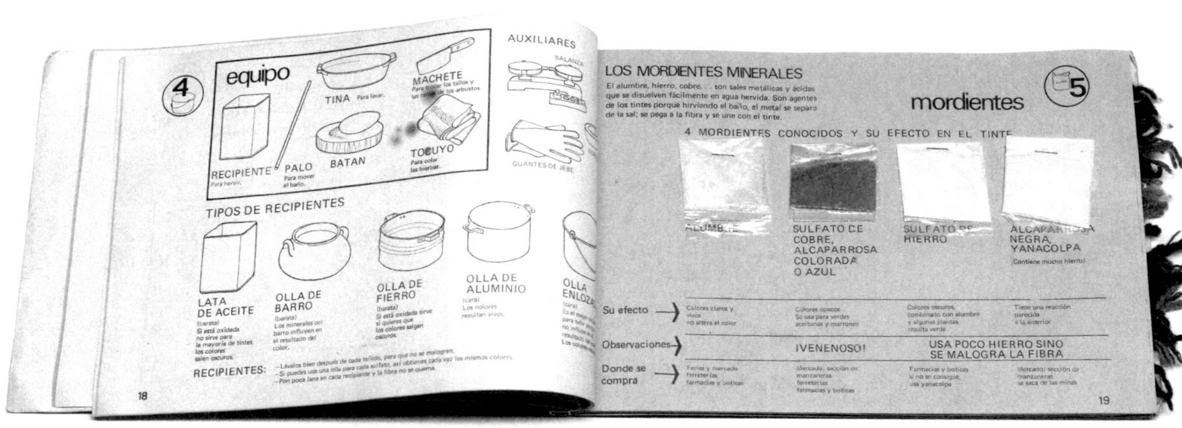

"El Arte Peruano En La Escuela": Elena Izcue: published by Editorial Excelsior-Paris, 27, Quai de la Tournelle 1926; "Tintes Naturales: Huaycano, Peru 1979": Hugo Zumbühl: Edicion para la Sierra Central Especial Para Lana do Oveja: published by 'KAMAQ MAKI' Auspiciado por S.E.P.A.S. Huncayo, Peru 1979; bought second-hand, 2011 and 2013. In 1920s Latin America a revival of ancient American art was part of a political move to re-establish the pre-Conquest identity of nations that had long been controlled by European colonisers. This so-called 'Indigenism' idealised and appropriated forms from the ancient American past. Archaeological excavations like the one conducted by Julio C. Tello at Paracas inspired Elena Izcue to produce her two-volume *El Arte Peruano en la Escuela*. She worked in a group project to create an educational and social model at the Chiclín estate, the property of Rafael Larco Herrera, a philanthropist and collector of pre-Hispanic objects. With this focus, Elena developed the two volumes, to be used for artistic instruction, published in 1926. The first copybook

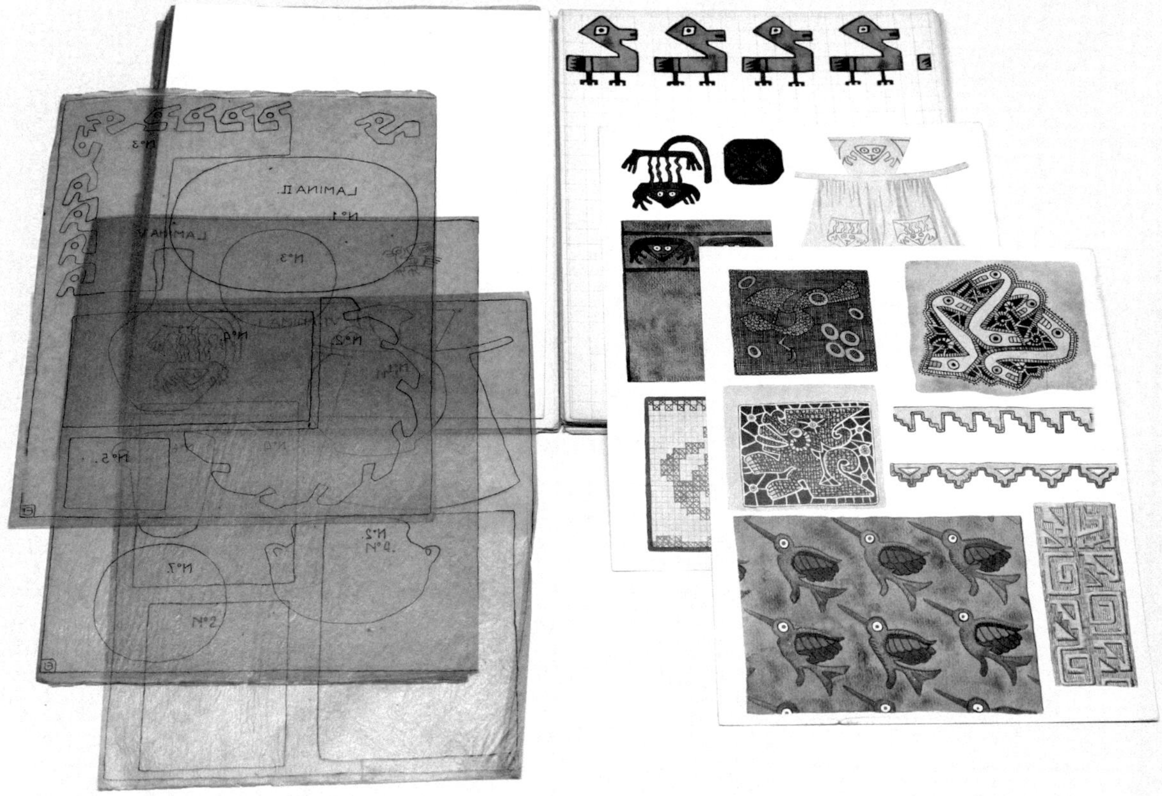

was primarily designed for children to encourage their desire to create art; while the second, with a section on the topic of the application of the decorative arts, was designed for craftsmen or more advanced students. In both, the figures are derived from pre-Columbian works but are presented as autonomous elements. Given the isolation of the figures from their original context, without any explanation about their origin or meaning, this presentation placed priority on the designs themselves. The copybooks were used for arts education in various schools around Peru and were also introduced into US schools and arts media.

In the 1970s, Hugo Zumbühl, a Swiss designer and textile enthusiast, produced two extraordinary books self-published with artisan cooperatives in Peru. One concerned plants that had produced dye colours, knowledge of which were in danger of being lost. It was extraordinary in that the book contained packets of either seeds and/or leaves of these plants in small plastic bags stapled to the pages on which their botanical details and the processes needed to make the dye were described. The other, also original in the presentation of content, was a DIY (do-it-yourself) guide to the construction of different kinds of weaving loom with technical drawings and step by step accounts of how to make them. They were not professionally ethnographic but manifestly a labour of love.

Nylon

"Better Living for Better Things through Chemistry" proclaimed a dramatic advertisement full of the promise of a new world by the USA chemicals company Du Pont when it launched nylon at the site of the forthcoming New York World Fair in 1938. A few years earlier the British firm Courtauld were proclaiming "loveliness fortified against air and sun and soiling", speaking of their own 'artificial silk' that it had first produced in 1905. Then in 1912, it opened a factory to make stockings from this new material and these – as the price became cheaper, dominated its sales and image. In 1921 Du Pont started to produce the same material and gave it the name Rayon, to give voice to its lustrous appearance. It was synthetic but based on the natural element cellulose though it was marketed as a 'man-made', an ironic label since in addition to women being the targeted consumers, they far outnumbered men working in the artificial

WOMEN UNITE
SOLIDARITY WITH WOMENS STRUGGLES ALL OVER THE WORLD
WOMENS DAY MARCH
SALLE D'EXPÉRIENCES
15. BOULEVARD DES ITALIENS
HUGHES
INDUSTRIES
Rocketing into the Future!
1939
NEW YORK WORLD'S FAIR
A LITTLE CHILD SHALL LEAD THEM
WE NEVER FORGET
A WOMAN'S PLACE
STOP THE WAR ON CHOICE

silk industry. Courtauld kept emphasising the material's seemingly contradictory virtues of durability and softness, "Lovely soft silken things that will wear and wear". The increasing cheapness also prompted outburst of a faux-socialism based on bourgeois disgust aimed at working class women as in a description of them at the holiday resort of Blackpool as "silly girls with their pathetic silk stockings". For others it was the very shininess of the silk that was somehow cheap and vulgar when worn by the same class of women who had been condemned by Daniel Defoe for wearing calico over 200 years earlier.
During the years between the two World Wars of the 20th century the global output of Rayon grew exponentially by 7600% despite the economic crises and depression, but in the USA from Du Pont's point of view there was still too big a market for real silk stockings and an accompanying import bill from Japan. From 1932 and with several false starts the company worked on developing a truly synthetic material. The testing stages were conducted "with a secrecy matching the Manhattan project" until the final public presentation of nylon. It had some initial PR problems: there were rumours of dead bodies having been used, and then more accurately that because of its basis in coal tar chemistry it was somehow dirty. Indeed a *Fortune* magazine review of the new world of synthetic textiles included a map which despite the glitter of Nylon and Rayon islands "rooted plastics in the extractive materials of the past ... it implied an odd denial of chemistry's promise to free the human race from the geographic accidents of supply and scarcity. The very outline of the map suggested the tropics, civilisation's colonial reserves ... areas of dark viscous flow predominated, evoking images of coal tar, asphalt, petroleum, all products of the planet's dawn of time organic waste." Nylon also suffered initially precisely because of the techno-utopianism of its presentation as a miracle of science and machine-age perfection, there was an expectation that this meant the kind of perfection that would mean no 'ladders' in the stockings. However when the stockings did reach the National market in May 1940 after an intensive marketing campaign it was a sell-out, within a year it had captured 30% of the full-fashioned hosiery market. Just 18 months later, after the USA's entry into the Second World War, Du Pont's nylon went almost entirely into parachutes and other war material when previously 90% had gone into stockings. When the war ended the news media were keen to report 'nylon riots' as women queued for the nylon stockings back on the market, publicity that can only have pumped up demand for the Du Pont product. More prosaically, and despite losing its patent monopoly on the material, Du Pont indulged in some safety-first vertical integration by buying up Conoco to ensure its supply of the necessary petro-chemicals in 1954. In the following period derivatives like bri-nylon boasting non-iron and long life were developed but there was a turn against such materials for the pragmatic reason that they did not 'breathe' and would become clammy regardless of the weather, but also because the USA cotton lobby developed a PR strategy on the back of a cultural shift to proclaim the naturalness of cotton as against the synthetic. Given the amount of chemicals applied to cotton in the textile and clothing industries there is a certain irony in this as has been the development of nylon and other synthetics as micro-fibres and yarns to be blended with the full range of 'natural' fibre.

1912

The Lawrence Textile strike, known as the "Bread and Roses", begins in Massachusetts, USA. It followed previous wage cuts and a speed-up of work with the introduction of the two-loom system, and began when the owner of one mill – Everett Cotton Mills – responded to a new law shortening the working week by cutting wages. The Polish women workers walked out and within a week 20,000 newly immigrant workers, mostly women, many aged between 14 and 18, joined them. A strike committee was formed that translated its proceedings into 26 languages. Despite the imposition of martial law, jail sentences, private militia goon squads, and provocations like the planting of dynamite, the strike was won. Even now what is so impressive is the way fund-raising in other textile towns, the creation of soup kitchens and medical care by volunteer doctors was organised. Innovative tactics countered the charge of loitering by forming a moving human chain around mills. Another pragmatic tactic was to send the children of strikers to the homes of supporters elsewhere. One such occasion became a pivotal moment in the conflict when the police and militia attacked both parents and children just when the children were set to go to Philadelphia. Both were clubbed at the railway station and dragged to court where they opted for prison rather than pay the fine. The publicity and subsequent government interest

Bodies of the sixty-two workers who jumped or fell from windows. "This is not the first time girls have been burned alive in the city. There are so many of us for one job it matters little if 146 of us are burned to death. The life of men and women is so cheap and property is so sacred." Rose Schneiderman, a survivor of the Triangle Shirtwaist factory in New York City, where 146 women working in the clothing business died in 1911 because the doorswere locked due to the owners' obsession with theft.

swung the balance of power for the time being, and textile companies throughout New England agreed to a deal which met many of the strike's demands of higher pay for the lowest paid, time and a quarter for overtime, and no discrimination against strikers.
It was the first time a strike by such a diverse group of new-wave immigrant workers had united in this way, and it was opposed by the Craft Union of earlier generation immigrants, English, Irish and German.
The success is mostly ascribed to the IWW, the Wobblies, worker organisers who didn't bother with craft unions or professional negotiation. This is highlighted in a long 'study' in the *Atlantic Monthly* soon after the strike, which put forward an unashamedly pro-employer point of view on what happened. It talked of the "dangerous use of sentiment in place of reasoning" as if it had a monopoly on reason; of how the market price of labour is governed *neutrally* by supply and demand, and how it is capital that takes all the risk.
The 'study' blamed the owners only for not allowing a responsible labour organisation to develop, and for "a failure in communication". The writer, Leland F. Deland, talked of worker intimidation and while attacking the Wobbly organisers also made a racist attack on the new-wave immigrants: "Many of them represent a low scale of Asiatic living"; they arrive "saturated with class hatred". Over time the victory was chipped away at by the employers, who also fired union activists and put in labour spies to keep a watch on workers. Conditions of 'supply and demand' were created to make for more speed-up and lay-offs.
But the women strikers' slogan for "Bread and Roses Too" echoed the feelings of textile workers of the past and resonated into the future. In the face of higher wages and better conditions, the response of capitalist mill owners was predictable. They shifted production to the old Confederate states of the South, where wages were half those of Massachusetts, where longer hours were worked, and where oligopolistic control of state legislatures meant especially weak labour laws.

Graham Townsley

Twisted Language. Yaminahua shamanism, located in the Peruvian Amazon, claims for itself extraordinary powers to cure and kill, which rest on understanding things better than other people and more profoundly. They really know (*tapiakoi*), and they really see (*ooiki*).
The Yaminahua ideas about the constitution of the world provide the framework of how shamans construct meaning from the actual experience of their ritual. This shamanism cannot be defined by a clearly constituted discourse of beliefs, symbols and meanings. It is not a system of knowledge or facts known, but rather an ensemble of techniques for knowing and chief among these ways of knowledge are those of song. In Yaminahua thought all things in the world are animated and given their particular qualities by *yoshi*, a spirit or animate essence.
Everything about the domain of *yoshi* is marked by an extreme ambiguity, associated with the night, the half-seen and dreams. They are implicated in all literally vital questions of human existence: birth, growth, illness and death. For humans too are animated by *yoshi*, entities just like the essences of other things, which grow with the body through life and finally cause its death by leaving it. Illness arises from the fact that each *yoshi* is subject to the influences of others, and that constitutes the field of shamanic activity. The basic parameters of shamanic knowledge are thus formed around this highly ambiguous relationship of animated essences and bodies. While *yoshi* are very much part of nature and the bodies they animate, they are at the same time beyond them, in a realm where even the *yoshi* of trees and insects live intelligent, volitional lives in a supra-sensory realm.
In one way, then, the *yoshi* is simply all the empirical characteristics of the thing with which it is associated, hypostatised and raised to the status of some independent being, an essence. This accounts for the very high degree of fine-tuned empirical knowing involved in shamanism, to know the *yoshi* of something is to know in detail the appearence, behaviour and characteristics of the thing it animates.
Creation myths are not simply regarded as tales of some distant past, but are regarded as still present in the spirit world. These myths, transformed into the elliptical language of shamanic songs, are seen as providing "paths" into this spirit world. All accounts of the paradoxical *yoshi*

stress their mutability and the fundamental difficulty of knowing them, without a possible unitary description. They are always "like ... and not like," "the same ... but different." This duality marks not only all accounts of them but is reflected in all ritual dealings with them, which are constructed in a multi-referential fashion so as to mirror the refractory nature of beings who are their objects. Shamanistic knowledge, beyond its empirical and mythic content, is constituted as a set of ideas and techniques related primarily to dreams, controlled hallucinations and all that a European would call the imaginary. One of the keys to this knowledge seems to lie exactly in an image of the person and knowing subject which has no place for a "mind" and associates "mental" events with animate essences which can drift free from bodies and mingle with the world.

In their notion of the person, the Yaminahua have a tripartite schema: a body; a social, human self associated with reason and language; an animate, perceiving self which is neither so social nor human, mingling easily with the non-human *yoshi* who are beings of the same type. The Yaminahua have no notion of anything that would approach our idea of "mind" as an inner store-house of meanings, thought and experience quite seperate from the world. All that is "mental" is the property of entities which, although closely related to particular bodies, are not permanently attached to them. Through the relationship between these two entities the whole arena of thought between the sameness and difference between the human and non-human develops. The idea of *yoshi* shapes the fundamental sameness of the human and the non-human and creates the space for animal transformations of the human and the attribution of mental and human characteristics to all aspects of nature.

Songs, usually conducted under the influence of a hallucinogenic brew Ayahuasca, *shori*, are a shaman's most highly prized possessions, the vehicles of his powers and the repositories of his knowledge. "A song is a path – you make it straight and clean and then you walk along it." Learning to be a shaman is learning to sing, to intone the chant rhythms, to carefully thread together verbal images couched in the abstruse metaphorical language of the shamanic song, and follow them. It is *shori* that is always considered to give primary access to the world of animated essences and the songs express the *yoshi* visions which the drug induces. Songs do not have fixed or invariant texts although, in songs created from myths, they may have a minimally fixed narrative sequence of metaphors and images. Beyond this, their language consists of circumlocutions or unusual words for common things which are either archaic or borrowed from neighbouring languages. The songs are metaphoric in two distinct ways. They make little reference to the illness or the real situation which the songs are intended to influence. Instead, they create elaborate analogies to it and almost nothing is referred to by its proper name and the importance of this is emphasised by all shamans. They are almost totally incomprehensible to all but other shamans. For example, night becomes "swift tapirs", the forest "cultivated peanuts", fish are "white-collared peccaries", jaguars "baskets", anacondas are "hammocks", rain becomes "big cold shelter" and so forth.

Shamans are clearly aware of the underlying sense of their metaphors and refer to them as *tsai yoshtoyoshto* - "twisted language" (literally: language twisting-twisting). "Singing, I carefully examine things – twisted language brings me close but not too close – with normal words I would crash into things – with twisted ones I circle around them – I can see them clearly." Through singing the shaman actively visualises the images referred to by the external analogy of the song, but he does this through a carefully controlled "seeing as" the different things actually named by the internal metaphors of the song. This "seeing as" creates a space in which visionary experiences occur. Only by using words which draw attention to the minute similarities between dissimilars, the shaman tries to sharpen his images at the same time as creating space for visions to develop.

As *yoshi* are real beings, both "like and not like" the things they animate without a stable or unitary nature, paradoxically the "seeing as" of "twisted language" is the only way of adequately describing them. Metaphor here is the only proper naming possible and the whole strategy of the song is precisely to drag these refractory meanings and images of the *yoshi* world out into this one and embed them unambiguously in a real body.

Graham Townsley in Jeremy Narby, Francis Huxley (eds): *Shamans Through Time, 500 Years on the Path to Knowledge*: Jeremy P. Tarcher / Penguin, New York, 2001.

Inkuña / Ritual Manta or Carrying Cloth

45

Sheep wool, natural and synthetic colours; late 20th century; acquired from an antique dealer, Puno, 2010. An *inkuña* is a rectangular warp-faced woven carrying cloth with 4 selvages and woven trim edging cloth used to hold coca leaves or food; it is used mostly by women in ritual offerings to the mother earth and other deities. The piece has a tan background decorated with bright stripes in pinks and greens, as well as yellow, blue, black, white and brown. The patterns nearest the centre are wide bands made of smaller stripes of gradated pinks near their centres and gradated greens on the outside. The centre of the band is patterned in double weave, in geometric reversing triangles. In the centre of each pattern band the double weaving ceases and bands are woven in warp-faced plain weave; this is the terminal area of the cloth. There are thin stripes of black, green, red, and, at the selvages, stripes of gradated blue, red, pink and natural. A plain red braided edging is joined continuously to all four selvages. According to the seller, the *manta* consists of a female and a male part. Before the Incas established a centralist empire in the 15th century, women and men of the people they colonised lived in independent parallel worlds, each with their own property and their own deities. The Incas robbed the women of their autonomy, separated them from sacred knowledge, and pushed them out of public life. The reorganisation of gender roles acquired crucial importance in the formation of Inca governments. The dynamic relationships that existed until then were recast as static hierarchies in an effort to assert control. As far as weaving was concerned, the Incas enforced a system of gender-specific specialisation: the men produced the luxurious cloths while women were only permitted to make ordinary textiles for everyday use. Inca textiles, then, served the socio-political designation of differences that were later used by the Spanish invaders in establishing their terrorist regime. Today two single persons 'become people' through marriage. A woman is referred to as a weft thread and the man a warp, and at the marriage the *ayllu* textile is finally completed. A single person is considered to be a loose thread, whereas a married one is plied. In the process of becoming plied, the couple grow to be two braided words and, after a while, half a ball of wool. After marriage the couple also become a plying spindle, wound tight and hard, because it has strength, whereas a single person's thread is still considered loose and weak. You can know a couple that is simply living together, because the thread knows that it is just so and is not well plied. The woman will ply her threads in vain – they will just begin to unwind again. A weaver makes a good daughter-in-law, as she is a real 'woman', whereas a non-weaver is both useless and unproductive.

Grey

In the language of socio-fashion, flitting from one summed-up decade to another, grey is always on the verge of being tomorrow's black, or as it is now, for the time being, *the* colour of the post-2008 banking crash. Austerity without the drama. Once upon a time there was no choice for most folk. The British King Richard I imposed a law in 1197 by which it was under penalty for 'simple' people to wear anything but grey. Given the price of good dyes in a colourless world, this may simply have been legislating how things already were for most 'simple' folk. This changed in the 15th century when it became popular amongst the upper classes, with superior dye tones obtained by the use of a mordant with baths of birch and alder with an addition of iron sulphates and sometimes a little oak apple. There was no competition with black which then was the clothes colour to spell out the wearer's sobriety and purpose. Grey instead became the colour of hope, joy and life and towns like Rouen, France, specialised in producing high quality grey cloth for the nobility. This increased subtlety of the colour in its dye form is picked up some centuries later by visual artists. Expressed, for one, by Vincent van Gogh, who wrote in a letter to his brother Theo in 1882, "Absolute black does not really occur. But like white, it is present in almost all other colours and forms the endless variety of greys – distinguished in tone and intensity – so that in nature one really does not see anything but tones and intensities there are only three basic colours – red, yellow, blue – 'composites' orange, green and purple. By adding black and some white one gets the endless variations of greys, red-grey, yellow-grey, blue-grey, green-grey, orange-grey, violet-grey. It is impossible to say, for instance, how many different green-greys there are, it varies endlessly. But the whole chemistry of colours is no more complicated than these few simple basics. And a good understanding of this is worth more than seventy different colours of paint, since one can make more than seventy tones and intensities with the three principal colours and white and black." Now, back as a consumer colour with some minimalist chic attached, it has escaped an early 20th-century return to poverty when French working women were referred to as *grisettes*, expected to be invisible in a drab grey that blended in with the urban background; then its 1950s grey suit conformity connotation. But, in modern times in the world of interior decoration although there are 20 named shades of grey, they are all reduced to background, what makes other colours 'sing'. In the world of what is called 'High Street' fashion, that which is for ordinary folk, it becomes a bodiless signifier, tucked neatly into socio-fashion's decades: light grey marl with its 1970s sportswear resonance; or as reminiscent of 1990s minimalism. Where it does come into its own, as understood by the weavers and dyers of Rouen over 500 years ago, is "to be the perfect shade to showcase truly luxurious fabrics" when having clothes that can't be replicated cheaply on the High Street, is one way that those for whom post 2008 austerity has been advantageous, can recognise each other.

178Q

"Men and women, children and old people spin, weave and elaborate cotton and wool in the workshops. The laws promise hours and wages, but the Indians thrown into these great slave quarters or prisons only leave them when their burial hour arrives." The original idea had been for the workshops *obrajes* to be sustained by Christian charity and to serve as centres for evangelism. In Peru were not only 'abominable' but the locked-in Indians "were destined for a quick civil death." In both the Viceroyalties of Peru and New Spain (Mexico) they relied on various forms of coerced labour to make woollen cloth for the colonialists, coercion needed because of the decimation of local populations and then of their disinterest in money and continued self-sufficiency in making cloth. They involved "the use of public power by private parties to obtain labour that market incentives could not provide", a case of Adam Smith's 'invisible hand' picking the locals' pockets. Or killing them. In this event, noted the Ducado de Linares early in the 18th century, the *obraje* in New Spain was likely to seize the corpse's wives and children as slaves. As in the present day, checks on conditions, *visitas*, did no more than line the pockets of inspectors. The ordinances were ridiculed by the owners.

Plastic fibres pollution is one of the biggest problems in marine conservation today, with more than 700,000 plastic fibres, such as rayon, acrylic, polyester, and nylon. Synthetic clothing produces 728,789 toxic fibres per every 6 kg of laundry.

A main aim of the uprising led by Tupac Amaru II and Micaela Bastidas Puyucachua, his wife, against the Spanish authorities of Peru, was to free them by burning down these 'prison workshops'. Tupac was himself a *kuraka*, giving him rights to land and conditional recognition by the colonialists as the head of several Quechua communities and was, in one sense, an agent of Spanish rule. He was also active as a regional merchant and muleteer, inheriting 350 mules from his father's estate at a time when the animals were crucial to trading transport. This gave him contacts in many other communities and knowledge of economic and working conditions in addition to a sense of responsibility to 'his' communities, from which people might be coerced into such labour. Micaela herself, described as "an exceptionally able leader of the rebellion", was an African-Indigenous women. When the uprising was underway, and despite the urgings of Micaela, who was left in charge of their forces near Cuzco, Tupac refused to attack and take that strategic city that had been the Inca capital. This was either on the grounds that he could not kill other Indians, specifically those who were defending the Spanish-held city, or because he was sidetracked elsewhere and did not understand the realities of troop morale. This has disastrous consequences and Tupac himself was captured after being betrayed by one of his own captains, Francisco Santa Cruz. His torture was supervised by the Spanish king's representative José Antonio de Areche: Micaela and their son Hipolito have their tongues cut out before being garrotted. Tupac's own body is tied to four horsemen riding in different directions, but his body does not split, *and a violent rainstorm begins.*

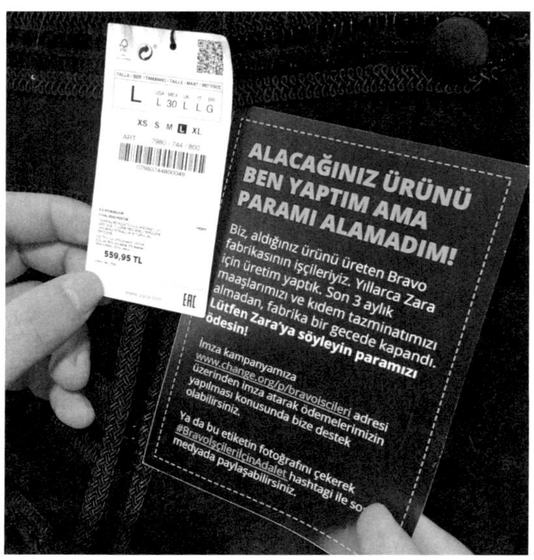

Shoppers in Istanbul at fashion retailer Zara, worth an estimated £8.6 billion and with more than 2,200 stores worldwide, have found unusual notes in their clothes from workers claiming they have not been paid for making their merchandise. Handwritten in the pockets of garments they ask for help in their campaign for better labour standards and unpaid wages from an outsourced producer for the label. Zara has been accused in the past for ripping off young designers, sued for poor working conditions and using slave and child labour in Syria.

Taking full advantage of this gruesome defeat of Tupac Amaru II and his supporters, Areche delivers a proclamation against Inca dress. A Spanish prohibition had been made as early as 1575, but was now repeated with force. "Indians are forbidden to wear the dress of the gentry, and especially of the nobility, which serves only to remind them of what the ancient Incas wore, bringing back memories that merely cause them to feel more and more hatred for the ruling nation; apart from looking ridiculous and hardly in keeping with the purity of our religion, since it features in various places the sun which was their first deity; this order extends to all provinces of this Southern Americas, totally abolishing such clothing ... and at the same time all paintings or portraits of the Incas ... And to that end that these Indians should rid themselves of the hatred they have conceived against Spaniards, that they should dress in clothing prescribed by law."

Irene Silverblatt

Threads speak. They entwine themselves into our hearts and dreams. Threads speak of many things. They talk about the present, about exotic tourism and about our own fixation with "other worlds"; they suggest hidden dialogues, interior to Andean histories and worlds – that speak to us only obliquely. They also talk of intimacy, of the human relations embodied in producing extraordinary art/textiles; they talk of enduring burdens of exploitation; they talk about the special joys and travails of women – who, after all, are the weaving artists of the Andes. Weaving is women's work and women's pleasure; women's modes of expression and creativity; women's history-writing of community and family. It is a knowledge, art, grace, geometry that has been transmitted over centuries from generations of women to generations of women: how to card wool, how to spin wool, how to dye wool, how to set up a loom, how to transform thread into meaningful fabric. Centuries-old Andean graves hold women buried with their spindle whorls. Textiles are culture-work in the Andes. Textiles are chronicles and history lessons; textiles bind kin and comadres; textiles are symbols of wealth and power; textiles are the source of wealth and power. Textiles, like this one, communicate with worlds beyond. Textiles represent a social vision of community – in time and space. They also personify the social ties of *ayni* (reciprocity) – between people and between people and the divine – that ultimately ground anything produced by Andeans. Textiles, and the women who produced them, could be translated into wealth by imperial forces that shaped Andean experience. Before Europe colonised the Americas, native Andean emperors demanded weavings made by women of the peasantry and by the elite women called the Inca's "chosen" or *aclla*. Indigenous monarchs, however, recognised obligations to those under their rule and honoured the integrity of women's work. Women, the producers of Andean textiles, including tribute, remained embodied in production. Guaman Poma de Ayala's 1000-page letter of protest to the Crown acknowledges the importance of textiles in Andean life. Look at his drawings of the *uncus* (ponchos) worn by Inca kings, symbols of Inca

1

2

3

4

5

6

dominion and the history of Inca dynasties (1). Look at the drawings of Inca queens dressed in shawls filled with meanings of their status and authority (1); or of the *aclla*, or chosen women, carrying the tools that brought these shawls and uncus into existence (2); or the Inca census, with iconic women, representing "stages of life", who are tied to weaving, with spindles and thread (3–5). Weaving substantiated women's powers, as Andeans knew well.

"The priests want money, money and more money, so they force women to serve them as spinners [and] weavers ..." says Guaman Poma. Spanish colonists brought very different understandings of textiles and institutions of textile production to the Andes. Women were forced to work in proto-factories, alienated from what they made and the creative means to produce their lives. Markets, money and "commodities" insinuated themselves into Andean life. Spanish economic practices distorted the tie between weaver and textile, transforming textiles and the women's labour that produced them into commodities. See Guaman Poma's devastating portrayal of how priests shamelessly beat women so they could have "money, money, and more money" in their coffers (6). But neither colonialism nor modern capitalism can obliterate a textile's soul. We don't know who created this extraordinary textile on display. Yes, this textile has become a commodity, passing from the woman who created it to others. Eventually this ritual cloth found its way to an exceptional Lima shop selling Andean artisanry, and, then, it crossed channels and oceans, and found its way to my door and to this exhibition. I hope and believe that in spite of the journeys traversed by this textile, the woman who spun the wool, dyed the yarn, set up the loom, and transformed her vision into a textile of beauty, is still, in Andean spirit, embedded in its threads, is still, in Andean spirit, laying claim to what she produced, is still, in Andean spirit, speaking to us.

Skirt, underskirt and bustier acquired from a transgender performer, Puno, Peru, 2010. The Dance of the Miners, first performed in 1790, evolved into today's *Diablada*, the Devil Dance, which was born during the colonial period in the entrance of a mine in Oruro. It symbolises the fight with Evil and the Seven Deadly Sins: only the sin of Lust has survived in Bolivia in the figure of the native *china supay*. During the Carnival she is escorted by the bears and the condor, using all her charms to seduce susceptible onlookers. The dances of the myths play a constituent part in Andean reality.

The New York Times reported in 1992: *Only a few months ago, Peruvians knew her as one of the country's prima ballerinas, slim and beautiful. But after Maritza Garrido Lecca was captured this month with Abimael Guzman Reynoso, leader of the Shining Path guerrilla group, the gracefulness of dance was lost. Peruvians were shocked to see her on a police videotape with raised fist and a fierce, hardened stare, shouting, "Communism will take over the world!" On the same night the police also arrested three members of the Shining Path central committee. They were all women, planning what was to be the most violent wave of killings yet in Lima. It was a reminder of a remarkable phenomenon: Peruvian women, many of Andean Indian background, play major roles in the violent revolution espoused by Mr. Guzman.*

The No. 2 person in the organization has almost always been a woman. Of the 19 members of the central committee, the governing body of the guerrilla group, at least 8 are women as are 40 percent of its guerillas.

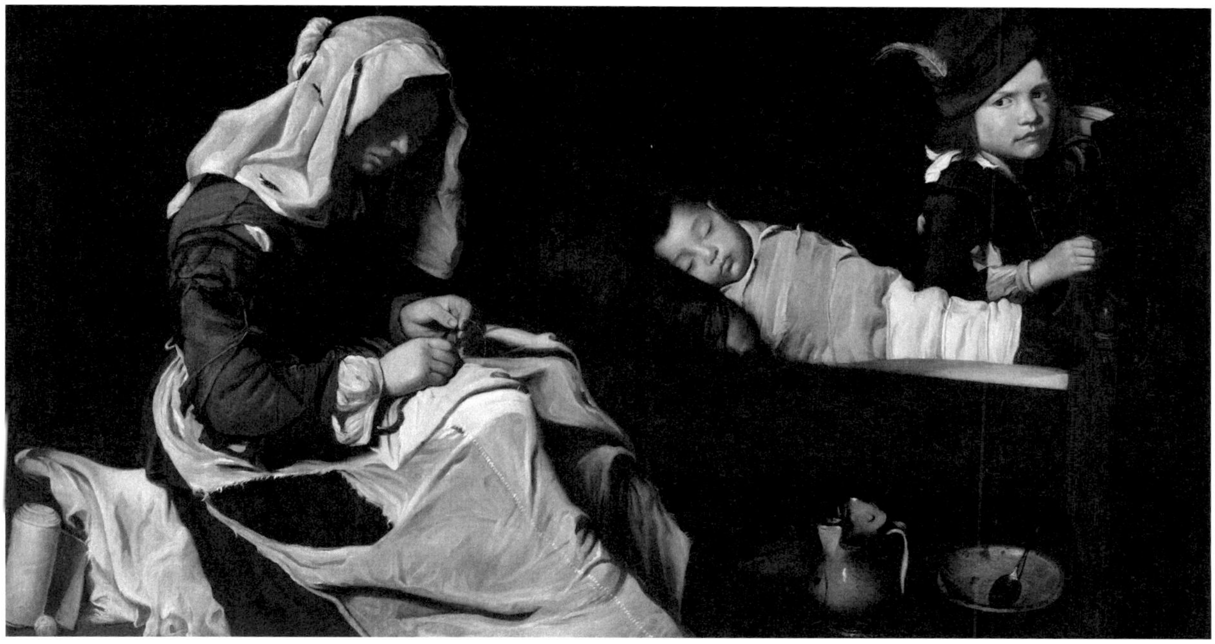

Blue Jeans

Once upon a time in the 16th and 17th centuries there were two cloths. One was from Genoa and was used by its far-travelling sailors. The French called it *bleu de Gênes* though the story is that it was originally more of a yellow. It became known as jean and was made from a mix of thread, which was imported into England and soon produced there. Meanwhile denim is alleged to have originated as *serge de Nîmes* and was made from silk and wool. What both had in common was that they were a twill weave – developed as early as 10 centuries BCE in Austrian Hallstatt – which makes for a fabric that is both flexible and resilient and has a distinctive diagonal ribbing. At the same time in the Dongari Killa area of Mumbai, a coarse plainweave fabric called dungaree was used also by sailors, both as sails and for their own clothes. All three clothes were worn by poor working people. Italian painting of the late 1600s like that of Giuseppe Bonito shows beggars and workers in blue denim. What they also had in common was that the two European fabrics came to be woven with cotton at the end of the 18th century, when slave labour on cotton plantations in the Americas made it available worldwide. By 1789, George Washington was able to see both jean and denim woven at the Beverly Mill in Massachusetts.

It is in name only that dungaree survived, both as the particular overall and still interchangeably with jeans until the 1970s. Back in the 1850s in the USA, jean as a fabric continued to co-exist with denim. General workers including those in non-manual jobs dressed in the lighter jean, but mechanics, painters and those doing heavy work wore blue denim. Now the two are married, one became the trousers, the other the cloth. The story of Levi Strauss is well known, but it is significant that even before the famous blue jeans with the metal rivets, denim came in blue. This was surely not accidental; a second marriage between denim and indigo was a natural. On the use of indigo Jenny Balfour Paul writes, "Indigo-dyed cloth in some parts of the world has had a largely decorative function. In southern Arabia, as for the farming communities of South East Asia, its prime importance has been practical. Hence the lengths to which dyers went to render the cloth as windproof and hard wearing as possible. It performed a function similar to the anorak or army jacket. Though primarily used by the humbler classes, its striking decoration quality was appreciated further up the social scale. In this it shows similarity with the development of blue jeans made from denim." And this is indeed the development that took place as jean changed from fabric to the Levi Strauss trousers style, the classic 501 still going strong, but the range of both style and the very fabric of denim inexhaustible. Which is another story to be told in Denim Triumphant.

Ladders are built and used mainly by sub-Saharan men attempting to jump over the barb-wired wall that seperates the Spanish enclave Melilla from North Africa. They are constructed using whatever is at hand, such as twigs and scraps of denim.

2006

"Where are the men? Here are the Women!" So shouted around 3000 women garment workers at the Misr Spinning and Weaving Company complex in Mahalla al-Kubra in the Nile Delta to those male workers who had not switched off their machines just when a strike was gathering momentum. The Company where "control by harsh discipline" was still considered as "economically rational in the short term", had a long history of labour militancy. In 1937 workers went on strike for an 8-hour work day and in 1947 to demand that they work under less severe discipline. During that strike the government brought in tanks and workers were killed, but the next year they finally won an 8-hour day. More strikes and repression occurred later under the regimes of Nasser and Sadat as wages did not keep pace with increased food prices.
In 2006 the cry of the women shamed the men, who stopped work and went to the Tal'at Harb Square outside the factory to join other workers who had assembled there. They had been promised an increase in the annual bonus given to public-sector workers by the Prime Minister, but when pay packets came in December, there was no increase. Soon riot police were deployed around the factory but they did not know what to do when there were 10,000 in the square. With the encouragement of the Egyptian state security apparatus, management offered 21 days pay. The women again took the lead in scorning the offer. Some of the men then re-occupied and locked themselves in the mill. The police cut off water and power to the occupied mill, but the following morning they had massive support from 20,000 workers outside. On the 4th day, a 45-day bonus was offered with an assurance that the company would not be privatised. This was accepted but a campaign began against the state-controlled 'Trade Union' of the Mubarak regime. In the 3 months that followed, 30,000 textile workers in ten mills in the Nile Delta and Alexandria went on strike or on slowdowns to get for themselves what had been won at Misr in Malhalla. In Misr mills in Kafr al-Dawwar strikers kept hold of a leader of the discredited official Union inside the factory, compelling him to be a striker too. It was some 17 months later that the general strike called by textile workers in Malhalla for April 6th, 2008 was blocked by a heavy police and military presence. In the fight back that day 300 strikers were injured and 3 died. It included local residents ripping down posters of President Hosni Mubarak, and this date has been seen as the real start of the movement that eventually brought about Mubarak's fall. The continuation of strikes in the city and its textile factories that continued from 2006 onwards against the regime's neoliberal policies and the accompanying imposed official trade union, and for an independent union, built up the momentum that resulted in his fall from power. Since then it has continued in the absence of significant regime change. As early as February 11th, 2011 workers called a general strike, and in September, 22,000 at the Egypt Weaving and Textile Company, also in Malhalla, went on strike with their own union for a better minimum wage. In 2012 workers protested against the Muslim Brotherhood's proposed constitution and the price rises they had instigated, showing a political initiative that was then hijacked by the al-Sisi military coup. The violence, and the comprehensive nature of the repression of popular protest and independent trade unions by the new military regime, exceeds that of the Mubarak period, but once again the workers, and especially the women of Misr in Malhalla, have taken a lead in disputes over the non-implementation of unpaid promised 'social allowances' in a period of rapid inflation. During a strike in 2015, seven women were "handed over for investigation" for allegedly "inciting the workers". In February 2017 a strike blackballed by the official union was brought to a halt when a further five women were arrested.

The taboo of violence against unarmed women is unusually strong in the Arab world. Egyptian army soldiers are beating a young woman in Tahrir Square in Cairo with batons, their fists, and boots. To pull the black *abaya* above her head and expose her midriff and chest is a profound and sexually charged humiliation.

opposite page

Stanislav Arlet, a Jesuit missionary in 1697, said of Peruvian Indians' perceptions of him that at first they see an amusing monster, and that later they told him they "thought the man, his hat, his clothing and the horse he rode were all one extraordinary animal". *Diablada*, Carnival of Oruro.

Guiseppe Campuzano

"As a homosexual, a philosopher too, and a cross-dresser, I research cross-dressing in the history, the culture of Peru, but with the Museo Travesti I make praxis and perform as a cross-dresser, that is I dress in many forms. I emphasise this for several reasons. For one thing, I don't call myself gay because the gay thing is linked to a lot of things about belonging, and I don't want to belong, but rather to stop belonging, in order go in for the next form of belonging. For another, because there is so much ethnic clothing in this country, each region has different clothing and each one is more beautiful than the next. And finally because of all the cross-dresser clichés that exist. Their distorting and demeaning power was clear to me at an

exhibition I presented about a museum of drag and all these journalists and TV gossip programme people came and they were full of presuppositions about what a cross-dresser is. They spoke very badly about it, even an important art critic, because for him, a drag queen was a cheeky scandal; that is he wanted a performer to shout and contort and undress. Otherwise, for him, it wasn't a genuine drag queen, which is more to do with the vulgar clichés of a dangerous woman.

Now at the same time there is great ethnic drag here in Peru, even on prime time television with the programme, the *Chola Chabuca*. And he is gay and HIV positive and a drag queen but people don't think about him as either gay or HIV positive because he really becomes his character, the defenceless *cholita*, an Indigenous Andean woman in the city wearing ethnic dress. He is very good, but what's especially significant is that he has another character who was *La Negra*, and whilst *La Chola* is very funny and everything, she's not sexual, whereas *La Negra* was an explosion of sexuality. But his character *La Negra* wasn't successful whereas the one of *La Chola* was successful. Because it's not something dangerous, I mean she can pick up your son and be with him and caress him but she's not going to do anything to him, you know what I mean? She's safe.

It's also related to what I would call marketing around the *cholo* world right now. It is being integrated, the *cholo* world, that is ethnic men and women from the country, it is being integrated into consumerism, but first of all, so that this can happen, this world is being stripped of everything dangerous. And he knows, this drag queen knows that he must project this image, while of course the women on the street begging, they also know that they have to project, don't they? I mean they are people who you have to help so what they definitely don't have to show you is their sexual side, because the sexual side is a side with power with strength, isn't it, and that would be the wrong projection, too dangerous.

But then, despite how good the TV performance is, I don't think a drag queen, an ethnic drag queen, needs to be created, because there already are drag queens in the dances of Peru. I'm talking here about *las chinas*, those characters that act as she-devils, and what's so impressive is the strength required for the performance. It's the same with the characters played by men in festivals, a lot of, their activity is very physical, I mean, they are like acrobats. They really are acrobatic, they turn in mid air and jump or climb one on top of the other.

What's also interesting is that every time I have spoken with the specialists in *Wititi* dances they would tell me, but no, in the *Wititi* the man dresses as a woman because he is going to kidnap the woman that he is in love with. That is, he is not gay, Oh no no no. He dresses up because he has to kidnap the woman he is in love with. But if the dance had ended with this line of men and women like in all dances now, then to get the spirit of the dance we should put the cross-dressers back at the centre of it. With the androgyne at the centre, then it was a way of reconstructing the dance. What is crucial to Andean choreography has to do with the opposites mediated by the androgyne. That is, men, women and the androgyne mediated in the ritual which then became dance, and you can see graphic representation of this in *talegas*, the woven bags for carrying potatoes or coca, and the way the different stripes of colour are placed against each other when they are woven.

Or look at the figure of *Manco Capac*. What they teach us at school when we're little, is that *Manco Capac* was a very macho man. And he fought, a real fighting man, but the historians now have challenged this idea. In fact *Manco Capac* was a *shamán*, who belonged to a caste of *shamáns*, who didn't go to war. Rather, it was through spells that they won wars. Of course it was another way of accessing power, another form of power but without the characteristics that macho idolises.

Ah, but if you look closely at this image, this person here, is an androgyne from the clothing, but it is never stated whether it is a man or a woman. And that is a very chauvinistic view on the part of anthropologists, isn't it? Because it says here is a character, the research says: "… there is a character dressed with men and women's clothes, having sex with another character dressed with the clothes of a God." So then, the God is God, and the other is a man dressed in men and women's clothing, but why is it a man dressed? It could also be a woman dressed in men and women's clothing, but there is always this idea within the Castilian language itself, which gives priority to the masculine. And at the same time I don't understand why they want to look at drag kings and drag queens as if they were the same, they are totally different things.

The drives, what lies behind the crossdressing act, is different."

Bought in a hardware store in La Paz, 2010. Designs found in Andean textiles and their names in Quechua: *alqo yupi* (a knitted design meaning dog's paw), *chaska* (star), *chili-chili* (a medicinal plant), *k'enko* (roses in the form of a zigzag), *ley pallay* (a dark design on a light background created using supplementary warps in two or three colours), *llama sillu* (llama footprint), *ñawi* (eye), *pakay* (pod with seeds), *pallay* (to pick up threads), *pata pallay* (an infinite number of designs can be created using just two or three colours), *pichincho* (a small Andean bird), *pumaq maquin* (puma footprint), *puyto* (a large diamond), *qenqo* (zigzag, often symbolises lightning or rivers), *raki raki* (fern), *t'ika* (flower), *tiqlla* (designs resulting from a complex warping system using discontinuous warps), *viscacha* (an Andean rodent), *wakaj ñawin* (cow eyes). Some dyes of Peru are: *chilq'ua* (a weedy bush that literally grows everywhere in Peru; used primarily to obtain a light green, *chilq'ua* can also be combined with the mordant cupric sulfate to create a much darker green), *q'uolle* (a yellow dye, usually used with a cochineal exhaust vat to get a golden yellow; it is most commonly picked and dried before use, rather than used fresh), *palo-palo* (a jungle vine that gives a range of peachy salmon colours), *kinsa q'uchu* (a substantive natural dye, similar to black walnuts; the dye properties are found in the fungus that grows on the plant's leaves and the mordant is found in the tannins in the leaves themselves. Because of this it requires no outside mordant, and it gives a surprising turquoise/teal colour), *indigo* (another native plant of South America that grows in the lower altitudes but is being introduced to the highlands). There are three ways indigo is used in the dyeing process: 1) fermentation (from fresh leaves) 2) reduced natural indigo and urea (chemical naturally found in urine) 3) reduced natural indigo and fructose (from over-ripe or rotting fruit, especially apples, pears, and bananas). *Cochineal* (a dye made primarily out of ground up beetles that live on prickly pear cacti), *awaypili* (a purple leaf that is dried and then used as dye. By itself, it gives a medium to dark blue-purple).

Pistachio

In 'The Colours of Abu Kir' – the *Arabian Nights* story of the dyers Abu Kir and Abu Sir, starting on the 483rd night – Abu Kir is a very bad person who leaves Alexandria with the virtuous Abu Sir for an unnamed kingdom where textiles were dyed only in blue. Even though the dyers have only heard of blue, they had their own guild. Abu Kir presents himself before the king and says, "I can give the most charming shades of every colour to any fabric: reds of all kinds, as rose and jujube; blacks of all kinds, as charcoal, pitch and kohl; greens of all kinds, as grass, pistachio, olive and parakeet; yellows of all kinds, as citron, orange, lemon and gold. All these colours I have at my command, and yet the dyers of this city will have none of me."
On Ranking the Gifts of Cloth Received by the Mughal Emperor Akhbar: "The garments stored in the Imperial wardrobe are arranged according to the days, months and years of their entries, and according to their colour, price and weight. Such an arrangement is now-a-days called a set. The clerks fix accordingly the degree of every article of wear, which they write on a strip of cloth, and tack it to the end of the pieces. Whatever pieces of the same kind arrive for the Imperial wardrobe on the Urmuzd day (first day) of the month of Farwardinj, provided they be of a good quality, have a higher rank assigned to them than pieces arriving on other days; and if pieces are equal in value, their precedence, or otherwise, is determined by the character of the day of their entry; and if pieces are equal as far as the character of the day is concerned, they put the lighter stuff higher in rank; and if pieces have the same weight, they arrange them according to their colour. The following is the order of colours: fus, safidalcliah, ruby-coloured, golden, orange, brass-coloured, crimson, grass green, cotton flower-coloured, sandalwood-coloured, almond-coloured, purple, grape-coloured, mauve like the colour of some parrots, honey-coloured, brownish lilac, coloured like the Ravaamanjani flower, coloured like the Kasni flower, apple-coloured, hay-coloured, pistachio, bhojpatra-coloured, pink, bright blue, coloured like the Qulghah flower, water-coloured, oil-coloured, brown-red, emerald, bluish like China-ware, violet, bright pink, mango-coloured, musk-coloured, coloured like the Fakhtah pigeon."

The traditional colours of Japan trace their historical origins to the Twelve Level Cap and Rank System which was established in based on the five Chinese elements. They form an elaborate sumptuary laws system relating colours and hierarchy. Nowadays, 465 traditional colours are known and used widely. It is said that there are more than 1300 old colours including nameless ones.
Some of them are: ibis wing colour, plum-blossom mouse, red bean colour, dawn-colour, orang utan-coloured, shrimp brown, dawn-colour, persimmon-juice colour, glazed persimmon, cypress bark colour, brewed mustard-brown, spicy red-brown (Chinese tea brown), rinsed-out red, foreign crimson, meat-colour, chestnut-leather brown, rich gardenia, polished brown, stylish persimmon, boiled red bean brown, daylily-coloured, legal dye (from when colour use was regulated by class), decaying leaves colour, yellow-trough shell-brown, weathered bamboo (lit. 'sooty'), egg-coloured, the colour of an undried wall, brown-nosers' brown (lit. 'the brown of flattery'), golden-grey bamboo (dried and weathered), golden oak, faded Sen no Rikyu's tea, thousand year old brown, eggshell paper-coloured, contemplation in a tea garden, steamed chestnut colour, pale young green onion, a thousand years-green, horsetail colour, greenfinch colour, willow tea, flirtatious indigo tea, indigo podium fragile seaweed brown , underside of willow leaves, inside of a bottle, thousand herb colour, blue black crayfish, harbour rat, iron storage, kimono storage, secret-colour / lapis lazuli blue, rusted light-blue, rabbit-ear iris, opposite flower colour, sky colour, peered into jar, coarse wool colour, mousy wisteria, dove feather grey, vine grape, fake purple, vanishing red mouse, wisteria and burnt-bamboo, indigo white, wet crow's wing.

2005

A fire at a textile sweatshop in the Caballito area of Buenos Aires killed six undocumented Bolivian immigrants, four children and two women. It was estimated that there are 100,000 such workers from Bolivia and Paraguay. The fire was triggered by a short circuit due to unsafe and excessive electrical wiring in the workshop where over 60 immigrants worked. The children had been locked in a room so they would not disturb the work. Previous reports and cases of slave-like conditions have been presented by the Union of Seamstress Workers, formed out of a

"Indigenous knowledge is not ... a 'why' knowledge or a knowledge of causes but rather a 'how' knowledge. It also cannot be filed away or be alienated from its subject. Rather, it demands the commitment of the subject who handles or manipulates it. In Indigenous thinking knowledge is closely related to ritual."

neighbourhood assembly at Parque Avallenada in the absence of official trade union representation. Just as the Unions won't accept undocumented affiliates, the police say they cannot act on these cases because the victims do not have their DNI, a National identity card. Some of the smallest shops are owned by undocumented immigrants themselves, who earn little more than the workers they employ. Contrary to the usual sociological narrative, these places are not producing cheap label-fakes but are making clothes for Argentine high-street labels including Soho, Montagne, and Cheeky, and it is they, the retailers, as in most parts of the world, who are making the bulk of the profit. This is a familiar situation in another respect wherein richer countries aim to keep a textile industry of their own which they can only do by allowing 'illegal' immigration so as to compete on wage levels. It is, for example, well documented in Los Angeles. The sweatshops of Los Angeles's downtown and Vernon in its periphery are one of the city's dirty secrets with an estimated half a million workers both in small 'sweatshops' or in home working. It's a natural location because of its strong connections with fashion and style but also because of its long anti-union tradition. Thus though the clothing industry doesn't like bad publicity, it objected to the city passing a living wage ordinance because though it didn't affect them directly they saw it as the first crack in the door towards raising wages. Instead retailers with all their power and manufacturers, by and large, enjoy a system whereby most "neither own nor operate their own factories. This intentionally confusing system serves the important function of diffusing legal and moral responsibility for working conditions". It is again Latino workers who are exploited often by Korean bosses who tend to take any of the bad publicity that does come around as contracts go through chains of sub-contracting. The pressure always comes from above with short delivery deadlines and very strict controls whereby small errors in the packing and placing of bar codes are subject to extortionate fines. One manufacturer complained that "retailers are making their profits at dockside rather than in the shop". With the pressure come the risks that in even less organised Buenos Aires can be fatal. To which the Argentine government's response was to want to force owners to turn their workshops into companies and the immigrant workers into formal employees. But as the activist group Alameda argued, in opposing it, "This reform intends to place all the responsibility for the workshop on the workshop owners. The owners however are in the same boat as the workers. They are exploited by the big labels and paid a pittance to produce clothes; in turn they have no choice but to exploit the workers. The reform aims to remove all liability from the labels". More recently, in 2010 Alameda has facilitated the textile cooperative Mondo Alameda, which, with a Thai cooperative, has set up the "No Chains" trademark.

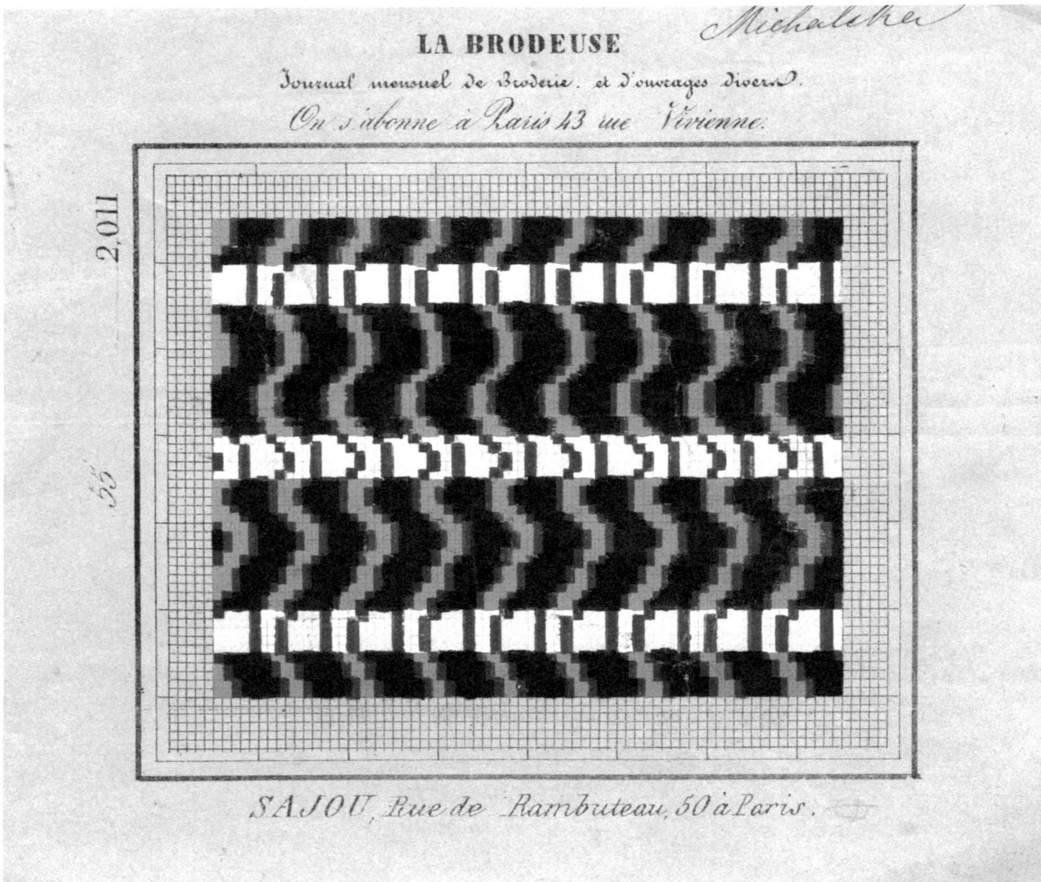
LA BRODEUSE
Journal mensuel de Broderie. et d'ouvrages divers.
On s'abonne à Paris 43 rue Vivienne.
2.011
55
SAJOU, Rue de Rambuteau, 50 à Paris.

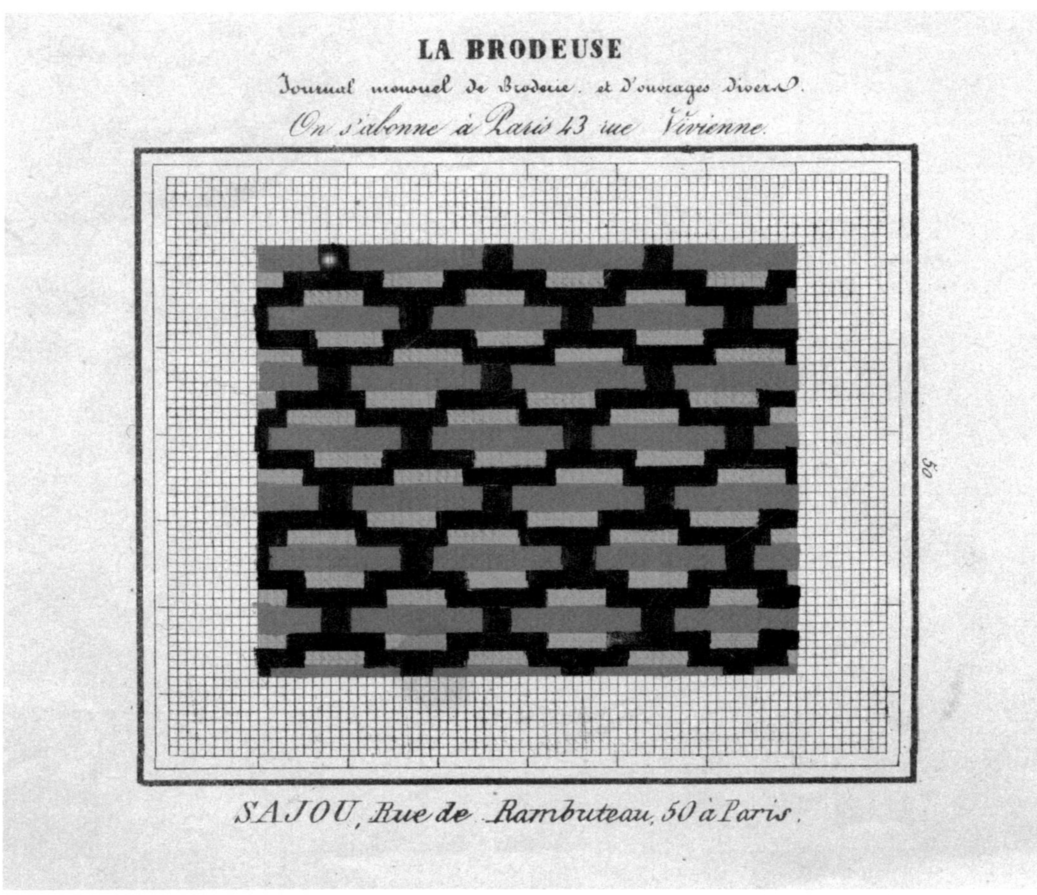
LA BRODEUSE
Journal mensuel de Broderie. et d'ouvrages divers.
On s'abonne à Paris 43 rue Vivienne.
50
SAJOU, Rue de Rambuteau, 50 à Paris.

Luciano

"I have worked as a shoeshiner for 45 years. I have always lived with this job, all my life, since I was 14 years old. I got married and had children, and well, you know, I had a family. After some time my wife, she died, and so now I live with my children. I have three children, they are big now, grown up. I have always made a living from this job, shining shoes.
I see a lot of families here in Bolivia having a very hard time. There are a lot of poor people here. It is very sad to see fellow Bolivians having such a hard time. These people, only God knows how they get by and how they live day to day. Right now, the economic situation here is not very good, and these people, they have nothing. There's a lot of poor people here. The only thing we can do is entrust ourselves to God, and have faith in God, you know? There's a lot of abandoned people here, left in the streets with nothing, they don't have a home, they live in the street, it is so sad. It gets very cold here, and they have to sleep in the street. It is very sad, even little children, orphans who have been abandoned, living in the street with nothing to eat. It is sad to live here and see these things. That is what I can tell you, what I see here in La Paz.
It is important that people know, that people understand, you know? Because people in other places don't know that people here live in need, in terms of housing and financially. So then, that is one thing that is important. This is a beautiful country, a big and beautiful country, but we are few inhabitants, you know? This country is beautiful, with a lot of land, but we are not well organised here, we need better organisation.
With the new president things have changed a little bit, of course, things are changing. But let's hope that they change a bit more, you know? And people then could live without worries, if the financial situation were better, they could have a job, and make a living from a job, and live without worries. And, why not say that other countries could also help, you know? They can lend us a hand, lend our country a hand, especially for poor people. Because – it is important that you know this – Bolivians are hard workers. What we need is good organisation, but people in Bolivia work hard, you know? And also, I'd like to say, we are missing sources for jobs. It could be that, if there were more companies here, then these poor people could make a living and live comfortably, don't you think? They could have a few pesos for their sustenance, for a soup. But it's never too late. We can come out of this, if and when we get some help from countries with money. Otherwise, I don't think we'll manage to come out of this. What we need is a future, an exit out of this situation, and a future, you know? We can do it, we need a future. We cannot change the past, the past is passed and we cannot change it. We need to look for a future, for a new future. And so, other countries could lend Bolivia a hand, could they not? I think so. It is important that they lend this country a hand, because we are all people of the world, we are all the same, God has made us all the same, of any colour, we are all the same. That's my opinion.
I have always enjoyed chatting to people, when people arrive from different countries, I always chat to them. I have many friends all over the world, tourists who have come here, from Germany, from the United States, Italy, Spain, Australia, Portugal. They know me from my job, and they have videotaped me and photographed me. They have even told me, when they've come back, 'You are an international shoe-shiner', that's what they said. I have many friends all over the world. And well, this is all I can tell you. I am 65 years old and have been working here for 45 years, in my post, by the hotel. You can always find me there. I always work, every day. When you arrive at the hotel, you will find me there. That's where I work, always, every single day, every day of the year. Whenever you come back, you'll find me there. And so, this is what I wanted to tell you while we chatted, it's not a great story, but it's important, I will tell you more next time. And I will give you this ball for you to remember me, a keepsake.
You can take this with you. In my country we do it like this, for knitting a pullover, a *chumpa*, we make a ball like this, look, like this. Take good care of it. Thank you very much."

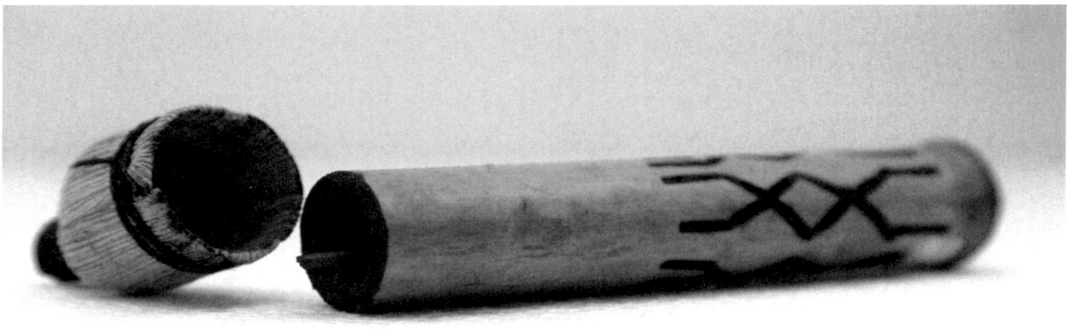

Cotton, dye 140 x 128 cm; urucum seed face paint; ca. 1960; Upper Ucayali River, Peru; both bought in São Paulo, 2014. The Asháninka often paint their faces; it is a tradition they use to exteriorise their feelings and moods. They use the seeds from the *achiote* trees, which provides them a pigment known as *urucum*. This pigment has now become one of the world's most important natural food colourants.

The *kushma* is worn by the Pajonal Asháninka in the Peruvian Amazon and they acquire them through trade with other Asháninka groups. Women learn to spin and weave cotton when they are young. The effort to make sufficient yarn for a single *kushma* may take an entire month. The garment is woven on a backstrap loom, and dyed stripes always figure in the design, vertical for men's garments and horizontal for women's. The *kushma* constitutes an important article of dress and cultural identity. Its continued use points to the persistence of shared Asháninka values and practices in the face of prolonged colonisation in the area. Some eight million people may have lived in the Amazon region in 1500, divided between dense coastal settlements, such as that at Marajó, and inland dwellers. By 1900 the population had fallen to one million and by the early 1980s it was less than 200,000.

The Asháninka population of 25,000–40,000 live in the Peruvian rainforest and in the state of Acre, Brazil. They are known historically to be fiercely independent, and were noted for their "bravery and independence" by the Spanish invaders. During the rubber boom (1839–1913) they were enslaved by rubber tappers, and an estimated 80% of the population were killed. For over a century now, there has been encroachment onto Asháninka land not just from rubber tappers, but also illegal loggers, drug traffickers, and oil companies. Since the 1950s, their territories have been reduced and their settlements systematically destroyed, resulting in a retreat by Asháninka people further into the jungle. During the 1980s and 1990s, internal conflict in Peru caused massive displacement, disappearance, and death among the communities. Their *chacres* (garden plots) were burned, their legal papers were destroyed, some were forced on pain of death to join the Maoist Shining Path, and others were enslaved. As Asháninka communities are usually very small this caused great disturbance. Because they could neither hunt nor fish effectively given the danger posed by armed groups in the forest, malnutrition became increasingly threatening. According to the Peruvian Truth and Reconciliation Commission, 10,000 Asháninka were displaced, 6000 died and 5000 were taken captive by the Shining Path during this time, and thirty to forty communities disappeared.

In the mid-2000s, the Asháninka gained legal title to a portion of their lands which they had mapped using GPS technology; these lands are now a National Park and a Reserved Zone. By now most have returned to their ancestral lands, some from as far afield as the Urubamba river. Current threats are amplified by illegal roads, conservation groups, missionary groups, and diseases brought by outsiders. Roads are being built into the forest to extract mahogany and cedar trees for export to markets in the United States and Europe despite an international embargo. Religious missionary groups are intent on changing Asháninka culture and belief systems. Some conservation programmes in the area have also been less than fair to the Asháninka in their move to create conservation zones in this "important ecologically diverse area", choosing plants and animals over Indigenous rights. Today, a large communal reserve set aside for the Asháninka is under threat from the proposed Pakitzapango dam, which would displace some 10,000 of them. The dam is part of a large set of hydroelectric projects planned jointly by the Brazilian and Peruvian governments.

At the same time an influx of industrial goods into the Asháninka trading system has boosted the circulation of traditional exchange items. Recent political organising has further strengthened their identity, and their leaders who had started to wear Western-style clothes now return to the *kushma* to display Asháninka-ness to influential outsiders. No longer can it be assumed that its use merely testifies to the cultural purity of its wearer. Its use may also be an indication of his or her sophisticated acknowledgment that the timely display of Indigenous identity may well be rewarded.

Blue

Like most colours, blues are subject to shifts of significance including those of class and gender. During the Roman Empire, blue was the colour of working class clothing as opposed to the blacks, whites, reds and purple of the nobility. It was more generally fashionable in the 12th and 13th centuries, starting with King Louis IX of France, but with the increasing use of a woad-based dye on cheap cloth it developed too democratically to be of use as a mark of any distinction, instead becoming the colour of artisan and servant clothing, so much so that Pope Pius V could reject its use for altar decoration on the grounds that it was too common. In more recent times it was used to mark out the factory working class as blue-collar.

A counter-trajectory, especially with darker blue, has been that of a mix of seriousness and authority seen today in the cloned blue suit of politicians and corporate executives, as well as in police uniforms. This mix could also be mocked along with the colour, so that in 17th-century England blue was used to point to over-zealous moralising. Specifically, the parliamentary supporters of Oliver Cromwell were labelled 'blue-stockings'.

This label, however, has another history, and mockery in its direction carries a distinctly reactionary male sneer. It refers to a seriousness that is not moralising, nor that of established authority, but rather one of freedom. By the late 1500s in Paris, the term *bas bleu*, bluestocking, was being used to describe literary women, the same kind of women who would form the politically important salons of the 18th century. By which time both in France and in England, where Mrs Elizabeth Montagu founded the first official bluestocking society in around 1750, the wearing of blue worsted stockings rather than the standard high-society black silk stockings was, as Jane Robinson puts it, like wearing jeans, practical and casual. Later the term was used to describe the first women in England who, in the face of standard misogyny, gained a university education.

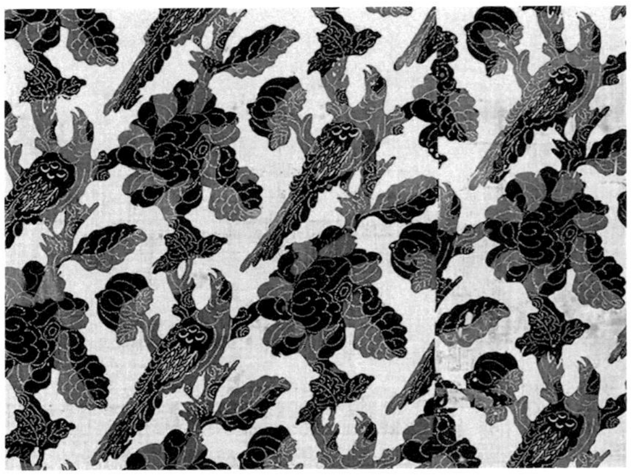

Blue-resist panel (detail). Probably produced in India for the American market, mid-18th century. Cotton, painted and block-printed resist, dyed.

These stand in sharp contrast to the male fantasies about women in European, especially German, Romanticism, which replayed the earlier fantasies of courtly love. These fantasies were supplemented by a secular use of blue, but with heavenly connotations recalling those borne by the colour in the European Middle Ages. Following Goethe, who had declared in his three-volume work on colour that "we love to contemplate blue, not because it advances to us, but because it draws us after it", the hero of Novalis's quest novel *Heinrich von Ofterdingen* (1800) finally finds a blue flower in a meadow in the midst of wild countryside; the flower is transformed into his beloved with sky-blue eyes and blue veins in her neck. As a cornflower it will take a more sinister twist: well-known as Hitler's favourite, it will be worn by MPs of the Austrian Freedom Party when they enter government in 2002. There was however a markedly different aspect to German Romanticism and Novalis himself who, as Friedrich von Hardenberg, was a geology student at the Freiburg mining academy.

In the same novel he heroises the miner, and his own work on brown coal, in which he saw nature as a dynamic entity in flux and with its own self-knowledge, was part of the process that led to coal tar becoming the source of synthetic colour dyes. Work in this mode was continued by Friedlieb Ferdinand Runge who, exploring both the potential of coal tar and the make-up of indigo, created blue 'cyanol' in 1832, arguably the first synthetic before William Perkin's mauve. "Colour glittered forth from blackness. It was a kind of magic." This sense of chemicals as having a life force was allied to a purposefully democratic urge to popularise their workings.

In the hands of the early-20th-century painter Wassily Kandinsky, via the theosophy of Rudolf Steiner and Annie Besant, blue is snatched back into the spiritual stratosphere: "The inclination of blue towards depth is so great that it becomes more dense the darker the tone, and has a more characteristic effect. The deeper the blue becomes, the more strongly it calls man towards the infinite, awakening in him a desire for the pure and, finally for the supernatural." It is definitely *man* and the pure infinite, male spirituality, so that Franz Marc, co-founder of The Blue Rider, could write that "Blue is the male principle, sharp and spiritual".

1913

20,000 textile workers go on strike in Barcelona, a major cloth-making centre since the 18th century. 13,000 of them are women and children and they are demanding a cut in working hours to a 9-hour day and an 8-hour night shift. In the face of steeply rising food prices, due in part to Spain fighting a war against Moroccan guerrillas, they are also demanding a 40% rise in piece rates, which is how many women are paid, and a 25% increase in wages. Some months earlier in October 1912, the Constancy Union was formed to organise unskilled men, women and children in the textile industry, but at a general meeting the following February, despite there being a majority of women in attendance, only one was given time to speak. The union was also slow to acknowledge both piece-work and the conditions of home-workers whose importance had also been articulated by a book, *Las Obreras de la Aguja*, in the same year. But in the course of the strike it was women who took the initiative and developed new forms of organising. Women had already been crucial to the mass strikes in 1890 for shorter hours, when mill owners' houses were bombed; the *Semana Trágica* (Tragic Week) of 1909; the textile workers' strike in Sabadell in 1910, but in Barcelona the social networks they had already formed – with mutual child care and food kitchens for other strikers – were developed so that the boundaries between community and workplace organisation were blurred: a process that also overcame the division between factory workers and home workers. At an assembly called on August 10th, they ensured that it was one for the community as a whole so that all were welcome and could speak as equals. At the same time they took responsibility to avoid repressive violence while giving no ground on demonstrations. On August 8th in a march on the Governor's office – and faced with a police block – they sent the men home and then defied police orders by regrouping, with 200 marchers reaching the office. Despite police blocks in the next

Strikers at the New Bedford Mills, USA, in 1928 oppose a 10% cut in wages that were already considered well below a living wage. After several months, constant police harassment and arrests and the introduction of the National Guard, a 5% cut was agreed, but union activists lost their jobs.

days they continued to demonstrate and hold daily public meetings. All this meant that there was conflict between them and the union strike committee, some of whom denounced them as a 'mob'. Even the most militant union men were put out by the women's way of dealing with women strike-breakers which was to cut their hair off and then sell it to wig-makers to financially support food kitchens. Reports at the time refer to women workers serving as "ringleaders well known to the crowd". On August 20th the strike committee made agreements, which the women did not accept, saying it was they who spoke for the community and that they wouldn't return until there was official publication of a new law, which mandated a 60-hour week. Such a Royal Decree was introduced after a return to work on 15th September, but as in many other cases there was then the matter of implementing it. Most employers simply ignored the decree, so that another major strike took place in Barcelona in August 1916 to make it stick.

Imogen Stidworthy

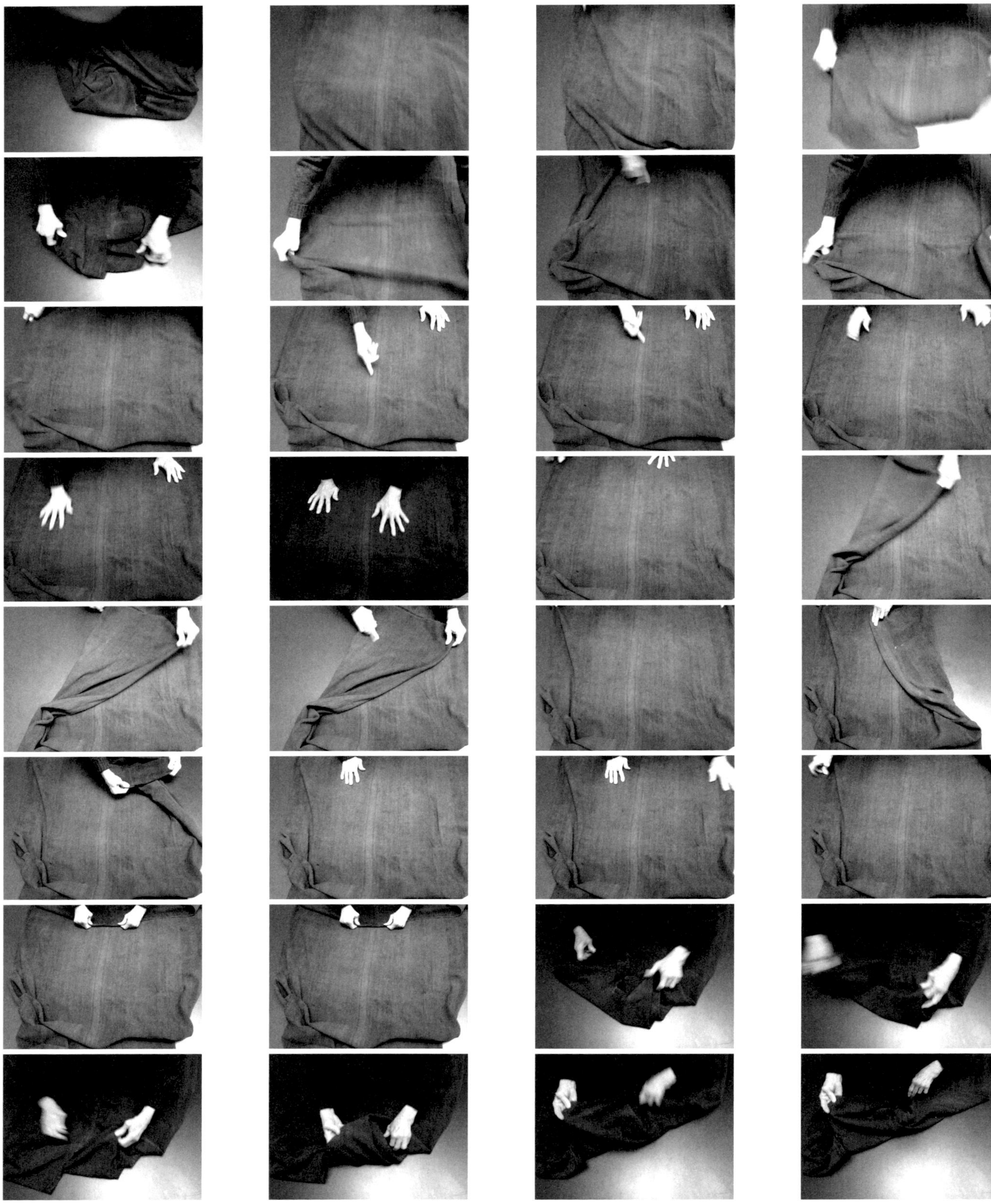

A woman investigates a garment of unknown origin. She has been sewing for the past seventy-five years, from running repairs to elaborate patchwork quilts which take years to complete. She notices the thick cord used to sew the seams in the garment. She points out the faded outside surface and deep colour of the inside, and the concentrated lines of light and dark in the fibres. It is the tropical colour of red earth. She turns the cloth over and over, moving it through her hands many times to sense its weight and dimensions, and to imagine the proportions of the body that wore it.

Where do we go to? Could you speed up? Just a little, will you, or the sun will burn our foreheads. Is this an utopian and counter-hegemonic walk, us being moved in accordance to a cultural script? Please speed up and tell me where we are going. How can I move thee? Or maybe it doesn't matter, the Andes are everywhere anyhow. But could you just move a bit quicker. Are you already tired or what? Yes, the Andes are everywhere and you're doing well to walk without stumbling in this altitude. But you look a bit pale and I shall not inhale your breath, bad vapors coming from your mouth polluting the air and my humour. Don't get sick on me, don't. If you die, I'll kill you. You people eaters can't handle our mountains veiled in clouds, the snow mountains which appear on no maps, are you mal del altura? Here we are, where history moves into geology, knowing that the capitalisation of land is part of the pre-history of capital. Dear old Karl, always good for a quote. Why don't you tell me your name? At least your first name. For I could never endure to be called by any other name than my own, although there are many names for différance and aporia. I'm handsome, don't you think? Do you? Do you have sisters? Where do you come from? Where are your parents? Are you married? Do you have children? How many? Sons or daughters? Do I really speak, speak with authenticity, originality even. Can my deepest self be detected behind all that, what difference does it make who is speaking? Who of you will smell the space between us, who of you will measure the crossroads, who of you will lift this heavy coat from my shoulders, from me, the necessarily lost object? I'm not used to sit around for such a long time. For us, members of the ethnocultural reality, all distances are long anyway. Yes, for the poor todos los caminos estan largos. Está bueno, está bueno, compadre, vivo estoy, me the resident alien, me the native informant.
Yo digo: pobre es igualito a borracho, ante de la autoridad. Para quién será borracho? Borracho de champán, de wiski, francés, alemán, yanki, de pisco venenoso ... Probably we are here admidst an epistemological and moral debacle, speculations of constructions and errors, suffering in translation, adrift on a sea of mistaken intententions, walking on this unmotivated soil. Exploitation, appropiation, contamination, assumptions and presuppositions. Us locked up together, you trembling as if with the ague in your hegemonic pretensions. Why don't you tell me your name, your christian name at least, or are we here just sharpening awareness of "difference"? Aqui estamos, here we are, you and me. You and me, combing the fringes of our situated knowledges. You must have once been something different from what you are now. Something has no doubt happened to you that can be given a voice. Who struck you such a blow? A trauma perhaps has imbalanced

you? Speak up, you will feel so much better, trust me. You and me. You and me. We–me. We–me–me–me–me. How does it feel to be part of a cross-cultural intersubjectivity? Maybe we could go to Spain? Aaah, eviva España! Or shall we head to China, I don't like los Chinos, but I still prefer China. I have a cousin who travels there twice a year, she buys bowler hats. We–me. Am I sitting here on a locus of enunciation? Can I finally be localised? Will they call my name? To tell you the truth, it feels small here. And I'm bored to death. My ankles get swollen and really stiff and my ass hurts. What do you think about my country? Do you like it here? Isn't this a very nice view? Can you see the village over there? My fathers family originally comes from this place. When the skies were heavy like the water in the cisterns my mother moved the clouds with her hands. We have everything here, everything. Like the mountain at Potosi, so much silver taken from it, they could have built a bridge from here to Europe with it. Solid silver.

And in return, ah what luxury. Granada, Priego and Jaen with taffeta Toledo with stockings and swords Valencia and Murcia with satin and silk Cordoba with silk and manteaus Seville with stockings
Portugal with fine linen
France with lace points made of silk, gold and silver, serge, beaver hats and lingerie
Flanders with tapestry, lace points and lace
Germany with table linen
Calabria and Puglia with silks
Naples with stockings
Florence with thick fabrics and satins
Tuscany with fine embroidered cloths and textiles of admirable exquisiteness Milan with elegant lace points made of gold and silver, and refined fabrics England with woollen cloths and hats
The East Indies with fine textiles, crystals, tortoiseshell, ivory and gemstones Ceylon with diamonds
Arabia with perfumes
Persia, Turkey and Cairo with carpets
Ternate, Malacca and Goa with spices, musk and civet
China with extraordinary silk garments
Cape Verde and Angola with Negroes

What do you think about the food? You like it? What do you like most? Las papas, el maiz, tan rico es, el ceviche, superrico. Why are you all by yourself, tan solito? Un hombre como usté, con respeto le digo, con todo respeto! Are we together in a geopolitical context stuck in a plurality of interpretations? Do you believe in god do you own land what do you plant there? How brave you are to set one foot in front of the other, I like your skin, I adore it. I really do. I always fell for los

blancos. Let me take a good look at you, what a delight. How big and fresh you are, I knew you were beautiful, I can see what is plain for all to see. Bueno, you like me too or has the Indian to please you yet to be born? I love you, I truly love you, but than, everyone knows about love these days and, ah, quel horreur! they practice it. Quiet creature.
No names in this place. We have the right to know nothing from each other. The right to be ignored and forgotten. The right to die unnkown. The right to devastate the graves of our ancestors. Lucky the guy, who is killed by the mugger before the good Samaritan arrives! Could you please just move a bit quicker, otherwise we will never arrive, never. Or are we moving through a dream? The earth below us vibrating from all the talk among the dead. My dreams are lying, always, I prefer not to close my eyes at all. And you, what about you? Last night I measured your sleep, compadre, your sleep that is too shy for the sorrow you carry around, it reaches only as far as the neck and no further.
I watched you and saw that your eyes then remain uncovered; and you can't fall asleep, the sleep doesn't reach your eyes, you rip it into pieces. Do you expect to sleep? No one will sleep anymore! NO ONE!! You think you are looking but you cannot see what is before you. I watch you from my background; the monster has the right to refuse the withholding of the master's returned gaze. Asi es, a world full of evil eyes. Are we obsessed, are we one single entity, divided into two? Two what? Parts? Who are you, are we almost the same? With you, my friend,
I don't have this kind of border thinking, no, I don't, I would not place myself in heuristic categories, I do have a relevant sensibility, even if you don't tell me your name I would never even think of giving you one, no. There are few of us, very few and our diseases are contagious. You'd like to buy a cap, it's handmade, pure wool, made by my sister, she has five kids and no husband. A jumper? What do you mean, it comes out of a factory, what do you want, we have a lot of mouth to feed here and the others are gone, looking for a future somewhere else, walking your dogs in Ibiza, we are the only ones left. My grandparents couldn't speak, they had no voice, just an ugly language, krda spracha, as you would say over there, but I can, I can tell everyone, what's happening, how they treat us, how they kick us off the pavement, how they treat us, when we wear our ponchos, but now things are going to change, because we can speak up, we have a voice and silence is not killing us anymore, as it did our ancestors. You taught me the language and my profit on this, I know how to curse. Yet, against all straws in the wind, one must talk in the hope that there is no deal done forever. You can listen to me but in exchange I take away your sight. Listen, are you hungry, I could do with a piece of bread myself, why are you not talking to me? I like food, always did. Just don't give me bananas, for seven years I was having to live in the jungle; they send us to secure the border, which fucking border I don't know, down there, nowhere.

We had bananas every day, every day, bananas. There are limits for everything and as it is, if someone threw bananas at me ow, mille grazie, I would go to prison because I would kill him. I will never touch them again, and all those mosquitos, I'm happy to be back here. We are mountain people, we belong here. You look a bit pale and you are sweating. I was sweating like a pig myself. I was no one down there, do you have a wife? I don't have a fixed identity, I'm not a stable entity, but I must know how to dress as the one who is carried, out of respect, this is important to me, you know. The other night I went out dancing. Estaba descalzo y vestido de overol apretado, limpiecito, y una camisa de color rojo geranio. For you, my dear friend I shall wear leather boots, fine leather boots, polished cow leather, certainly no dust on them, everyone has to see that my feet never touched the dirt road and that I am a free man. I will be recognised as somebody. Que será de mi? Shall I go and leave you? Shall I stay? Yes, I'll go. Because if you stumble I may fall down and muddy my shiny boots. Pero hay que caminar firme cuando hay pelea con la carchancha muerte. Maybe I should walk by myself and then I will walk away with no forgiveness in my heart. Remember, you never never never touched me at all. How old are you by the way? An endless question that's what you are and our relationship is hopeless. Did I tell you already that I adore untranslatable Pushkin, he is such an illumination in all this heavy rain. I'm wet, I am, wet down to my bones. The sun is not attending our walk anymore but the crows are following us. This walk is such a insane project. What is it, are we driven by a nostalgia for lost origins? I will never recover from it, never. Do you really think you can have more existence only by living less? Do you love yourself is this self-love suicidal do you want to master the world is this will ultimately self-destructive do you spit out what you desire do you torture yourself, do you? Do you take pleasure in pain, imperial pleasure, do you mourn your losses do you face your fear is your rectum a grave? Is it? Do you think you can cross rivers without getting wet? Do you lose sight of yourself do you want to have sex with me are you obsessed with love do you maintain your appetite for appetite, do you find pleasure in pain do you have a disease are you devoted to the true, the good and the beautiful, is your soul immortal can the power of evil be defeated? Is there a narcisstic pleasure involved carrying me? Are we here in an oedipal exchange and is carrying me a labour of love? Is it a sacrifice? Can you be disciplined? Would you call your lover little wild potato-flower? Would you like to have a feather of gold and a silvery paper to write to your most beloved? Can you feel reality before you see it? Are you living in the darkness, waiting for the axe to fall? Are you an utterly confused and slippery character, more dead than alive? Do you think that when you eat yourself alive you will live forever? Are you a dominant Western, ... wait a minute, I just forgot what I wanted to ask,

... Do you realise how tiring it is to talk to oneself all the time, never getting an answer, a feeble mumble at least, something anything, give me something! I hate you, believe me, I am an oral person, I need the other. My grandmother always told me, Was du nicht im Kopf hast, musst du in den Füßen haben. I tell you this, because I hated it as a kid, no, I am not trying to mock you, I am not. Nunca. You know what, I get used to you. Karajo! Linda se habla, en silencio, con el pensamiento, como el Dios. Igual. Me permite, even if I can't see it, you have such a quiet face, su rostro tranquilo, gracioso, lovely. Una cara de palo. By the way: what is your favourite animal? Puede ser el chanco, compradito? Could it be the pig, my friend? The pig is majestic in its expression. I have been a pig farmer, with farm or barn pigs, you know, pigs enclosed in a farm. I have learned a lot from pigs. The feeling, the joy that it is to eat knowing, the snout, this long, the tongue, the warmth, the smell of the food, fish flour mixed with other little things; the sound, from "deep in the throat" as you say, bold, with a melody that is like silk or like gut, in which fires and roots of the world, of the ass of the earth itself, are revealed, that grunt, my friend. There, in the different grunts of the pig, you can feel, my friend, the hot and the cold water, the mud, the fresh air; in the "stench", and, as you call it, the good old relief of defecation, of the belch and the flatulence. And when the pigs are set free for their bath, my friend? They whip the air with their small tails; their fat bodies don't jump much, but there is no animal, or person, that enjoys as much their body's movements. Ready to die, like no one, no other!* ... sorry, I got carried away, I just love them too much. Too much. Demaciado. Do you people have songs? Do you have the grace to compose yourself? What if you haven't tasted money and blood? Do you think the face itself is a mask? Do you think you can make whatever scares you less threatening by wearing it? The facialisation of the entire body, the landscapification of all milieus, arghhh. They didn't want to see my face. But I'm here. Are you truly terrified of me and therefore pretending not to hear me? Listen, if I would want to scare you I would fire a shot next to your ear! BANG I'm getting so annoyed now that I will introduce you to my friends as my dog. Jump, you dog! Let's see your teeth! Open the mouth! Make him lift up his legs! Make him sing good and loud! Run! Run! Run! Sing! How much, sir? You my dear dog, will be my weapon against the morose and the monological. How'd you like that? Well, can we rest for a while, even if I hate this damn rain. It's raining hammers and nails, the heavens are dumping buckets, it rains pitchfolks, it rains cat and dogs, a pestilence of rain, it rains lizards, snakes and ears. This is real, all too real. My speech was rehearsed for so long, a bread knife, swaggering, full of righteous fury, oh, how do I bear to go on living! Your whorish eyes dragging the ground to appear holy, you, compadre of cruel hands who chooses with fire to conquer your burning. Anyone

*José Maria Arguedas: El Zorro de Arriba y el Zorro de Abajo. Editorial horizonte, 1983

who will see you without the mask will die from laughing. I hate this place, you are ugly, you murdered your own daughter, you probably fuck your own sister, you wanna fuck my sister?, you can suck my cock, hijo de puta, and you stink! Ah, where am I here and who are these people? Do you all stuff your pockets with whatever you can? Gluttons! The devil choke thee with that thou hast eaten! Thou hast given me my bread for today; now as I live, I am ready to rid my stomach, and to cast up all that I have in my body. By the way, I never made any pact, explicit or tacit, with the devil. Where is my bread? What happened to that? Who took it? Who stole it? Was it you? Where is my bread? Whores! Daughters of a whore! Tell me, who took my bread? May whoever ate it be eaten by rabies! What will become of me now, poor forlorn wretch that I am? Why don't I just die and get it over with? And where do we go to? Could you speed up? Just a little, will you, or the sun will burn our foreheads. Is this a utopian and counter-hegemonic walk, us being moved in accordance to a cultural script? How successfull are we with our attempt to confront the ethnocentric and reverse-ethnocentric benevolent double-bind? Please speed up and tell me where we are going. Or maybe it doesn't matter, the Andes are everywhere anyhow. If I would have a horse instead of you brainless chicken I would hold tight to it, trampling, killing and wounding everything and you, you I would brand your left cheek with hot coal and string you up from a tree. So could you just move a bit quicker or this will never become a proper walk. Are you already tired or what.

The Investigator and Her Friendos

During the *Loomshuttles, Warpaths* research the figure of *The Investigator* was created to explore and subvert conceptions of the researcher in the ethnographic and artistic worlds, a role with origins in medieval fantasies of unknown and then recently discovered geographies. In a reversal of roles, made hypervisible by a costume that plays with notions of the alien gaze, the phantasm returned from Europe to South America, in an attempt to rupture the image archives that have, and still define highly asymmetrical, iconographical relationships. In February 2011, a workshop was held by *The Investigator* in La Paz with a group of masked shoe shiners. A song was composed and a performance developed presented at the Museo de Etnografía y Folklore in La Paz. Starting from the museum, the figure then travelled through Bolivia where she was a happy particpant in the Carnival at the mining town of Oruro.

Back in Europe *The investigator* appeared in different places with her newly gained perverse community: the wandering and murmuring K2 mountain, a puppet in her hands and an Indian automat, carried on her back. In the face of *The Investigator*'s silence this appendage whines, screams, nags, complains, insults, theorises and laughs while halluzinating a crossing of the Andes. Its monologue encompasses notions of travel, strange encounters, monsters, the history of the conquered, and the notion of différance. The puppet interrupts the flow with a shortened description of the products imported to the nouveaux riche of Potosí between 1676 and 1736, which show a globalised world of luxury trade. It was a class made grossly wealthy from the city's mountain of silver that flowed to Europe from 1545 onwards and involved the deaths of millions of enforced Indigenous Andean and enslaved African labour in its mines.

A few years later *The Investigator* returned to Latin America, this time to Brazil, where, newly hyper-visible in 'disruptive pattern', to join in dance with 'funk ball' devotees in the *favelas* of Rio de Janeiro.

Full
MOLLENDO
SALIDAS: Navidad, AÑO NUEVO,
Carnaval, Semana Santa y feriados
U.E. LUIS ADOLFO SILES SALINAS
CURSO ESPECIALIZADO
MANEJO Y CONTROL DE
ALMACENES
INVENTARIOS
VENTA
ORION
PLANILLAS
PERFORMANCE
GUERRERA

CEMENTERIO GENERAL
PLACAS CONMEMORATIVAS
Genesis
N°970
N°1274

Appendix

page 34

1 German airship, 1928. 2 Boys of Tayancani, Cuzco, picture postcard. 3 *Qhapac Qolla* dancers signify the rich merchants from the Lake Titicaca region. Photo: Andrea M. Heckman, 2003. 4 Lead by the *Ukukus* Peru's *Q'oyllur Rit'i* or 'Star Snow' festival takes place each May in the Sinakara Valley. Photo: Eric Lafforgue/Constantine James. 5 Workers at Omi Kenshi silk spinning factory go on strike in protest at the company's feudal working conditions. 6 *Schiaparelli Pour le Sport*, hand-woven ski hood, 1930s, worn by Bettina Bergery. Photo © collection BillyBoy*.

page 38

1 Parents and children would sleep naked inside the heavy sleeping coat, the *donja*, as the shared body heat would protect them from dangerously cold winters. This *boro* clothing, roughly translated as "castaway rag", comes in many indigo shades and was worn by peasants, merchants or artisans in Japan from Edo up to early Showa (17th–early 19th century). For peasant families, each garment would last long enough to be passed down through generations. 2 1899, Arizona. During her sentencing after robbing a stagecoach, Pearl Hart declared, "I shall not consent to be tried under a law in which my sex had no voice in making." 3 The human machine. Fritz Kahn (1888–1968). 4 Cowboy in the accessories section at Fortnum & Mason, London, 2016. 5 The *Mama Sinakara* (Virgin of Fatima) is thought to be the awaq *mamancha*, the little weaver mother. Women sit next to her shrine, weaving small doll-sized samples of their handywork to leave as offerings. They say as they weave their hands "learn" from the *mamancha*, and they depart more accomplished in their craft. (Allen, 1985: 74) 6 Indian farmers commit suicide because of debt. The governmental agriculture department offers free modern education to the eligible family members. A committee comprising financial experts and psychiatrists is supposed to interact with farmers and their families to relieve them from such anxiety. 7 *Vicuñas* live near the snowline of the Andes and since 1970 they are on the Endangered Species List as their wild nature made it easiest to obtain the fibre by killing the animals. Their fibre is among the most valuable luxury fibres and each animal only provides about 114 grams of fine fibre, which measures 12 microns in diameter, which is finer than cashmere and around 284 to 340 grams of shorter, less choice fibre. Its colour ranges from red-brown to light tan to yellow-red. The fibre's softness, luster, strength, and warmth without weight result in highly desirable fabrics and has sold at auctions for $400 per kilo. 8 Cut and voided silk velvet coat, Safavid Iran, first half of 17th century. A gift to Queen Christina of Sweden from the Czar of Russia in 1644.

page 137

1 Corita Kent (1918–1986) was an artist, educator, and advocate for social justice. She was teaching in the art department of the Immaculate Heart of Mary College in Los Angeles and worked almost exclusively with silkscreen due to her wish for democratic outreach, urging viewers to consider poverty, racism, and injustice. 2 Haiti one year after the earthquake. "The great question now before our people is how to appropriate all the African labor of the country." *The Macon Telegraph* of Georgia, 1865. 3 The lapis lazuli mines of the northeastern province of Badakhshan are one of the richest assets of the Afghan people and should be a powerful resource for development. Instead they are a major source of conflict and grievance, supply millions of dollars of funding to armed groups, insurgents, and strongmen, and provide a tiny fraction of the benefit they should to the Afghan people. Source: https://www.globalwitness.org/ru/campaigns/conflict-minerals/war-treasury-people-afghanistan-lapis-lazuli-and-battle-mineral-wealth/ 4 Bill and Hillary Clinton have outdone themselves in self-praise for their role in post-earthquake Haiti. It consists of a hand in getting $400 million of global aid to set up an industrial park in an area untouched by the quake and now soley occupied by a Korean textile firm, Sae-A, which contributed financially to the Clinton Foundation but has a record of violent intimidation of workers in its Guatemala factories. In Haiti it has underdelivered on projected jobs and accused of

management bullying and sexual harassment. Image: Larry Downing/ AFP/Getty Images. **5** "Managers measured production values that were formerly unmeasurable and held workers to more difficult standards than any imposed by the industry to date via statistical process control. This permits the continuous monitoring of performance of each operator over time." **6** A demonstrator on Oct. 7, 2011 supporting the unionisation campaign holds a sign that says, "Respect the rights of working people". Credit: Ansel Herz/IPS. **7** "Those who journeyed along the Silk route gained useful information about competitors, as did the 7th c. AD Chinese traveller Husuan-Tsang who noted Persian silks were twice as wide as those of his own country. This mild form of industrial espionage was reinforced by artisans themselves; weavers were analysing competitors' weave structures in order to imitate them long before scholars were doing the same to understand them." **8** Street market in Brazil. **9** "Because I don't believe that Europe can resurrect its own textile industry, since the price of manpower on its territory does not allow it anymore, the only possibility for Europe is to trust countries like ours ... I think Europe needs Morocco, Tunisia and nearby countries. We are slowly becoming the suburbs of Europe." **10** Picture of an 18th-century *obraje* in the Otavalo region, which was one of the most valued and prosperous in what is now Ecuador. This institution rapidly became the core of colonial economy. **11** Strategic colonial classification designates the group of natives that shows itself to be most aggressive to them as intruders with respect to a more docile group, and asserts that they are setting things right again by expelling the so-called intruders. **12** Members of the UNITE (Union of Needletrades, Industrial and Textile Employees) from New York turn out in support of 19 workers fired from Peerless Clothing company in Canada for organising a union to replace a company association called the Fraternity. 2000 workers speaking 35 languages are employed at Peerless, the largest clothing manufacturer in Canada. Foreign-language-speaking women among the sacked assert that they were especially badly treated. **13** Tender Buttons [A Long Dress]. "What is the current that makes machinery, that makes it crackle, what is the current that presents a long line and a necessary waist. What is this current. What is the wind, what is it. Where is the serene length, it is there and a dark place is not a dark place, only a white and red are black, only a yellow and green are blue, a pink is scarlet, a bow is every color. A line distinguishes it. A line just distinguishes it." *Gertrude Stein, 1874–1946*

page 139

Liz Conor

Banks, Joseph. 1896. Journal of the Right Hon. Sir Joseph Banks. Edited by Joseph D. Hooker. London: Macmillan. Breton, Lieutenant R. N. [1834] 1970. Excursions in New South Wales, Western Australia, & Van Diemen's Land, During the Years 1830, 1831, 1832 & 1833. London: Richard Bentley. Burroughs, E.R. 1912. Tarzan of the Apes. First serialised in The All-Story. Comaroff, Jean. 1996. 'The Empire's Old Clothes: Fashioning the Colonial Subject.' In Cross-Cultural Consumption: Global Markets Local Realities, edited by David Howes, 19–38. London: Routledge. Cook, James. 1955. The Voyage of the Endeavour 1768–1771. Edited by J.C. Beaglehole. Cambridge: Cambridge University Press. Cunningham, Peter. 1827. Two Years in New South Wales: A Series of Letters, comprising, Sketches of the Actual State of Society in that Colony ... Vol. 2. London: Henry Colburn. Frazer, J.G. 1890. The Golden Bough: A Study in Magic and Religion. London: Macmillan. Gregory, Edmund. 1896. Narrative of James Murrells' seventeen years' exile among the wild blacks of North Queensland, and his life and shipwreck and terrible adventures among savage tribes; their manners, customs, languages, and superstitions; also Murrells' rescue and return to civilisation. Brisbane: Edmund Gregory. Hobsbawm, Eric, and George Rudé. 1968. Captain Swing: A Social History of the Great English Agricultural Uprising of 1830. Toronto: Norton. Hunt, Lynn. 1993. The Invention of Pornography: Obscenity and the Origins of Modernity, 1500–1800. New York: Zone. Jones, Dorothy. 2001. 'Defining Self and Others through Textile and Text.' Women's Writing 8 (3): 375–390. Johns, Reynell Eveleigh. 'Concerning Religion.' R.E. Johns Papers, SLVPAC-10005304. State Library of Victoria. Konishi, Shino. 2009. 'François Peron and the Tasmanians: An Unrequited Romance.' In Inside Story. http://inside.org.au/an-unrequited-romance/. Maynard, Margaret. 1994. Fashioned from Penury: Dress as Cultural Practice in Colonial Australia. Melbourne: Cambridge University Press. McCombie, Thomas. 1840. Latest Information With Regard to Australia Felix. Melbourne: Arden and Strode. Mudie, Robert. 1829. The Picture of Australia: Exhibiting New Holland, Van Diemen's Land, and all the Ross, Robert. 2008. Clothing: A Global History. Cambridge: Polity. Settlements, From the First at Sydney to the Last at the Swan River. London: Whittaker, Treacher. Weeks, Jeffrey. 1981. Sex, Politics and Society: The Regulation of Sexuality since 1800. London: Longman. Wollstonecraft, Mary. [1792] 1982. Vindication of the Rights of Woman. London: Penguin.

page 147

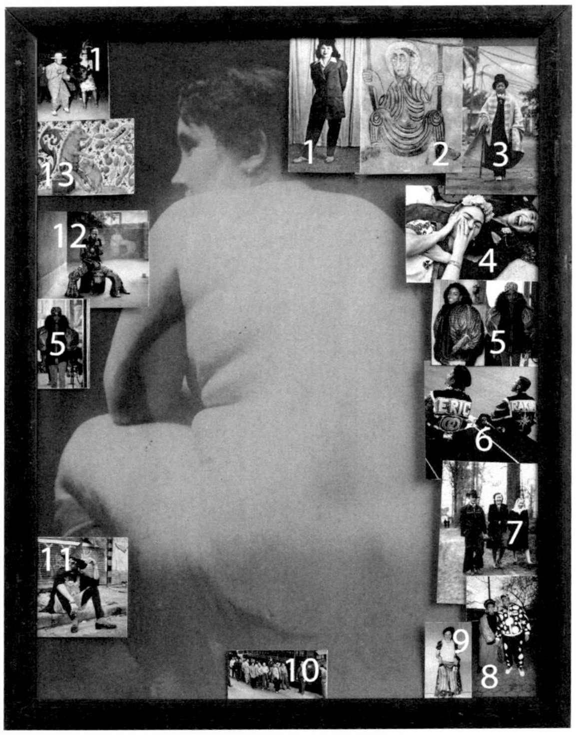

1 "Hobble Skirts Hide Razors / Zoot Suiters Run for Cover but Their 'Cholitas' Carry On" (*The Washington Daily News*, June 1943); "Zoot War Called 'Near Anarchy' / Armed Police Patrol City In Effort to Stem Fighting / 'Black Widow' Girls Beat, Slash Woman; Soldiers Civilians Enter Private Homes" (*The Washington Post*, June 1943). **2** An early Middle Ages fresco (around 800) showing the escape of archbishop Prokulus over the city wall of Verona. **3** Women *Sapeurs [Sapeuses]* from the Democratic Republic of the Congo are making a statement by using styles from the former colonial masters and making them into their own. photo: Junior D. Kannah. **4** Frida Kahlo and Chavela Vargas in 1937. **5** Is it possible to bootleg a bootleg? Dapper Dan, who described his re-conceptualisation of brand symbols as an Africanisation of high fashion, made a design with a Louis Vuitton fabric for Olympic runner Diane Dixon in the 1980s. Dixon posted an image of herself in her jacket with the 2018 Gucci Cruise Collection next to it, writing: "'Bish' stole my look! Give credit to @dapperdanharlem He did it FIRST in 1989!" **6** Eric B. & Rakim's 1988s album *Follow the Leader* (cover). **7** Stilyagi, Russia, 1950s. Men were wearing zoot suits or fitted pants and shirts, flashy ties and shoes with thick soles that were originally worn by Russian factory workers. Women wore American inspired dresses, pant suits and high hairstyles. **8** KRS-One in Dapper Dan of Harlem with his wife, Ms Melodie, in 1989, in Marcus Garvey Park, in Harlem. Photo: Ernie Paniccioli. **9** Estelle Zemon shows the vest and pant-apron used to conceal bottles of alcohol to deceive border guards during the US alcohol prohibition on March 18, 1931. **10** Zoot suiters lined up outside Los Angeles jail en route to court after a feud with sailors. Tacitus gives account of the Roman courtier Petronius c. 27–66 CE) in his *Annals* (XVI.18): He spent his days in sleep, his nights in attending to his official duties or in amusement ... (with) his life of vicious indulgence, he became one of the chosen circle of Nero's intimates, and was looked upon as an absolute authority on questions of taste in connection with the science of luxurious living. **11** Fashion Rebels'. Young Entrepreneurs in Pretoria, South Africa. **12** "Desert Super Power", 26, Hellbanger from Botswana. **13** Spinning sow.

page 163

1 Fool's World Map, 1590, unknown maker, based on Ortelius's third 'Typus Orbis Terrarum'. **2** Edgar Degas's 1873 painting of his uncle's cotton brokerage in New Orleans in the post-Civil War boom. It was his first sale to a museum and changed him from struggling to comfortably off artist. The brokerage on the other hand went bankrupt a few years later, sunk by the opening of the city's Cotton Exchange. **3** This 1885 photograph shows a German in an unnamed colony. © Bildarchiv Preußischer Kulturbesitz. **4** During a victory speech in Havana after the 1959 revolution a dove landed on Fidel Castro's shoulder and two others hovered around the stage. Santeria followers believed that he was blessed by their gods. Between the 16th and the 19th centuries over onemillion Africans were brought to Cuba as slaves. Torn from their homeland, they held on to their belief system despite many attempts by the Spanish colonial lords to repress it and from this the name of their belief system became known as Santeria. **5** "From the fortress (Sacsahuaman above Cuzco) one can see many houses. There are houses where the tributes the vassals bring in are stored ... and there is a house in which are kept more than one hundred thousand dried birds for from their feathers articles of clothing are made." **6** Sicuri dancer playing the pan flute in the Peruvian highlands. **7** The swan dress, designed by Marjan Pejoski, resembles a white swan and was worn by the Icelandic artist Björk at the 73rd Academy Awards on 25 March 2001. During the ceremony Björk mimicked laying an egg on the red carpet. The dress was widely criticised seen as outrageous and outlandish, an outfit that "became the year's fashion faux pas". Jay Carr of the *Boston Globe* wrote, "Bjork's wraparound swan frock ... made her look like a refugee from the more dog-eared precincts of provincial ballet". In response to the hype, Björk said "It's just a dress". **8** Vegetable lamb of tartar, a legendary plant growing sheep as fruit, acted as a medieval explanation for the existence of cotton. Actually a real plant, the fern *Cibotium barometz*. A zoophyte. **9** Weaving students of Anni Albers on backstrap looms, Summer Art Institute 1945, Black Mountain College. The art of pre-industrial tribal cultures – then known as 'primitive' – was held in high esteem by the German artist group Der Blaue Reiter, and by the Die Brücke. After World War I, industrialism was viewed with ambivalence, even abhorrence, and the handcrafted products of supposedly pre-lapsarian, pre-rational societies became models for the ideal integration of art and life, spirituality and daily use. **10** A worker at the Klein Karoo Feathers Factory in South Africa dries coloured ostrich feathers.

page 192

Anja Büchele / Matthew Hyland

[translators' notes] der Stoff. After considering the alternatives we decided that *Stoff* MUST be rendered as 'stuff'. Not just for metrical/stylistic reasons but because it's the only word that literally means textile material AND carries all the broader connotations as they run through the poem. Although the colloquial usage of 'stuff' (an otherwise unspecified substance or pile of things) has become the most common over recent decades, the word originally refers to textiles and *woven* textiles in particular (related to the French *estoffe*, which likewise goes back at least to the 14th century), and this connotation hasn't disappeared altogether. The way the word gradually came to be used more broadly also suits the expansion from literal to figurative reference in the poem: by the time (16th century) of Francis Bacon's *New Atlantis* it could be broadened from woven (i.e. *worked-on*) textiles to other materials transformed by the work of hand/eye/mind, though with the emphasis still on textile production:
We have also diverse Mechanicall Arts, which you have not; And Stuffes made by them; As Papers, Linnen, Silks, Tissues; dainty Works of Feathers of wonderfull Lustre; excellent Dies, and many others. 'Stuff' is also necessary because without it the the *Räume/Träume* section of the poem would lose the play on Shakespeare's *such stuff as dreams are made on* (and its derivations, e.g. in John Huston's *Maltese Falcon*, though not Hammett's, in the Johannes Mario Simmel novel *Der Stoff, aus dem die Träume sind*, and in general cliche/journalese – 'the stuff of dreams' etc). If this were just a clever trick (and if the line *Das ist nicht übersetzbar* that follows were just irony) it might not matter so much, but this sequence addresses between the literal and tangible that runs throughout: *Der Stoff, aus dem die Träume sind*, or *such stuff as dreams are made on*, is the *translatable* phrase for the *non-translatable*, socially woven matter of life. Un/endlich, die Wolle/das Wollen, Räume/Träume. No need to rewrite whole passages drastically just to avoid quoting German words within the translation, especially when the passages in question are all about the problem/s of translating. In this case, anyway, it wouldn't work to choose arbitrarily one of at least four adjectives and adverbs to stand for the ambivalent *endlich* in its first appearance, and then to argue about whether 'finally' and 'finite' are 'similar' (let alone the adj./adv. ambivalence, which takes *mehrere Bedeutungen* to another level). Therefore in all these three sections we've quoted the German words where necessary, but only where the poem is self-referentially discussing their multiple meanings and problems of translatability. (In each of these cases, the poet is already making it easier by mentioning the difficulty, especially in the wry comment to the effect that 'rooms' and 'dreams' don't match quite as neatly as *Räume/Träume*, but don't sound all that far apart either, at least in the context: *es klingt ja ähnlich.*) It's important to remember that the translation is not pretending NOT to be a translation. What matters is that any non-English words be understandable in the context for a monoglot anglophone reader, that nothing said in the original be lost, and that the rhythm/style not be ruined. [One related detail: we translated *mehrere Bedeutungen* and *mehrere Wörter* as 'more' meanings/words in full awareness that mehrere and mehr are not identical. The reason is that the indeterminate 'more' includes any limited but undecided number implied by *mehrere*. Whereas something like 'several' would be inadequate because it implies a small range of more-or-less equivalent alternatives: in the case of *endlich* ignoring the qualitative dimension of the adj./adv. ambivalence for a start, then also flattening all the other gradations of meaning within 'final', 'finally', 'finite' & 'finitely'. Likewise with *unendlich*: the string of potential synonyms (in German or in English) is itself almost unendlich, and as the string continues it starts to fray: not all synonyms of 'unendlich' match each other, not all synonyms of each match 'unendlich', and so on with the particular synonym-strings of each. ('Multiple' might almost have done in this second case – if it didn't sound like ugly academic pedantry – but the two sequences do need to match as closely as possible, and 'multiple' wouldn't work at all with the *Bedeutungen*

attached to *endlich*, because there the difference is not just quantitative (one, several, many meanings of the same grammatical sort) but qualitative: different *kinds* of meaning: adjective and adverb.)] die Bande (plural)/die Bande (singular). The problem here isn't really the homonymous singular and plural, but the need to maintain the connection between the various *band-bind-bound-bond* forms (also *ribbon/band*) when the English sense of 'band' that would once have corresponded more or less to *die Bande* (s.) has almost passed out of memory, to the extent that it might be recognised in connection with, say, the 'merry band' of Robin Hood, but otherwise it would look like a reference either to a binding/encircling object (rubber band, wedding band/ring) or a musical group. 'Gang' seems closer semantically to *die Bande* (s.), but by itself it would break the connection with bind/bond/ribbon etc, and it isn't an exact semantic fit either inasmuch is it can also suggest a big organisation like the Crips, Hell's Angels or whoever: the kind of structure that might be referred to in German with the English word 'gang'. Hence the compromise whereby 'band' is used but qualified parenthetically by 'gang', keeping the resemblance to *Verbindung* and so on without reducing the 'band'/'group' to a bunch of hapless guitar players, and at the same time attaching 'gang' to its still valid small-scale sense. Erkennen ist tun. 'Acknowledge' may not be the word most obviously corresponding to 'erkennen', but this context calls for it. Even apart from any possible confusion with the sense closer to *wissen*, rendering *erkennen* as 'know' might suggest established knowledge/familiarity already possessed by the knowing/acquainted subject, rather than the complex act (*tun* here, but also a process described throughout the poem) of encountering something with eyes/hand/language/mind and coming to 'know' (or acknowledge) it not by adding it unchanged to a stock of privately owned 'facts', but by understanding it through its interweaving with what's already subjectively and socially known, so that both the object and the subject are remade: the knowledge arrived at this way can't be mistaken for possession/mastery, any more than the process of learning from the object is a matter of simple imitation or submission to its authority. Learning/knowing/doing converge in the act of *acknowledging* the work & ability of the weavers: the wish to be *auch so geschickt* is expressed not in a bad copy of the woven object, but in the binding of the words. (The other possibility, 'recognise', was rejected because it tends to sound too much like an automatic reflex, rather than a process of work that binds and changes subject and object.)

page 242

1 Geometric designs on canvas, Asurini do Xingu tribe, Brazil. Asurini means "red people" and Xingu is the river they live alongside. They inhabit the Koatinemo Indigenous reserve and have an approximate population of 160 people. 2 Men on their way to the market. 3 A Woman puts flowers on the grave of Berta Cáceres. © Orlando Sierra/AFP/Getty Images. 4 Berta Cáceres Flores, Lenca leader who fought for the preservation of her peoples' natural and ancestral resources, was murdered by at least two individuals who broke down the door of the house where Berta was staying in the Residencial La Líbano in La Esperanza, Intibuca. Since 2006, Berta and COPINH have been entrenched in a struggle with DESA, a private Honduran company, building the Agua Zarca dam in Rio Blanco, Honduras. The project has been plagued by human rights abuses from its inception, when it bypassed a consultative process with the affected communities. https://actionnetwork.org/letters/tell-the-state-department-and-usaid-justice-for-berta-and-policy-change. 5 There is nothing new about the patenting of black hues. Bayer's early-20th-century advertisement is for one such. Nor is it a surprise that they came from German industry, which dominated the production of dyes. Katigen Black's use of the tiger suggests strength of colour while reproducing the standard racism of the time. 6 *Tierra en armas que se hace mujer /Amazona de la libertad / Quiero formar en tu escuadron / Y al clarin de tu voz atacar ...* Mercedes Sosa sang about Juana Azurduy, who was a Bolivian guerrilla leader fighting for independence from Spanish rule in the early 19th century. 7 By the time Bayer had become part of the notorious IG Farben, proudly hoisting the Nazi flag above its offices, the image was even more explicit in its representation of the 'extra strong', the hunter and its prey, strength and weakness. 8 A portrait of the 18th-century Indigenous rebel Bartolina Sisa made out of local potatos, carrots, corn and other vegetables on display at the Tiwanaku inauguration of Evo Morales. Photo: Benjamin Dangl. 9 The women of the French Revolution, the sans-culottes, were the poor of Paris empowered as the sovereign people. They did knit, as in the post-revolution portrayal of them as hags enjoying executions during the period of the Terror, but their knitting took place most often at meetings and political discussions with neighbours, and its purpose was to make clothes for the soldiers of the Republic who were defending it against invasion. In 1793, to avoid their political demands, the Jacobins insisted that a woman's place was in the home. 10 A *challa* is an Andean ritual of reciprocity. Offerings are prepared to feed the Pachamama which contain aguayo, fruits, candies, spices, grains, sweets, nuts, alcohol, flower petals, streamers, llama fetus, flower petals, cigarettes, and coca leaves. While burned and smoked with aromatic Koa and palo santo wood, people drink and offer songs and dances. It is common to set off firecrackers during the ceremony because the noise will chase away bad spirits. 11 Chinese ladies making silk. 12 Lucas Cranach the Elder and Workshop, ca. 1520–25, oil on linnen (detail), Metropolitan Museum of Art. Originally the wing of an altarpiece, this panel represents Maurice, the Roman legion commander martyred for refusing to slaughter Christians.

page 278

1 Petr Štembera, Sleeping on a tree, Prague, 1975. 2 Most associate nylon with stockings, but this 'miracle fibre' has a storied history and a variety of critical applications. Nylon was the first synthetic fibre to become a major commercial hit. Its low cost, versatility, strength and disposability gave it an edge over other fibres such as rayon and led to its widespread use from fashion runways to even the battlefields of WWII. Today nylon is everywhere – from medical devices and cell phones to guitars, carpets, food packaging and car parts. The automobile industry in particular continues to be a driver of the nylon market set to reach $30 billion sales by 2020. 3 Photo: Women corset workers on strike, 1937. From the collection of the International Ladies Garment Workers Union Photographs. 4 New York World's Fair 1939 poster. © Hughes Industries. 5 Nylon stockings were sold to the public for the first time 1939 in Wilmington, Delaware, where the Du Pont company was headquartered. 6 After announcing plans for a US nationwide women's general strike in 2017, the people behind the Women's March have officially set the date for March 8 – which is International Women's Day and was called "A Day Without A Woman". © Getty images. 7 Christian Bendayan. From Pantaleón and the Visiting Girls, 2010. Oil on canvas. 8 On March 8, 1857, garment workers in New York City marched and picketed, demanding improved working conditions, a ten hour day, and equal rights for women. Their ranks were broken up by the police. Fifty-one years later, March 8, 1908, their sisters in the needle trades in New York marched again, honouring

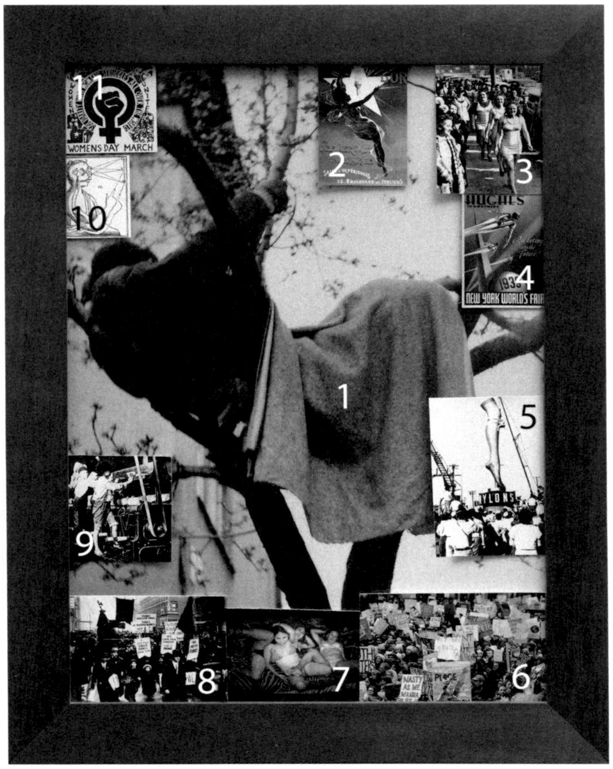

the 1857 march, demanding the vote, and an end to sweatshops and child labour. **9** child labour. **10** Diagram illustrating Cartesian Principles, between 1596 and 1650. According to Descartes, the pineal gland (shown here behind the eyes) transmitted messages from the eyes to the muscles mechanically, but also linked humans to the one non-material part of the universe, the mind. Photo Credit: The Warder Collection, NY. **11** Red Women's Workshop, Women's Day March poster, 1975.

References

Important readings, among others, have been

Phipps, Elena, Johanna Hecht, and Cristina Esteras Martín (eds.). *The Colonial Andes, Tapestries and Silverwork, 1530–1830.* New Haven: Yale University Press, 2004; Schevill, Margot Blum, Janet Catherine Berlo and Edward B. Dwyer (eds.). *Textile Traditions of Mesoamerica and the Andes: An Anthology.* Austin: University of Texas Press, 1996; Pratt, Mary Louise. *Imperial Eyes: Travel Writing and Transculturation.* London: Routledge, 1992; Montoya, Rosario, Lessie Jo Frazier and Janise Hurtig (eds.). *Gender's Place: Feminist Anthropologies of Latin America.* Basingstoke: Palgrave, 2002; Root, Regina A. (ed.). *The Latin American Fashion Reader*, Oxford: Berg Publishers, 2005; Rishel, Joseph J., Suzanne Stratton-Pruitt. *The Arts in Latin America, 1492–1820.* Published in association with the Philadelphia Museum of Art, Antiguo Colegio de San Ildefonso, Mexico City, and the Los Angeles County Museum of Art, 2006; Heckman, Andrea M. *Woven Stories: Andean Textiles and Rituals.* Albuquerque: University of New Mexico Press, 2003; Katzew, Ilona (ed.). *Contested Visions in the Spanish Colonial World.* Los Angeles County Museum of Art, 2011; Femenías, Blenda. *Gender and the Boundaries of Dress in Contemporary Peru.* Austin: University of Texas Press, 2004; Gisbert, Teresa, Silvia Arze and Martha Cajijas. *Textiles En Los Andes Bolivianos.* La Paz: Agencia Boliviana de Fotos / Asociación Cultural Quipus, 2003; Gisbert, Teresa, Silvia Arze y Martha Cajías. *Arte textil y mundo andino.* La Paz: Plural Editores, 2010; Arnold, Denise Y. *The Metamorphosis of Heads: Textual Struggles, Education, and Land in the Andes.* Pittsburgh: University of Pittsburgh Press, 2006; Meisch, Lynn A. (ed.). *Traditional Textiles of the Andes: Life and Cloth in the Highlands.* Fine Arts Museum of San Francisco, 1997.

Colours and Textiles

Velvet Landini, Roberta Orsi. The Triumph of Velvet. In *Velvet: History, Techniques, Fashions*, Fabrizi de Marinus (ed.). New York: Idea Books, 1994 **Blue Jeans** Paul, Jenny Balfour. *Indigo in the Arab World.* London: Routledge, 1996 **Indigo** Roberts, James. Narration of James Roberts, A Soldier Under George Washington, 1856. In *Fathering the Nation: American Genealogies of Slavery and Freedom*, Russ Castronovo. Berkeley, CA: University of California Press, 1996; Voltaire. *Essays on Morals and Customs*, 1756 www. megaessays.com/viewpaper/21012.html **Calico** Smith, Woodruff D. *Consumption and the Making of Respectability 1600–1800.* London: Routledge, 2002 **Negro Cloth** Ellison, Ralph. *Invisible Man.* New York: Random House, 1952 **Gold** Bondy, Salazar. *Ballad of Cuzco in Poesia Quechua.* Mexico City: Fondo de Cultura Económica, 1947 **Acryl** Zorn, Elaine. Dressed to Kill. In *Latin American Fashion Reader*, Regina A. Root (ed.). Oxford: Berg, 2005 **Camouflage** Martin, David L. *Curious Visions of Modernity: Enchantment, Magic and the Sacred.* Cambridge Mass: MIT Press, 2011; Cocteau, Jean. In *Cocteau's World: an Anthology of Writings*, Margaret Crosland (ed.). London: Owen, 1972; Yoruba Spell Against the Enemy. In *Poesia Anónima Africana*, Martinez Rogelio Fure (ed.). La Habana: Editorial Arte y Literatura, 1977; Galeano, Eduardo. *Memory of Fire I, Genesis.* New York: Pantheon Books, 1985 **Grey** Vincent van Gogh. Letter to his brother Theo. In *Colour*, David Batchelor. London/ Cambridge, MA: Whitechapel Gallery/ MIT Press, 2008 **Feathers** Waterton, Charles. *Wanderings in South America: The North-West of the United States and the Antilles, in the Years 1812, 1816, 1820 & 1824: With Original Instructions for the Perfect Preservation of Birds, Etc., for Cabinets of Natural History*, Rev. J. G. Wood (ed.). New York: Hippocrene Books, 1983; Wilson, Lee Ann. Nature v. Culture: The Image of the Uncivilized Wild-Man in Textiles from the Department of Cuzco, Peru. In *Textile Traditions of Mesoamerica and the Andes.* Margot Blum Schevill, Edward B. Dwyer and Janet Catherine Berlo (eds.). Austin: University of Texas Press, 1996 **Crinoline** Earnshaw, Pat. *Lace in Fashion.* London: Batsford, 1985; Ross, Robert R. *Global Clothing: A History, or The Imperialist's New Clothes.* Cambridge (UK): Polity Press, 2008 **Berafula Cloth** Krieger, Collen E. Mapping the History of Cotton Textile Production in Pre-Colonial West Africa. *African Economic History* No. 33 (2005) **Lace** Earnshaw, Pat. *Lace in Fashion.* London: Batsford, 1985; de Ulloa, Juan, Jorge and Antonio. *Noticias Secretas de America (Siglo XVIII).* Madrid: Editoria América, 1918; Phipps, Elena. *Cumbi to Tapestry in The Colonial Andes: Tapestries and Silverwork 1530–1830.* New York: The Metropolitan Museum of Art, New York, 2004 **Cashmere** Rizvi, Janet and Ahmed, Monisha. *The Kashmir Shawl and Beyond.* Mumbai: MARG Publications, 2009 **Turkey Red** Lowengard, Sarah. *The Creation of Colour in 18th Century Europe.* Project Gutenberg: http:// www. gutenberg-e.org/ lowengard/; Bancroft, Edward. *Experimental Researches Concerning the Philosophy of Permanent Colours: Volume II.* Philadelphia: Thomas Dobson, 1794, updated 1813; Mazéas, Guillaume. *Recherches sur la Cause Physique de l'Adhérence de la Couleur Rouge aux Toiles Peintes: qui Nous Viennent des Côtes de Malabar et de Coromandel.* Paris: Imprimerie Royale, 1793; Irwin. J. and P.R. Schwartz *Studies in Indo-European Textile History.* Ahmedabad: Calico Museum of Textiles of Ahmedabad; Vuaya Ramaswamy. Coromandel Textiles. In *Global Textile Encounters*, Marie-Louise Nosch, Zhao Feng and Lotika Varadajaran (eds.). Oxford and Philadelphia: Oxbow, 2014; Robert Chenciner. *Madder Red: A History of Luxury and Trade.* London: Taylor and Francis, 2004 **Remix** Eicher, Joanne B. From India to Africa: Indian Madras and Kalabari Creativity. In *Global Textile Encounters*, Marie-Louise Nosch, Zhao Feng and Lotika Varadajaran (eds.). Oxford; Krieger, Colleen E. Guinea Cloth: Production and Consumption of Cotton Textiles in West Africa before and during the Atlantic Slave Trade. In *The Spinning World*, Giorgio Riello and Parsannan Parthasarathi (eds.). Oxford: The Pasold Research Fund/OUP, 2009; Landini, Roberta Orsi. The Triumph of Velvet. In *Velvet: History, Techniques, Fashions*, Fabrizi de Marinus (ed.). New York: Idea Books, 1994; Berlo, Janet Catherine. Beyond Bricolage. In *Textile Traditions of Mesoamerica and the Andes*, Margot Blum Schevill, Janet Catherine Berlo, Edward B. Dwyer (eds.). Austin: University of Texas Press, 1996; Escobar, Ticio. Issues in Popular Art. In *Beyond* *the Fantastic*, Gerardo Mosquera (ed.). London: Iniva, 1995; Bouttiaux, Anne-Marie. The Porosity of Objects. In *Fetish Modernity*. Royal Museum for Central Africa, Teruven (Belgium), 2013; Saenz, Jaime. *Felipe Delgado*. La Paz: Plural Editores, 1979 **Linen** Schneider, Jane. Rumpelstiltskin's Bargain: Folklore and the Merchant Capitalist Intensification of Linen Manufacture in Early Modern Europe. In Cloth and Human Experience, Annette B. Weiner and Jane Schneider (eds.). Washington DC: Smithsonian Institution Scholarly Press, 1989 **Wool** More, Sir Thomas. *Utopia*. Project Gutenberg: http://www.gutenberg.org/ ebooks/2130; Prebble, John. *The Highland Clearances*. Harmondsworth: Penguin, 1961; Melville, Elinor G. K. *A Plague of Sheep: Environmental Consequences of the Conquest of Mexico*. New York and Cambridge: Cambridge University Press, 1994 **Alpaca** Mallon, Florencia E. *The Defense of Community in Peru's Central Highlands, Peasant Struggle and Capitalist Transition*. Princeton, NJ: Princeton University Press, 1983 **Black** Pastoureau, Michel. *Black: The History of a Colour*. New Jersey: Princeton University Press, 2008; Heaton, Herbert. A Merchant Adventurer Abroad. *The Journal of Economic History* 6, 1 (1946) **Scarlet** Hawthorne, Nathaniel. *The Scarlet Letter*. Boston: Ticknor, Reed, and Fields, 1850; Chenciner, Robert. *Madder Red: A History of Luxury and Trade*. London, Taylor and Francis, 2004 **King Cotton** Northup, Solomon. *Twelve Years a Slave*. New York: Derby and Miller, 1853. Reprinted. Baton Rouge, LA: LSU Press, 1968; Yafa, Stephen H. *Big Cotton: How A Humble Fiber Created Fortunes, Wrecked Civilizations, and Put America on the Map*. New York: Viking, 2004; Beckert, Sven. *Empire of Cotton: A Global History*. New York: Alfred A. Knopf, 2014 **Bogolanfini Cloth** Thompson, Robert Farris. *Flash of the Spirit*. New York: Vintage Books, 1984 **Indian Yellow** Frietag, Sandria. Sacred Symbols as Mobilizing Ideology: The North Indian Search for a 'Hindu' Community. *Comparative Studies in Society and History* 22, 4 (Oct 1980), 597–625 **Pistachio** Nagasaki, Seiki. *Nihon no dentoshoku: sono shikimei to shikicho, Seigensha*, 2001. http://kidorakujapan.com/know/others_color.html; *The Book of The Thousand Nights and One Night, Volume 3*. J.C. Mardrus and E.P. Mathers (trans). London: Routledge Keegan Paul, 1964; Abu'l-Fazl ibn Mubarak. *Ain-i-Akbari*. Henry Blochmann (trans). Kolkata: Asiatic Society of Bengal, 1873 **Silver** Galeano, Eduardo. *Memory of Fire, Volume 1, Genesis*. New York: Pantheon Books, 1985; Chaudhury, Sushil. European Trade, Influx of Silver and Prices in Bengal (1650–1757). In *Global Connections and Monetary History*, Flynn et al (eds.). Aldershot: Ashgate, 2003 **Devil's Food** McKinley, Catherine E. *Indigo, In Search of the Colour that Seduced the World*. London: Bloomsbury, 2011; Janet Hoskins. Why Do Ladies Sing the Blues. In *Cloth and the Human Experience*, Annette B. Weiner and Jane Schneider (eds.). Washington, DC: Smithsonian Institution Scholarly Press, 1989 **Muslin** Austen, Jane. *Northanger Abbey*. London: John Murray, 1815; Vicente, Marta V. *Clothing the Spanish Empire*. Basingstoke: Palgrave MacMillan, 2006; Riello, Giorgio. *Cotton*. Cambridge UK: Cambridge University Press, 2013; Perkins, E. E. *Treatise on Haberdashery*. London: Thomas Hurst, 1832 and 1839; Irwin. J., Schwartz, P.R. *Studies in Indo-European Textile History*. Ahmedabad: Calico Museum of Textiles of Ahmedabad; Chaudhury, Sushil. European Trade, Influx of Silver and Prices inBengal (1650–1757). In *Global Connections and Monetary History*, Flynn et al (eds.). Aldershot: Ashgate, 2003 **Wood Dyes** Armstrong, Wayne P. Logwood and Brazilwood: Trees that Spawned Two Nations. *Pacific Horticulture* 53 (1992), 38–43; Camille, Michael A. *Historical Geography of the Belizean Logwood Trade*. Monroe, LA: Department of Geoscience, Northeast Louisiana University, 1996 **Blue** Leslie, Esther. *Synthetic Worlds: Nature, Art and the Chemical Industry*. London: Reaktion, 2005; Robinson, Jane. *Bluestockings, The Remarkable Story of the First Women to Fight for an Education*. New York: Viking, 2009; Gage, John. *Color and Meaning*. Berkeley CA: University of California Press, 2000 **Ultramarine** Browning, Robert. *The Bishop Orders His Tomb at St Praxed's Church*, Project Gutenberg: http://www.gutenberg.org/files/16376/16376- h/16376-h. htm#page107; Ball, Philip. *Bright Earth: Art and the Invention of Colour*. Harmondsworth: Penguin, 2001; Maerz, A. and Paul, M. A. *A Dictionary of Colour*. New York: McGraw Hill, 1930; Taussig, Michael. *What Color is the Sacred?* Chicago: University of Chicago Press, 2009; Ball, Philip. *Bright Earth: Art and the Invention of Colour*. Chicago: University of Chicago Press, 2004 **Hats** Allman, Jean. *Fashioning Africa: Power and the Politics of Dress*. Bloomington: Indiana University Press, 2004; Faría, Haroldo and Flavia Castro. Los Mil y un Sombreros de la Cultura Boliviana. In *Geomundo* 8, 6, Santiago de Chile, 1984; Earnshaw, Pat. *Lace in Fashion*. London: Batsford, 1985 **Green** Bartholomeus Anglicus: De Proprietatibus Retrum, cited in John Gage, *Color and Meaning*. Berkeley, CA: University of California Press, 2000; Kandinsky, Wassily. *Concerning the Spiritual in Art*, 1913. Project Gutenberg: http://www.gutenberg.org/ ebooks/5321; Finlay, Victoria. *Colour*. London: Sceptre Books, 2002 **Silk** Needham, Joseph. *Science in Traditional China*. Cambridge, MA: Harvard University Press, 1981; Tristan, Flora. London Journal. Jean Hawkes (trans.). London: Virago Press, 1982 **Denim Triumphant** Downey, Lynn. *Levi Strauss and Co.* Mount Pleasant, SC: Arcadia Publishing, 2007; Comstock, Sandra Curtis. *The Place of Blue Jeans in the Consolidation and Transformation of American Power in the 20th Century*. Ithaca, NY: Cornell University Press, 2008 **Human Hair** Hemming, John. *The Conquest of the Incas*. Harmondsworth: Penguin, 1983; Wade, Peter. *Race and Ethnicity in Latin America*. London: Pluto Press, 2010; Malcolm X, Haley, Alex. *The Autobiography of Malcolm X*. New York: Grove Press, 1965; Wait, Rose. Women and Their Hair: Seeking Power through Resistance and Accommodation. *Gender and Society* 15, 5 (2001) **Tartan** Trevor-Roper, Hugh. The Invention of Tradition: The Highland Tradition of Scotland. In *The Invention of Tradition*, Eric Hobsbawm and Terence Ranger (eds.). Cambridge, UK: Cambridge University Press, 1992 **Sky and Water** Cary, Joyce. *The Horse's Mouth*. London: Michael Joseph, 1944 **Colour Control** Kandinsky, Wassily. *On the Spiritual in Art*. Project Gutenberg: http://www.gutenberg.org/ebooks/5321; Nordau, Max. *Degeneration* (Entartung) 1892. https:// archive.org/details/degeneration1895nord; Schauss, Alexander G. Tranquilizing Effect of Color Reduces Aggressive Behaviour and Potential Violence. Presented at 13th *Advanced Seminar on Clinical Ecology*, San Diego, 1979 **Nylon** Proctor, Hannah. Synthetic Dreams: Gender, Modernity and Silk Stockings. www.metamute.org (31/07/2015); Meikle, Jeffrey L. *American Plastic: A Cultural History*. New Brunswick: Rutgers University Press, 1995; Wolfe, Audra J. *Nylon: A Revolution in Textiles*, Chemical Heritage Foundation, 2007 **Twill** Grömer, Karina. Tradition, Continuity, Innovation: The Development of Textile Expertise from the Bronze Age to the Hallstatt Period. In *Textiles from Hallstatt*. Karina Grömer at al. (eds.) *Archaeolingua* 29 **Dye Spy** Leslie, Esther. *Synthetic Worlds: Nature, Art and the Chemical Industry*. London: Reaktion, 2005.

Dates

1377 Moore, R.I. *The Formation of a Persecuting Society: Power and Deviance in Western Europe 950–1250*. Oxford: Basil Blackwell,1986; Cohn Jr, Samuel. *Protest in Medieval Europe*. Manchester: Manchester University Press, 2004 **1378** Cohn Jr., Samuel. *Protest in Medieval Europe*. Manchester: Manchester University Press, 2004, Machiavelli, Niccolò. *Florentine Histories*, Laura F. Banfield and Harvey C. Mansfield (trans.). Princeton: Princeton University Press, 1988; Cohn, Samuel K. *Lust for Liberty*. Cambridge, MA: Harvard University Press, 2006 **1580** Van Nedervween Meerekerk, Elise, et al. Textile Workers Covering the World. In *The Ashgate Companion to the History of Textile Workers, 1650–2000*, Herrma van Voss et al (ed.). Farnham: Ashgate Publishing Company, 2010; Traub, Valerie. *The Renaissance of Lesbianism in Early Modern England*. Cambridge, UK: Cambridge University Press, 2002 **1680** Interview with Harry Burnside, Crownpoint, New Mexico. In *Weaving a World Textiles and the Navajo Way of Seeing*. Albuquerque: Museum of New Mexico Press, 1996 **1738** Pynchon, Thomas. *Mason & Dixon*. London: Cape, 1997 **1780** Galeano, Eduardo. *Faces and Masks: Volume II of Memory of Fire*. New York: Norton, 1998; de Ulloa, Juan, Jorge and Antonio. *Noticias Secretas de America (siglo XVIII)*, 2 Volumes. Madrid: Editoria América, 1918; Salvucci, Richard J. *Textiles and Capitalism in Mexico: An Economic History of the Obrajes 1539–1840*. New Jersey: Princeton University Press, 1987 **1794** Beckert, Sven. *Empire of Cotton: A Global History* New York: Alfred A. Knopf, 2014 **1795** Ramaswamy, Vuaya. Coromandel Textiles. In *Global Textile Encounters*. Marie-Louise Nosch, Zhao Feng and Lotika Varadajaran (eds.). Oxford and Philadelphia: Oxbow, 2014;

Beckert, Sven. *Empire of Cotton: A Global History*. New York: Alfred A. Knopf, 2014; Parthavasarathi. Prasannan. *The Transition to a Colonial Economy: Weavers, Merchants and Kings in South India 1720–1800*. Cambridge, UK: Cambridge University Press, 2001 **1796** Larsen, Brooke. *Cochabamba 1550–1900. Colonialism and Agrarian Transformation*. Durham, NC: Duke University Press, 1998; Berg, Maxine. *Markets, Trade and European Manufacture in Early Industrial Europe*. London and New York: Routledge, 1991 **1819** Thompson E.P. *The Making of the English Working Class*. London: Victor Gollancz, 1963 **1859** Mitra Dinabandhu. *Nil Darpan or The Indigo Planting Mirror*, 1859, Michael Madhusudan Dutt (trans.). Sudhi Pradhan and Sailesh Sen Gupta (eds.). Kolkata: Paschimbanga Natya Academy, 1997 **1844** Vatter, Sherry. Journeymen Textile Weavers in Nineteenth Century Damascus: A Collective Biography. In *Struggle and Survival in the Modern Middle East*, Burke and Yaghoubuan (eds.). Berkeley: University of California Press, 2005 **1851** Koester, Joachim. *Of Spirits and Empty Spaces*. Mousse Publishing, 2012 **1859** Leslie, Esther. *Synthetic Worlds: Nature, Art and the Chemical Industry*. London: Reaktion, 2005; Philip Ball. *Bright Earth: Art and the Invention of Colour*. Chicago: University of Chicago Press, 2004 **1862** Featherstone, David. *Solidarity; Hidden Histories and Geographies of Internationalism*. London: Zed Books, 2010; Beckert, Sven. *Empire of Cotton: A Global History*. New York: Alfred A. Knopf, 2014 **1866** Hunefeldt, Christine. *A Short History of Peru*. New York: Facts on File, 2006; Jacobsen, Nils. *Mirages of Transition: The Peruvian Altiplano, 1780–1930*. Oakland, CA: University of California Press, 1993; Taylor, Lewis. Indigenous Peasant Rebellions in Peru during the 1880s. www.cedla.uva. nl/50_publications/pdf/.../pp-183-215-Lewis_Taylor.pdf **1904** Zimmerman, Andrew. *Alabama in Africa, Booker T. Washington, the German Empire and the Globalization of the New South*. Princeton, NJ: Princeton University Press, 2007; Beckert, Sven. *Empire of Cotton: A Global History*. New York: Alfred A. Knopf, 2014 **1907** (England) Bruley, Sue. Gender, Class and Party: the Communist party and the crisis in the cotton industry in England between the two World Wars. *Women's History Review* (1993); Liddington, Jill. *Rebel Girls, Their Fight for the Vote*. London: Virago, 2009; Parker, Rozsika. *The Subversive Stitch: Embroidery and the Making of the Feminine*. London: I.B. Taurus, 1989 **1907** (Mexico) Lear, John. Labor Regime Change in the Mexican Revolution. *Revista de Historia Social y Literatura de América Latina* 7, 2. Raleigh: North Carolina State University (2010). http://dialnet.unirioja.es/servlet/revista?codigo=7318 **1911** Cohn, B.S. *Colonialism and its Forms of Knowledge*. Princeton, NJ: Princeton University Press, 1996; Naughton, Jim. *Conflict and Costume: the Herero Tribe of Namibia*. London: Merrell, 2013 **1913** Smit, Angel, Carles Enrech, Carme Molinero and Fere Ysas. 'Spain'. In *The Ashgate Companion to the History of Textile Workers, 1650–2000*, Lex Herrma van Voss et al (ed.). Farnham: Ashgate Publishing Company, 2010 **1917** Ghandi, Mahatma. The Story of My Experiments With the Truth, Navjivan 1925–29. In *Collected Works*. Publications Division, Ministry of Information and Broadcasting, Govt. of India, 1970; Bayly, C.A. The Origins of Swadeshi. In *The Social Life of Things*, Arjun Appadurai (ed.). Cambridge, UK: Cambridge University Press, 1986; Uzramma. Cotton to Cloth: An Indian Epic. *Textile Society of America Symposium Proceedings* 330 (1996). http://digitalcommons.unl.edu.tasconf; Beckert, Sven. *Empire of Cotton: A Global History*. New York: Alfred A. Knopf, 2014 **1932** Rossman, Jeffrey J. *Worker Resistance Under Stalin: Class and Revolt on the Factory Floor*. Cambridge MA: Harvard University Press, 2005 **1944** Aranda and Escalante, cited in Marisol de la Cadena. *Indigenous Mestizos: the Politics of Race and Culture in Cuzco, Peru 1919–91*. Durham, NC: Duke University Press, 2009 **1954** Kim, Janice C. *To Live to Work: Factory Women in Colonial Korea 1910–45*, Palo Alto, CA: Stanford University Press, 2009 **1967** Arnison, Jim. *The Million Pound Strike*. London: Lawrence and Wishart, 1970 **1978** Kim, Janice C. *To Live to Work: Factory Women in Colonial Korea 1910–45*, Palo Alto, CA: Stanford University Press, 2009; Ogle, George E. *Dissent Within the Economic Miracle*. London: Zed Books, 1990; Chun Soon Ok. *They Are Not Machines: Korean Women Workers and their Fight for Democratic Trade Unionism in the 1970s*. Farnham: Ashgate, 2005 **1981** Rajni, Bakshi. *The Long Haul*. Bombay: BUILD Documentation Centre, 1986; Strikes and Strikebreakers: Bombay Textile Mill Strike 1929. *India Economic and Political Weekly* 17, 14/16 **2005** Bonaicich, Edna and Applebaum, Richard. *Behind the Label: Inequality in the LA Apparel Industry*. Berkeley: University of California Press, 2000 **2005** Galeano, Eduardo. *Days of Love and War*. New Delhi: Aakar Books, 2009 **2006** Maudlin, Barbara. *Folk Art of the Andes* exhibition. Museum of Folk Art Santa Fé, 2012 **2008** Campuzano, Guiseppe. *Museo Travesti del Perú*, 2008; Tristan, Flora. *Peregrinations of a Pariah 1833–4*. London: Virago Travellers, 1986 **2009** Brooks, Andrew. *Clothing Poverty*. London: Zed Books, 2014; Uzramma. Cotton to Cloth: An Indian Epic. In *Textile Society of America, Symposium Proceedings* 330 (1996). http://digitalcommons.unl.edu.tasconf; Beckert, Sven. *Empire of Cotton: A Global History* New York: Alfred A. Knopf, 2014 **2011** Bonfigioli, Chira. Structures of Feeling After Yugoslavia. *IWM Post* Spring/Summer 2017.

Textile Descriptions

Khipu Pérez Bocanegra, Juan, Geronymo de Contreras (eds.). *Ritual formulario; e institución de curas para administrar a los naturales de este reyno, los santos sacramentos del baptismo. Confirmación, eucaristía y viático, penitencia, extremaunción, y matrimonio: con advertencias muy necessarias*. Lima, 1631 (trans. Rosa Nogues) **Glove** Romero, Simón. Sacaca Journal – Ritual Fades Into Blur of Drinking and Fighting. *New York Times*, 2007; Allen, Catherine J. *The Hold Life Has: Coca and Cultural Identity in an Andean Community*. Smithsonian Institution Press, 1988 **Isoshëta / monkey-teeth bracelet** Roe, Peter G. *The Cosmic Zygote. Cosmology in the Amazon Basin*. New Brunswick: Rutgers University Press, 1982 **Eke'ko** *Stand der Verhandlungen mit Bolivien bezüglich der Steinfigur BHM Inv. Pe 145*. Press release published on the website of the Historical Museum of Berne, 2014; Barben, Dölf. Bolivien schickt hohen Politiker nach Bern – um Ekeko zu holen. *Der Bund*, 2014 **Chuku / head shawl, ch'ullu soltero / single man's cap** Ypeij, Annelou, and Zorn, Elaine. Taquile: A Peruvian Tourist Island Struggling for Control. *European Review of Latin American and Caribbean Studies* 82, 2007 **Llama figure** Bolin, Inge. *Rituals of Respect. The Secret of Survival in the High Peruvian Andes*. Austin: University of Texas Press, 1998; Flores Ochoa, Jorge A. The classification and naming of South American camelids. In *Anthropological History of Andean Polities*. Murra, John V. Nathan Wachtel and Jacques Revel (eds.). London-New York: Cambridge University Press, 1986 **Man's shawl** Rösing, Ina. Religion, Ritual und Alltag in den Anden. Die zehn Geschlechter von Amarete, Bolivien. Zweiter Ankari- Zyklus: Kollektivrituale der Kallawaya-Region in den Anden Boliviens. In *KZfSS Kölner Zeitschrift für Soziologie und Sozialpsychologie* (01/2002) **Gauze cloth** Amery, Irene. *The Primary Structure of Fabrics*. London: Thames & Hudson, 1964; Gerschultz, Jessica. The Serpentine Essence of a Chancay Gauze Headdress. Textile Society of America Symposium Proceedings, 2008. http://digitalcommons.unl.edu/tsaconf/94 **Ch'uta, carnival suit, wire mask** McFarren, Peter. *Mascaras de los Andes Bolivianos*. La Paz: Editorial Quipus, 1985 **Women's Shirt** Powless, Ben. Peru. Battle Lines Drawn over the Amazon. https://nacla.org/node/5879; http://rabble.ca/blogs/ bloggers/ben-powless/2009 **Kushma Ashárinka** Veber, Hanne. External Inducement and Non-Westernization. The Uses of the Cushma Asheninka. *Journal of Material Culture* (1996) http://mcu.sagepub.com **Montera Tarabuqueña / felt helmet** Galeano, Eduardo. *Century of the Wind*. London: Minerva 1990. **Wichi wichi / 3 slings** Vasari, Giorgio. *The Lives of the Most* Excellent Painters, Sculptors, and Architects. New York: Modern Library, 2006 **Textile fragment / Nazca** D'Harcourt, Raoul. *Textiles of Ancient Peru and Their Techniques*. Mineola, NY: Dover Publications, 1962; de Lavalle, Jose and J. Garcia with papers by James W. Reid, et al. *The Textile Art of Peru*. Lima: L. L. Editores; Industria Textil Piura S.A., 1991; Rowe, Ann P., John F. O'Neill. *Costumes and Featherworks of the Lords of Chimor*. Washington DC: Georgetown University of Washington Textile Museum, 1984 **Chumpi / 2 belts** http://digicoll.library.wisc.edu/ UWDCNew/view/ uwdc:TIRIS.1998.09.011 **Inkuña / ritual carrying cloth** Silverblatt, Irene. *Moon, Sun, and Witches: Gender Ideologies and Class in Inca and Colonial Peru*. New Haven NJ: Princeton University Press, 1998; Silverblatt, Irene. Andean Women in the Inca Empire. In *Feminist Studies* (1978); Costin, Cathy L. Housewives, Chosen Women, and Skilled Men: Cloth Production and Social Identity in the Late Prehispanic Andes. In *Craft and Social Identity*, C. Costin and R. Wright (eds.). Washington, DC: The American Anthropological Association, 1998 *Band* Davis, Wade. *One River, Explorations and Discoveries in the Amazon Rain Forest.* New York: Simon & Schuster, 1996 **Carnival dress / China Supay** Nash, Nathaniel C. Shining Path Women: So Many and So Ferocious. *New York Times* 1992; McFarren, Peter. *Mascaras de los Andes Bolivianos / Masks of the Bolivian Andes.* La Paz: Editorial Quipus, 1993 **Chitonti** Odland, Claire. Shipibo Textile Practices 1952–2010. *Textile Society of America Symposium Proceedings.* DigitalCommons@University of Nebraska – Lincoln, 2010 **Lliclla / 2 carrying cloths / Qero** Pollard Rowe, Ann, Cohen, John. *Hidden Threads of Peru: Q'ero Textiles.* London: Merrell, in association with The Textile Museum, Washington, DC, 2002; Wilson, Lee Ann. Nature v. Culture: The image of the Uncivilized Wild Man in Textiles from the Department of Cuzco, Peru. In *Textile Traditions of Mesoamerica and the Andes: An Anthology*, Margot Blum Schevill, Janet Catherine Berlo and Edward B. Dwyer (eds.). Austin: University of Texas Press, 1996 **Alacitas / 3 dolls** McFarren, Peter. *Mascaras de los Andes Bolivianos / Masks of the Bolivian Andes.* La Paz: Editorial Quipus, 1993; Catherine J Allen. When Pebbles Move Mountains: Iconicity and Symbolism in Quechua Ritual. In *Creating Context in Andean Cultures*, R. Howard-Malverde (ed.), pp. 73–84. Oxford University Press **Acrylic rope** Center for Traditional Textiles of Cusco. www.textilescusco.org; www.incaglossary.org **Asháninka kithaarentze / tunic and urucum seed face paint** Park, Chris C. *Tropical Rainforests.* London: Routledge, 2003 **Scarf** Inspiration or plagiarism? Mexicans seek reparations for French designer's look-alike blouse. http://www.theguardian.com/global-development-professionals-network/2015/jun/17/mexican-mixe-blouse-isabel-marant **Note head / mummy mask with wig** Finlay, Victoria. *The Brilliant History of Color in Art.* Paul Getty Museum, 2014 **K'eperina / manta / carrier cloth** Denise Arnold. Making Men in Her Own Image: Gender, Text, and Textile in Qaqachak. In *Creating Context Andean Cultures*, Rosaleen Howard-Malverde (ed.). Oxford University Press, 1997 **Costal / large food sack** Charles C. Mann. What Endures From the Ancient Civilizations That Once Ruled the Central Andes? *Smithsonian Journeys Quarterly*, 2015; Cereceda, Verónica. The Semiology of Andean Textiles. The Talegas of Isluga. In *Anthropological History of Andean Polities*, John V. Murra, Nathan Wachtel and Jacques Revel (eds.). London-New York: Cambridge University Press, 1986.

Communications from

Ines Doujak and **John Barker** live in London and Vienna, and work together through a common interest in the political dimension of cultural exchanges. Since 2010 they have collaborated on exhibitions like 2015 *The Beast and the Sovereign*, MACBA, Barcelona; *Ape Culture*, HKW, Berlin; 2014 *Universes in Universe*, Biennial São Paulo; 2013 *Not Dressed for Conquering*, Royal College of Art, London; 2012 *Garden of Learning*, Busan Biennale, Korea. **Barker** is a fiction writer, essayist and performer who, since the 1970s, has been focused on economics, geopolitical dynamics and the exploitation of labour. **Doujak** received two research grants from the Austrian Science Fund, *Loomshuttles / Warpaths* (2010–18) and *Utopian Pulse: Flares in the Darkroom* (with Oliver Ressler 2013–15), which resulted in an exhibition in the Secession, Vienna (2014) and a publication (Pluto Press, London). Exhibitions (selection) 2017 *Masterless Voices*, Bunkier Sztuki Gallery of Contemporary Art, Kraków; *The Conundrum of Imagination*, Leopoldmuseum, Vienna; 2016 *Aqua Viva*, SBC Gallery of Contemporary Art, Montreal; *Transcultural Flux*, Stiftelsen 3, Bergen; 2015 *Follow the Leader*, Johann Jacobs Museum, Zürich; 2010 *The Potosi Principle*, Museo Nacional Centro de Arte Reina Sofía, Madrid; Museo Nacional de Arte La Paz, Bolivia; 2009 *Ladies Almanack**, Tranzit CZ, Prague; 2008 *Peripheral vision and collective body*, MUSEION, Bolzano; 2007 *documenta 12*, Kassel. **Markus Wörgötter** is an artist, photographer and graphic designer. He lives in Vienna. **Cordula Daus** is a cultural scientist and author. She was editor in the team for the Documenta 12 magazines. Since 2009 she has been investigating the relations between places and words, acts of speech and their consequences in the frame of the *Neue Gesellschaft für Angewandte Toponymie.* **David Riff** is an art critic, artist, curator, translator, and member of Chto Delat. He lives in Berlin. **Alice Creischer** studied Philosophy, German literature and Visual Arts in Düsseldorf. Her artistic and theoretical agenda within institutional and economical critique has focused more recently on the early history of capitalism and globalisation. She is co-curator of such exhibitions as *Messe 2ok* (1995), *ExArgentina* (2004) and *The Potosi Principle* (2010). **Andreas Siekmann**'s works have been shown at numerous exhibitions, e.g., at Kunsthaus Bregenz, Bregenz (2013); Museum Abteiberg, Mönchengladbach (2012); Museum Ludwig, Cologne (2012); MACBA, Barcelona (2009), Documenta XI (2002) and XII (2007), Kassel; Skulptur Projekte Münster 07, Muenster (2007); Haus der Kunst, Munich (2005); 50th Venice Biennale, Venice (2003); Portikus, Frankfurt/Main (1999). **Fahim Amir** is a Viennese philosopher with Afghan origins. Recent publications include *Dwellers and Strayers: Multispecies Criminality in Postcolonial Worlds and 1000 Habitats: Warm Wars and Tiny Architects.* **Waldo Jordan** began in the 1970s to rescue the ethno-technologies, meanings and communication elements related to traditional Andean weaving. He is director and founder of the *Museo de Textiles Andinos Bolivianos* in La Paz, Bolivia. **Cristina Bubba Zamora** organised Aymará Indians in the area of Coroma to identify, archive and recover communally owned ceremonial weavings that have been stolen or sold to dealers who illegally traffic in these weavings throughout the world. Trained as a social psychologist, she studied under Cornell University professor of anthropology John Murra, who was one of the first academics to study the cultural importance of Andean textiles. **Irene Silverblatt** teaches Cultural Anthropology at Duke University, USA. She studies relations of culture and power in the Andes and contemporary Europe. She has written *Moon, Sun, and Witches: Gender Ideologies and Class in Inca and Colonial Peru* and *Modern Inquisitions: Peru and the Colonial Origins of the Civilized World.* **Max Jorge Hinderer Cruz** works as an independent editor, researcher and curator. Together with Alice Creischer and Andreas Siekmann he curated the exhibition and publication project *Principio Potosí / The Potosí Principle* (MNCARS Madrid, HKW Berlin and MNA/MUSEF La Paz, 2010–2011). **Simon Sheikh** is a freelance curator and critic. He is a researcher for the ongoing Former West project, initiated by BAK in Utrecht. Sheikh is a Senior Lecturer in Curating at Goldsmiths College, London. **Catherine Lord** is Professor of Studio Art at the University of California. She is an artist, fiction writer and critical essayist. Currently she is working on a text/image project titled *The Effect of Tropical Light on White Men.* **Guiseppe Campuzano** was a Peruvian artist, philosopher and crossdresser and the founder of the *Museo Travesti* in Lima. **Judith Fischer** lives in Vienna as an artist, philosopher and lecturer in the fields of (horror) film, visual art, literature, liminality and theory. Her latest publications include: *Reading the Hidden, Writing the Liminal*, p. 30–43, in Andrei Siclodi (ed.), *Private Investigations – Paths of Critical Knowledge Production in Contemporary Art*, Künstlerhaus Büchsenhausen, 2011 and the artist book *some women houses phantoms*, Schlebrügge Editor, Vienna 2010. **Boris Ondreička** (1969) is an artist, curator and author, former director of tranzit.sk, based in Bratislava, Slovak Republic. He co-curated *Manifesta 8* and *The Event* 2011, and exhibited his works in Venice, Prague, Gyumri Vienna and Torino. **Jens Risch** (1973) born in Rudolstadt/Thüringen; 1993–95 HfG Offenbach am Main; 1995–99 Städel, Staatliche Hochschule für Bildende Künste, Frankfurt am Main with Thomas Bayrle; since 2001 in Berlin. **Thomas Kilpper** was born 1956 in Stuttgart, lives in Berlin, Germany; studied Fine Arts at the Staatliche Kunstakademie in Nuremberg, Düsseldorf and Städelschool, Frankfurt on Main (Professor Georg Herold). Since 2006, together with Franziska Böhmer, he runs the not-for-profit project space *after the butcher.* **Lukas Pusch** lives and works in Vienna and studied painting in Vienna, Moscow and Dresden. Founder of the *White Cube Gallery Novosibirsk*, the first centre of contemporary art in Siberia, and of *SLUM-TV* in Mathare. **Simryn Gill**, born in Singapore, lives and works as an artist in Sydney, Australia and Port Dickson, Malaysia. **Juan Quispe** is a resident of the island of Taquile, Lake Titicaca, Peru. He is a storyteller who works as a farmer and cap-knitter. **Shooshie Sulaiman** was born in 1973 in Malaysia. She received a Bachelor of Fine Art degree from MARA University of Technology. Her art ranges from drawings, collages and architectural installations to performance art. Recent exhibitions include in Art Stage Singapore 2012 (Singapore), 6th Asia Pacific Triennial 2009 (Brisbane, Australia), and Documenta 12, 2007 (Kassel, Germany). She also curates exhibitions and runs 12, an alternative art space in Kuala Lumpur. **Sonia Abian**'s work starts with a visit to archives and research. In whatever medium – video, painting, object, installation – she analyses discourses and historical pictures as vehicles of an ideology. Her special interest is in the power structures demonstrated in these pictures through the legitimisation of specific gender positions and their current relevance. **Luis Jacob** was born in Lima, Peru in 1971, and lives in Toronto, Canada. Working as an artist, curator, and writer. Recent exhibitions of his work include: *A finger in the pie, A foot in the door, A leg in quicksand*, Kunsthalle Lingen (Germany); *Pictures at an Exhibition*, Museum of Contemporary Canadian Art (Toronto). **Ruth Noack** trained as a visual artist and art historian; she has acted as art critic, university lecturer and exhibition-maker since the 1990s. She was Curator of Documenta 12 (Kassel 2007) and Head of Curating Contemporary Art at the Royal College of Art in London. **Edgar Huracán Ramírez**, a former miner, is a member of a collective which has and is making the COMIBOL mining archive in El Alto, the industrial area of La Paz. The project began in 2003 and spread out to other mining towns in Bolivia. **Helga Weber** was the muse and technician of the project, responsible for the archiving and documentation and assisting in the production of the images. **Zdenka Silvia Ballon** is a sociologist who is defending and promoting traditional Indigenous cultures of the Andean region. She is the co-founder and director of the Coca Museum in La Paz. **Anja Büchele** is clear but potentially icy. **Matthew Hyland** loiters in the margin for error. **B. Traven** *An author should have no other biography than his books*. **François Rabelais** was the 16th-century humanist writer of the epic *Gargantua and Pantagruel*, which mixed satire, scholarship and risqué jokes. His spirit was truly carnivalesque. **T.J. Clark** is an English art historian and writer. He taught art history in a number of universities in England and the United States, including Harvard and the University of California, Berkeley. He has been influential in developing the field of art history, examining modern paintings as an articulation of the social and political conditions of modern life. **Ferdinand Schmatz** writes poems, prose, essays and audio drama. He lives in Vienna and teaches at the University of Applied Arts. Awards: 2004 Georg Trakl-Preis. 2006 H.C. Artmann-Preis. 2009 Ernst Jandl-Preis. **Antke Engel** is director of the *Institute for Queer Theory* in Berlin; a site where academic debate meets up with activism and artistic practices (www.queer-institut.de). She has published two monographs and numerous essays, some online available at *e-flux journal*, and co-edited *Hegemony and Heteronormativity* (Ashgate 2011) and *Bossing Images* (NGBK 2012). **Evelyn Steinthaler**, born 1971, is an Austrian journalist, writer and editor. Her work focuses on the Austrian Exile in the United Kingdom and women in the Austrian resistance during the Nazi régime. In 2011 she published a biography of the singer Richard Tauber. **Graham Townsley** is a British anthropologist who lived among the Yaminahua people. He is the first one to make an effort to decode the 'secret language' of the shamans. Townsley calls the Yaminahua way of knowing *unthinkable* within the Western model of cognition. He wrote the text in 1993. **Grant Watson** teaches Curatorial Theory at the Royal College of Art in London and is Roaming Academy core-tutor and curator at the DAI in Arnhem. He was Senior Curator at the Institute of International Visual Arts (Iniva) London (2010–14), Curator at the Museum of Contemporary Art (MuHKA), Antwerp (2006–10), Curator of Visual Arts at Project, Dublin (2001–05). Recent exhibitions include *How We Behave* (Nottingham Contemporary and The Showroom in London), *Social Fabric* (Iniva, Lunds Konsthall and Dr Bhau Daji Lad Museum, Mumbai). **Peter Linebaugh** taught at Rochester, New York University, University of Massachusetts-Boston, Harvard and Tufts before joining The University of Toledo in 1994. Among others he is the author of *The London Hanged* (1991), *The Magna Carta Manifesto: Liberties and Commons for All*, University of California Press: Berkeley, California, 2008, and co-author with Marcus Rediker of *The Many-Headed Hydra: Sailors, Slaves, Commoners and the Hidden History of the Revolutionary Atlantic*, Beacon Press Boston, 2000. He is currently at work on a study of an Irish insurrectionary during 'the great transformation' of the Atlantic revolutions. magnacartamanifesto.blogspot.com **Edgar Endress** studied at ARCOS in Santiago, Chile, graduating with the B.F.A. equivalent. In 2001 he received his MFA from Syracuse University with a concentration in Art Video. **Imogen Stidworthy** is interested in language and the voice, which she works with as physical and spatial material. Her work has been exhibited at venues such as the São Paulo Biennal (2014), Museum Leeuwarden, NL (2014), Bergen Triennale 2013: Monday Begins on Saturday (2013). **Pedro G. Romero** has been an artist since 1985 Starting in the late 1990s he has worked on two different projects: Archivo F.X. and Máquina P.H. Since 2007 he has been working in the national section of the archives of the MACBA and MNCARS; he also directs the project Al-Athar, Arab features in Latin America. **Cornelia Klinger** studied Philosophy, Literature and Art History at the University of Cologne. Since 2003 she has been Visiting Professor of Philosophy at the University of Tübingen. While working in several research areas, she focuses mainly on Political Philosophy, Aesthetics, and Gender Studies. **Anja Kirschner** and **David Panos** are artists living in London. They have collaborated on a number of films and video installations that created speculative histories and spectacular fantasies that interrogated the relation of art to power. Their work has been exhibited widely in the UK and abroad and was recognised with the Jarman Award (2011). Their films are distributed by LUX (UK) and are in the Artists' Moving Image Collection of the British Film Institute. **Beatriz Canedo Patiño** The Bolivian fashion designer was named by the international press as *The Queen of the Alpaca*. Her world-renowned creativity leads her to dress European and Asian Royalty, high political authorities in Bolivia and abroad, business leaders and celebrities. **Elena Izcue** was born in 1889 in Peru and died there in 1970. She played a key role in the dissemination of pre-Colombian artistic culture by means of schoolbooks and through her work in the decorative arts, which included textile and paper printing with wood and linocuts. She spent 12 years in Paris with her sister Victoria working successfully in a variety of graphic media before returning to Peru as the Second World War approached. **Nora Izcue** is a film director and writer born in Peru in 1934. She was a founding member of the Cinéastes de America Latina at a time of massive repression in the region and helped found the Foundation of New Cinema, a prestigious film school in Cuba. Her films include *El Vino del Ayahuasca* and *Elena Izcue: La Arminia Silenciosa*, the subject of the imagined conversation. **Luciano** is a 65-year old resident of La Paz, Bolivia. He is a widower and has three children. He has worked as a shoe-shiner in La Paz for the past 45 years. **Konstantin Goncharov**, 1969–98, lived in St Petersburg. In 1989 he founded the fashion house *Strict Youth* with Timur Novikov. From 1989–90 he worked as a stylist for the rock group Kino. He won the prize *The Best Artist of the Avant-garde* at the fashion competition in Metelitsa Club in Moscow, 1995 for the collection *Passiones Luci*, which was produced in collaboration with Alexei Sokolov, Ekaterina Andreeva and Olga Tobreluts. The pictured costume was made for the priest of Isys. **Hedwig Saxenhuber** is a curator and co-editor of the arts periodical *springerin Hefte für Gegenwartskunst*, Vienna. From 2003–15 she was the founding director (with Christian Kravagna) of Kunstraum Lakeside, Klagenfurt. Her recent projects include *The School of Kyiv*, Kiev Biennal 2015, *Unrest of Form – Imagining the Political Subject* (with Georg Schöllhammer and Stefanie Carp), Vienna Festival, MQ, 2013; *Bertha von Suttner Revisited*, Schloss Harmannsdorf (with Susanne Neuburger), 2009; *A Ladies Almanach*, Tranzit Prag, 2009; *Art + Politics*, MUSA, Vienna, 2008; Gyumri Biennal, Armenia, 2008; VALIE EXPORT, Moscow Biennal, NCCA, 2007; Parallel Histories, ACF, New York, 2006; and *Postorange, Contemporary Art from Ukraine*, Kunsthalle, Vienna 2006. **Hermann Seiwald** aka **Nipples Hasno Gender**, born 1972 in Austria. Working in Vienna as an artist, costume designer and dragqueen performer. **Andreas Riegler** aka **Mara Gheddon**, born 1973 in Germany, since 2009 living and working in Vienna as a performance artist, dragqueen and upcycling designer. **Julia Fuchs** was born in Bregenz, Austria. After studying cultural sciences, theatre and philosophy in Vienna and Berlin she attended the School for Artistic Photography by Friedl Kubelka and the Academy of Fine Arts Vienna in the contextual painting class of Ashley Scheirl. She works as an artist and performance artist in Vienna. **Prabhkar Pachpute** lives and works in Bombay and participated, among others, in the following exhibitions: *no, it wasn't the locust cloud* (Te tolanche dhaga navhate) at National Gallery of Modern Art, Bombay (2016), 14th Istanbul Biennial *Saltwater: A Theory of Thought Forms* (2015), *Black OR White*, Van Abbemuseum, Eindhoven, Netherland (2013). **Liz Conor** in an ARC Future Fellow in History at La Trobe University on the *Graphic Encoun-*

ters: Prints of Indigenous Australians project. She is the author of *Skin Deep: Settler Impressions of Aboriginal Women*, UWAP, 2016 and *The Spectacular Modern Woman: Feminine Visibility in the 1920s*, Indiana UP, 2004. Liz is co-editor of the *Aboriginal History Journal*, a columnist at *New Matilda*, and essays have appeared in *The Age*, *The Conversation*, *The Drum*, and *Arena*. She is also a community campaigner.

Photo Credits

(pages) **6** In Hugo Zumbühl, *Manual for the Construction of a Pedal Loom*, distribution Huancayo: SEPAS, 1981 **30** Peruvian newspaper, 2005 **31** Courtesy Luis Gonzalés, CARETAS. In *The Peru Reader*, Orin Starn, Carlos Iván Degregori, and Robin Kirk (eds), Duke University Press 2005, p. 405 **38** *1* Amuse Museum Boro Exhibition, Tokyo, 2011, collection of Chuzaburo Tanaka; *8* In *5000 years of textiles*, Jennifer Harris (ed.), London: The British Museum Press, 1993 **39** CSIRO Science Image 10736 www.wikimedia.org **42** 18th-century wool-weaving manufactory **43** *Baltasar Jaime Martinez Compañón: Trujillo del Perú, 1782–86*, Real Biblioteca del Palacio Real de Madrid **50** Republicana Boliviana. Paz. Chunco. Cusillo, Indians. Partial copy of the original in Melchor María Mercado, *Album of the human types and costumes of Bolivia (1841–69)*, Banco Central de Bolivia/Biblioteca Nacional de Bolivia, 1991 **57** Text: Eduardo Galeano, *Century of the Wind*, 1998 **58** Photo: Taslima Akhter **61** In Nilda Callanupa Alvarez. *Weaving in the Peruvian Highlands: Dreaming Patterns, Weaving Memories*, Cuzco: Center for Traditional Textiles, 2007 **63** *The Zombies*, by Hector Hyppolite (1894–1948), Museum of Haitian Art of St. Peter College, Port-au-Prince; Los Angeles County Museum of Arts, LACMA **66** Attributed to Abu'l Hasan, 1605–08 Johnson Album 1,30 © The British Library Board **67** http://www.history.com/this-day-in-history/february-revolution-begins-in-russia **70** in Irene Emery, *The Primary Structures of Fabrics*, Washington DC: The Textile Museum and Thames and Hudson, 2009 **71** Chancay Central Coast. Three-dimensional figure depicting weaver with loom, Camelid wool and coastal cotton, MNAAHP. In *Pre-Columbian Peruvian Textiles: The First Modern Art*, James Reid. Piura: Industria Textil Piura S.A. **72** http://diepresse.com; Walter P. Reuther, Library – Wayne State University **75** Image: Edelstein Collection, Hebrew University; *Dyers*, 15th century, Flemish. British Museum, Royal Ma. 15, E III, fol. 264 **76** Image via www.dailymail.co.uk; Prabal Gurung via Forbes **77** Photo: Paul Huf, 1998 **80** Farbenfabrik Otto Baer, 1929, Bibliothéque des Arts Décoratifs, Paris **81** solidaritystorieskr.wordpress.com **85** L. Raitser, *The Turkestan-Siberia Railroad*, cotton print from the Red Rose Factory, circa 1930 **89**, 160 Andrea M. Heckman. *Woven Stories: Andean Textiles and Rituals*. Albuquerque: University of New Mexico Press, 2003 **90** Joseph Parry, *Eccles Wakes: Racing for the Smock*, 1808, Manchester Art Gallery **91** Rafael Castro in a Carnival Costume, 1861. Biblioteca Nacional de España, Madrid; vintage photo http://www.homohistory.com/2015/08/ **92** Kisasü'l-Enbiyá SK Hamidiye 980 **95** photo: Raveendran; http://www.mcclatchydc.com/news/nation-world/world/article24730981.html **96** *Artisans Tailors*, drawing in a manuscript of the *Postillae Nicolai de Lira supra Pentateucho, Josue et Judicibus*. Arras, Municipal Library, Ms. 252 **98** courtesy of the Museum of Leimebamba, Peru **100** Adrian Piper, *Catalysis III*, performance (1970) **105** Biblioteca Nacional de Antropología e Historía, Mexico City **106** in Elena Phipps, *Cochineal Red: The Art History of Color*, Metropolitan Museum of Art New York/Yale University Press **126** Photo: Arkarapova Ghish/Barcroft India **131** Exchange of gifts, including Ypres cloth. Leningrad, Saltykov-Shchedrin Library, F. IV.LDIX 232, fol. 150; Brushes, cloth, spices, and hats are on offer. Miniature from a manuscript, 15th century. Rouen, Municipal Library **132** *The process and progress of a weaving*, by Dieter Roth and Ingrid Wiener. Published by Karin Shick, Kerber Art, 2008 **137** *10 Taller Visual, Equador 12* photo: Cara Metz/UNITE **141** Photo: Flurina Rothenberger **142** http://nomadicpolitics.blogspot.com **146** © dapperdanofharlem.com **147** *11* http://afropunk.com **152** After a copy of the stolen 17th-century original from Jesús de Machaca, Dep. La Paz by Monika Baer, Berlin 2010, in the *Potosí Principle* exhibition **155** Photo taken around 1900 **157** Textile design, factory of Jean-Michel Haussmann, Colmar, 1797 **158** www.libcom.org **167** Barthel Beham, *The Spinning Room*, 1524, graphic arts collections, Albertina, Vienna **168** *Drum Magazine Ghana*, 1969 **169** photo: Ruth Noack **170** in *Weltgeschichte der Bekleidung*, Patricia Rieff Anawalt, Haupt Verlag Bern, Stuttgart, Wien **171** *Gold of the Andes*, Jorge Flores Ochoa, Kim MacQuarrie and Javier Portús, Jordi Blassi, Barcelona 1995, photo: Jaume Blassi, Jordi Blassi **172** Illustration via National Geographic **177** *Circle of James Pollard: Queen Victoria, Prince Albert, and Victoria, princess royal in Windsor Great Park*, oil on board, 1792–1867. London, Saffran Collection; Daniel Rabel, 1626, Musée du Louvre, Paris **182** *Train to Busan*, 2016, film still **186, 187** Image: Coram Foundling Museum **189** Text: Cummins, Tom, in *Writing Without Words: Alternative Literacies in Mesoamerica and the Andes*, Durham: Duke University Press, 1994; image: *Child Virgin at the Spinning Wheel*, c. 1680–1710, Museo Pedro de Osma, Lima, Peru **190** Photo: Kristy Sparow **191** Photo: Archivio Carbone **195** Photo: José Gabriel Gonzáles, Cuzco, 1926 **195** Lina Bo Bardi, image via Fondazione MAXXI **196** Atlanta Washerwomen's Strike, 1881. www.old-photos.blogspot.com **199** William Hogarth, *Finis, or The Tail Piece. The Bathos, or manner of sinking in sublime painting, inscribed to the Dealers in Dark Pictures*, engraving, published 1764 **201** Bartolozzi after John Webber, *A young woman of Otaheite, bringing a present*, engraving, 1784, from Cook and King, A Voyage to the Pacific Ocean. **202** Joseph Cornell, *The Pulse of Fashion*, 1957 **203** Photo: National Archive, College Park, Maryland, in *The Narcotic Farm*, Nancy D. Campbell et al. Abrams Books, 2008 **222** Photo: *New York Tribune* **223** Paolo Uccello, *La Bataille de San Remano: Bernardino della Ciarda* (detail), 1456, Galleria degli Uffizi, Florence **224** Musée Gadagne, Lyon **227** Science Museum London **228** Ewa Jaroszynska, *Trousers*, 1969, sisal and hemp, crochet. **231** http://www.licadho-cambodia.org/ **232** www.cambodiadaily.com **234** Text: Tom Raworth, *Logbook*, N.P. Poltroon Press, 1970 **236** Victoria and Albert Museum, London; Lucas Cranach d. Ä., *Venus*, 1532. Städtische Galerie, Frankfurt, photo: Blauel/Gnamm-Artothek **237** Soviet fabrics design, 1933, mechanisation. **238** www.mkgandhi.org **242/243** *11* early 12th-century painting by Emperor Huizong of Song, a remake of an 8th-century original by Zhang Xuan, China *5* image: Gary Moch *7* www.basf.com **246** Robb, G. 2007, *The Discovery of France*, Picador, London **248** Text: Eduardo Galeano, *Los hijos de los días*, 2012; image: Huari Glove, 650–800 AD Peru, Pre-Columbian **249** Gaëtan Gatian de Clérambault, 1914–18. Musée de l'Homme, Palais de Chaillot, Paris **252** Vintage picture postcard, Swiss-Foto, 1958 **255** © Pedro Armestre/AFP/Getty Images **259** © Maison Martin Margiela **260** In Jim Naughten *Conflict and Costume: The Herero Tribe of Namibia*, Merrel London, New York, 2013 **263** #Kuwaithttp://ara.tv/5a52u **265** Image: J.A. Fuertes Lopez, *Molinos de Sangre*, Potosí 1998. Text: Fanon, Frantz. *Black Skin, White Masks*, 1952. **267** *Hidden Threads of Peru*, Anne Pollard Rowe and John Cohen (eds.), London: Merrell in Association with the Textile Museum Washington DC, 2002 **270** Calico hood from 1875, worn by all prisoners in solitary confinement, photo: Ciell, 2008 **274** www.turnkey.com. **275** Digital Archive of Documents Related to Mills www2.cs.arizona.edu [Cotton Textile Mill Training], China Pictorial, 1965, No. 3 **278** *9 Young workers in a Georgia cotton mill, early 1900s*, photo: Lewis Hine; Library of Congress **280** Library of Congress **287** Ladder (detail). Spain/Marocco. 2001 or 2002. Museum of World Cultures, Gothenburg; anonymous, *Il Maestro dellatela jeans*, North Italy, approx. 1675–1700 **288** Photo: Reuters **289** In: Johannes Lein, *A German Photographer in Bolivia 1939-67*, M. Strecker et al (eds.) **292** Illustrations of the *Arabian Nights* by Duilio Cambellotti **293** Kodra *cut-out* (fragment), Ztaków Borowy, 1986 **298** In: *Interwoven Globe: The Worldwide Textile Trade, 1500–1800* © www.metmuseum.org **299** www.workersed-ucation.org **posters** CAMBIO, 2nd March 2011, page 4/5. In May 2008 in Sucre civilians forced *campesinos* to undress and march into town as a racist act. Sancho Gutiérrez: MAPAMUNDI, 1561, Fundación Museo Naval, Madrid **29, 36, 41, 51, 60, 65, 74, 79, 104, 180, 194, 221, 259, 276, 277** Markus Wörgötter.

Thanks

foremost to all the contributors and: Markus Wörgötter, who stayed with the project throughout this long period and supported it with inspiration and skill; Cornelia Klinger, who enabled the application to the FWF through hosting the research at the IWM; Helga Weber who was assisting my work for many years with dedication; Katharina Blaas, who believed in the undertaking early on; Alexander Damianisch, who was in charge of PEEK at the Austrian funding scheme for arts-based research at the FWF; Hildegund Amanshauser and Ruth Noack who advised the formulation of the application; Vitalie Lesan throughout; Denise Y. Arnold, who invited us to give a talk at a very early stage of our research at the conference 'Textiles, Techne and Power in the Andes', Birkbeck University, London and whose work has been an inspiration; as was Eduardo Galeanos' Memory of Fire Trilogy throughout the research. Birgit Haehnel, who gave the opportunity to write down first thoughts in FKW // Zeitschrift für Geschlechterforschung und visuelle Kultur (Heft 52 / 2011); Soledad Mujica, Museo National de Cultura; Claudia Augustat, curator of the South America Collection, Weltmuseum Wien; and Eva Fischer, Francisco Godoy, Hansel Sato, Leonhard Eder, and to the models: Miwa Burger, Lena Hofmann, Lenny Hierländer, Gan Jambaa, Lukas Vospernik.

to the curators who showed the *Eccentric Archive* in its various stages: 2018 Cosmin Costinas (Dhaka Art Summit; Para Site, Hong Kong; Museum of Modern Art, Warsaw) 2017 Ursula Maria Probst (WELT KOMPAKT? Q21, Vienna) 2016 Malin Barth (Transcultural Flux, Stiftelsen 3, Bergen); Pauline Doutreluingne (The Next Big Thing is Not a Thing, Bureau Europa, Maastricht) 2015 Hans D. Christ, Iris Dressler, Paul B. Preciado, Valentín Roma (The Beast and the Sovereign, MACBA, Barcelona); Hemma Schmutz (Räume und Ressourcen, Kunstraum Lakeside, Klagenfurt) 2014 Pablo Lafuente, Nuria Enguita Mayo, Charles Esche, Galit Eilat, Oren Sagiv (Universes in Universe, São Paulo Biennal); Armin Medosch (Fields, National Art Museum, Riga); 2013 Ruth Noack (Not Dressed for Conquering, Royal College of Art, London); Nathalie Boseul SHIN, Iris Dressler, Hans D. Christ, Christine Peters (Acts of Voicing, Total Museum, Seoul); Cosmin Costinas (Acts of Voicing, Para Site, Hong Kong); 2012 Simon Sheikh (Unauthorized, Inter Arts Center, Malmoe); Iris Dressler, Hans D. Christ, Christine Peters (Acts of Voicing, Württembergischer Kunstverein, Stuttgart); Susanne Neuburger (Reflecting Fashion, MUMOK, Vienna).

to those who invited the *Investigator*: Pauline Doutreluingne, Bonaventure Soh Bejeng Ndikung (The Conundrum of Imagination, Leopoldmuseum, Wiener Festwochen, 2017); Boris Ondreička (The Indian-Investigator-Machine visiting the TBA, 'Ephemeropterae', Thyssen-Bornemisza Contemporary Vienna, 2012); Iris Dressler, Hans D. Christ, Christine Peters (Acts of Voicing, Württembergischer Kunstverein, Stuttgart, 2012); Alice Creischer, Andreas Siekmann, Max Jorge Hinderer Cruz (Con el Viento, Museo Nacional de Etnografia y Folklore, La Paz, Bolivia, 2011).

Almost 40 years ago I made my first journey to Latin America, which lasted over a year, and this is where everything probably already started. Even though I had very little money I bought some textiles, enchanted by the rich textile tradition of the Quechua and Aymará people, and these were the foundation of my extensive studies and production of works over the last years. From 2010–2012 an artistic research called *Loomshuttles, Warpaths* was granted by FWF Austrian Science Funds, for which I applied together with Catrin Seefranz. Finally the first part, the Eccentric Archive, is finished.

conceived by
Ines Doujak

edited by
Württembergischer Kunstverein Stuttgart
LENTOS Kunstmuseum Linz

posters
Ines Doujak

texts realised by
Ines Doujak, John Barker,
with the exception of *An Investigator, an Indian Automat and a Puppet*, written by Ines Doujak

graphic design, photography, collages, digital imaging
Markus Wörgötter

translation
Matthew Hyland, Anja Büchele, Rosa Nogues

proofreading
Danny Hayward, Matthew Hyland, Georg Bauer

printed by
Holzhausen Druck GmbH, Wolkersdorf, Austria

published by
Spector Books
Harkortstraße 10
04107 Leipzig
www.spectorbooks.com

distribution
Germany, Austria: GVA, Gemeinsame Verlagsauslieferung Göttingen GmbH&Co. KG, www.gva-verlage.de
Switzerland: AVA Verlagsauslieferung AG, www.ava.ch
France, Belgium: Interart Paris, www.interart.fr
UK: Central Books Ltd, www.centralbooks.com
USA, Canada, Central and South America, Africa, Asia: ARTBOOK | D.A.P. www.artbook.com
South Korea: The Book Society, www.thebooksociety.org
Australia, New Zealand: Perimeter Distribution, www.perimeterdistribution.com

The artistic research was hosted by the Institute for Human Sciences, Vienna, funded by the FWF-PEEK, Austrian Science Fund (AR 19-G21) and initiated by Ines Doujak.

ISBN 978-3-95905-218-4

bibliographic information published by the Deutsche Nationalbibliothek
The Deutsche Nationalbibliothek lists this publication in the Deutsche Nationalbibliografie; detailed bibliographic data are available on the Internet at http://dnb.dnb.de.

Württem bergischer Kunst verein Stuttgart
LENTOS Kunstmuseum Linz
BUNDESKANZLERAMT ÖSTERREICH
Kunst im öffentlichen Raum Niederösterreich
STUTTGART
Baden-Württemberg
IWM Institut für die Wissenschaften vom Menschen Institute for Human Sciences
FWF Der Wissenschaftsfonds. Austrian Science Fund
INNOVATIONSFONDS KUNST BADEN-WÜRTTEMBERG
LBBW Stiftung Landesbank Baden-Württemberg
WÜSTENROT STIFTUNG